The Spinozistic Ethics of Bertrand Russell

KENNETH BLACKWELL

The Bertrand Russell Archives, McMaster University

London
GEORGE ALLEN & UNWIN
Boston   Sydney

© Kenneth Blackwell, 1985
This book is copyright under the Berne Convention.
No reproduction without permission. All rights reserved.

**George Allen & Unwin (Publishers) Ltd
40 Museum Street, London WC1A 1LU, UK**

George Allen & Unwin (Publishers) Ltd,
Park Lane, Hemel Hempstead, Herts HP2 4TE, UK

Allen & Unwin, Inc.,
Fifty Cross Street, Winchester, Mass. 01890, USA

George Allen & Unwin Australia Pty Ltd,
8 Napier Street, North Sydney, NSW 2060, Australia

First published in 1985

British Library Cataloguing in Publication Data

Blackwell, Kenneth
   The Spinozistic ethics of Bertrand Russell.
1. Russell, Bertrand – Ethics   2. Ethics –
History
170'.92'4   B1649.R94
ISBN 0-04-190008-1

Library of Congress Cataloging in Publication Data

Blackwell, Kenneth.
   The Spinozistic ethics of Bertrand Russell
Bibliography: p.
Includes index.
1. Russell, Bertrand, 1872–1970 – Ethics. 2. Ethics,
Modern – 20th century. 3. Spinoza, Benedictus de,
1632–1677 – Influence. I. Title.
B1649.R94B52 1985   170'.92'4   84-16892
ISBN 0-04-190008-1 (alk. paper)

Set in 10 on 12 point Plantin by Computape (Pickering) Ltd
and printed in Great Britain
by Biddles Ltd, Guildford, Surrey

Contents

Preface   *page* vii

Chapter I   Introduction   1
1 Metaethics and normative ethics. **2** Relevance of Russell's normative ethic. **3** His metaethic. **4** Non-cognitivism in metaethics. **5** Previous attempts at systematizing Russell's normative ethic. **6** Russell's criteria for judging an ethic. **7** Connection with Spinoza and monistic ethics. **8** Commentators linking Russell with Spinoza. **9** The concept of impersonal self-enlargement.

Part A. Russell's Writings on Spinoza

Chapter II   The Early Period (1888–1901)   21
10 Introduction to Part A. **11** Russell in old age admits Spinoza's influence. **12** Russell's earliest religious reflections and nature-worship. **13** Self-abnegation. **14** Notes on lectures in the history of philosophy. **15** Pollock's *Spinoza*. **16** Graduate essays in the history of philosophy. **17** Rebellion against neo-Hegelianism. **18** Spinoza in Russell's *Leibniz*; and Joachim's *Study*. **19** Summary.

Chapter III   The Middle Period (1907–12)   53
20 Transition. **21** Review of Picton's *Spinoza*. **22** Review of Spinoza's *Ethic* (translated by White and Stirling). **23** Russell's copy of White and Stirling's translation. **24** Correspondence with Lady Ottoline Morrell. **25** Nasispo's speech in "The Perplexities of John Forstice". **26** Summary.

Chapter IV	**The Late Period (1914–64)**	79
	27 Miscellaneous references to Spinoza, 1914–40. **28** A radio discussion of the *Ethics*. **29** *A History of Western Philosophy*: preliminary aspects. **30** *A History of Western Philosophy*: chapter on Spinoza. **31** Miscellaneous references, 1945–64. **32** Summary.	

Part B. Russell's Spinozistic Ethic

Chapter V	*Amor Dei Intellectualis*	109
	33 Introduction to Part B. **34** Spinoza's concept of the intellectual love of God: Russell's first interpretation. **35** Russell's second interpretation. **36** Other interpretations: Pollock, White and Picton. **37** Joachim. **38** Wolfson, Bidney, Hampshire and Harris. **39** Wetlesen and Wienpahl. **40** Summary.	
Chapter VI	**Development of the Ethic of Impersonal Self-Enlargement**	129
	41 A developmental approach. **42** The element of mysticism. **43** "The Free Man's Worship". **44** "Prisons" and "The Essence of Religion". **45** *The Problems of Philosophy*. **46** "The Perplexities of John Forstice". **47** *Principles of Social Reconstruction*. **48** *The Conquest of Happiness* and *Marriage and Morals*. **49** Miscellaneous ethical writings, 1916–41. **50** *New Hopes for a Changing World*, *Human Society in Ethics and Politics* and later writings. **51** Summary.	
Chapter VII	Evaluation of a Normative Ethic	169
	52 Introduction: normative ethics. A. **53** Critical Summary of Russell's Ethic. **54** Related Theories. **55** Application of Evaluative Criteria. **56** Russell's additional criteria.	

57 Non-Russellian criteria. **58** Further non-Russellian criteria. **59** Impersonal self-enlargement and philosophic calm. **60** Conclusion

Notes	203
Bibliography	232
Index of Citations	246
Russell's Works	246
Spinoza's Works	249
Index of Names	251
Index of Subjects	255

Preface

Throughout the years I have studied Russell I have had a respect for him that has proven to be independent of his particular moral and political stands. It seemed to me a worthwhile project to dig for the roots of his normative ethic and to evaluate it. Russell never sets out his normative ethic systematically, but I believe I have discovered its underlying conceptual scheme.

This study traces the conceptual unity in Russell's normative ethic to the influence of Spinoza's central ethical concept, the "intellectual love of God", and then evaluates the ethic, which I call one of "impersonal self-enlargement". The evaluation is based on five criteria supplied by Russell himself when he considers the normative ethics of Aristotle, Santayana and Spinoza, and nine additional criteria.

The Introduction sketches the metaethical background to Russell's ethic. Its analysis poses difficulties not encountered with most ethical theories, since Russell does not hold ethical knowledge to be possible and is never systematic. At the same time, one of his most cherished endeavours is "to find some philosophy which should make human life endurable" (*Autobiography*, vol. I, p. 142). Russell often associated Spinoza's central ethical concept with this endeavour, but no commentator has hitherto asserted more than an affinity between their ethical views.

Part A examines Russell's writings on Spinoza from 1894 to 1964, dividing them into three periods. Besides the *History of Western Philosophy* chapter, there are reviews, a characterization of Spinoza's views in a novel, correspondence, and other items. There are also passages concerning Spinoza's *Ethics* scattered throughout Russell's ethical writings. Because of their uncollected and sometimes unpublished nature, I reproduce many of the passages. Russell is indebted to Spinoza chiefly, I argue, for his concept of the intellectual love of God.

Part B analyzes Russell's two interpretations of the "intellectual love of God", traces the concept of impersonal self-enlargement in Russell's own ethical writings, and evaluates the ethic. Spinoza and

Russell share a concept of the moral self that expands with knowledge (Spinoza and Russell) and with generous feeling (Russell especially). Russell's chief interpretation of the intellectual love of God is similar to that of the idealist H. H. Joachim. I claim that early training in neo-Hegelianism left a permanent residue in Russell's ethics.

In tracing Russell's ethical theory I identify two normative ethics. The first, expressed in "The Free Man's Worship", focuses on suppression of the self's demands. The second is the ethic of impersonal self-enlargement, which accepts the self's demands but emphasizes the widening of interests irrespective of this or that person. The ethic is at its most Spinozistic in 1911–12, when Russell tries to fashion a personal religion at once godless but acceptable to his confidante, Lady Ottoline Morrell. The ethic of impersonal self-enlargement is the way of living recommended in such works as *Principles of Social Reconstruction*, *The Conquest of Happiness* and *New Hopes for a Changing World*.

In evaluating the ethic I first discuss its relation to other ethical theories, and then apply the fourteen criteria. There is initial difficulty in applying any criterion to a non-cognitivist's ethic, but many of mine would be applicable in judging an ethic based upon cognitivism in the inconclusive sense. Russell's Spinozistic ethic satisfies some, but not all, of the criteria. Russell appears to be aware of some of the problems, but his modifications result in a degree of arbitrariness in his ethic. Nevertheless, impersonal self-enlargement is a way of living that encourages generosity and rationality, thereby tending to reduce human conflict. Given the present perilous state of human conflict, the ethic warrants serious consideration. As by-products of this study, the concept of impersonal self-enlargement should lead to greater understanding of other value-laden areas of Russell's thought (especially his political philosophy), and my set of criteria could be used to evaluate alternative normative ethics.

For reading this work in earlier stages as a dissertation at the University of Guelph, I am indebted to Jay Newman, Douglas Odegard and Nicholas Griffin. For more recent comments I wish to thank Jack Pitt, Harry Ruja and John G. Slater. George Sessions encouraged me at a very early stage, as did the late Paul Wienpahl. Roland Hall kindly brought Russell's copy of Joachim's *Study of the Ethics of Spinoza* to my notice.

References to Spinoza's works are explained in Chapter II, note 2. The Bertrand Russell Archives at McMaster University are the source of most of the unpublished documents cited. Quotations from them are © McMaster University, 1985. Quotations from Russell's letters to Lady Ottoline Morrell are printed also with the permission of the Harry Ranson Humanities Research Center at the University of Texas at Austin, where they are held.

I dedicate the work to Kadriin and our children, Joanna, Benjamin and Elizabeth.

Greensville,
Ontario
November 1984

CHAPTER I

Introduction

1   Metaethics and Normative Ethics

Bertrand Russell had certain difficulties in his personal life: the familial loneliness into which he was plunged as an orphan, the consequent lack of union with others (be they groups or individuals), and the lack of peace caused by the restless torment of his particular set of passions. Russell sought love because through love he felt the hard shell of his ego dissolve and experienced the mingling of personalities. He sought even sexual love for this reason, as is evidenced by the coinciding of his early asceticism of both the emotions and the body and his later expansiveness of the emotions and welcoming of sexual love. In the realm of thought, Russell is well known for his insistence on certain standards of belief. Allowing yourself to believe without good evidence is to yield to paltry personal desires to which a largeness of vision would never succumb. And just as he wished to escape from the prison of purely personal desires, he wanted man to escape from the anthropocentric viewpoint, the perspective that judges all in terms of man's desires. When, however, it became a question of man's existence being threatened by man himself, Russell's ability to think of the human race without distinctions, supported by an expansive generosity, led him into strife in his old age, to do battle not with other men but with hostile forces in man himself. In private life he was a generous man whose impersonal intellect was tempered by caring for the persons involved in the issue at hand. The record of his life shows him, as he puts it in his advice on growing old, making his "interests gradually wider and more impersonal, until bit by bit the walls of the ego recede, and [his] life becomes increasingly merged in the universal life" (quoted in full in **50**).

The foregoing description uses language associated with what I identify in this enquiry as the Spinozistic ethic by which Russell tried to live and which underlies his normative writings. The identification and evaluation of that ethic jointly comprise the topic of this enquiry.

Since my topic is normative ethics and not metaethics, some distinctions and a summary of Russell's metaethical views are in order. The study of ethics can be distinguished from morality on the one hand, and metaethics on the other. When there is a theoretical basis to a morality, that basis is called "ethics", or more usually "normative ethics". A morality, or code of conduct, can be generated by a normative ethic. Normative ethics, therefore, is more fundamental than morality. Take, for example, classical utilitarianism as a normative ethic. With respect to the morality of promise-keeping, two positions have developed. The rule-utilitarian holds that the greatest good in the long run results from always keeping one's promises. The act-utilitarian holds that the keeping of each promise must be examined on its merits, with the greater good in the long run very likely including some broken promises. The formulation and defence of such positions belong to normative ethics. I referred to utilitarianism as a "normative *ethic*". The singular term is less common than the collective term, but Russell uses "ethic" in this sense and also in the sense of a particular metaethical theory, or "metaethic". For the sake of clarity, I use "normative ethics" for the field of study and "normative ethic" for the fundamentals of a particular morality. When I use just "ethic", I mean "normative ethic". At its most general, an ethic is a recommendation of a way of life. Russell writes in this sense in his book *Power* of the doctrine of the Tao. It consists, he says, "not of specific duties, but of a way of life, a manner of thinking and feeling, from which it will become plain, without the need of rules, what must be done on each occasion."[1] Hence there can be ethics based on love, power, self-realization, etc.—whatever is sufficient to inspire "a manner of thinking and feeling" and therefore acting.

Metaethics "consists entirely", in William Frankena's words, "of philosophical analysis".[2] Metaethics deals with the nature of moral reasoning and the analysis of concepts such as "right", "ought", and "good", without prescribing what it is right or good to do. It is at this level that we find such classificatory terms as "naturalism", "cognitivism", "emotivism", "prescriptivism" and "intuitionism". The classification of metaethical systems suggests a study of even greater generality, namely meta-metaethics. H. J. McCloskey, in his work *Meta-Ethics and Normative Ethics*, includes under meta-metaethics enquiries "concerning the status of the meta-ethical theory, about the method of arriving at a meta-ethic, and about what constitute the facts which the theory is to explain and upon which it is to be grounded."[3]

He includes also the question whether metaethics can be normatively ethical.[4] This is not an unusual question, despite the assumption by some metaethicists that in doing metaethics they are ethically neutral. P. H. Nowell-Smith, for example, in distinguishing "theoretical ethics"—our metaethics—from "practical ethics"—our normative ethics and morality—contrasts "Knowledge" with "Practice".[5] As a philosopher enquiring into the logic of moral discourse (to which, he holds, his concern as a philosopher is limited), he refrains from interfering with what people do in situations in which practical ethical questions arise. This approach seems to assume that philosophical reflection cannot recommend a way of life, that, to put it bluntly, philosophers can have no special access to wisdom. Suppose, however, that your metaethical enquiry leads you to subjectivism— the emotivist doctrine that ethical expressions are really only expressions of (or sometimes about) a state of approval or disapproval in the mind of the speaker. George Santayana, in criticizing the intuitionistic ethical objectivism of G. E. Moore and Russell in 1911, maintains that subjectivism has the non-logical consequence of greater tolerance.[6] If true, that is certainly an ethical matter. Roger Hancock, in a useful textbook, points out that a normative ethic such as utilitarianism can also be a metaethical theory.[7] This is the case when "right" is taken to *mean* "tending to increase happiness". The only argument is over whether or not that is how the word is ordinarily used. But the normative implication remains. For if we ask whether someone acted rightly in doing x, all we have to do is examine whether x increased happiness (an examination that is not necessarily easy to make).

2 Relevance of Russell's Normative Ethic

My interest in Russell's ethics is not metaethical, despite the importance of metaethics and the different metaethical theories Russell holds at various times. Nor does my interest lie primarily in his morality, or the biography of his personal moral behaviour. Russell's morality, and his politics for that matter, are not deducible from his normative ethic—which is not to say they are inconsistent with his ethic. People do not simply deduce a morality or a politics from a normative ethic. There are too many situational variables, including the perception of the situation by those involved in making moral or political decisions. What I am interested in, in Russell's case, is something of greater generality than a morality, a principle or set of principles that can generate suggestions for moral action, political decision and even a way of life.

In dealing with the notion of a way of life, this study straddles ethics and philosophy of religion—taking "religion" broadly. In the midst of the devastation of the Second World War, Russell writes: "What is needed is something in the nature of religion, not in any dogmatic sense, but as a source of serious and determined effort towards something better than the present."[8] Russell says that "the least unsatisfactory" statement of his philosophy of religion is in *Principles of Social Reconstruction*,[9] published in the midst of the First World War. That he was dissatisfied with this book is shown by a letter he wrote from prison to his mistress, Lady Constance Malleson ("Colette"), two years after publication of the book:

> I must, I *must*, before I die, find *some* way to say the essential thing that is in me, that I have never said yet—a thing that is not love or hate or pity or scorn, but the very breath of life, fierce, and coming from far away, bringing into human life the vastness and the fearful passionless force of non-human things.... I want to bring back into the world of men some little bit of new wisdom. There is a little wisdom in the world: Heraclitus, Spinoza, and a saying here and there—I want to add to it, even if only ever so little.[10]

During a period of study of Spinoza's *Ethics*, I began to notice conceptual affinities between the ethics of Spinoza and Russell. Russell's ethical views seemed to have an underlying unity in the light of an increasingly apparent debt to Spinoza. For the references in Russell to Spinoza turn out to be both numerous and important. One of the most significant comes mid-way in the first year of Russell's study of philosophy; another, in his 92nd year (see 11 for both references). It seemed that Russell's early monistic idealism left an important Spinozistic residue in his ethic.

3 His Metaethic

Over a long life Russell held a large number of opinions on moral and political questions. These questions range from the very particular to the very general, from those which concern the private individual to those which concern the largest communities of men. Since Russell never presents these opinions systematically, most commentators have failed to see systematic connections between them. Ronald Jager, in his major study, accomplishes somewhat more. For example, he draws analogies between Russell's treatment of the epistemological individual and the political individual.[11] But he, too, does not attempt to find unity in Russell's value judgments. In the widespread assumption that there is no worthwhile unity to be found in Russell's ethics, commentators take their cue from Russell himself. In replying to the critics organized by Schilpp, Russell declares that "I should like to exclude all value judgments from philosophy, except that this would be too violent a breach with usage.... Where ethics is concerned, I hold that, so far as fundamentals are concerned, it is impossible to produce conclusive intellectual arguments."[12] He adds that, with respect to his most systematic work of value judgments, *Principles of Social Reconstruction*, he wrote it not as a philosopher, but as an individual who suffered from the state of the world and wished to do something about it (p. 730). In accordance with this view of his work, Russell does not treat ethics in his philosophical autobiography, *My Philosophical Development* (1959).

Despite this "official" discouragement from Russell, other writings and other facts about him encourage a different view. From his books we can infer at least a sporadic concern with metaethical topics. Metaethics is discussed at length from 1900 (*The Philosophy of Leibniz*) to 1954 (*Human Society in Ethics and Politics*). From the preface to *Human Society* we learn that the metaethical part was originally composed as part of *Human Knowledge: Its Scope and Limits* (1948). It was discarded when Russell decided, not for the first time, that ethics is not part of knowledge. Indeed, the part almost never appeared, at least in a work on ethics and politics in the mid-1950s. For Russell's original plan for such a work was to collect in one volume his major writings on political philosophy, and in this plan he did not have a place for metaethics.[13]

Thus a lifelong concern with metaethics can be traced in Russell's published writings. A number of unpublished writings on metaethics survive as well. But it is not my purpose to trace Russell's metaethical development, which (as published) proceeds from intuitionism through emotivism to a tentative naturalism. That task has already been done, in regard to the major published theories, by Lillian W. Aiken.[14] Russell's metaethics, after he broke with Moore's intuitionism about 1913, is always an attempt to climb out of noncognitivism. He is never quite satisfied with his attempts. In his

History of Western Philosophy (1945) he bemoans the "subjectivistic" trends since Descartes.[15] (Russell generally identifies ethical subjectivism with non-cognitivism.) But he has to admit, at that time, that he has no alternative.[16] And despite the attempt in *Human Society* to provide an objectivist, or cognitivist, basis for his ethic,[17] Russell expressed dissatisfaction after publishing the book. On D. H. Monro's account in 1960 of Russell's last metaethic, he commented just as he had in 1944 and 1957: "I cannot see how to refute the arguments for the subjectivity of ethical values, but I find myself incapable of believing that all that is wrong with wanton cruelty is that I don't like it."[18] There is some pressure on the non-cognitivist label Russell bears, which I discuss at length in 42. In so far as certain experiences can convince him of values, Russell could be construed as a cognitivist. But this is cognitivism of a very strange kind, since Russell holds that he can offer no intellectual arguments in its favour. I mention the topic because, despite Russell's intellectualist non-cognitivism, it is not the case that he is unsure of his ultimate values, or that he cannot sometimes put forward *some* reason, albeit a quasi-intuitionistic one, for his holding them.

4 Non-Cognitivism in Metaethics

Russell's test of a successful ethic is its ability to prove, or justify conclusively, that wanton cruelty is bad. If an ethic offered a plausible proof (or even allowed for its possibility) that such cruelty is good, Russell would arguably have spent his life seeking to undermine that proof. However, he holds that ethics is not capable of proving cruelty—or happiness, for that matter—to be either good or bad. This view of the limitations of the reasoning of normative ethics belongs to metaethics. Metaethics, until such a proof either way is found, is therefore, for Russell, morally neutral. Reason in ethics, in addition to being analytical, can be persuasive, but not conclusive, even in the mild fallibilist sense. But the fact of its inconclusiveness (if, with Russell, we accept it as a fact) is often said to imply that those who take this non-cognitivist metaethical position are irrational if they express normative ethical views in the usual ways.[19] They—especially Russell, who writes in reply to this point—are said to be irrational in this regard because they continue to make ethical statements in the indicative mood which they believe are not really descriptive.[20] Either such philosophers are irrational, or they are dishonest. The reply, it seems to me, is clear. First, such statements are beyond the sphere of conclusive reason. Hence they are not subject to its controls, and a critic such as George Grant should say Russell is "non-rational", not "irrational", in ethics. Second, the illusory indicative mood of the grammar is dealt with by a doctrine about its true logical form. Russell need not declare, in his "Reply to Criticisms", that "I am not prepared to forego my right to feel and express ethical passions; no amount of logic, even though it be my own, will persuade me that I ought do so."[21] Finally, the apparent insincerity of continuing to use the indicative or imperative mood of statement is excused by the realization that such statements are not, by their very nature, susceptible of proof; and by the further realization that persuasive considerations may nevertheless be advanced. A non-cognitivist may, therefore, hold reasoned beliefs as to what he ought to do; but as his reasons for these beliefs are not put forward even in a fallibilist sense, he cannot be said to *know* what he ought to do. Moral persuasion becomes, for Russell's non-cognitivist metaethic, a matter of appealing to both reason and emotion.

Non-cognitivism in metaethics, therefore, has a consequence for ethics which cognitivism lacks. While the latter can rest after presenting its proof (fallibilist or infallibilist) of what people are obliged to do, the former must continue to persuade. Russell is especially strong on the need for persuasion under the assumption of non-cognitivism. Large parts of *Human Society in Ethics and Politics* are devoted to making this need clear. Ethical persuasion depends upon finding common grounds for discussion which henceforth may be entirely rational. Common grounds may be created in two ways: (1) through sympathy in feeling, or the sharing of ultimate goals for mankind; (2) through the removal of appeal to special, or exclusive, interests. Such removal, in practice, amounts to the avoidance of proper names in ethical arguments. This is Russell's "universality" principle,[22] which becomes the "impersonal" element in his ethic (see especially 53). The avoidance of proper names works wonders for ethical objectivity. If your opponent knows you reject cognitivist ethics, you are at a disadvantage in setting out to convince him that you ought to be the major recipient of the world's goods, whatever they might be. If your argument contains, instead of your name, the symbol "A", much less passion is generated and the argumentation less clouded by emotion. More importantly, your opponent can see that his name can replace "A"; but he can also see that it will be as difficult for him to get you to agree to such a substitution as it was for you to engage him in discussion when your name was in the place of "*A*".

This procedure is not one which is guaranteed to avoid error in ethics. It *may* be the case that Aryans, the late Shah Mohammed Pahlevi Reza, Ayatollah Ruhollah Khomeini, or some other group or individual, ought to be in the place of "*A*".[23] But there is no known procedure of arguing cognitively for such a position. And even if there were a procedure, we may be sure that it would not be accepted by all the ambitious groups and individuals who would still be vying "illogically" for the position of top dog. Non-cognitivism in meta-ethics, therefore, has the advantage of being a safeguard against moral authoritarianism and of requiring the advocates of non-cognitivist ethics continually to justify their recommendations in the logically inconclusive style still left to such advocates. In the widest schemes of non-cognitivist ethics, the recommendations must be based on a theory of human nature. If your opponent in argument can be got to agree to your theory of human nature, then it becomes easier to achieve agreement on what course of behaviour is appropriate, in the light of that theory, to recommend. Under a shared theory of human nature there is greater chance of agreement, since the range of possible goods for man becomes narrower. There is lacking simply what I call the "obligatory force" characteristic of a cognitivist ethic, in virtue of which it is putatively known how you should act. Non-cognitivism is here in greatest contrast with the Kantian approach of infallibilist cognitivism. When the cognitivist claim is dropped, an ethic can no longer assert that we are obliged to act as it recommends, since the ethic is no longer claiming that it is known that we are obliged to perform a given act.

Russell much regretted his non-cognitivist metaethic. In books from *Principles of Social Reconstruction* through *A History of Western Philosophy* to *Human Society* he tried to find ways out of it. This is ironic. For what some would regard as good features of his normative ethic are consequences of his non-cognitivism. Those features regarding norms of conduct, however, could be included in a cognitivist-based ethic—if they were known to be right, or even if ethical knowledge were held to be possible in principle. The issue of cognitivism versus non-cognitivism is, however, not overwhelmingly important in evaluating ethics. Normative ethics that presuppose fallibilist cognitivist and non-cognitivist metaethics respectively can be evaluated by many of the same criteria, as will be evident in Chapter VII, section 55.

5 Previous Attempts at Systematizing Russell's Normative Ethic

The quantity of Russell's moral, social and political writing is enormous. There are writings on such diverse topics as free trade, women's suffrage, the Vietnam War, sexual conduct, freethought, euthanasia, and the achievement of happiness. There has even been an attempt to link Russell's sexual conduct theories to his internationalism.[24] While attempts to link aspects of Russell's normative ethic and his politics are rare, a more standard enterprise is to link his metaphysic to his politics. In his 1946 essay, "Philosophy and Politics",[25] he himself observes a psychological connection between empiricism in philosophy and liberalism in politics—their common tentativeness towards belief. The scientific attitude displayed in seeking knowledge is said to be akin to the non-authoritarian attitude of political liberalism. This is the sum of the psychological connection Russell observes.

It is difficult to believe that Russell's ethical and political writings are largely heterogeneous, in the sense that they lack unifying principles. Not only metaethics but also normative ethics concerned him seriously from an early age. I submit the following as a working hypothesis in examining Russell's ethical and political beliefs: philosophers strive to find conceptual connections, and they strive for conceptual unification, or systematization, of their beliefs; their beliefs *may* be heterogeneous and piecemeal, but for us to seek for systematization in them could well be rewarding. I reject the objection that, in his ethical and political writings, Russell is not writing as a "philosopher". In a great deal of his writing on topics which do not fall within a narrow conception of philosophy, he nevertheless discloses a search for conceptual fundamentals. In political writings he usually brings in the more general because persuasion in politics is almost impossible if you start with the particular, and political disagreement usually concerns the particular. We may, then, hope to find fundamental conceptual connections in the value judgments contained in Russell's normative ethic. And, depending on our degree of success, Russell's work in ethics may become the subject of further philosophical enquiry. There may also be a certain soundness or applicability to his ethic, which I shall discuss in my evaluation of it.

Russell is not the only one to probe this area for connections. Jager has gone further than Russell himself into the connections between his technical philosophy and his theoretical work in ethics, education, politics and religion, and has grasped the connection which Russell hints at in "Philosophy and Politics". This is the connection between the individual, the recipient or locus of sensations, as epistemological centre; and the individual as political unit (of which states are only compounds), the centre and standard of ethical worth and political value. Jager writes that it is "no accident that an atomist in metaphysics turns out to be an individualist in ethics and politics" (*Development*, p. 428). This leads Jager to emphasize the notion of individual freedom in Russell's political theory. He claims that this notion is to political theory "what the privacy of sense experience is to epistemology", and he devotes two chapters to connections suggested by this insight. The insight is, in my opinion, a flawed one. We shall find that the emphasis ascribed to Russell on the individual as the ethical and political unit is exaggerated and obscures the primary conceptual foundation of his normative ethic and politics. Since Russell is more of a socialist than a liberal, some modification of autonomous individuality should be expected.

The most powerful claim that Russell's political theory is related to his metaphysic is made by Benjamin R. Barber, who fastens on the "polarity" which results from seeking certainty through sceptical means:

> To insist, as liberals have always done, that the criteria by which we elucidate standards of knowledge must somehow correspond with criteria by which we fashion a common life, is a particularly pernicious kind of folly. To think that the attitudes with which we approach nature must reflect on the attitudes with which we approach the civic polity promotes an extremism of the mind incompatible with the social requirements of common living.[26]

Interestingly, Barber recognizes another trend in Russell, the trend towards what Barber calls "mutuality" (p. 473). But as an empiricist liberal, Russell "hoped for a politics of love, but could anticipate only a politics of anarchy or a politics of dominion or some weak, unstable compound of the two" (p. 475). Barber does oppose the view that Russell's political writings are heterogeneous. He is, however, mistaken in assuming that Russell employs the same conception of self in normative ethics and politics as he does in epistemology; in the latter case, the charge of atomism is appropriate, and the tendency to solipsism admitted, though always combated.

Russell has been recognized by some as a sage on the question of how human life can be improved. But this recognition has stopped short at what might be called the poetic or inspirational level. Russell has not been viewed as a philosopher on questions of value.[27] It is often concluded that, following his views on metaethics, his normative ethic is an atomistic jumble of individual preferences.[28] This conclusion does not follow from his holding a non-cognitivist metaethic. If it is thought that the normative ethic of a non-cognitivist might still have underlying conceptual connections, then the attempt to find them has rarely been made. Probably it is the lack of obligatory or prescriptive force which any systematization of such an ethic would have that has been the discouraging factor here: a non-cognitivist cannot say "You should" with the same impact as a cognitivist. In the context of a non-cognitivist metaethic, however, there is greater philosophical interest in the possibility of a systematic normative ethic. If its foundations in human nature are secure, and its reasoning correct, it ought to be persuasive. This is the sort of "naturalism" Robert J. McShea has ascribed to Spinoza.[29] It is a naturalism based on the satisfaction of the desires human beings do, in fact, have.

6 Russell's Criteria for Judging an Ethic

Let us explore the notion of a non-obliging or non-cognitivist normative ethic further. We may be helped by Russell's writings, for the question is of more than passing interest to him. In trying to transcend non-cognitivism in ethics and politics he is led to analyze the characteristics of ethical systems. One characteristic, on his view, becomes clear when he analyzes the term "philosophy":

> What is conventionally called "philosophy" consists of two very different elements. On the one hand, there are questions which are scientific or logical; these are amenable to methods as to which there is general agreement. On the other hand, there are questions of passionate interest to large numbers of people, as to which there is no solid evidence either way.... For one reason or another, we all find it impossible to maintain an attitude of sceptical detachment on many issues as to which pure reason is silent. A "philosophy", in a very usual sense of the word, is an organic whole of such extra-rational decisions.[30]

What we are looking for in Russell is the "organic whole of extra-rational decisions" which constitutes his ethic. In particular, we are looking for that aspect of his ethic which makes it "organic"—i.e. a unifying principle or principles which for Moore made the whole different from the sum of its parts.

In the work just quoted, *A History of Western Philosophy*, Russell does not confine his treatment of the major philosophers to their metaphysic, logic, and epistemology. Besides their metaethic, he deals with their normative ethic and political theory if they have either of them. The problem of a non-cognitivist evaluating others' normative ethical systems has clearly occurred to Russell. He discusses it in relation to Aristotle and Nietzsche; and there may be other discussions. The statement is fullest with respect to Aristotle:

> Let us now try to decide what we are to think of the merits and demerits of the [*Nichomachean*] *Ethics*. Unlike many other subjects treated by Greek philosophers, ethics has not made any definite advances, in the sense of ascertained discoveries; nothing in ethics is known in a scientific sense. There is therefore no reason why an ancient treatise on it should be in any respect inferior to a modern one. When Aristotle talks about astronomy, we can say definitely that he is wrong; but when he talks about ethics we cannot say, in the same sense, either that he is wrong or that he is right. Broadly speaking, there are three questions that we can ask about the ethics of Aristotle, or of any other philosopher: (1) Is it internally self-consistent? (2) Is it consistent with the remainder of the author's views? (3) Does it give answers to ethical problems that are consonant to our own feelings? If the answer to either the first or the second question is in the negative, the philosopher in question has been guilty of some intellectual error. But if the answer to the third question is in the negative, we have no right to say that he is mistaken; we have only the right to say that we do not like him. (Pp. 181–2; p. 193)

In the same period that he wrote the above, Russell makes a similar statement preparatory to judging Santayana's ethic, but in it he also raises the question of the "importance" of the ethic. Importance, he implies, is independent of consistency, for Spinoza's ethical judgments, Russell claims, while not wholly consistent, are important.[31] The two statements have two criteria in common, internal consistency, and consonancy to our own likes or dislikes. Unfortunately,

Russell does not elaborate on the claim of importance in the essay on Santayana. However, what seems to be the same question is discussed in relation to Aristotle. It appears in the last paragraph of the chapter on Aristotle's ethic, after the three formally posed questions are answered. Russell judges that the *Nichomachean Ethics* is "lacking in intrinsic importance". The reasons he gives are of considerable interest to any study of Russell's own ethic. They all concern the *Ethics*' "emotional poverty":

> ... everything that makes men feel a passionate interest in each other seems to be forgotten. Even his account of friendship is tepid. He shows no sign of having had any of those experiences which make it difficult to preserve sanity; all the more profound aspects of the moral life are apparently unknown to him. He leaves out, one may say, the whole sphere of human experience with which religion is concerned. What he has to say is what will be useful to comfortable men of weak passions; but he has nothing to say to those who are possessed by a god or a devil, or whom outward misfortune drives to despair.[32] (P. 184; p. 195)

What Russell seems to mean by the "importance" of an ethic in this context is its ability to deal with what he calls the "profounder" experiences of life. I return to this criterion in 56 (4). He claims, in the passage referred to on Santayana, that Spinoza's ethic is important. Because Russell so often mentions Spinoza in normative ethical contexts, I have sought to discover why he regards that man's ethic as important.

7 Connection with Spinoza and Monistic Ethics

Now that Spinoza's ethic has been mentioned, I shall begin to trace its connection with Russell's ethic. In the account of his "conversion" experience of 1901, Russell recalled that he emerged "filled ... with a desire almost as profound as that of the Buddha to find some philosophy which would make human life endurable."[33] This philosophy was never published as such, though I believe Russell thought he had found it. He made an attempt at writing it out in 1911; but the book-length manuscript that resulted has disappeared and was probably destroyed (see 44). For this negative reason and for many positive ones, Russell's reputation is as an analytic philosopher outside the analysis of value. He ruefully remarks in his "Reply to Criticisms" in respect to Philip Wiener's paper on Russell's study of Leibniz: "One may read Spinoza in order to learn how to live, but not Leibniz.... But Leibniz, though he wrote on practically everything, is (so at least I think) only worth reading when he is wholly abstract. Perhaps the same is true of myself; at least, this is Mr. Santayana's opinion" (p. 695).[34]

Russell's books have sold in the hundreds of thousands. Possibly millions of people have read them. A large number of those readers would deny that he is worth reading only in the abstract. But that is not to say philosophers would second this claim. In order to explain the connection which underlies Russell's ethical writings, I propose to trace a conceptual inheritance from Russell's early adherence to a monistic philosophy. Well after his rebellion against neo-Hegelianism, Russell confessed to another mistress, Lady Ottoline Morrell, that he was inclined to "Monism in feeling, dualism in judgment, [which] covers much reconciliation of religion and truth".[35] This can be taken as a remark about two conceptions of self in Russell. One conception—the narrow one—is important as the pluralist focal-point in epistemology and the locus of feeling in ethics, and there are striking similarities, or at least consistencies, between Russell's final position on the self in his philosophy of mind and his normative ethic; the other is a wider notion of self that can be found in Spinoza. Nevertheless I shall not attempt to bridge the gap between metaphysics and ethics for Russell. I take seriously the bifurcation he makes between what he calls his technical philosophy and what he thought about the plight of persons and their world. What I have sought to discover is what one non-cognitivist ethic has to offer. Russell once summed up what remains after the rejection of idealist metaphysics. The context is a review of *The Value and Destiny of the Individual* by Bernard Bosanquet, the neo-Hegelian. Russell published the review anonymously in 1913:

> Essentially independent of Dr. Bosanquet's metaphysic, there is in his work an ethic and an attitude towards human destiny which—at least to the present reviewer—appears both profoundly true and profoundly important. Man, as we know him, Dr. Bosanquet says, is a compound of finite and infinite, of separate selfhood wrongly claiming independence, and consciousness of the whole struggling after greater comprehensiveness and harmony. The feelings which underlie mysticism appear curiously constant in different ages and countries; but the

intellectual superstructures to which they give rise are extraordinarily various. Of these superstructures, Hegelianism is the most surprising. Overlaid by a long academic tradition, clothed in logical forms alien from its spirit and shocking to many logicians, the old vital mystic impulse may still be discerned in these lectures. Accept the world, live in the world, adapt your wishes and demands to what the whole permits, and you will achieve a certain wisdom, and a liberation from much evil that would seem otherwise inevitable—this is, in effect, what Dr. Bosanquet's philosophy becomes when the apparatus of metaphysic is cleared away. And it is thus possible to agree with much of what he urges, even when the doctrines from which it seems to flow are utterly rejected.[36]

This expression of continuing allegiance to monistic ways of feeling and of viewing the place of the self in the world may prepare the reader for conclusions to be reached in this study.

Having dealt with the separation between metaethics and normative ethics, we turn our attention to the systematization of Russell's ethic. Since I hold that Spinozism is the key to that ethic, I shall focus first on the major element of Spinoza's influence. I have reached the conclusion that Russell and Spinoza—despite vast differences in their metaphysics—share a certain view of the self. In part this is also the self of the monistic idealists, with a tincture of the notion of self-realization to be found in F. H. Bradley but avoiding the specifics of Bradley's ethic, as expressed in "My Station and Its Duties".[37] The notion of the wider self that is involved in Russell's normative ethic is hinted at in *The Problems of Philosophy* (1912), in a passage discussing the rewards of philosophical study. The gist is that through that study the boundaries of your mind are extended in proportion to the greatness of the object contemplated (and the object here is the universe); then the mind "becomes capable of that union with the universe which constitutes its highest good."[38] Enlargement of self is thus achieved through contemplation of what is not-self, with the result that your interests are widened. The spatial metaphor of "enlargement" is to be noted.

8 Commentators Linking Russell with Spinoza

A few commentators have mentioned Russell and Spinoza in the same breath. There are those, like Stuart Hampshire and Lewis S. Feuer,[39] who note a resemblance between the two philosophers. I quote Hampshire: "Russell is very conscious of nobility as a virtue, and of the proper role of a sage, who stands, like Spinoza, alone, near to nature in half-intellectual, half-mystical, understanding and therefore in opposition to society. Again he writes, 'Spinoza, always, is right in all these things.'"[40] There are a very few commentators such as Nicholas Rescher who have seen a connection bordering upon influence between the ethical philosophies of the two.[41] Hampshire goes as far as any well-known Spinoza scholar in relating Russell to Spinoza—which is not very far.[42]

What the commentators note is an affinity between Spinoza and Russell, not an influence of the former upon the latter. Russell's only prominently published writing on Spinoza is the chapter in his *History of Western Philosophy*. Reviewers of that work sometimes noticed the respect in which Russell holds Spinoza (see Chapter IV, n. 24). In 1964 D. J. O'Connor noticed the affinity again, in an essay on Russell: "Even if we disagree with the detail of his arguments, we can absorb, to our advantage, a certain quasi-religious reverence for truth and objectivity which is the mark of the true philosophic mind ... in his attitude to the world there is something of a religious attitude of a detached and impersonal kind, reminiscent perhaps of Spinoza more than of any other great philosopher."[43]

In recent years there has been evidence of a different interest in Russell and Spinoza. Three of the authors are thesis writers, while the fourth is primarily interested in ecological ethics. I shall discuss only the fourth.[44] The "ecophilosopher", George Sessions, has not provided a systematic connection between Spinoza and Russell, but to my knowledge he is the first to draw attention to a popular ethical work by Russell as being influenced by Spinoza:

> Russell claimed that his well-known *The Conquest of Happiness* was patterned after Spinoza's ethics although it is not clear Russell was entirely consistent in this effort. He tells us, "Spinoza long ago wrote of human bondage and human freedom: his form and his language make his thought difficult of access to all [but] students of philosophy, but the essence of what I wish to convey differs little from what he has said."[45]

The weakness of Sessions' claim is that he nowhere says in what precisely the attraction of Spinozism for Russell lies. Indeed, I am unsure whether he regards it as anything more than an affinity.

Moreover, he offers no evidence for his claim that the attraction was "life-long".

9   The Concept of Impersonal Self-Enlargement

The notion of self-enlargement is one of two notions that are needed to systematize Russell's normative ethic. Self-enlargement does not suffice to establish the connection of the ethic with Spinoza. A complementary notion, the "intellectual love of God", has to be taken from Spinoza's writings. On the one hand, Russell is searching for an ethic of "impersonality"—one that escapes the egocentric focus of desire. (Russell gives desire the honour of being the *raison d'être* of all ethics—for without the conflict of desires, he holds, there would be no need of ethics.) On the other hand, Spinoza suggests a rational approach to loving others as we may love ourselves. The common ground is the possible objectivity of thought. Russell would add feeling, or "impartial love" as he calls it in his classic essay, "Man's Peril" (1954), and elsewhere.

What I have found at the root of Russell's normative ethic requires the marshalling of historical evidence and analysis of the concepts of self-enlargement and the intellectual love of God. To show that Russell was influenced by Spinoza, it will be necessary to find in Spinoza's writings the notion of self-enlargement or its equivalent. Even that, however, is not sufficient. It will be necessary also to trace a direct debt from Russell to Spinoza. Finally, to show that the Spinozistic connection characterizes Russell's ethic in general, the connection must be found to hold, more or less strongly, throughout not only the conceptual core but also the chronological span of Russell's normative ethical thought. In dealing with a corpus of writing as large as Russell's, due care must be taken in selecting representative expressions of his views. After establishing the influence, I evaluate the ethic. True, it is an ethic about generosity and altruism, but it is also expressed as one of "impersonality". Do we really want to be treated impersonally by those who would do us good? Must we treat ourselves impersonally? These and other questions are considered in the light of criteria I bring to bear.

Part A (Chapters II–IV) examines Russell's writings on Spinoza. As a serious connection between Spinoza and Russell has not hitherto been proposed, the examination will be thorough. These chapters offer a critical history of Russell's concern with Spinoza's ethic and his notion of self; I shall pause occasionally to evaluate Russell's knowledge of Spinoza's doctrines. The division into three chapters is based on breaks which occur in Russell's writings between 1901 and 1907 and between 1912 and 1914. I begin Part B by assessing Russell's understanding of the "intellectual love of God" (Chapter V). Then I scrutinize Russell's own ethical writings for Spinozistic elements (Chapter VI). Russell's ethic of impersonal self-enlargement will be found to be heavily indebted to Spinoza. In Chapter VII, I evaluate the ethic, employing Russell's criteria in addition to my own, some of which are: suitability to human nature, clarity of the concepts involved, the claims of kinship versus impersonality, the ethic's completeness as a way of living, arbitrariness of any modifications made to the ethic to maintain its viability, and soundness of the ethic's claim to produce philosophic calm. These criteria should be borne in mind in the intervening chapters.

Some conclusions are that Russell's normative ethic forms, in the large, an "organic whole of extra-rational decisions", that it is indebted to his study of Spinoza's *Ethics,* and that the fundamental principle uniting the ethic's seemingly disparate parts is the principle of impersonal self-enlargement through diminution of the egocentric focus in desire. Some consequences are that, despite the views of commentators, Russell's normative ethic is a systematic whole, and that it shares much with the ethic of one of the great seventeenth-century rationalists. The evaluation of the ethic of impersonal self-enlargement, shared as it is by at least two very important figures in the history of philosophy, suggests that it is a plausible alternative to some more widely known ethical theories, particularly that of self-realization in the narrow sense.

PART A

Russell's Writings on Spinoza

CHAPTER II

The Early Period (1888–1901)

10 Introduction to Part A

The fundamental concept of Russell's normative ethic, as suggested in the Introduction, is that of impersonal self-enlargement. Russell derived this concept from two sources: the monistic idealism of British neo-Hegelianism, and Spinoza. There are, thus, two claims about Russell and Spinoza to be supported by reference to Russell's writings: the first is that the concept is embedded in Russell's normative ethical writings; the second, that he derived it from Spinoza. I shall begin by considering the extent of Russell's acquaintance with the life and writings of Spinoza. Part A is devoted to this task. The chapter divisions come after 1901 and after 1912 as a result of shifts in Russell's interests in Spinoza. The chronological approach will enable us more easily to uncover any development of Russell's ideas in these writings. Because of their uncollected nature, frequent quotation will be necessary.

Russell's acquaintance with Spinoza began early in his study of philosophy. Consequently, several sections will be concerned with unpublished documents from Russell's post-graduate years, well before his major published discussions of Spinoza. And it will be useful to refer to even earlier documents. First, however, I call upon the witness of Russell in very old age.

11 Russell in Old Age Admits Spinoza's Influence

In a widely distributed film interview, Russell, at the age of 92, declares: "Spinoza has been a great influence in my life and an influence of a practical sort." Russell makes the declaration after a series of questions from Robert Bolt, the playwright, about the relative importance of philosophy and the game of chess. He answers them by saying that, unlike chess, philosophy can "suggest ... further action". He then elaborates on Spinoza's influence: "You see, Spinoza's contention is that everything is determined and that it's absurd to find fault with a man for anything he does because he is bound to do that; whatever he does he's bound to do; and it teaches you tolerance, it teaches you to view actions that seem to you obviously absurd as inevitable; like a thunderstorm."[1] (*Cf.* Spinoza, E2P49S: "This doctrine contributes to the welfare of our social existence, since it teaches us to hate no one, to despise no one, to mock no one, to be angry with no one, and to envy no one."[2]) The interviewer goes on to draw the admission from Russell that he could never "reasonably" feel indignation or reverence.

The film offers no clue to the duration of Spinoza's influence on Russell, but the unedited transcript of the film does. The following lines were deleted in editing the film immediately before the longer quotation above:

BOLT: "Um, when did you first come under the influence of Spinoza? Approximately?"
RUSSELL: "I was an undergraduate, no, in my first graduate year."
BOLT: "And he affected you, as you say, in a practical sense?"
RUSSELL: "Yes."[3]

Since Russell obtained his B.A. in 1893, his first graduate year was in 1893–94 (ending when he was 22). Thus Spinoza's influence on him had a possible duration of over 70 years. No other philosopher exerted so long an influence on Russell, with the possible exception of J. S. Mill, whose lasting influence was in political philosophy.

A few years prior to the film interview, Russell explains in greater detail how the conflict between determinism and free will

> ... was partly resolved for me, though in a way which I no longer think valid, when I read Spinoza's *Ethics*. Spinoza allayed my suspicion of sentiment by his geometrical method. The apparatus of definitions, axioms, and demonstrated propositions lulled my doubts to sleep. The rigid determinism of his system allowed me to think that there was nothing in him that the most austere scientific rigour need view with distrust. And yet despite all this he arrived in the end at a degree of ethical sublimity which I found unequalled in those who advocated free will for the sake of morals. I still feel that Spinoza was a very great man, whose life

was consistent with his belief, and was lived always in a profoundly admirable manner. Morally he stands for me where he did, but intellectually, in spite of his parade of mathematical cogency, I find his doctrines almost wholly unsatisfactory.[4]

The quotation makes it almost certain that at the beginning of this passage Russell is referring to his first study of Spinoza's *Ethics*. His well-known reflections as an adolescent on the problem of determinism and free will, published as his "Greek Exercises", are not far in the past. His first study of Spinoza's doctrines almost certainly took place in January 1894. The notebook listing the books he read between 1891 and 1902 records the reading of Sir Frederick Pollock's work on Spinoza in that month.[5] It appears, from the following passage in a letter to Alys Pearsall Smith, who became Russell's first wife later in 1894, that Russell also read Spinoza himself, though no entry to that effect was made in the notebook. He writes Alys: "But I wish I had got hold of Spinoza two years ago instead of Thomas à Kempis: he would have suited me far better: he preaches a rich voluptuous asceticism based on a vast undefined mysticism, which even now has seized hold of my imagination most powerfully."[6] The phrase "a rich voluptuous asceticism" is obscure. It may be that Russell has in mind Spinoza's permitting of some of the minor enjoyments of life while not consenting to be in bondage to the stronger passions. Spinoza recommends: "It is the part of the wise man, I say, to refresh and invigorate himself with moderate and pleasant eating and drinking, with sweet scents and the beauty of green plants, with ornament, with music, with sports, with the theater, and with all things of this kind which one man can enjoy without hurting another" (E4P45S). At any rate, it is sufficient to recognize in this and the preceding passage a temporary satisfaction of the two motives Russell often claims brought him to philosophy. These motives were "the desire to find some knowledge that could be accepted as certainly true . . . and the desire to find some satisfaction for religious impulses."[7]

12 Russell's Earliest Religious Reflections and Nature-Worship

Russell's religious impulses were at once ethical and intellectual. He wished to believe that God guides the world towards some good end, but he increasingly found difficulties in believing in immortality, free will and hence moral responsibility, and finally God himself. He writes in his "Greek Exercises" between the ages of fifteen and seventeen on all three topics. What he writes on free will is relevant to understanding his later attraction to Spinozism:

> ... it seems impossible to imagine that man, the great man, with his reason, his knowledge of the universe, and his ideas of right and wrong, man, with his emotions, his love and hate, and his religion, that this man, should be a mere perishable chemical compound, whose character, and his influence for good or for evil, depends solely or entirely on the particular motions of the molecules of his brain, and that all the greatest men have been great by reason of some one molecule hitting up against some other a little oftener than in other men!
>
> For if we examine any action whatsoever, we find always motives, over which we have no more control than matter over the forces acting on it, which produce our actions. The Duke of Argyll [in *The Reign of Law*, 1866] says we can present motives to ourselves, but is not that an action, determined by our character, and other unavoidable things.
> The argument for free will from the fact that we feel it, is worthless, for we do not feel motives which we find really exist, nor that mind depends on brain, etc.[8]

He retained his belief in God for two more years, when he lost it upon reading Mill.[9] The argument in the last quotation above is reminiscent of a passage in Spinoza's *Ethics* (1Ap.): "[Man] thinks himself free because he is conscious of his wishes and appetites, whilst at the same time he is ignorant of the causes by which he is led to wish and desire, not dreaming what they are...." Thus at this early age Russell reached positions which would make him receptive to the *Ethics* a few years later. Russell later admitted the parallel to be found in his early reflections with what he called Spinoza's "quasi-mathematical psychology" in Part III of the *Ethics*.[10] The actual origin of Russell's early determinism, however, stems from his interest in nineteenth-century scientism and mechanism.

At about the same time (1888–89), a strong impulse to nature-worship manifested itself in Russell. He reports in old age that "Beauty, especially beauty in nature, caused me at times to lean towards pantheism."[11] (Russell's favourite nature-poet was Shelley, who, as Pollock points out, translated Spinoza.¹²) A passage from the "Greek Exercises", headed "Nature-worship", reveals a pantheistic outlook:

> Herein indeed lies the beauty of nature, and the comfort it can afford when the spirit is vexed with doubt, when peace seems a thing never more to bless the soul; then the blessed influence of the stars or the moon descends like balm upon the soul; a peace and calm seem to reign over all, and all jar and discord flee away—and is it reasonable to suppose such influence to lurk in mere lifeless matter? What is the beauty in art, in painting or sculpture, unless it be·the soul that manifests itself in the canvas or the marble? And is not the same true of nature? Can inanimate speak to animate? Is not rather the soul which is manifested in nature as much more perfect than the soul of painter or sculptor, as nature is more perfect than art? In human handiwork perfection can never be attained; in nature, perfection appears at every turn, manifesting the perfect soul of the creator.

At the end of the entry from which the above is an extract, Russell allows that his belief in nature may be "mere poetic sentimentalism". He was much influenced at this time by Wordsworth's "Ode: Intimations of Immortality from Recollections of Early Childhood", and Wordsworth, too, was familiar with Spinozism (Pollock, p. 402).¹³ The disparaging reference to "poetic sentimentalism" raises the question of means to truth. Russell was not yet a complete rationalist, in the sense which is not opposed to empiricism. He did not yet hold the principle, which became a fundamental part of his intellectual world-view and of his epistemology and metaphysic, that human emotions reveal nothing about the nature of the external world, and indeed not very much about ourselves in so far as "they interfere with the receptivity to fact which is the essence of the scientific attitude to the world."¹⁴ At the beginning of the "Greek Exercises" he pledges that "in finding reasons for believing in God I shall only take account of scientific arguments. This is a vow I have made which costs me much to keep, and to reject all sentiment" (19 Mar. 1888; *Camb. Essays*, p. 5). Near the end of the journal, however, in a passage concerning the possible immortality of the soul, Russell, while not admitting faith as a means to truth, does admit "poetic arguments"—i.e. inferences based upon sentiment or emotion:

All these facts tend to make one imagine that the bond of body and soul is indissoluble, both living and dying together.... Let us not however dogmatically deny man's immortality, for innumerable "poetic" arguments may be urged in its favour, as that from man's greatness, (ably put forth by Tennyson ... ,) and poetic arguments often have something in them. But let us despise those whose reason tells them they know nothing about it, but who fall back on "faith", which seems to me always to mean belief in something unreasonable, and is a most cowardly thing to call down upon us all as a divine gift. (31 July 1888; *Cambridge Essays*, p. 20)

I shall return to this point shortly. It would be interesting to know at what point in his life Russell completely rejects "poetic sentimentalism" as a means to truth. In the meantime natural beauty remained a strong interest for the young Russell. Upon entering Cambridge the following year (1890), he chose to answer an examination question on the subject. The question was: "Compare the effects produced upon the mind of the beholder by beauty in nature and beauty in art."[15] We do not possess his answer, but it may be said that, in general terms, appreciation of natural beauty to the near-mystical extent that Russell felt it indicates a profound feeling of closeness, perhaps of union, with nature. The later Russell might have expressed this identification with nature as "enlargement of self". Before that development, however, for a considerable period he strove for abnegation of self.

13 Self-Abnegation

An important manifestation of the religious impulse lies in the attitude to the self, or ego in a non-Freudian sense. Religion has often inspired the attitude of self-abnegation. This is particularly true of Eastern religions and Roman Catholic mysticism. The root of it is the wish to merge one's self with something greater than oneself, but it can take morbid forms, such as the urge to deny, and even destroy, the self. That "something greater" is usually God, though it may be the state. In the case of pantheism, self-abnegation is expressed in the attempt to merge one's personality with the world, since God is conceived as numerically identical with all that exists. A self merged with the world would be a person who did not draw a distinction between himself and any other apparent entity in the world.[16]

13 Self-Abnegation

This manifestation helps to explain the allusion to Thomas à Kempis in the letter to Alys Pearsall Smith quoted in 11. Russell wished he had come upon Spinoza "two years ago" instead of Thomas à Kempis. There is no mention of Thomas à Kempis, or even evident need of someone like him, to be found in Russell's few surviving writings of the winter of 1891–92, the time implied to Alys. There is, however, evidence of a substantial influence a little earlier, in a journal entry of 14 July 1890, shortly before Russell entered Cambridge:

> I have just been reading that wonderful chapter in the *Mill on the Floss* where Maggie finds Thomas à Kempis. I wish I could take his lesson to heart even in the misunderstood way in which Maggie does. For although she is still perhaps in some sort selfish in her self-renunciation, as is proved by her yielding to the first temptation worth the name which comes across her path, still she does carry some sort of holiness about with her throughout that time, and her life is calmer and unquestionably happier. Like her, I feel that all my life has been selfish: even my best acts have had some background of selfish motives, as my miserable habit of introspection shows me; but unlike her, though convinced of the truth of the blessedness of self-renunciation, I have not enough self-control nor enough steadiness of purpose to be able to practise it for any length of time. I always hanker after a fuller life, after a satisfaction of my highest wants which I know to be inconsistent with the highest life. Of course the want of faith, which I feel to be no fault of mine, does increase the difficulty of life for me; but even so, if I could put away that miserable longing for happiness, I might instead thereof find blessedness. For with the faith in immortality and in a reward of virtue hereafter, the utter and entire self-denial of those who do good without that hope is much diminished.[17]

The Mill on the Floss (1860) is a novel by George Eliot, who was herself influenced by not only Thomas à Kempis but also Spinoza, whom she too translated.[18] This chapter in question occurs in Book IV, "The Valley of Humiliation", and is called "A Voice from the Past". The voice is that of Thomas à Kempis (1380–1471), whose life was lived chiefly as a monk in Germany. As a monk he was exemplary: according to his successor, "from the outset of his monastic life he endured great poverty, temptations, and labours."[19] He so succeeded in repression of self that he was an exception to the rule offered by

Spinoza that even authors who write against the self identity themselves when they publish (E3Df.Aff.44Ex.)—Thomas à Kempis's chief work, *The Imitation of Christ*, was published anonymously.[20] The thesis of this work is that you move closer to God through imitating the suffering of Christ. As Christ's suffering consisted in the mortification of self, you should imitate that form of suffering. The manifestations of self to be suppressed are those which involve one in "worldly things"—such as fellow creatures and creature comforts.[21] By such self-denial the gamut of ascetic practices may be inspired. Asceticism, however, takes many forms. On the one hand, there is the physical self-assault of early Christians such as St. Simeon Stylites, who joyously (it is said) tore out his flesh. On the other, there is the outer-directed selflessness of Albert Schweitzer after the age of 30, when he began to follow the ethical principle of "good fortune obligates".[22] And there is also what we might call "prudential asceticism", which denies some aspects of self in order to promote others. This kind of asceticism is by no means uncommon. Russell's later rejection of asceticism does not involve prudential asceticism in all its forms.

The passages which George Eliot quotes from Thomas à Kempis inculcate the near-total suppression of self. I say "near", for several times, in these passages, he states that the purpose of such suppression is to satisfy the desire for peace of mind. Peace of mind is a common goal of mystics and others who try to calm the self's turbulent demands; Spinoza's phrase for it is *acquiescentia mentis*. Some of her quotations are: "Know that the love of thyself doth hurt thee more than anything in the world" and "On this sin, that a man inordinately loveth himself, almost all dependeth, whatsoever is thoroughly to be overcome; which evil being once overcome and subdued, there will presently ensue great peace and tranquillity."[23] It is, then, partly a prudential asceticism which Thomas à Kempis invokes. The renunciation or abnegation of self is very different from the enlargement or expansion of self in an impersonal way encouraged by Spinoza and soon Russell. The chief difference between Thomas à Kempis and Russell lies in their views of selflessness as a general means of salvation. Russell, following Spinoza, builds upon the facts of man's nature an ethical and political philosophy of considerable scope; Thomas à Kempis refused to accept those facts, preferring the attempt to alter man's nature. As Russell cautions in 1918: "The sum total of the matter is that one's idealism must be *robust* and must fit in with the facts of nature; and that which is horrible in the actual world is mainly due to a bad system. Spinoza, always, is right in all these things, to my mind."[24]

With the advent, in 1893, of his study of philosophy at Cambridge, Russell began looking to traditional philosophical texts for the combination of metaphysical and religious enlightenment. He was in luck, for the school then in vogue was British absolute idealism, or neo-Hegelianism. This school provided a normative ethic—though its content was not always easy to determine in the writings of Bradley and others—and treated Spinoza's monistic idealism as a respected precursor.

14 Notes on Lectures in the History of Philosophy

In 1893–94 Russell attended several lecture courses in philosophy at Trinity College. Among them were Stout's "History of Philosophy" and Ward's course of the same title. Russell's extensive notes on the lectures have survived. George Frederick Stout (1860–1944), editor of *Mind* from 1891 to 1921, did his major work in philosophical psychology and was the author of a noted textbook on psychology. His own teacher, James Ward (1843–1925), was an idealist; Ward also wrote notably on psychology. Neither philosopher published general works on the history of philosophy, although Ward wrote a study of Kant. Stout devoted two lectures to Spinoza in January 1894 between six on Hobbes and nine on Descartes. Ward spent part of one lecture on Spinoza in a survey extending from Descartes to Reid and Spencer. In general, Stout covered Spinoza's philosophical psychology, relating it always to Hobbes', while Ward dealt with his metaphysic. Ethics *per se* was neglected, doubtless because Henry Sidgwick had just offered two courses on the subject. (Russell kept his extensive notes on Sidgwick's lectures, but the discussions of Spinoza are insignificant. For Sidgwick's notion of impartiality, see **54**.) I shall examine first the notes on Stout's lectures, then the notes on Ward's.

Stout was chiefly concerned with Spinoza's theory of man. He emphasized *conatus*, the drive for self-preservation, and its relation to man's power, freedom and perfection. Stout is reported by Russell as holding that Spinoza and Hobbes shared the same goal, to understand the passions of men:

Both suppose fundamental impulse or nisus constitutes very being of individual: this in Hobbes endeavour after self-preservation or self-assertion rather. Spinoza says "each individual thing endeavours to persist in its own being: this effort nothing else than that thing being what it is" [E3P6–7]. Pollock says: Effort might be supposed mysterious power embodied in things: but Spinoza carefully excludes these: effort merely thing's being what it is: can't get it out of the way without doing work on it. This *persistence* from point of view of thing operated upon.[25]

Though inclined to monistic idealism at this time, Russell here received support for his later atomism, which he not only holds in metaphysics but seems to hold in political philosophy. The liberal, atomistic, individualistic view of man in society requires a psychology crediting each person with autonomous agency. Stout, however, in the monistic spirit of the time, offered a criticism of the atomistic view of man. He had told the class, in the previous lecture, that the "notion that individual as claiming separate being [is] doomed to failure because [he] derives existence from what's not himself" (lecture notebook, p. 129). Stout stressed the notion of power in Spinoza. He pointed out that "Power gives joy" and is equivalent to freedom and perfection (p. 131). We are free "in so far as what happens to us is our own doing"—a typical statement of the negative doctrine of freedom in its focus on the absence of external compulsion. Stout also discussed the definitions of some of the passions, and Spinoza's attack on the concept of will. The latter topic included a lesson in determinism. Although the views discussed are Hobbes', they are an important forerunner of Spinoza's deterministic psychology. Stout touched on ethical and even religious matters in Spinoza. He mentioned Spinoza's relativistic account in certain passages of the common usage of "good" and "bad" (though he did not call it relativism); he controversially added that Spinoza would "allow nothing absolute in distinction between good and evil" (p. 127). He obscurely said, or so Russell reports him as saying: "Doctrine that power of one excess above that of another constitutes religious problem for Spinoza, need of salvation: means of that he claims to lay down in his philosophy" (p. 129).

The notes Russell took of lectures introducing him to Spinoza show two long-lasting influences upon his own views. First, Stout quoted from Pollock; Russell read Pollock straightaway and even seventeen years later was recommending the book to others (see **15**). Second, Ward began his lecture by telling the class how to read the *Ethics*: "Read Ethics, longer scholia, prefaces, excursus. Propositions are tedious."²⁶ If Ward said the propositions were tedious, what then did he think of the demonstrations? It is likely he shared Stout's view. In reviewing G. S. Fullerton's *The Philosophy of Spinoza* the following year, Stout remarked that "... from the point of view of Philosophy and History of Philosophy, the formal correctness or incorrectness of Spinoza's demonstrations could, at the present day, be of interest to no mortal."²⁷ Ward's attitude to the "tedious" parts of Spinoza is echoed half a century later in the chapter on Spinoza in *A History of Western Philosophy*. Russell writes there that the detail of the demonstrations is "not worth mastering"; it is the scholia, he claims, "which contain much of what is best in the *Ethics*" (p. 572; p. 554). Third, even Russell's later judgment that Spinoza's metaphysic is inconsistent is present in Ward's lecture. After a grand introduction—"Philosophy near akin to poetry: imagination in the abstract has got hold of some philosophers, notably Spinoza and Plato"—Ward declared, "But as philosophy can't disguise from oneself that Spinoza falls to pieces" (notebook, p. 28). Acccording to Ward, Spinoza falls to pieces in the following ways; his rationalistic, geometrical method was exposed by Kant as inappropriate, since mathematics proceeds largely by "clearness of mathematical intuitions" and philosophy cannot intuit; his mathematical model fails in its treatment of causation ("cause" being made equivalent to "logical condition"); and the "gulph" (*sic*) between finite and infinite modifications of an attribute cannot be traversed. As for Spinoza's concept of God, Ward held that he "means only what is meant nowadays by Absolute or Unconditioned" (p. 29). Ward told the class that Spinoza's writings were suppressed by the Church until the "first edition" of Kant, i.e. the publication of the *Critique of Pure Reason* in 1781, which made Kant historically prior in terms of impact. And he spoke of Spinoza's pantheism and of his influence on Hegel, and said at that point that "Erdmann [is] good on Spinoza" (p. 29). Ward concluded his stimulating lecture thus: "Have in him first hint of doctrine of two aspects. Scouts free-will, but uses liberty as synonymous with necessity, in which a good deal of subtlety. God does things from inherent necessity of his own nature, which same as freedom.—For criterion of knowledge has only the Cartesian principle of clearness and distinctness" (p. 30). Thus Ward influenced Russell's understanding of Spinoza—from the view he was to express of Spinoza's demonstrations through his tendency to classify Spinoza as a proto-absolute idealist.

Before examining Pollock's book and Russell's own writings after these lectures, we shall look at Erdmann's "good" account.[28] Russell evidently used Erdmann's *History* in 1894 for the purpose of gaining insight into Spinoza's subtleties, as his markings reflect. For example, he marked several passages explaining Spinoza's attribute of thought.[29] They are not the sort of passages marked by the student aiming at a minimal understanding of Spinoza's metaphysic. Erdmann also devotes space to Spinoza's political philosophy. This topic interested Russell, who wrote "Hobbes" beside a passage stating, "Men were always and are everywhere the same; and therefore, if things go badly, the political arrangements alone can be responsible" (trans., p. 81; orig., p. 69). In his discussion of moral philosophy, Erdmann combined accounts of Spinoza's doctrines of freedom, will and knowledge. Russell marked several passages, some of them being:

> His Moral Philosophy, on the other hand, has for its purpose to show how the few who do not require the State and for whom accordingly civil liberty is insufficient, raise themselves to the highest form of liberty, [Russell's mark appears to end here, but Erdmann continues:] spiritual freedom, which is a private virtue (*Tract. polit.* i., 6).[30]

> Thus the relation that subsists between the individual who understands and the being understood, is that between one who is free and something which he has himself approved of or willed. Increase of understanding, therefore, brings increase of (spiritual) freedom, for it adds to the amount of that of which I am master. On the other hand, the more I understand, the more I am bound to accept of what does not depend upon my approval, and, therefore, the more constrained I am. This contrast between constraint (servitus), treated of by Spinoza in the *Fourth Book* of his chief work, and spiritual strength and spiritual freedom [here the translation omits "(libertas)"], discussed in the *Fifth*, is the cardinal point of his *Ethics*, which thus becomes really a *Tractatus de intellectus emendatione*, to adopt the title of one of his earlier writings.[31]

> If we keep firm hold of that fact that to conceive is to approve, or to will for oneself, we can easily understand how Spinoza, in spite of his fatalism, can still assert that,—in fact can even show the way in which,—man may attain to ever greater freedom and rid himself of all passivity.[32]

These passages all concern the relationship of personal freedom and understanding. To a student hoping to find a combination of metaphysics and religion in philosophy, they must have been intriguing. Russell also marked passages setting out Spinoza's three kinds of knowledge: sensation and opinion, reasoning, and intuition. Understanding of the latter two kinds must result in assent, for they relate to the perception of necessary connections. The man who perceives necessary connections between things is not, Spinoza trusts, going to will that they be otherwise. Hence he will be free of all desire in relation to these things.

Erdmann's chapter is lacking notably in a treatment of Spinoza's psychology of the self and of the passions, which, we shall find, Russell values highly. Even at this time of first acquaintance with Spinoza, Russell has a fairly high opinion of Spinoza's psychology. He writes Alys Pearsall Smith: "I have been reading Hobbes and Spinoza, and tomorrow I am going to read DesCartes [sic], on the subject of the passions; Spinoza is good"—though he added a qualification not unexpected in one who had just got himself secretly engaged, "one cannot help feeling that both of them write of a good many passions from hearsay and not from personal experience." Russell rejects, in a passage he effectively retracts many times in later years, Spinoza's normative ethic of the intellectual love of God:

> ... a heaven without emotion, spent in passionless contemplation of propositions of Euclid, which seems to be Spinoza's ideal (though he calls it intellectual love of God to make it sound better), makes any modern shudder: a heaven without all-absorbing emotional love seems a far less desirable thing than earth with all its drawbacks. This opinion is not mine peculiarly, but that of almost all the younger people I know, and that of philosophers, like Bradley. (28 Jan. 1894)

It is at just this point, however, that Russell makes the remark (quoted in 11) about wishing he had got hold of Spinoza earlier.

15 Pollock's *Spinoza*

Russell soon read the other commentary recommended in the lectures. A week after first writing of Spinoza to Alys, he tells her:

Sir Frederick Pollock, whom thee mentions in thy letter to Logan [Alys's brother] as the rudest man in England, is the author of a book on Spinoza which I have lately read and which seems to me every way admirable; besides being very well and interestingly written it displays an amount and variety of learning before which my brain reels. It is a very apostolic book, being written by one brother and dedicated to another (W. K. Clifford). (4 Feb. 1894)

Whether or not Sir Frederick Pollock (1845–1937) was then the rudest man in England, he was one of the most intellectually distinguished.[33] For years Pollock regularly reviewed major works on Spinoza for prominent journals. At the age of 90 he published a new little work on him. It is not known whether Russell read Pollock's minor contributions, but, as we have seen, he long esteemed Pollock's major critical work, *Spinoza: His Life and Philosophy*.[34] To a friend in 1902 he writes: "Yes, Spinoza is hard: I strongly advise reading Pollock's book about him first; you will then find it easier to discover his heart."[35] In reviews he later writes: "He [Spinoza] therefore requires commentaries to translate him into easier language, if his main ideas are to be appreciated as widely as possible. Sir Frederick Pollock's book has performed this task with rare skill...",[36] and "the task of interpretation has been performed for the technical reader by Mr. Joachim, and for a wider class by Sir Frederick Pollock...."[37] To Lady Ottoline Morrell, he advised early in their affair: "Don't bother about reading Spinoza yet a while. I should be sorry if you took the time away from writing to me! I think if you do have any time, you will do better to read Pollock than to read Spinoza himself, at first" (no. 98, [June 1911]).[38]

The most important effect upon Russell of Pollock's book was that it instilled in him a permanent admiration for Spinoza. As he writes also to Lady Ottoline in 1911, "Ever since I first read Pollock's book, which was when I was an undergraduate [sic], Spinoza has been one of the most important people in my world" (no. 169a, 11 Aug. 1911). Several features of Pollock's *Spinoza* could cumulatively have had such an effect. Pollock is first of all a very readable author, being both critical and enthusiastic. His work has an excellent selection of quotations from Spinoza, translated by Pollock himself. What Russell told Alys about the extent of Pollock's learning was based doubtless on his evident wide research, multilingualism, knowledge of history, knowledge of past philosophies, and up-to-dateness in science. Consider as an example of the last feature: Pollock makes it a canon of interpretation that "the physiological correlations of mental action are never overlooked by him [Spinoza] for a moment" (p. 284); this scientific outlook was then being directed to the verification of the results of psychology, "as far as possible", by physiological observation (p. 195). Pollock works in even the discovery of anaesthetics (p. 225), and is aware of non-Euclidean geometries (p. 174)—which Russell, at this time of first reading Pollock, was just beginning to investigate and on which he would soon write his fellowship dissertation.[39] Pollock himself accepted determinism—"the choice I exercise in writing these lines is determined and in nowise arbitrary" (p. 205)—and had little respect for orthodox, and even theistic, religion (pp. 356–7). While not discernibly an absolute idealist himself, Pollock followed T. H. Green and others in taking Spinoza's monistic idealism seriously. And his book praises Spinoza's character and adduces sufficient information about his life to justify that praise. We have seen that Russell was inclined at this time to asceticism: Pollock writes of Spinoza's "almost incredible frugality of health and economy" (p. 41). Russell is always critical of churches: Pollock talks about "martyrs and confessors in the cause of free thought", at the same time anticipating one of Russell's favourite cynicisms: "no sooner has a persecuted community secured its freedom than it takes to persecuting in its turn" (p. 9).[40] He tells us details of the persecutions suffered by Spinoza and how his books were prohibited and neglected for a century (pp. 34, 41, 379), and then how his works regained intellectual favour. *A propos* of Goethe's interest in Spinoza, Pollock quotes a passage which seems to have stuck permanently in Russell's mind.[41] The passage has Goethe quoting Spinoza (E5P19): "Whoso truly loves God must not expect God to love him in return" (p. 395). In later years Russell derides Goethe for what he considers is a serious misunderstanding. In his review in 1910 of the White and Stirling translation of the *Ethics*, Russell merely refers to "the moralistic priggery of Goethe's praises".[42] But by the time of *A History of Western Philosophy*, Russell still remembers Pollock's section on Goethe or has lately reread it: "Goethe, who admired Spinoza withint even beginning to understand him, thought this proposition an instance of self-abnegation. It is nothing of the sort, but a logical consequence of Spinoza's metaphysic. He does not say that a man *ought* not to want God to love him; he says that a man who loves God *cannot* want God to love him" (p. 576; p. 558). Russell is correct in his translation of the verb *potest*.

The suggestion is that logical necessity is Spinoza's strength, not mere moral advice.

Thus, in his treatment of Spinoza the man, Pollock set up an intellectual model for the young Russell. As a role model, Spinoza had not only intellectual but ethical significance. Russell rarely fails, in many references to him throughout his life, to treat Spinoza with reverence. It was, of course, Spinoza's life itself, and not Pollock's presentation of it, that had this effect, but Pollock's sympathetic presentation surely got Russell's reverence off to an early start. Even in the matter of religion Pollock's account must have appealed to the young Russell. Russell had not been a theist since reading the refutation of the first cause argument for God's existence in Mill's *Autobiography* four years earlier, but he still looked to philosophy to provide religious consolation. "It was largely the hope of getting a religion out of philosophy that led me to take it [neo-Hegelianism] up ...",[43] Russell writes to Lady Ottoline (no. 199, 28 Sept. 1911). Yet Pollock's characterization of Spinoza's attitude to religion is almost precisely that of the later Russell:

> It is evident that he considered religion as something very real in a man's life, and the charge of irreligion or atheism as the grossest and most wicked of calumnies. But this religion, as he understands it, is not the religion of churches and sects. It is independent of dogmatic theology, independent of any particular knowledge or belief as to revelation, independent even of the so-called natural theology which holds to the conception of God as a Person after all other definitions of his nature have been renounced, and to the expectation of another life which shall redress the balance of the present one in some manner of which all specific knowledge is disclaimed. The essence of religion is in Spinoza's mind a cheerful and willing cooperation with the order of the world as manifested in the nature of man and society. (P. 69)

I said "almost precisely", because Russell hardly regarded "the charge of irreligion or atheism as the grossest and most wicked of calumnies". But observe how close he comes. "What makes my attitude towards religion complex", he writes in 1944, "is that, although I consider some form of personal religion highly desirable, and feel many people unsatisfactory through the lack of it, I cannot accept the theology of any well known religion, and I incline to think that most churches at most times have done more harm than good."[44] Russell even sometimes calls for a new "religion": "What is needed is something in the nature of religion, not in any dogmatic sense, but as a source of serious and determined effort towards something better than the present";[45] and: "The movement in favour of war resistance is not to be viewed primarily as political, but rather as a matter of personal conviction, like religion."[46]

While Pollock treats the whole of Spinoza's philosophy in his work, in this study we must confine ourselves to ethics. Some discussion of Spinoza's metaphysic is necessary, but only in relation to Russell's transitional work in his rebellion against monistic idealism (17) and his understanding of Spinoza's key concept, the "intellectual love of God" (Chapter V).

Pollock devotes considerable space to Spinoza's conception of the nature of man. The fundamental idea in that conception is "the tendency or effort (*conatus*) of all things towards self-preservation" (p. 86). As is evident from this quotation, man is held to share this feature with all creatures, and inanimate objects, too. Pollock twice calls Spinoza's resulting account of man's passions a "masterpiece" (pp. 86, 216). Spinoza's account is productive as a theory, for he proceeds to define desire in terms of it: "desire is appetite [i.e. *conatus*] with consciousness thereof" (p. 221). The mature Russell, as I noted above (9), never ceases to regard desire as the fundamental fact of ethics. From desire Spinoza derived what he considered to be the two chief "affections", or emotions, namely pleasure and pain, or joy and sadness (*laetitia* and *tristitia*). The simple emotion of pleasure accompanied by the idea of an external cause is love (*amor*), and the simple emotion of pain accompanied by a like idea is hatred (*odium*). In this way Spinoza builds up explanations of the common and not so common human emotions. An essay written later in 1894 shows Russell to have been influenced considerably by Spinoza's theory of the emotions. In "Cleopatra or Maggie Tulliver" (cited at n. 62) Russell uses Spinoza's statement that "a passion can only be overcome by a stronger passion" (E4P7). The point of this proposition is to exclude *mere* reason from an active role in determining the ends one pursues. This is, again, a permanent feature of the mature Russell's metaethic. For instance, in *Human Society in Ethics and Politics* he writes: "'Reason' ... signifies the choice of the right means to an end that you wish to achieve. It has nothing whatever to do with choice of ends.... Desires, emotions, passions (you can choose whichever word you will), are the only possible causes of action" (p. 8). Thus, had

Hume not written his account of the role of reason in ethics,[47] Spinoza's would have sufficed. Pollock makes the point well: "... knowledge, as such, is incompetent to restrain the passions: it can have that effect only in so far as it is an emotion" (p. 252). Russell doubtless agreed that the joyful exercise of reason turns a reasonable man into a potent force for action.

The purpose of a theory of the emotions is to enable us to understand man. Understanding man's emotions can lead to prediction of his actions. If you know how I am going to act on the basis of knowledge of me in the present, then there are conditions in the present which can be said to "determine" the future and which can be manipulated to control behaviour. Spinoza was a determinist in this sense, and so is the mature Russell[48] and, as we have seen in **12**, even the adolescent Russell; so, too, was Pollock. Pollock was a cheerful determinist. He writes that "determinism, in short, if only one applies it thoroughly, leaves all the common uses of life exactly where they were" (p. 204). Spinoza would not have agreed. It is essential to his ethic that understanding how people must behave contributes to *acquiescentia mentis*. Russell is less strong on this point, but nevertheless holds that the view lessens indignation, or ought to do so. In a political context, he writes nearly 30 years later:

> The final outcome [of what Russell calls his "reflection on war hypocrisy"], so far as I am concerned, is a Spinozistic moral philosophy. To apply moral terms to human beings—to call them knaves or scoundrels or what not—is unscientific, expressing our own ignorant surprise at what we should have foreseen if we had been a little wiser. "Each thing," says Spinoza, "in so far as it is in itself, endeavors to persevere in its being" (Ethics, III, 6). It follows that a politician will try to stay in office. One might as well blame the earth for sticking to its orbit though other parts of the universe would be more agreeable to us.[49]

Yet I have some hesitation in regarding Russell as a thorough determinist. It is not only the infrequency of his explicit use of the notion, but also the doubtful adoption of the large ethical claim, made by Pollock, that a deterministic attitude "leaves all the common uses of life exactly where they were."

A major part of Spinoza's normative ethical theory concerns *scientia intuitiva*, the third kind of knowledge (for Spinoza's kinds of knowledge, see **34**). Pollock rightly connects the third kind of knowledge with Spinoza's key ethical concept, the "intellectual love of God". A brief examination of this connection may help us later (34–5) in understanding how Russell comprehends this concept. Such an understanding is important, for Russell later claims that while commentators quarrel over the meaning of this phrase, he feels *he* knows what it means (letter to Lady Ottoline, no. 82, p/24 May 1911). As Pollock notes, Spinoza's exposition presents great difficulties: "Spinoza proceeds to lay before us a theory of intellectual immortality, or rather eternity, the perfection whereof consists in an intellectual love of God which is likewise eternal, and 'is part of the infinite love wherewith God loves himself'" (E5P36). Pollock thinks Spinoza "carefully isolated" the section on the intellectual love of God in the latter half of Part V of the *Ethics* from the more readily understood section in the first half on the love of God arising from clear and distinct knowledge of our emotions. The eternality of mind he regards as "a kind of supplemental speculation" (p. 282). The more mundane love of God consists in intuitive knowledge of our own nature, and it provides various remedies against the emotions which seem to control us.[50] The intellectual love of God involves knowledge *sub specie aeternitatis*. Eternality is characteristic of the third kind of knowledge—seeing things at once as they *must* always be. The "contemplation" of things as they must be is a pleasure accompanied by the idea of God as its cause (p. 300). We have, then, in Spinoza as interpreted by Pollock, the ideal of the life of contemplative activity, whose reward is emotional peace (E5P42). This ideal must have been very attractive to a youth who sought religious consolation from philosophy. Pollock sums it up:

> ... the substance of the propositions thus expressed is still purely and simply the human mind's contemplation of itself and its own certain knowledge as part of the infinite and necessary order of the universe; that for Spinoza the divine love is nothing else than conscious acceptance of universal law, the "welcoming every event" of the Stoics;[51] and that the secret of blessedness and glory (for those titles are expressly claimed and justified) is none other than a mind steadfastly bent on truth. (P. 302)

Despite his somewhat critical attitude, Pollock holds that Spinoza's "doctrine of the eternity of the mind must remain one of the most brilliant endeavours of speculative philosophy, and it throws a sort of poetical glow over the formality of his exposition" (p. 308).

16 Graduate Essays in the History of Philosophy

Soon after reading Pollock's *Spinoza*, Russell was obliged to write a number of graduate papers on the history of philosophy, metaphysics and metaethics, and following his year of philosophical study at Cambridge he wrote several other philosophical papers. Many of these papers are extant. Several are comparative in nature, and we find Russell comparing Spinoza's doctrines with those of other rationalists. In Spinoza, he writes in one paper, there is "no loophole in rigid Determinism" and "the individual can hardly find a place." Leibniz, on the other hand, is an "individualist": "Every individual monad seems like a Spinozistic world in itself;" "the Deity acts from logical necessity, and the whole development of the universe flows from the principle of contradiction...."[52] Russell does not justify his use of "Deity"; but although his use suggests a deity apart from the world, that can hardly have been his understanding of Spinoza, since the grossest error of interpretation would be involved, and Russell was well enough aware of pantheism.[53] At the end of the paper Russell makes a puzzling remark to the effect that Leibniz "requires a satisfaction of ethical requirements" which is not available in Spinoza's writings. This must refer to Leibniz's principle of sufficient reason. Russell holds that this principle requires that all causation be the result of some desire for the good (see **18**). Leibniz held that among equally possible alternative worlds, God would select that world whose existence would realize the greatest good; the potentiality of that good, therefore, was sufficient reason for bringing the world into existence. Since other worlds than our own were possible to God, ours must be the best of all the possible worlds, given God's use of the principle of sufficient reason in the selection process. In Spinoza there is a total absence of ethical considerations, not only in the choice of worlds—there is only one possible world—but also in the "choice" of events occurring in that world. Several years later, as we shall also see in **18**, Russell reverses his view of the principle of sufficient reason in Leibniz, holding that it lacks ethical content after all.

Russell makes explicit his view of Spinoza's God in his "Paper on Descartes II", written a few months later. "God is immanent in the world, and is the whole of what is...."[54] Spinoza, Russell says, took Descartes' God and gave him "undue prominence, to the final destruction of the individual" (p. 184). It is unclear whether Russell is giving this statement an exclusively metaphysical content, or also an ethical one. He develops a metaphysical point he noted in reading

Erdmann: "... Spinoza's monism is not so complete as it might be, since extension, for us, exists only as thought about, and the two attributes of God are therefore unnecessary; thought alone would have been sufficient" (pp. 181–2). There is an interesting passage on the derivation of Spinoza's ethic:

> ... [Descartes] speaks as if virtue consisted in freeing ourselves from the bodily passions and devoting ourselves to a life of pure contemplative intellect, in which our actions are all determined by pure reason; this doctrine, if worked out, would lead to a theoretic asceticism, though it might allow practically such indulgence in the pleasures of sense as the reason was willing to permit, provided these were never pursued for their own sakes but always only after the reason had had its say. His doctrine seems to contain the germ of Spinoza's intellectual love of God and indeed of Spinoza's ethical system generally; but it is not logically worked out, and is only here and there hinted at in a fragmentary fashion.... (P. 183)

This passage helps us understand what Russell means at this time by "asceticism", namely, control of all desire for sensual pleasure; but that brings us no closer to comprehending the phrase he used in the letter to Alys, "a rich voluptuous asceticism", except for a probable weakened emphasis on self-abnegation. By "the germ of Spinoza's intellectual love of God" Russell must be thinking of devotion to "a life of pure contemplative intellect".

Another essay topic required Russell to compare Spinoza and Hobbes.[55] Both, he asserts, deduce all the passions from one desire, that desire being the desire for power, "except that Spinoza throws a tinge of mysticism into his whole account and into his view of power" (p. 192). Both study the passions scientifically, without praise or blame. Hobbes, however, "has no hint of the ascetic self-abnegation by which alone Spinoza thinks this continual striving can be overcome" (*ibid.*). Evidently Russell views what he then regards as Spinoza's notion of self-abnegation as an ascetic doctrine, and he criticizes it: "... for as these [passions] point into the future, and depend on an imagined good not represented as actual, the better way to view them would be as a striving after some perfection in which all desires are represented as satisfied, not extinguished by asceticism as in Spinoza, but allayed by attainment" (p. 193). Russell then suggests that in the case of what he later calls compossible desires, such as love and benevolence, the opposition between self and world ceases. He considered saying—the passage was struck out—that "Self-assertion and self-denial become one in such a state" (p. 477 at 193:17). The attempt to unify opposites shows Russell's dialectical approach to philosophy at the time. In this paper we see the seed both of Russell's later metaethical naturalism with its concern with the *satisfaction* of desires (of whatever nature they may be), and of part of his normative ethic, with its acceptance of basic human desires.

In a journal entry made later in 1894, Russell mentions Spinoza in a way showing that the latter had become part of the former's mental furniture: "Wrote to Alys about abstract intellectual nature of my passions—I grow more abstract every day—I believe I'm drying up, like Spinoza in Pater—but perhaps it's only a phase, due to self-preservation—any more human passions cannot be satisfied here [a forced stay in Paris]" (Journal, 6 Oct. 1894; *Cambridge Essays*, p. 66). Walter Pater's only extended writing on Spinoza is in "Sebastian van Storck", a portrait of an imaginary Dutch painter in Spinoza's time who takes plausible implications for self-abnegation in Spinoza's ethic to an extreme and consequently "dries up"—i.e., he seeks an end to his life through lack of interest in it.[56] As I. C. Small has shown, the invented aspects of Spinoza's ethic are those encouraging the individual to merge himself with the world through the ultimate form of self-abnegation, namely suicide.[57] But Russell speaks of "Spinoza" drying up. Probably he is, with some justice, transferring Pater's account of Spinoza's protégé in the story, van Storck, to Spinoza himself. Russell himself never pursued the abandonment of passion to the point of van Storck's state of desiccation, though, as we have seen, he was temporarily attracted to asceticism.

One of the results of Russell's study of philosophy during his fourth year at Cambridge was a brief adherence to neo-Hegelianism. This lasted approximately three years, but was rejected only gradually. There were several varieties of neo-Hegelianism in Britain at the time, among which there were subtle variations.[58] Several of Russell's teachers were neo-Hegelians, notably Stout and McTaggart. Harold H. Joachim was another neo-Hegelian influence. In 1892 he wrote Russell about the latter's intentions to study philosophy and provided him with a reading list.[59] After naming various works by Plato and Aristotle and some histories, Joachim suggested: "Then you might go on to Descartes, Leibnitz (which I regret to say I haven't read—except in Erdmann!)—and Spinoza—especially the latter's Ethics (= Metaphysics with him) and his Tractatus de Emendatione intellectus, and (as an ingenious curiosity) his tractatus Theologico-Politicus. These are all in somewhat hard Latin, but one soon gets into the style." Russell does not seem to have read any of Spinoza's works in 1892–93. Joachim also recommended that Russell read Bradley's *Principles of Logic*, which he did. When *Appearance and Reality* was published in 1893, Russell read it, too—Stout having told him the work "accomplished as much as is humanly possible in ontology".[60] It is Spadoni's judgment that "There can be no doubt that during Russell's fourth year at Cambridge, Bradley overwhelmingly dominated Russell's philosophical thinking."[61] Russell studied not only Bradley's metaphysic, logic and theory of knowledge, but his ethic as well, reading his *Ethical Studies* in May 1894. Bradley had a normative ethic of self-realization. With Bradley, however, much turns on what he regarded as the self. In the next paper I shall discuss, Russell writes: "I am vastly tempted to regard the Subject, as apparently Bradley does, as a mere fluid nucleus of Feeling, of uncertain and constantly changing boundaries, and so adopt an almost Spinozistic monism. ..."[62] This doctrine could well lead to the concept of self-enlargement, simply by pushing out the boundaries of the narrow self. Bradley held that self-realization was limited by the necessity of one's conduct being consistent with that of other individuals. Theoretically, that was not difficult to achieve. In "My Station and Its Duties" he proposed that each one of us has a definite place and set of duties in society. We cannot be moral except by identifying our will with the moral spirit of the community.[63] Russell was never attracted to a normative ethic for its advocacy of duty, let alone a prescribed list of duties; but there were other attractions in Bradley's ethic.

The most important ethical notion reinforced by Bradley, aside from his concept of the self, was that philosophy could provide "metaphysical comfort", that it could provide "intellectual integrity" for religious belief, instead of mere "sentimental apologies".[64] Spadoni criticizes the expression "metaphysical comfort" as "exceedingly vague".[65] It is not vague, though the thesis behind it may well be untrue. The expression refers to the provision of desired ethical and emotional consequences grounded in speculation upon the ultimate nature of reality. Russell is disappointed when he finds that his speculations no longer yield comforting consequences (see 17).

To the "Society", or Apostles,[66] Russell read a paper on control of the passions called "Cleopatra or Maggie Tulliver". Cleopatra was hardly one to suppress her sensual desires, whereas Maggie Tulliver, the heroine of *The Mill on the Floss*, was notably self-controlled. In tackling problems of desire in the paper, Russell always has in mind the metaphysical relations of the ethic he is trying to work out. He writes Alys about the paper:

> The dilemma at the end has puzzled me for a year—I think there is no solution short of the Hegelian Dialectic. I am thinking of saying more on the independence of desire and knowledge: how they form coordinate realms, and how, just as no isolated truth is wholly true, so no isolated object of desire is wholly good—and as thought leads one dialectically to the Absolute, so desire, by alternative satisfaction and disappointment, leads one to the Absolute Good. And then I might discuss how to bridge the gulf between knowledge and desire—i.e. how to pass from morality to religion. But I'm inclined to leave this to McTaggart, as I've never quite understood the transition myself.[67] (26 Oct. 1894)

The paper is chiefly metaethical, and provides an early record of Russell's taking desire as fundamental. A "passion" he defines as "a body of particular desires coordinated by direction to a single end or to a closely related system of ends", and "emotion" as "the State of Mind accompanying the fruition or frustration (final or temporary) of a Passion, with special reference to its aspect of pleasure and pain" (*Camb. Essays*, p. 92). We saw (15) that Russell cites Spinoza (E4P7) in maintaining that a passion can only be overcome by a stronger passion. Russell's ethical point concerns the giving of dominance, in one's life, to passions with greater universes over passions with smaller universes and, as Ruja observes (p. 140), the point anticipates the concept of compossibility. By the "universe" of a passion, Russell appears to mean the extent of its possible effects. This term leads to difficulties. Thus he says, "if we are capable of realizing the future, a passion will overcome an isolated desire, and a passion with a larger universe will overcome one with a smaller universe" (p. 94). Like Spinoza (E5Pref.), Russell proposes remedies for "vividly bringing to mind the larger and perhaps remoter universe of the less intense desire, and so resisting the more intense but more limited one" (*ibid.*), a notion which contains the germ of self-enlargement. Russell's remedies, however, are not Spinoza's.

The paper is interesting also for Russell's view of the psychology of human motivation: "nothing can be accomplished without powerful passions—the more efficient men are the men wholly in the grip of some great passion which carries them over difficulties and obstacles and makes them neglect all but what conduces to their end" (p. 95).

His view includes a theory of repression. It is evident that he already holds that action is prompted by, and only by, desire. But it is not only the conflict of desires or passions that is of ethical importance; Russell observes that some "perfectly pure" desires are undesirable. He attempts a way out through ignoring a desire's possessor, and gauging only its possible total satisfaction through compatibility with other desires whether the possessor's or anyone else's. But this principle requires, he perceives, proof that "the satisfaction of the individual is necessarily that of the Universe". The explanation of this requirement is, I believe, that the individual must be persuaded of the ultimate, higher, "universal" satisfaction to be derived, in some cases, from the non-satisfaction of some desires he possesses. Such self-abnegation or self-sacrifice is a difficulty in any ethical theory which proceeds by the total satisfaction of desires. If it were not for the multiplicity of individual selves, who are, after all, the enjoyers of satisfaction, Russell says he would be tempted to "adopt an almost Spinozistic monism, in which our terms become merely Desire on the one hand and Satisfaction on the other" (p. 98). "Thus if I am allowed, in estimating a desire's universe", he adds, "to consider things outside the agent himself, all becomes easy." The problem of extending a desire's "universe" is a perennial one for Russell, and his solution, I hold, centres upon removal of the egocentric focus in desire. Russell concludes that the satisfaction required to make desires ethically good is not necessarily satisfaction of the self. There must, instead, be a "universal harmony" of desires (p. 98).

The ethic in "Cleopatra or Maggie Tulliver" is a compound of Spinoza and Bradley. In it Russell does not discuss "how to pass from morality to religion", as he told Alys he would do. Nothing so synthetic was possible to him, even during his adherence to a form of neo-Hegelianism. It is of interest for Russell's later development to find him repeating a cardinal point of Spinoza's, and discussing, as a live option, a monistic view of desire and satisfaction. For the "Spinozistic monism" he is tempted to adopt is one in which there would be no selves, Bradley's "mere fluid nucleus of Feeling" being a considerable step in the direction of self-enlargement.

The last, and fullest, expression of Russell's ethical views during his neo-Hegelian period is in a paper of June 1895, "The Free-Will Problem from an Idealist Standpoint".[68] It is nominally an explanation and defence of determinism in an idealist philosophy, in response to a criticism of that position in A. J. Balfour's *The Foundations of Belief*. Balfour dismissed discussing Bradley's views on freedom of the will in favour of T. H. Green's, and as a Bradleian at this time Russell complains that Green is out of date (p. 230). The paper is valuable to us because in it Russell offers a greater understanding of the Bradleian ethic than he does in "Cleopatra or Maggie Tulliver". And while Spinoza is not mentioned in the paper, views close to his are offered.

Considering man's freedom to attain and not merely wish for his goals, Russell examines the notion of "man's relation to his environment, and his share in the life of the whole" (p. 236). The universe is both perfectly free and perfectly determined. It is perfectly free because "as the sum of all that is . . . there is nothing outside by which its freedom could be interfered with" (p. 237). This statement is consistent with Spinoza's definition of "freedom" (E1Df.7). The universe is perfectly determined "for no one, now-a-days, would maintain that there is any part of the universe not amenable to law" (*ibid.*). Further, the universe is an organism—a change in one part involves a change in every other. In the human sphere, this may be expressed as an endless series of dependencies on our fellow men. It may, at first, appear that there is little chance of freedom in that sphere. That is not the case. The whole is merely the sum of its parts, so every part has a share in determining the character of the whole: "Hence, finally, we are free in proportion as we are self-determined, and we are self-determined in proportion as we are in harmony with the whole. To be in harmony with the Universal Will is, therefore, the full and sufficient condition of our freedom" (p. 238). Having considered the altruistic (or impersonal) satisfaction of desire, Russell reaches his fundamental moral principle: "In any case of a conflict of desires, that desire is to be followed which will bring with it the largest satisfaction—the satisfaction being great in proportion to the possibility of fully realizing the object of desire" (p. 239). His principle (which stated baldly is classical utilitarianism[69]), reduces itself, Russell continues, to harmony with the universal will.

The social implications of this idealist ethic are comforting to those who are most conventional. Those whose actions are not in harmony with the universal will are neither free nor virtuous. Nor are they self-determined. This idealist ethic allows no room for individual moral innovation, courage in standing alone against the multitude, or even a narrow self-realization with an individual appeal. Russell the later moral actor would not find a place in this framework. Of realization there is plenty, but it is the realization of the satisfaction of desires irrespective of desirers. That is the only way in which the sheer quantification of satisfaction of desire can be understood. The universal will turns out to be identical with that state of affairs in which there is greatest satisfaction of desire. In a paper written a year earlier, Russell had not yet jettisoned the personal element in desire, though he admitted that "self-realization may of course be best attained by what is commonly called self-sacrifice...."[70] But although there is nothing in the later essay explicitly said about Spinoza, that, I think, is the way in which Russell at this time understood him, and Bradley as well. Of all the monistic idealists, these two seem to have been his favourites.

17 Rebellion against Neo-Hegelianism

Russell's rebellion against neo-Hegelianism seems to have occurred at the end of 1897. The rebellion did not suddenly alter the whole range of philosophical views he held. For example, early in 1898 he was still attempting a dialectical, or neo-Hegelian, approach in his writings on philosophy of science.[71] Yet the breakthrough is clearly detectable in a paper, "Seems, Madam? Nay, It Is", written for delivery to the Society in December 1897.[72] It is not the wider topic of Russell taking his leave of idealist metaphysics that we are interested in, however, but the effect of that action upon his study and use of Spinoza. Russell's essential objection to idealism, he says, is that it bears no relation to the world of experience, "in which world all our interests lie" (*Camb. Essays*, p. 108);[73] hence the philosophy of monistic idealism cannot provide religious comfort. He then lists a number of ways in which comfort may still be provided by philosophy. The first is that we may find it a pleasant activity. The second is that "We may, again, take philosophy aesthetically, as probably most of us take Spinoza." The rest of the paragraph elaborates:

> We may use metaphysics, like poetry and music, as a means of producing a mood, of giving us a certain view of the universe, a certain attitude toward life—the resulting state of mind being valued on account of, and in proportion to, the degree of poetic emotion aroused, not in proportion to the truth of the beliefs entertained.... For aesthetic satisfaction, intellectual conviction is unnecessary, and we may therefore choose, when we seek it, the metaphysic which gives us the most of it. For religious comfort, on the other hand, belief is essential.... (Pp. 109–10)

Russell adds that this explanation of philosophy's ability to provide comfort is complicated by the "mystical theory of the aesthetic emotion", i.e. that certain "experiences approach it [Reality] as it really is." He means, by this phrase, philosophy's transformation of the world—he uses the term "beatific vision". But such a transformation is on the aesthetic level, not the ontological.

We learn, then, that by the time of Russell's revolt against neo-Hegelianism he is taking Spinoza "aesthetically", i.e. for the attitude toward reality that his writings may inspire. This may be why at this time he names Spinoza as one of the two men in history who attract him most.[74] We have, for this time, little information on the details of Moore's influence, which Russell credits for bringing him out of the monistic morass. But apart from that, we can agree with Russell's confession to Lady Ottoline fourteen years later: "When I adopted Moore's views, the last hope of getting any creed out of philosophy vanished. That was of course a great disappointment. . . . Since then I have only hoped that philosophy could show that we know something; and to find out whether this is so has been my main business" (no. 199, 28 Sept. 1911).

18 Spinoza in Russell's *Leibniz*; and Joachim's *Study*

A period of historical interest in Spinoza began for Russell when he agreed to give a course of lectures on Leibniz at Trinity College in the spring of 1899. Much is known about the genesis of the work that resulted, *A Critical Exposition of the Philosophy of Leibniz* (1900).[75] Although Russell in that work makes many comparisons between Leibniz and Spinoza, it has not been realized how extensive was his study of Spinoza for that purpose. It had to be extensive, for in introducing the book Russell asserts: "In these last chapters [on Soul and Body, God, and Ethics] we shall find that Leibniz no longer shows great originality, but tends, with slight alteration of phraseology, to adopt (without acknowledgement) the views of the decried Spinoza" (p. 5).[76] He read the *Ethics* in March 1899.[77] It may also have been at that time that he acquired the three-volume van Vloten and Land edition of Spinoza's *Opera* and the second edition, published in March 1899, of Pollock's *Spinoza*.[78] For translations from Spinoza in *The Philosophy of Leibniz*, Russell sometimes used the copious translations of individual passages in Pollock, and sometimes the White-Stirling translation.[79] In researching the book he used two works specifically on Spinoza, Foucher de Careil's *Réfutation inédite de Spinoza par Leibnitz*, and Stein's *Leibniz und Spinoza*.[80]

Russell's analysis of Leibniz's philosophy is chiefly metaphysical and logical. The references to Spinoza are mostly of this nature, the few other connections in which Spinoza is brought in being ethical. Russell's *Leibniz* reveals little, therefore, of his attitude to Spinoza's contribution to ethics. And there is nothing touching on the concept of self-enlargement. The plentiful citations of the *Ethics* do show Russell thoroughly familiar with Parts I–III. This is useful, for in later writings he lets it be known that the first two Parts were of least interest to him.

The purpose of the *Leibniz* is to explain Leibniz's philosophy in terms of five principal premisses. The most important of these, in Russell's analysis, is the principle of sufficient reason. Russell brings Spinoza in thus:

> In Leibniz's philosophy everything, from the Law of Sufficient Reason onwards, depends, through the introduction of final causes, upon Ethics. But Ethics, being a subject on which theology is very definite, could not be dealt with by Leibniz in a free spirit. The Ethics to which he was entitled was very similar to Spinoza's; it had the same fallacies, and similar consequences. But being the champion of orthodoxy against the decried atheist, Leibniz shrank from the consequences of his views, and took refuge in the perpetual iteration of edifying phrases. The whole tendency of his temperament, as of his philosophy, was to exalt enlightenment, education, and learning, at the expense of ignorant good intentions. This tendency might have found a logical expression in his Ethics. But he preferred to support Sin and Hell, and to remain, in what concerned the Church, the champion of ignorance and obscurantism. This is the reason why the best parts of his philosophy are the most abstract, and the worst those which most nearly concern human life.[81] (P. 202)

It is seldom realized that Russell held two views of the principle of sufficient reason in Leibniz. It is Russell's 1900 view of the principle of sufficient reason that is relevant to the influence of Spinoza upon Leibniz. At that time Russell distinguishes two principles under the same name. "The former", he says, "is a form of the law of causality, asserting all possible causes to be desires or appetites; the latter, on the other hand, is the assertion that all *actual* causation is determined by desire for the good" (p. 30). Desire, or volition, is the link between the principle of sufficient reason and Leibniz's ethics—although Russell makes Leibniz's ethic the last topic in his book, it has to be worked in from the beginning. Not only is this the best of all possible worlds, but all of us, in whatever we do, are working toward the best—everything evil being necessary for the best. As Russell notes, "this principle confers upon the good a relation to existence such as no other concept possesses. In order to infer actual existence, whether from another existent, or from mere notions, the notion of the good must be employed" (p. 34).[82] Russell points out that Spinoza held a principle of sufficient reason which was independent of final causes: "For the existence or non-existence of anything, it must be possible to assign a cause or reason" (E1P11D2), and Spinoza was specifically anti-teleological (E4Pref.).

Russell claims that Leibniz's views on body and soul, God's existence, and ethics owe much to Spinoza. He asserts (p. 139) that Leibniz, in dealing with these topics, adapted to his monadology Spinoza's theory of activity and passivity. This is a theory of change and is the basis for his idea of human freedom. When changes in us originate from within ourselves, we are "active" and "free"; when changes originate from without, we are "passive" and in bondage. In Leibniz's application, monads more perfectly mirror, or perceive, the world when they are active, less perfectly when they are passive. A sharp line, Russell thinks, should be drawn between topics in Leibniz he has treated until this point and those dependent upon Spinoza's notion of passivity.[83] In concluding that Leibniz was entitled to a much more liberal normative ethic than the one he chose, Russell says, significantly, that he was entitled to all the ethical consequences of determinism (p. 197). But instead of accepting his entitlement, he aimed to reconcile his doctrine with free will as well. This seems to me the reason for Russell's final judgment that "the best parts of his philosophy are the most abstract, and the worst those which most nearly concern human life" (p. 202).

In 1901 Russell read Joachim's *A Study of the Ethics of Spinoza*.[84] Nine years later Russell remarks that "the task of interpretation has been admirably performed for the technical reader by Mr. Joachim" (see 22), but aside from a few notes that is all we know of Russell's response to the book.[85] In view of his praise Russell surely concurred with Joachim's main points of interpretation. Three features dominate his *Study*: it is idealist; it treats Spinoza's normative ethic as one of self-realization in the wider sense; and it provides a detailed treatment of the technical workings of his metaphysic. Joachim was an absolute idealist. He saw a massive, interconnected reality behind appearances, one worthy of devotion. Only the Absolute is real, because only it is "self-dependent" (*Study*, p. 37). Like Spinoza's notion of substance, the notion of the Absolute is said to be "complete in itself", there being nothing extraneous to afford a completion. As Joachim puts it: "The conception of self-dependent Reality forces us to the conclusion that there is nothing self-dependently real except the Absolute, the whole system; and the conception of the Absolute forces us to conclude that it alone is self-dependently real" (p. 37). As for the individual self, "In proportion, therefore, as there is absolute continuity in all being—as no 'single thing' can really be separated from its context—the human mind and the human body are devoid of distinct being: their individuality is illusory and untrue" (p. 130).

Joachim was a follower of Bradley, so it is not surprising to find the former interpreting Spinoza's normative ethic as one of self-realization. The Spinozistic application is that man's self-realization is proportionate to the degree of union he feels with Reality. The concept of union is pervasive in Joachim's *Study*. His interpretation (which will be examined at greater length in 37) concludes in the "intellectual love of God": "The course of man's progress towards freedom and knowledge—towards that absorption in God which is the realization and the transcendence of man's self—is traced by Spinoza in his ethical doctrine and in his theory of the stages of knowledge" (pp. 143–4). Man has to grasp the union of all things in God—that is, in one another. This supreme understanding absorbs our emotional nature. Being conscious of God as the cause, we love Him. "This 'love', since it rests on intelligence and not on imaginative apprehension, may be called 'the intellectual love of God'" (p. 305). When we are in this state, we are in the state of our fullest being. But although we may suppose that such discussions interested Russell despite his rejection of monism, we know nothing of his response to individual points.

19 Summary

In this chapter exploring Russell's early acquaintance with Spinoza's life and writings, books relating to the study of Spinoza which Russell is known to have read, and Russell's writings on Spinoza during the period ending in 1901, my paramount concern has been to locate and trace whenever possible the concept of impersonal self-enlargement which Russell—especially in the periods to be covered by the next two chapters—drew out of Spinoza's *Ethics*. Russell approaches the notion but misunderstands it as "self-abnegation". A similar concept was found in Russell's writings expounding Bradley's idealist ethic. While complicating the notion of influence with which we have been operating, it raises the possibility of greater generality in our conclusions. It seems that the kind of philosophy from whose metaphysic Russell ceases to derive religious comfort in late 1897 is the kind which in general supplies him with the concept of an expandable self. Spinoza's role, therefore, may be that of a particular, and personally appealing, source for that concept after Russell ceases to adhere to the metaphysic of monistic idealism.

CHAPTER III

The Middle Period (1907–12)

20 Transition

In the last chapter we traced Russell's writings on Spinoza to 1901. The focus was on Russell's knowledge of Spinoza as a source of the normative ethic Russell later espouses. Since my claim is that this ethic is founded on the concept of impersonal self-enlargement, we looked for evidence of Russell's recognition and use of the concept in his reading and writing on Spinoza. This chapter continues that search. Russell's reliance on Spinoza becomes explicit by the years 1910–12. The main evidence is two published reviews on Spinoza, an important correspondence, and an autobiographical novella. These sources will complete our survey of Russell's acquaintance with Spinoza's writings and ideas through 1912 and establish his reliance on them through this period.

The years between 1901 and 1907 will be examined in Chapter VI, on the development of Russell's ethic apart from the explicit Spinozistic influence. They are relatively barren years for references to Spinoza in Russell's published writings, for Russell was hard at work on *Principia Mathematica* and writing little (e.g. "The Free Man's Worship") on ethics except privately. Two references to Spinoza are relevant here. In December 1902, on the brink of composing "The Free Man's Worship", Russell writes to Gilbert Murray: "If only one had lived in the days of Spinoza, when systems were still possible. ..."[1] The context of this statement is a discussion of the value of *The Principles of Mathematics* (1903).[2] It is said to possess a general value, but one of access only to the specialists who can master the work as a whole. Russell may have felt that, unlike Spinoza, he could not combine his most abstract speculations with the concrete work he was at the same time doing in ethics. Another interpretation of this passage, however, could be that, while Russell's absolute realism did have a correlative ethic, a total system was not possible because of various difficulties he ran up against in writing *The Principles*—e.g. the contradiction concerning the class of all classes that are not members of themselves. The other reference is in a 1906 review of McTaggart's *Some Dogmas of Religion*:

> The principle that the kingdom of heaven is hidden from the wise and prudent and revealed unto babes "is sure to be popular, for it enables a man to believe that he is showing his meekness and humility by the confident assertion of propositions which he will not investigate and cannot prove" (p. 298). In contrast with this principle of indolence, the discussion ends with the noble words of Spinoza: "Omnia praeclara tam difficilia quam rara sunt."[3]

These noble words are from the end of the *Ethics* (E5P42S).

In addition to "impersonal self-enlargement", other key concepts to which attention will be drawn in this chapter are the "intellectual love of God", "philosophic calm", and "self-preservation". Noting how Russell uses the terms will aid us in Chapter V, where we shall evaluate his understanding of Spinoza, and in Chapter VI, where we shall search for the development of these elements of Spinoza's ethic in Russell's own ethical writings.

21 Review of Picton's *Spinoza*

The first document to be studied is a review of a little-known work on Spinoza. The review and the work itself will be useful for the light they can shed so early in our new period on Russell's attraction to Spinoza's ethic. In 1907 the London *Nation* published a short review[4] of J. Allanson Picton's *Spinoza: a Handbook to the Ethics*. The review is unsigned, and there is no external evidence in the way of correspondence, record of payment, or annotated copy of the book in Russell's library to attribute the review to Russell. Nevertheless, I hope to convince the reader that Russell is the author. Reviewing anonymously in the *Nation* was not unprecedented for him. Six weeks before the review in question Russell had published an unsigned review of F. C. S. Schiller's *Studies in Humanism*, a review which is known to be Russell's from the fact that the phrase "By Bertie Russell" is written across the head of a copy of the printed review kept by him, and the phrase is in the handwriting of his wife. The existence of this review, however, only slightly improves the possibility that Russell may again have written anonymously for the *Nation*. In the subsequent thirteen years he did review anonymously on a good many occasions for that journal, but for most occasions strong external evidence is now available for the identification of his reviews.

In presenting the internal evidence for Russell's authorship, I cannot do better than begin by quoting the review's first paragraph, numbering five tell-tale phrases.

> Of all the great modern philosophers, Spinoza is probably the most interesting in relation to human life[1], and is certainly the most lovable[2] and high-minded. Unfortunately, the difficulty and crabbedness of his writing[3] make it very hard for people who are not serious students of philosophy to understand even what is not inherently difficult in his doctrines. He therefore requires commentaries[4] to translate him into easier language, if his main ideas are to be appreciated as widely as possible. Sir Frederick Pollock's book has performed this task with rare skill[5], and might be thought to have rendered Mr. Picton's work unnecessary. But I do not think such a view would be just. Mr. Picton's book is shorter and easier; it confines itself wholly to the "Ethics"; and it can be read by those who have no previous acquaintance with philosophy.

[1] "[T]he most interesting in relation to human life" is similar to a judgment Russell offers Lady Ottoline Morrell four years later, when he tells her that Spinoza "is the only one of the modern philosophers who has anything of that sort of say" (no. 169a, 11 Aug. 1911); that is, he is the only one with something of interest to say on the conduct of life. [2] "[T]he most lovable" of the great modern philosophers is the phrase Russell uses in beginning his chapter on Spinoza in *A History of Western Philosophy*. "Lovable" is a word Russell uses rarely—another occasion was in speaking of Einstein, also an admirer of Spinoza.[5] [3] "[T]he difficulty and crabbedness of his writing" is another judgment echoed in the correspondence with Lady Ottoline: "it is difficult digging the good out of his writings, because it is all concealed in a horrible pedantry of geometrical demonstration ... " (no. 82, p/24 May 1911). A similar judgment can also be found in the 1910 review—"so difficult that even the best philosophers cannot be sure of having understood him"—and two decades later in *The Conquest of Happiness*—"his form and his language make his thought difficult of

access to all but students of philosophy".⁶ [4] "[R]equires commentaries" is another judgment found in Russell's signed review, three years later, of White and Stirling's translation of the *Ethics*. He begins that review by saying: "The work of the populariser, though sometimes depreciated by professional students, is a very useful and necessary work, and in few cases more useful or more necessary than in the case of Spinoza."⁷ [5] The mention of Pollock's *Spinoza* is just what we might expect of Russell, given the material in 15. A last indication of Russell's authorship appears in the review's final paragraph. It is there declared that "Spinoza's philosophy ... remains one of the noblest monuments of human genius...." The signed review of 1910 concludes with the words "he achieved a nobility, both in life and in speculation, which has not been equalled by his predecessors or successors in the realm of philosophy", and the chapter in his *History* opens by calling Spinoza "the noblest ... of the great philosophers". The rest of the 1907 review contains nothing inconsistent with Russell's known views at the time. Indeed, there are touches of his characteristic wit, e.g. the remark that Picton has "a tendency to urge that what Spinoza says is common sense, when it is really something better." Russell did not respect common sense *per se*. Additional support for Russell's authorship of the review would be provided if we knew whether he was the *Nation*'s main reviewer of philosophy at this time, but we do not know this, and the publisher's marked file of the journal has vanished. It is very unlikely, in fact, that Russell was the main philosophical reviewer, for the *Nation* carried many more philosophical reviews at this time than internal evidence can attribute to Russell. By 1912, however, Russell does seem to have become the main philosophical reviewer.

Something must be said on behalf of the negative case for Russell's authorship. I shall not consider the very unlikely hypothesis that Russell was not the author of the *Nation*'s review of Picton but read and so absorbed the review that, when he came to write on Spinoza in 1910, 1911, and 1945, he repeated phrases and sentiments which he had picked up in casual reading of 1907. Russell's admission to Lady Ottoline in 1912, "I have never written anything on Spinoza except the *Nation* review, of which I have no copy" (between nos. 362 and 363, p/1 March 1912), may be dismissed as applying to the review of Picton: by 1912 Russell was the author of a large number of short reviews, and there is no particular reason why he should have remembered this brief one written five years earlier. I assume, of course, that "the *Nation* review" denotes the review of the *Ethics* published in 1910. But as that piece of writing is outstanding and the Picton review is not, as Russell had not published anything of the nature of the former for some years, and as the 1910 review is on Spinoza himself rather than a commentator, it is not assuming too much to conclude that he had the 1910 review in mind in writing to Lady Ottoline. Should this attribution fail, however, my overall argument is not affected.

Much of the remainder of the review concerns an "is"–"ought" confusion in one of Spinoza's proofs. Russell (i.e. the reviewer) objects to drawing the conclusion that the love of God above everything *ought* to occupy the mind (E5P16) from the premiss that the love of God *does* occupy the mind (E5P11). Russell shows himself here very conscious of the fallacy first pointed out by Hume.[8] As further evidence of Russell's authorship—it being consistent with his habits—the same proposition (E5P16) and its proof are discussed in detail, as the sole example of Spinozistic demonstration, in *A History of Western Philosophy* (pp. 575–6; p. 558). As the elucidation of the phrase will concern us later, it is useful to know that Russell considers that Picton "in the main ... successfully extracts his master's teaching on the conduct of life and on *the intellectual love of God*" (my italics). While the phrasing suggests a certain distance from Spinoza on Russell's part, it is in keeping with the lack of discipleship found in the latter's maturity. (In his youth, Russell confessed to being a disciple of Bradley.) The review continues: "Much of the moral teaching of the 'Ethics,' being inspired by a general tolerant large-heartedness, remains *valid* [my italics], whether we accept or reject the metaphysic by which it is 'proved'; but the more interesting and characteristic portions stand or fall with that metaphysic, and remain unconvincing to readers who are not pantheists." As Russell proceeds to discuss the application of the "is"–"ought" fallacy, it may be surmised that he means by "the more interesting and characteristic portions" Spinoza's derivation of how we ought to act from his account of the nature of reality. Russell cites the proposition, "By reality and perfection I understand the same thing" (E2Df.6). He also discusses this proposition in "Mysticism and Logic" (1914). There he holds that Spinoza uses the word "perfection" when he means "the good that is not merely human". Russell contrasts perfection with the definition "By good, I understand that which we certainly know is useful to us" (E4Df.1). He concludes: "Thus perfection belongs to Reality in its own nature, but goodness is relative to ourselves and our needs, and disappears in an impartial survey."[9] We may conclude from this discussion that in saying reality is perfect Spinoza is conveying an attitude of acceptance toward the world as a whole, and that in Spinozism that attitude is based upon an understanding of the world's necessary character. However, from the fact that in 1907 we find Russell disagreeing with the literal sense of E2Df.6, it seems that some change of mind took place between that time and the writing of "Mysticism and Logic". It is clear, at any rate, that the topic is not of great interest to a lapsed monist such as Russell had become. There is far more interest evident in the phrase "a general tolerant large-heartedess". We can detect in it the spatial metaphor that is the nucleus of the ethic based upon impersonal self-enlargement.

It remains to consider what Russell can mean by "valid" as applied to the expression "Spinoza's moral teaching". The word in substantive form occurs again in the 1910 review: " . . . the general attitude towards life and the world which he [Spinoza] inculcates does not depend for its validity upon a system of metaphysics." The thought, though not the word, recurs in Russell's essay "The Philosophy of George Santayana". There Russell claims that, since the purpose of Spinoza's philosophy is to "suggest a way of life less wayward and less accidental than that of the unreflective", it does not lose its "importance" upon the discrediting of his metaphysic.[10] By "valid", then, Russell seems to mean "important to human life", or "appropriate to the conduct of human life".[11] He certainly does not mean here "correctly derived from the premisses", as the term is used in logic. I shall return to the problem of what constitutes a "valid" ethic for humanity in evaluating Russell's ethic in Chapter VII. Russell views it as possible to preach an ethic which demands too much or even too little of human nature, and such an ethic he would say is invalid. We shall find that one of the strengths of the Spinozistic ethic, in Russell's view, is that it is appropriate to human nature, which is the sense in which it is "naturalistic". That is why Russell praised Spinoza's emphasis upon self-preservation as the dominant motive. The motive itself is not praiseworthy, but if it exists it must be recognized for what it is, and it is its recognition that Russell praises. As he writes in 1922 in a political article concerning the United States' moral standing in international affairs:

> I have referred to Spinoza to show that the view which I am advocating is neither cynical nor novel. The view is that men's purposes, in fact, though often without their own knowledge, are egoistic—not quite invariably, but so preponderantly that the exceptions do not count in dealing with large numbers, as in

politics. The belief that this is not so is the cause of hypocrisy, of moral indignation, and also of the theory that a benevolent despotism is possible.[12]

Let us turn now to Picton's work itself. James Allanson Picton (1832–1910) was a disciple of Spinoza. He had earlier published *Pantheism: Its Story and Significance* (1905) and writes throughout his *Spinoza* of "the Master". He even once calls him "the brother of Jesus".[13] His purpose is moral, or religious in a broad sense, and he leaves exegesis and philosophical dispute to Pollock's book, to which he refers many times, concentrating his own exposition on the last two Parts of the *Ethics*. "My object", he writes, "is simply to bring within reach of ordinary people like myself the religious peace and joy that result from his [Spinoza's] identification of God with the Universe" (p. 29). Despite Picton's religiosity, there are reasons why Russell would have favoured his exposition. It is not only joy in the exercise of mental power which Picton celebrates in Spinoza (p. 106); it is not merely his liberal politics,[14] though his statement on behalf of "the apostles of popular liberty and freedom of trade"[15] would have pleased Russell. The chief reason Russell commends the book is that it presents Spinoza's psychology and ethic in a way that is both popular and agreeable to Russell's own interpretation. Picton repeats Spinoza's dicta on possessive and creative impulses (pp. 153–4), a division which Russell himself later develops at length, and he anticipates Russell's principle of growth (p. 183). These topics are essentially political ones, and Russell gives them a political interpretation in *Principles of Social Reconstruction* (1916). Picton also explains the concept of the intellectual love of God sympathetically:

> The doctrine is that the confused and inadequate ideas associated with passion are excluded. This being so, a man who clearly and distinctly recognises his place in the Universe, or God, necessarily regards God as the cause of whatever joy or satisfaction he has in existence; or if little of such pleasure has fallen to his lot, he can look beyond himself to "the glory of the sum of things." The glow of feeling with which such a man responds to the universe is what I understand the Master to mean by "the intellectual love of God." (P. 187)

Picton's understanding of this vital concept is inadequate. He undervalues Spinoza's emphasis on "intellectual". In so doing Picton fails to grasp that absorption in and acceptance of the necessity of things which characterize the Spinozistic understanding. Absence of passion is in no way equivalent to understanding in Spinoza.

22 Review of Spinoza's *Ethic* (translated by White and Stirling)

From this short but suggestive review we pass to the much longer one published three and a half years later, again in the *Nation*. "Spinoza", as it is titled, is a review of the new, fourth edition of White's translation, revised by Stirling, of the *Ethic* (as they translate the title). In addition to the review, we possess Russell's annotated copy of the volume reviewed; 23 is devoted to what can be learnt from his marginal annotations. The volume is a presentation copy, perhaps from one of the translators, William Hale White (1831–1913), though it could be the *Nation*'s review copy. The review is a superb expression of Russell's appreciation of Spinoza, and it did not go unnoticed by White. After the review appeared, White wrote to the *Nation*'s editor requesting that he publish an appreciative note. No such note was published, though the editor did forward White's letter to Russell. The latter must have been pleased by the sentence, "As might have been expected from him [Russell], it is the best brief word or two which, as far as I am aware, has been said about Spinoza, and worth far more than some bulky volumes."[16] The same day White wrote directly to Russell:

> I cannot help thanking you for your paper on Spinoza in the *Nation* of last week. I began to read him fifty years ago and I have not for any length of time ceased to read him. I have also read a good deal about him, but I have not found, even in bulky volumes, anything more instructive than what you have said in two or three columns. I know but little of metaphysics as a science. I study Spinoza because he teaches me how to live and you in this article make me better understand in what way he excels in teaching it. The two sentences "he sees no end to strife except by persuading men to choose as their ends things which all may enjoy in common," and "it seems that in the knowledge of what is necessary we place ourselves" in harmony "with what is greatest in the universe" are worth much lengthy exposition.
> Thank you also for the kind words about the translation.

You will remember giving me nearly three years ago your *Principles of Mathematics?* This gift has encouraged me to write to you.

Russell left his usual indication in the upper left-hand corner that he answered the letter, but the reply has not been found in either of the repositories of White's papers. Nor is anything known about the occasion for the gift of *The Principles of Mathematics*. We do know that Russell valued this letter highly, for he showed it to Lady Ottoline (no. 43, p/26 April 1911). It is a misfortune that Russell did not write a "lengthy exposition" of Spinoza. We shall find, however, in Chapter VI, in dealing with the development of Russell's own normative ethic, that he did not refrain from an exposition of the core of what he found valuable in Spinoza.

Russell's "instructive" essay—which may owe part of its enthusiasm to his recently won freedom from the writing of *Principia Mathematica* (1910–13)—begins by justifying the need for both popularizers and translators of Spinoza. "Even the best philosophers cannot be sure of having understood him", Russell claims. After praising Joachim and Pollock (see **18** and **15**, respectively) as interpreters, Russell comments on the quality of the translation as one who has himself worked through Spinoza's Latin: "The translation, though not wholly devoid of errors, seems in the main accurate and careful. It is, perhaps, a pity that the translators have chosen the manufactured word 'affect' to translate *affectus*, rather than the word 'emotion,' which is used by Sir Frederick Pollock and Mr. Joachim." Russell goes on, however, to offer the standard justification of innovators in translation: the neologism makes "the reader aware that Spinoza's meaning cannot be accurately rendered by any existing word in its common signification."[17] The translation's 93-page preface Russell says is "useful", not least for emphasizing that "Spinoza's purpose, as his title indicates, was ethical, and that he only introduced metaphysics in so far as seemed essential for his ethical doctrine." Russell concludes his introductory comments by a rare mention of another of Spinoza's writings, the *Short Treatise on God, Man, and Man's Well-Being*, and to Colerus's life of Spinoza, which he may have read in 1894 as one of Pollock's appendices.

Russell then briefly characterizes the first three Parts of the *Ethic*, sympathizing with the casual reader who is unlikely to persevere until he reaches the last two Parts. And then, as if he cannot be restrained any longer, Russell breaks into a passionate exposition of Spinoza's central ethical doctrine. In the following extract I have numbered the points to be discussed.

> Spinoza, more than any other modern philosopher, writes always with a strong sense of the importance of philosophy in the conduct of life[1], and with a firm belief in the power of reason to purify men's conduct and purify their desires[2]. Like many men of great independence of mind, he feels the need of something great enough to justify him in submitting to its authority. Like all who contemplate human life without sharing its baser passions, he is oppressed by the endless strife produced by conflicting aims and unrestrained ambitions. Believing, as he does, that self-preservation is the very essence of everything that exists, he sees no end to strife except by persuading men to choose as their ends things which all may enjoy in common[3]. Contempt and moral condemnation stand in the way of toleration; he therefore sets out to prove that what men do they do from a necessity of their nature. ... His theory of the emotions, in which, by his geometrical method, he demonstrates that men *must* act in ways which it is common to condemn, contains much admirable psychology; but it was not this that made him value his theory: what he valued was the conclusion that moral condemnation is foolish[4]. It is for this reason partly that Spinoza inveighs against free-will, and finds pleasure in showing the necessity of everything. But there is also another reason: what is transitory, though it may be tolerated, cannot be worshipped[5]; but the proof of its necessity connects it with the Divine nature, and thereby removes its pitifulness. To a certain type of mind there is something sublime about necessity: it seems that in the knowledge of what is necessary we place ourselves in harmony with what is greatest in the universe[6]. This constitutes, to those who feel it, a great part of the value of mathematical demonstration[7]; even Spinoza's geometrical method, which has been almost universally condemned, will be held appropriate by those who know the "intellectual love of God"[8].

[1] "[T]he importance of philosophy in the conduct of life" is not something the Russell of analytic philosophical reputation is thought to rate highly, because of his radical separation of reason and value. Yet even in "On Scientific Method in Philosophy" (1914) he concedes philosophy this role albeit under stringent conditions, in addition to

that of being an outlet for cognitive speculation.[18] [2] The "purification" of conduct and especially of desire is a concept important for the stage in Russell's normative ethic just coming to a close. In "The Free Man's Worship" he writes, "for Fate itself is subdued by the mind which leaves nothing to be purged by the purifying fire of Time."[19] In "The Study of Mathematics", written at the same time, we are told that "the austerer virtues have a strange power, exceeding the power of those not informed and purified by thought."[20] The word "purify", which occurs several times in that essay, is linked to his then dominant ethic of pain as the gateway to wisdom (see **43**). [3] "[C]hoose as their ends things which all may enjoy in common" appears to be a trivial answer to the question of how to end strife between men. To the suggestion that men may enjoy strife as an end, it may be replied that, as a common end, strife can only provide very temporary enjoyment. For unlimited strife soon results in the cessation of any enjoyment for some men, i.e. death. Thus strife cannot be one of the ends that all men may enjoy in common. It is, indeed, true that strife is generally over things which all men may *not* enjoy in common; and trivially true that: If all persons wished to enjoy only those things (class c) whose enjoyment by person A_1 does not preclude their enjoyment by persons $A_2 \ldots A_n$, and if strife between persons occurs only with respect to things not of class c, then strife between persons would cease. The question whether Spinoza's solution to the problem of strife is indeed trivial cannot be decided on technical grounds. It may well be that the solution is technically "trivial" but important. It may well be that people should have the solution constantly reiterated to them. They might then concentrate on providing content for the solution in the form of ends that are both satisfying and non-exclusive—"compossible" in Russell's later terminology. Russell, as we shall find in a later chapter, adopted the solution as one of the fundamental tenets of his ethical and political philosophy. It is best known as his doctrine of creative and possessive impulses.

[4] "[T]hat moral condemnation is foolish" did not prevent Russell from frequently indulging in it. But he just as frequently made remarks like that in **11** on this topic. Another instance of his acceptance of determinism in human affairs is: " . . . when men's actions are understood, they appear inevitable, and therefore no more worthy of praise or blame than sunshine or a thunderstorm."[21] [5] The desirability of worshipping anything may be questioned. For Russell it is linked to the need, "in men of great independence of mind", to submit to a greater authority. "The Free Man's Worship" concerns

the selection of objects of worship, with Russell selecting the ideals man has fashioned. [6] It is not quite true that Russell through Spinoza is advocating worship of the necessary progression of the universe; what he is advocating is living with, not against, that ebb and flow of events, without at the same time issuing an apology for the *status quo*. It should be noted that in such contemporary writings as "On the Notion of Cause", in *Mysticism and Logic*, Russell strips the concept of necessity from the concept of causality as used in science. If pressed on this point, he would have to say that the use of "necessity" was a way of referring to the frequent conjunction of similar events in a determined system with the addition of an element of compulsion that is superfluous to science. [7] "[T]he value of mathematical demonstration", for Russell, is first set out in "The Study of Mathematics", in which he writes: "But mathematics takes us still further from what is human, into the region of absolute necessity, to which not only the actual world, but every possible world, must conform; and even here it builds a habitation, or rather finds a habitation eternally standing, where our ideals are fully satisfied and our best hopes not thwarted."[22] There is admittedly a tension between Russell's understanding here of the purpose of Spinoza's geometrical framework, and his criticism of it elsewhere (**21**, point 3). [8] Let us hope that we are here provided with a clue to Russell's understanding of what Spinoza meant by the "intellectual love of God". For the moment I shall note that it seems to include an appreciation of the necessary order of the universe.

Following the exposition of Spinoza's central ethical doctrine, Russell discusses Spinoza's application of it to his life. If a saint is someone who lacks bad passions, Spinoza was a saint. Russell observes: "... he himself loved what he judged to be best, and lived, so far as one can discover, without effort in the way which he held to be conformable to reason. There seems to have been in him, what his philosophy was intended to produce in others, an absence of bad desires; hence, his nature is harmonious and gentle, free from the cruelty of asceticism, of the monkishness of the cloister, or the moralistic priggery of Goethe's praises."[23] Russell then attacks those who want to see Spinoza as inculcating resignation. He is, therefore, attacking his own previous ethic, which had been one of Stoic resignation in the face of ultimate despair, despite the optimistic veneer to his outlook evidenced by his political work for free trade and women's suffrage. The defect of an ethic of resignation is that it is devoid of joy and of faith in an ultimate reconciliation. "To represent such a philosophy [as Spinoza's]", Russell continues, "as one of renunciation is surely to miss the whole of the mystic joy which it is intended to produce, and to misunderstand the reconciliation of the individual with the whole, which is the purpose of so much elaborate argument."

Next comes a passage suggesting that the ethic that Russell himself advocates is an intellectualist one. An ethic of knowledge would be an ethic centred around the beneficial effects upon the self of the accumulation of understanding. Russell does encourage the acquisition of knowledge with such an effect in mind:

> He [Spinoza] believes that all human ills are to be cured by knowledge and understanding; that only ignorance of what is best makes men think their interests conflicting, since the highest good is knowledge, which can be shared by all. But knowledge, as he conceives it, is not mere knowledge as it comes to most people; it is "intellectual love," something coloured by emotion through and through. This conception is the key to all his valuations.

Here we have content supplied to the admonition to men to choose ends which all may share. Knowledge is the supreme end on this interpretation. Russell proceeds to quote Spinoza's *Short Treatise upon God, Man, and Man's Well-Being*: "[I]t is knowledge which is the cause of love, so that when we learn to know God in this way, we must necessarily unite ourselves to Him, for He cannot be known, nor can He reveal Himself save as that which is supremely glorious and good."[24] But this proposition hardly says enough, and is couched in mystical language. It was left to Russell to develop a normative ethic along these lines but independent of Spinoza's metaphysic, based upon the joyful acquisition and contemplation of knowledge as the supreme end of man, and tracing its implications for human selfishness.

In concluding the review Russell mentions Spinoza's love of humanity, which he says was provided by his pantheism. By this remark Russell probably means that when all that exists is viewed as being God, and when we love God, we therefore love all that exists—including humanity. Spinoza's supreme nobility among philosophers derives, in Russell's opinion at the end of the review, from "the union of the love of truth and the love of humanity".

23 Russell's Copy of White and Stirling's Translation

Russell's phrase in respect to his knowledge of Spinoza's life, "so far as one can discover", is curious. There is no evidence that by this stage he had gone to sources other than Pollock (with Colerus), Stein, and White's preface for Spinoza's biography. Freudenthal's *Die Lebensgeschichte Spinozas* had appeared in 1899, and various other works had appeared or were to appear, and yet there is no evidence Russell read them—which is not, of course, to say that he did not.[25] The conclusion must be that Russell felt he knew enough of the circumstances and details of Spinoza's life for the lessons he saw fit to draw (whether he *did* know enough is another question). Some 30 years after this review he writes: "Until one knows much intimate detail about a prominent man, it is impossible to judge whether he was really as great as appears or not. Some great men become greater the more they are studied; I should mention Spinoza and Lincoln as instances."[26] This statement suggests that Russell did read at least one detailed biography and, at the time of writing the essay just quoted from, he had recently read Lucas's biography (see **29**). Biographical annotations in Russell's copy of the translation do not help much. The only annotation in White's preface is a line beside these sentences about an event in 1673: "On his [Spinoza's] return he found the mob at the Hague greatly incensed against him, as France and Holland were at that time at war. His landlord was alarmed, and feared lest his house should be plundered and his tenant murdered" (p. xiii). I do not know why Russell marked this passage—a possible reason is empathy, if the mark was made after Russell encountered his own mob in 1917 (see **27**). The same event had been related in greater detail by Pollock (p. 37). Nothing more can be said on the biographical question for our purposes.

Altogether there are 80 annotations in Russell's copy of the White-Stirling translation: 3 are verbal, 72 are vertical lines, and 5 are crosses ("X"). And there are two page markers.[27] The highest ratio of marks to pages occurs in Part IV. However, the 1910 reading of the *Ethics* was at least Russell's third. (I assume here that all the pencilled markings not only are by Russell but also were made in 1910; yet it is quite possible some date from 1911–12, when he reread the *Ethics* with Lady Ottoline, or even later.) He may have been thoroughly familiar with the doctrines of Part V, and thus had little need of marking them. There is no annotation, for example, by the famous last sentence of the last proposition—"But all noble things are as difficult as they are rare"—or by another statement of considerable moral beauty, proposition 67 of Part IV—"A free man thinks of nothing less than of death, and his wisdom is not a meditation upon death but upon life." The annotations seem to cluster about major, but obscure, doctrines and explanations that Russell was not confident of understanding when he began this reading; insightful passages which had not struck him before; and minor passages of these kinds. The crosses may indicate passages of special importance to him. In addition to the cross by E4P37, concerning the slaughter of animals, there is one by E1P28, which proposes universal determination; by E2P40, concerning the nominalistic formation of universal concepts; by E2P95, that the doctrine of determinism "is of service in so far as it teaches us that we do everything by the will of God alone . . . "; and by E4P45S, on the distinction between mockery and laughter. Of the verbal marginalia, two concern the translation and a third consists of the word "Kant" beside E4P72S. White's preface (p. lxxix) has a discussion of the "remarkable anticipation of Kant" in this scholium, which concerns universalization of the hypothetical permission given one man to lie.

We may note briefly the remaining marginalia of any importance, all of which consist of a single pencilled line. E1Ap.: Russell marked two passages concerning the salutary effects of mathematics. E2P2: concerning the non-interaction of mind and body. E3P32: "If we imagine that a person enjoys a thing which only one can possess, we do all we can to prevent his possessing it." E3P43: "Hatred is increased through return of hatred, but may be destroyed by love"; and E3P45: "Hatred which is altogether overcome by love passes into love, and the love is therefore greater than if hatred had not preceded it."[28] E3P57: " . . . the joy by which the drunkard is enslaved is altogether different from the joy which is the portion of the philosopher. . . . " In the preface to E4 Russell marked Spinoza's new definitions of "good" and "evil". In E4P18S, he marked a passage bearing a possible romantic application: "There are many things, therefore, outside us which are useful to us, and which, therefore, are to be sought. Of all these, none more excellent can be discovered than those which exactly agree with our nature. If, for example, two individuals of exactly the same nature are joined together, they make up a single individual, doubly stronger than each alone." Despite this view Spinoza never married. As his next sentence indicates—"Nothing, therefore, is more useful to man than man"—Spinoza's application was probably to his later discussion, also marked by Russell, of the inestimable value to man there is of "a man who lives according to the guidance of reason" (E4P35C1), agreement in natures coming only "so far as men live in conformity with the guidance of reason" (E4P35). Thus it is that all reasonable men share a common end, which is the joyful pursuit of understanding—for as long "as men are subject to passions, they cannot be said to agree in nature" (E4P32; marked by Russell). Indeed, it will be seen that Russell marked a number of passages linking Spinoza's notion of good with self-preservation and increase of understanding, and linking the latter with the notion of harmony among men. Russell develops these points into a central ethical tenet, when he combines it with the notion of impersonal self-enlargement.

It is of interest that Russell marked Spinoza's most nearly Christian proposition, namely E4P46: "He who lives according to the guidance of reason strives as much as possible to repay the hatred, anger, or contempt of others towards himself with love or generosity." I do not mean, in introducing this proposition, that living according to reason is a concept that can be traced in the sayings of Jesus; I am thinking rather of his precept to turn the other cheek (Matt. 5:39). Russell did not invariably succeed in following this precept. As for other virtues associated with Christianity, such as humility and repentance, Russell marked Spinoza's criticisms of them (E4P54). He also marked a statement on pride and parasitism, as well as the analysis of despondency as pride (E4P57S).

In Part V, which concerns the power of the intellect, Russell marked relatively few passages. Two of those he did mark concern the power of the mind over the passions through understanding them (E5P3), especially through understanding them as necessary (E5P6). He marked also the definition of "blessedness": "And if joy consists in the passage to a greater perfection, blessedness must indeed consist in this, that the mind is endowed with perfection itself" (E5P33S).

The 1910 review and the marginalia in Russell's copy of the *Ethics* show him taking the ethic of Spinoza very seriously indeed. The following year he returns to the *Ethics* because he has entered into a relationship in which it seems to him that that ethic can be developed, taught, and shared. Much of the relationship was conducted by correspondence, since the participants could not live a common life; we have this circumstance, so frustrating to Russell, to thank for what can be revealed in the following section.

24 Correspondence with Lady Ottoline Morrell

The correspondence between Russell and Lady Ottoline Morrell (1873–1938) began in earnest in March 1911, although they had known each other since childhood. The relationship itself, which as a love affair lasted until 1916 and as an intimate friendship until Lady Ottoline's death, has been treated in ample detail by the participants themselves and their biographers.[29] Brink, in his study of the correspondence, reaches the judgment that "Together they cultivated feeling through reading Plato and Spinoza, Vaughan and Blake, among other philosophers and poets, in search of the enlargement vision brings" ("Russell to Morrell", p. 8). Such "enlargement", I hold, is the enlargement of self. Brink remarks later: "By fearless probing and stock-taking of self—without an immediate view to publication—Russell moved in his being toward 'wisdom' of the kind once associated with philosophers" (p. 15). It is crucial to an understanding of self-enlargement here that "self" be conceived impersonally. Spinozism seems to have entered early into the correspondence. Lady Ottoline makes it clear to Russell, very soon after their love becomes manifest, that she will continue all aspects of her life with her husband. Russell replies that in all the affairs he has heard of he has never come upon such an arrangement as this, and it perplexes him. "I must understand to acquiesce", he writes Spinozistically to her. "Till I understand, I shall not have that mental union with you which is necessary to love" (no. 8, p/28 March 1911). Being "somewhat at a loose end" after finishing *Principia Mathematica* (*Autobiography*, Vol. I, p. 201), Russell was casting about for another project. He tells Lady Ottoline that he wishes to write things embodying more of what he feels:

> So much that goes into religion seems to me important, and I want somehow to make people feel what survives dogmas. Most of the people who think as I do about the dogmas seem able to live in the every-day world without windows into a greater world beyond. But to me that would be a prison. Much of what I feel is in Spinoza, but he is difficult, and very few people can get what he has to give. I do not know how to express myself so as to appeal to people, and yet I am certain there is a way, if it could be found. I tried in the free man's worship, but that is only for people in great unhappiness. One wants also something for people whose vision is fading because their daily life is all prose. (No. 19a, p/6 April 1911)

Russell goes on to make the point that economic prosperity is not the criterion by which he would measure the quality of human life. Some two months pass before Russell opens his heart about

Spinoza's importance to him. Lady Ottoline seems to have had warning of the impending lecture.

> I find it hard to forgive people who compel one to think of small things in a small way. Spinoza (the lecture is coming now at last) is *the* man to teach love of mankind to people like me. He begins with two books of pure metaphysics, in which he tries to show that everything is necessary from the nature of the universe—these two books are not to me the most interesting. Then he goes on to show in particular (in the Third Book) how human actions are necessary—he deduces all the passions in the most formal way, and *seems* to be merely proving that human nature is vile. But what he is really doing is teaching one not to be indignant, but to understand people instead. He takes self-preservation as the root of the passions, and shows how it leads to strife. Then he goes on at last to point out how strife would cease if people put their Self into things which all may enjoy together—things in which one person's enjoyment does not prevent another's. The ultimate good which he holds before people is what he calls the "intellectual love of God"—commentators quarrel as to what he means by it, but I feel I know. He thinks men as individuals are not immortal, but in so far as they love God, their love of God is something deathless, but impersonal. He is filled full with an emotion towards the universe which is at once mystical and intellectual—it must have grown up in him through the feeling of god-like calm that comes when one passes from passionate strife to an impersonal reasoned view of the matter of strife. He thinks strife the fundamental evil, and reason informed by love the cure. His mind and heart are always great—he looks at each individual thing always in the light of the whole. His life was of a piece with his teaching. If one is in danger of indignation, or of letting desire destroy one's poise, he is just the man to think of. It is difficult digging the good out of his writings, because it is all concealed in a horrible pedantry of geometrical demonstration. Yet even that, in the end, one comes to love—it gives the sense of necessity, and it has the austere impersonal quality that he desires to get. (No. 82, p/24 May 1911)

Much of what Russell says in this letter is by now familiar to us. But there are important new points. The use of the term "small" in the first sentence is to be noted; presumably Russell wants people to think of large things, and in a large way. The answer to strife—putting "self into things which all may enjoy together"—is illuminating as to the emphasis Russell sees Spinoza making in his solution to the problem of conflict. And then Russell links it to the "intellectual love of God" through impartial reason—"reason informed by love [being] the cure" to strife. Although the solution is not explicit in the letter, it appears that the impersonal enlargement of self through "reason informed by love" is the solution Russell shares with Spinoza not only to the problem of conflict but also to the problem of attaining the optimum human condition.

Nearly three months later, during part of which time Russell wrote *The Problems of Philosophy*, a letter from him shows that he has made progress in teaching Spinoza to Lady Ottoline. "We must read some more Spinoza", he writes. "His 'intellectual love of God' is so much the thing we care for.... Spinoza says self-preservation is what makes everything be what it is and preserve its identity. He means I think the sort of self-assertion that prevents it from being absorbed in God and so ceasing to exist as a separate thing." We find Russell criticizing Spinoza: "But Spinoza is too pantheistic for the truth, and allows too little substantiality to individual things: nevertheless his view about self-preservation is interesting" (no. 165a, 6 Aug. 1911). They do read more Spinoza, for five days later Russell writes:

> I loved reading the Spinoza with you. Ever since I first read Pollock's book, which was when I was an undergraduate, Spinoza has been one of the most important people in my world. But I find his importance grows greater and greater to me—all my own thought makes me understand him better, and see the things he is meaning to say more clearly and with more knowledge of their importance. I felt an uneasiness until we had shared him. What I want to say is extraordinarily like what he says. He is the only one of the modern philosophers who has anything of that sort to say. (No. 169a, [11 Aug. 1911])

The reference to his own thought here is not likely a general one, but rather a specific reference to the thought he was then putting into a book on ethics, known familiarly in the correspondence as "Prisons". I outline this lost work in 44.

Russell brings Lady Ottoline into his innermost intellectual life. On two occasions he discusses reviews[30] of *Principia*, and Russell confesses to feeling himself at home among the great philosophers. He has pictures of Spinoza and Leibniz on his mantelpiece: "... I have conversations with them in which I explain how I am carrying on their work, and I can hardly resist the feeling that they hear and approve—sometimes it is all but delusion, it grows so strong" (no. 185, [Sept.? 1911]). It is a little odd that a major figure in the history of British empiricism should admire Leibniz so; but there is an affinity between them in their very strong logical interests. Spinoza, however, is on this consideration a most unlikely figure to be found on Russell's mantelpiece. It might be thought that interest in him would have vanished when Russell developed his refutation of the subject-predicate analysis of propositions on which he claimed monistic philosophies are based. (The refutation is that all propositions are reducible to a logical form in which a predicate is ascribed to a subject. From that it allegedly follows that all truth is analytic, or necessary. Hence, all propositions concerning relations between subjects are analyzable into propositions in which a predicate is ascribed to one or other of the subjects. Eventually all propositions are predicable of one subject, or substance.) The place of honour can be explained only by the extremely high regard in which Russell holds Spinoza's ethical contribution. Not all of the discussion of Spinoza with Lady Ottoline is conducted with such seriousness, however. On one occasion Russell sets out a geometrical proof "in the manner of Spinoza" of a proposition she should know.[31] On another, after she has returned from a rest cure, Russell threatens to set her an examination in philosophy. The questions were to be such as: "Explain Spinoza's doctrine of modes. How does an infinite eternal mode differ from an attribute?" (no. 178, [Aug.? 1911]). The fact that Russell discusses this metaphysical topic even playfully suggests that the two lovers spent at least a little time on it.

After the summer of 1911 there is less frequent mention of Spinoza in the correspondence. Russell has written "Prisons", his Spinozistic book on "The Religion of Contemplation", and has resumed tasks in technical philosophy. In addition to refuting Bergson he is readying himself to write on matter and on theory of knowledge.[32] In ethics and philosophy of religion he becomes dissatisfied with "Prisons" and attempts other literary means of conveying his insights. One of them, a short novel, will be discussed in the next section, since one of the characters corresponds to Spinoza. In looking back on 1911, Russell did not forget his reading of the *Ethics* a second year in succession. "Once in a way", he tells Lady Ottoline, "a book is important to me, but very seldom. Of books I have read in the last 11 months, not counting poetry, Synge and Spinoza and the Phaedrus and perhaps Trelawny's letters made a real impression on me ... " (no. 335, p/6 Feb. 1912).

Shortly after this summary of his year, Russell learned that Lady Ottoline was reading Spinoza on her own. First she read Pollock's book (see Chapter II, n. 38). Then she tackled the *Ethics*, in the Everyman edition. She puts various points to Russell in her letters, and he responds with what explanation and guidance he can.

> I am *so* glad you like the Spinoza so much. I think when he speaks of "intellect" he doesn't mean what one usually means. I don't quite know what he does mean, but the essence of it is to be universal, not particular, to be somehow in touch with the whole. I don't believe he means to shut out what you want to keep in. What he wants is that one think and feel a part of God, not as a separate Self. But he is very hard to understand fully, though one gets what is most important without very great difficulty. (No. 375, 10 March 1912)

The "intellectual love of God" is, it would seem, a way of uniting oneself to God through the kind of knowledge that comes from the intellect, not the senses. As she proceeds in her reading, Russell stresses the integrity of the *Ethics*: "Spinoza Bk. II as far as I can remember is not *very* interesting. Bk. III is meant to make you patient of people's defects by realizing that they are *necessary*. Bk. IV and still more Bk. V are the wonderful ones, but one ought to approach them through the earlier ones" (no. 384, p/15 March 1912). The kind of knowledge Spinoza values is necessary knowledge. Russell is not clear about the exact nature of Spinoza's third kind of knowledge, but he goes on to stress the necessary character of Spinoza's edifice:

> I have been looking up the passages in Spinoza. Yes, the passage about the three sorts of knowledge [E2P40S2] is fundamental, a vital part of his philosophy. There are all sorts of different views as to what he means by the third kind of knowledge: it is obviously in some sense mystical knowledge, but it is hard to get at it clearly. The other passages you speak of are important too. Part I is important; apart from his proof that there is nothing except God, his arguments about necessity are vital. Do look up in Part I Prop. XVII with Corollaries and Scholium; Prop.

XXIX, XXXII, XXXIII with Scholia, and the Appendix. (No. 386 [16 March 1912])

Mystical knowledge is obtained through the intimacy of the union of subject and object—of self and God. Thus, in all likelihood, Russell understood the third kind of knowledge as an essential step in the Spinozistic transcendence of self. His emphasis to Lady Ottoline on the propositions from Part I indicates the connection he saw between a necessary, or deterministic, view of the world and the intellectual love of God. Lady Ottoline had difficulty in understanding the *Ethics* and bemoaned the lack of access of its wisdom to the uneducated. Russell sympathized, thought that his doctrines could be taught more simply, but ultimately sided with the philosopher: "But I do feel quite convinced that Spinoza's spiritual life was richer and fuller and more in harmony with the universe than any ignorant person's could be" (no. 382 [14 March 1912]).

25 Nasispo's Speech in "The Perplexities of John Forstice"

Russell's affair with Lady Ottoline was, despite his wishes, childless. But in a metaphorical sense there were offspring. The lost manuscript, "Prisons", was often spoken of between them as their "child" because they thought of it as the fruit of their spiritual union, which was at least as important to them as their physical union.[33] But "Prisons" was in the end, i.e. by the spring of 1912, rejected as unsuccessful. The exception was a summary chapter published as "The Essence of Religion". Russell then tried again to convey a similar set of ethical insights, this time in fictional form. The result was a novella called "The Perplexities of John Forstice", which he wrote with Lady Ottoline's help in June 1912.[34] He showed it to several distinguished literary friends. One of them, Goldsworthy Lowes Dickinson, had, according to Clark, one of "his critical off-days" when he told Russell, "I do really think it has the quality of the best seventeenth-century prose, which is the highest praise one can give" (p. 180). Joseph Conrad was less enthusiastic.[35] The novella's literary merits are, however, clearly secondary to Russell's purpose, which is to present sympathetically certain ideas of a religious or ethical nature. The novella, to those who know Russell's life, is obviously autobiographical. Moreover, the autobiographical elements are just as patent at the level of theory as at the level of events. Only a section of the former will concern us here. It should be noted that Russell left the novella unpublished during his lifetime.[36]

John Forstice is a scientist who, devoted to his profession, has ignored even the people closest to him. Upon finishing an absorbing piece of work he attends a garden party, where he hears startling views about man's selfishness, class-warfare and colonial exploitation. He has never thought on such topics before. He returns home to tell his wife, but learns from her that she has a fatal disease. The result is a transformation of his character. It is nothing less than the transformation or "conversion" Russell claims he underwent at the bedside of Mrs. Whitehead in 1901. "With a sympathy which he [Forstice] had never known before, he saw the thoughts and feelings of others; the force of one great devotion set free the pent-up waters of love towards all the world" (*Collected Stories*, p. 23). In the *Autobiography* Russell writes: "I felt that I knew the inmost thoughts of everybody that I met in the street, and though this was, no doubt, a delusion, I did in actual fact find myself in far closer touch than previously with all my friends, and many of my acquaintances" (vol. I, p. 146). Those whose thoughts Forstice now penetrates are "full of the bitter determination that Self should succeed at whatever cost to others" (*Collected Stories*, p. 23). In search, therefore, of a new wisdom, Forstice takes sabbatical leave and travels abroad. In Florence he attends a meeting of a secret intellectual society, the "Amanti del Pensiero", or lovers of thought. Each speaker is a spokesman for a particular philosophy of life derived from the intense practice of a single discipline. The speeches are not imaginary; they represent Russell's own varying perspectives on the world. Moreover, the speakers' names seem to be anagrams and the like of the names of favourite personages of Russell's.[37] The mathematician's name is Forano. As Leithauser proposes, Forano could be an amalgamation of "Frege" and "Peano".[38] Jager adds: "It is no surprise that the mathematician seems to have cribbed generously from Russell's earlier essay 'The Study of Mathematics' (1902)."[39] The philosopher is Nasispo. That name is an exact anagram of Spinoza's name when spelt, as it sometimes was, with two *s*'s. ("Nasispo" is also an anagram of "passion", as Harry Ruja has pointed out to me; but "passion" is inappropriate to the Spinozistic stance Nasispo takes.) Jager is therefore off the mark in claiming that the "philosopher [was] invented by Russell".[40] The poet is Pardicreti. Leopardi and Lucretius were two of Russell's favourite philosophical poets.[41] There is a

Russian novelist, Chenskoff. Possibly he is Dostoyevsky, of whom Russell read a great deal, or Chekhov, though he was not a novelist; at any rate, the name in this case does not seem to be anagrammatical. The final speaker is Giuseppe Alegno, who represents the common man. He demands that the thinkers provide something for the common man, their highly intellectualized visions of reality being out of his reach. Forstice comes away from the meeting wondering: "Was it possible that even he [Alegno] was blind to something which could exist in the humblest lives, some good as infinite as that of the philosophers and the poet, but not dependent, like theirs, on a knowledge and a capacity only possible to a few?" (p. 34). The purpose of the story's third part is to answer that question.

Here I must admit a difficulty. I do not believe Nasispo's speech represents the essence of Russell's debt to Spinoza, or even his conscious debt. Other sections of "The Perplexities of John Forstice" are required to complete a description of that essence. There has been ample material presented in earlier sections of this chapter to support this belief. The completion of the analysis of the Spinozistic elements in the story will, therefore, have to wait until we return to it in **46**. Meanwhile, it will be useful to see what Nasispo has to say. He speaks after Forano. Leithauser regards this as appropriate, and no doubt she is right. Forano's speech concerns the refuge he takes in the necessity of the eternal truths of mathematics: "... the mathematician enters upon a calm world of ordered classic beauty, where human will, with its violence and uncertainty, counts for nothing; with joyful resignation he contemplates the unchanging hierarchy of exact, certain, shining truths, subsisting in lofty independence of Man, of time and place, of the whole universe of shifting accidental particular things" (p. 25). This is Russell's pre-Wittgensteinian view of mathematics, when it did not seem to consist entirely of tautologies. It is appropriate that the next speaker takes the model of mathematics as a starting-point for philosophy. Nasispo begins by acknowledging the beauty of the world of the "mathematicial ascetic" (p. 26). But such beauty is insufficient for life. What is needed, he holds, is an "ennobling" of our attitudes towards ordinary things. The way to achieve it is to view ordinary things as timeless, just as mathematical truths are timeless. Everything that exists, or has had existence, still has subsistence in the world of being. Focusing on this world is a corrective to the despair that takes existence to be of paramount importance. Implicitly invoking Spinoza's third kind of knowledge, Nasispo says: "Perhaps, if we could survey all time in one divine intuition, if we could rise above our hopes and fears into the region of untroubled contemplation, we should see the flight of Time as a thing of far less importance than it seems to actors entangled in the unknown drama" (p. 26). By "untroubled contemplation", Nasispo explains that he means "contemplation not fettered by desire". By overcoming desire we free ourselves from "slavery to Time" (p. 27).

This holistic, contemplative view of the universe regards everything as necessary and determined. Nasispo continues: "The joy and peace of this contemplation is Spinoza's intellectual love of God, that 'infinite love with which God loves himself' [E5P35], and the soul which is filled with the intellectual love of God is at one with all other souls inspired by the same love" (p. 27). At this point we find Russell's interpretation of Spinoza's notion of immortality, and it is bound up with the transcendence or enlargement of self: "In this contemplation consists our eternal life; for in this contemplation, Self and Time and all that makes for division is transcended." The result of the attainment of such a contemplative attitude to all things is freedom from fear of the transitoriness of individual existents. "Good and evil, to this vision, are swallowed up in the infinity of the world; and a boundless joy, the joy of union, fills the soul with worship and love and the peace of eternal life" (p. 27). We may ask, however, whether "the world" is this world, or merely the world of being.

Subsequent speakers all attempt to add something to Nasispo's philosophy of life. Pardicreti adds action to Nasispo's apparent passive receptiveness to the universe. Chenskoff adds the wisdom—derived from Russell's old ethic of pain—said to be learned by confronting "the infinite pain that lies at the heart of life" (p. 29), "driving me hither and thither in restless passion" (p. 31).[42] That is, all the subsequent speakers but Alegno attempt this. He tells the Amanti the story of his old washerwoman, whose children have whooping-cough. There is no consolation for her in Nasispo's philosophy. For "Nasispo would tell her that, although the whooping-cough may pass out of the world of existence, it will whoop on for ever in the world of Being" (p. 33). The outcome is that Forstice remains in doubt. He continues his search for ultimate wisdom.

The search takes him to the home of his uncle. We hear the story of Uncle Tristram's unrequited love for a woman who has become a nun. Tristram dies. Forstice reads his journal. Reflections upon self-enlargement begin. They are brought to a climax by his visit to the nun, who teaches him ultimate truths about "free[dom] from the prison-house of Self" (p. 42). Details of the truths taught will again have to wait until **46**, where we shall find that they amount to much more than a means of attaining what Leithauser claims Russell admires most in Spinoza's thought, namely philosophic calm ("Principles and Perplexities", p. 153).

26 Summary

This chapter, devoted to the middle period in Russell's acquaintance with Spinoza's life and thought, has shown us that Russell was a student of the *Ethics* far beyond his university days. In addition to minor references, Spinoza is the object of two book reviews and of representation in a novella by Russell. Perhaps most importantly, Spinoza has a role in a relationship between Russell and Lady Ottoline Morrell which is of crucial importance not only for Russell's personal development, but also for his attempt to unite the virtues of intellect and love. "Spinoza has it all—intellect and love. It [the unification] can be done", Russell tells her in an optimistic mood (no. 372, [early March 1912]).[43] The attempt fails and the mood passes, but the period embeds a permanent Spinozistic influence in Russell's ethical thought. That influence centres on Russell's understanding of the "intellectual love of God". He views it religiously, as a means of transcending purely personal aspirations. Although it is impossible to say exactly when it takes place, at some point in the middle period Russell ceases to view Spinoza as advocating mere self-abnegation (or the ascetic renunciation of self). In the concluding chapter of Part A, we shall trace the extent of Russell's acquaintance with this and other Spinozistic doctrines in the remainder of his life.

CHAPTER IV

The Late Period (1914-64)

27 Miscellaneous References to Spinoza

For 30 years after "Forstice" Russell did not write at length on Spinoza. Occasionally, however, his writings contain limited discussions of Spinoza's life and thought. The events he refers to in Spinoza's life are not numerous—the most common historical allusion being that for a century after his death "hardly anyone dared to say a good word for him".[1] The discussions of his thought are concerned primarily with ethics, rather than metaphysics or logic. Then Russell took two opportunities to review Spinoza's philosophy as a whole. The greater part of this chapter will be devoted to an analysis of these contributions, particularly that in *A History of Western Philosophy*. The chapter will conclude with a survey of minor references to Spinoza in writings during the remainder of Russell's life.

The first discussion of Spinoza in the later period occurs in "Mysticism and Logic", an essay written in January 1914.[2] Monistic metaphysicians, like mystics, Russell notes in the essay, deny the reality of time. Russell wishes "only to preserve the mental outlook which inspired the denial, the attitude which, in thought, regards the past as having the same reality as the present and the same importance as the future" (*Mysticism and Logic*, p. 24; 1963 ed., p. 26). He quotes Spinoza on eternality: "In so far as the mind conceives a thing according to the dictate of reason, it will be equally affected whether the idea is that of a future, past, or present thing" (E4P62). The essay has also a discussion of Spinoza's doctrine of the perfection of reality (discussed in **21**). In the same year Russell wrote the essay "On Scientific Method in Philosophy". Here he endeavours to separate further the cognitive from the emotive conceptions of philosophy and the results they can bring. He had, by this time, adopted a non-cognitive metaethic,[3] and one of his wittier statements is to be found in this essay expressing that theory: "Ethics is in origin the art of recommending to others the sacrifices required for co-operation with oneself" (*Mysticism and Logic*, p. 108; 1963 ed., p. 82). As for the ethical conception of philosophy,

> I do not deny the importance or value, within its own sphere, of the kind of philosophy which is inspired by ethical notions. The ethical work of Spinoza, for example, appears to me of the very highest significance, but what is valuable in such work is not any metaphysical theory as to the nature of the world to which it may give rise, nor indeed anything which can be proved or disproved by argument. What is valuable is the indication of some new way of feeling toward life and the world, some way of feeling by which our own existence can acquire more of the characteristics which we must deeply desire. The value of such work, however immeasurable it is, belongs with practice and not with theory. (P. 109; 1963 ed., p. 83)

Russell seems to be according such philosophy the "aesthetic" value he did in "Seems, Madam? Nay, It Is" (**17**).

Russell's normative ethical writing henceforth is an attempt to convey this way of feeling toward life and the world. In late 1914 he was again studying Spinoza, this time with his political research assistant, Irene Cooper Willis.[4] A year or so later Russell's skills as a writer were being put to use on behalf of conscientious objectors. His task was to draft letters designed to win the support of influential people. In defence of non-Christian objectors he writes that they,

> ... while not being members of any definite religious organisation, have a profound belief in the brotherhood of man, and a belief (perhaps fanatical, but shared by many of the greatest religious teachers, and finding intellectual expression in the philosophy of Spinoza) that hatred can only be conquered by love, that the reign of force cannot be destroyed by force, and that only spiritual weapons can destroy militarism.[5]

We have here another allusion to E4P46. About the same time he was engaged in writing *Principles of Social Reconstruction* (1916). There are some who see this book as influenced by a short-lived collaboration with D. H. Lawrence.[6] As to the book's fundamentals they are mistaken. The following central passage is fairly well known, but the last two sentences are not always included when it is quoted.[7] The passage is from the work's last chapter, entitled "What We Can Do".

Russell is writing in opposition to European society, which was in the midst of fighting a bitter war.

> The world has need of a philosophy, or a religion, which will promote life. But in order to promote life it is necessary to value something other than mere life. Life devoted only to life is animal, without any real human value, incapable of preserving men permanently from weariness and the feeling that all is vanity. If life is to be fully human it must serve some end which seems, in some sense, outside human life, some end which is impersonal and above mankind, such as God or truth or beauty. Those who best promote life do not have life for their purpose. They aim rather at what seems like a gradual incarnation, a bringing into our human existence of something eternal, something that appears to imagination to live in a heaven remote from strife and failure and the devouring jaws of Time. Contact with this eternal world—even if it be only a world of our imagining—brings a strength and a fundamental peace which cannot be wholly destroyed by the struggles and apparent failures of our temporal life. It is this happy contemplation of what is eternal that Spinoza calls the intellectual love of God. To those who have once known it, it is the key of wisdom.[8]

What is especially interesting about this passage is the claim that viewing everything *sub specie aeternitatis* may be merely an act of the imagination, and not a metaphysical belief as in Spinoza. It is unnecessary for one who is a monist in feeling, Russell is claiming, to be a monist in doctrine. From at least this time through his old age, Russell stands fast by the claim that Spinoza's "intellectual love of God" is the key to wisdom. In a passage I quote at **31**, he reiterates the claim in a book written in 1951. And in his *Autobiography*, in a passage written in 1931 but first published in 1967,[9] Russell confesses: "What Spinoza calls 'the intellectual love of God' has seemed to me the best thing to live by, but I have not had even the somewhat abstract God that Spinoza allowed himself to whom to attach my intellectual love" (Vol. II, p. 38).

Later in the war, when he was himself the subject of governmental persecution, Russell writes more personally of Spinoza, disclosing his affection for the man: "There is in most men a certain natural vindictiveness, not always directed against the worst members of the community. For example, Spinoza was very nearly murdered by the mob because he was suspected of undue friendliness to France at a time when Holland was at war with that country."[10] It will be remembered that the only passage Russell marked in White's preface was the one concerning this incident. Russell was himself subjected to the wrath of the mob in July 1917, some months before writing this, as he was suspected of undue friendliness toward Germany.[11]

After this time Spinoza seldom appears in Russell's technical works of philosophy. When he does it is usually as the subject of a statement like the following: "Spinoza is in many ways one of the greatest philosophers, but his greatness is rather ethical than metaphysical."[12] There is, however, a striking metaphysical use of him in "The Philosophy of Logical Atomism" (1918):

> One should always remember Spinoza's infinite attributes of Deity. It is quite likely that there are in the world the analogues of his infinite attributes. We have no acquaintance with them, but there is no reason to suppose that the mental and the physical exhaust the whole universe, so one can never say that all the instances of any logical sort of thing are of such and such a nature which is not a logical nature: you do not know enough about the world for that.[13]

We have here a direct debt on the part of Russell to one of Spinoza's most speculative metaphysical propositions (E1Df.6; *cF*. E1P11).

I have twice quoted references to the *Ethics* from a political article published on 15 March 1922 (in 15 and 21). Perhaps Russell was rereading the *Ethics* at this time, for just the previous week he published another article referring to Spinoza. The context is similar to that of the later article. Russell is at pains to deny accusations of cynicism just because he does not expect men to act morally. He mentions Americans in particular, now that their nation has become a great power:

> I hope no reader will think that my outlook is that of a cynic. Whoever will read the third Book of Spinoza's Ethics will find there a view of human nature identical with my own; whoever will read the fourth and fifth Books will see how little cynicism this view implies. The two qualities which I consider superlatively important are love of truth and love of our neighbour. I find love of truth obscured in America by commercialism, of

which pragmatism is the philosophical expression; and love of our neighbour kept in fetters by Puritan morality.[14]

I do not know whether it is more extraordinary to find Russell saying his view of human nature is (without reservation) "identical" with Spinoza's in E3, or to find anyone referring to so difficult and unpopular a work as the *Ethics* in political articles. Russell evidently thought his audience of American liberals and radicals knew their Spinoza.

In the late 1920s and early 1930s Russell was no longer writing what he regarded as technical philosophy, but instead popular books of moral advice. He had become a member of that class of "professional moralists" he had so often strongly condemned. Books such as *Sceptical Essays* (1928), *Marriage and Morals* (1929), *The Conquest of Happiness* (1930), and *The Scientific Outlook* (1931) flowed quickly from him. An important streak of Spinozism runs through them all. Love—the concern both of *Marriage and Morals* and of Russell's private life at this time—turns out to be one of the most important manifestations of impersonal self-enlargement. Happiness is conquered by widening the walls of the ego. The debt to Spinoza is explicit: "Spinoza long ago wrote of human bondage and human freedom; his form and his language make his thought difficult of access to all but students of philosophy, but the essence of what I wish to convey differs little from what he said."[15] In an essay "On Youthful Cynicism", which was written at about the same time as *The Conquest of Happiness*, Russell laments the loss of "sublimity" in our beliefs. For "when Spinoza believed anything, he considered that he was enjoying the intellectual love of God. The modern man believes either with Marx ... or with Freud.... In neither case can he enjoy Spinoza's exaltation."[16]

The final references to Spinoza to be considered in this section are in a splendid but seldom read essay, "The Philosophy of George Santayana" (1940). I have already had occasion to refer to it (**6**). Russell and Santayana wrote a good deal about each other in reviews and autobiographies, and they had known each other since 1893. Santayana had a strong interest in Spinoza, and introduced the Everyman's Library translation of Spinoza's *Ethics* in 1910. He recognized in the *Ethics* many of the same values Russell did. One of his judgments, however, is inconsistent with Russell's Spinozistic writings of the 1910–12 period. Santayana claims that "Nothing so well vindicates the genuine Hebraism of Spinoza as the fact that he avoided all Platonism...."¹⁷ The inconsistency lies in Russell's strong Platonism of that period; and how Santayana managed to ignore the Platonic notion of an eternal world in Spinoza is difficult to understand. By 1940 it was natural for Russell to think of Spinoza in connection with Santayana.¹⁸ Russell begins his essay by treating of Spinoza and Santayana's value as philosophers:

> Santayana, like Spinoza, is to be read, not so much on account of his theoretical doctrines, as on account of his view as to what constitutes the good life, and of his standard of values in art and morals. I do not mean to suggest that either his opinions or his values resemble Spinoza's. Spinoza, he says, failed to reconstitute the life of reason, because "everything impassioned seemed to him insane, everything human necessarily petty. Man was to be a pious tame animal, with the stars shining above his head." The likeness to Spinoza consists in concern for the life of reason, not in theory as to what it consists of. (*The Philosophy of George Santayana*, pp. 453–4)

He concludes that Santayana's religious opinions are "surprisingly reminiscent" of Spinoza's (p. 469): they have no theological content, and they evoke a notion of immortality similar to Spinoza's. Immortality, for both, is a matter of living in contemplation of what is eternal, by gradually caring for nothing but the rational pursuit of essences (Santayana) or necessary knowledge of the ways of the universe (Spinoza). Spinoza adds that there is something eternal in us that survives death. The result on Santayana's part is a passivity, Russell concludes, not unlike that with which he charged Spinoza.

28 A Radio Discussion of the *Ethics*

The source for the present section is the transcript of a radio discussion programme in which Russell participated—the Columbia Broadcasting System's "Invitation to Learning". About the year 1941, Russell was a guest on programmes on Hegel's *Philosophy of History*, Descartes' *Discourse on Method*, Carroll's *Alice in Wonderland*, and Spinoza's *Ethics*. Russell's antipathy to Hegel was known in advance to the other participants in the first programme, and he was encouraged by them to enumerate other philosophers with the same distinction. He replied: "I think that philosophy has suffered four misfortunes in the world's history: Plato, Aristotle, Kant and Hegel. If they were eliminated, philosophy would have done very well." To the question who would be left, excluding present company, he answered: "There would be very many people left. There would be Locke, Berkeley, Hume, Leibniz and Spinoza."[19] So despite the fact that Russell holds the monistic metaphysics of Hegel and Spinoza to be false, he separates the two philosophers in evaluating their contributions to philosophy.

In the discussion[20] of Spinoza's *Ethics*, the other participants were Scott Buchanan and Mark Van Doren, both academic literary critics and the former also a philosopher in the general sense. They seemed to have all the standard information about the figures they discussed, the guest on the programme usually contributing some freshness of approach. Russell was no exception. His contributions cover the topics of determinism, eternity, the intellectual love of God, Spinoza's third kind of knowledge, and a weakness he finds in Spinoza's ethic.

Russell's first contribution is the denial that Spinoza's deterministic view of the world "bears very much upon whether you should have an ethic" (p. 107). Russell means that the world's being determined is no reason against having an ethic. An ethic, he claims, enables the human passions "to work in a way that produces a minimum of disaster" (*ibid.*). Then he ascribes to Spinoza the view that one of the determinants of your actions is your reading or not reading his *Ethics* (a view doubtless derived from E2P49S). If Spinoza were present, "he would say that we are determined, but that those who realize that we are determined will be happier than those who do not" (p. 109). Moving on to "eternity", Russell states Spinoza's point in more commonsense terms than previously: "Well, Spinoza thought that in man there are temporary elements and eternal elements, and in proportion as the eternal elements in your nature preponderate, in that proportion you become a happier man and a better man, and he did think that philosophy could enlarge the eternal part of you" (p. 109). That is, philosophy can promote impersonal self-enlargement. In contrast to eternity, time is at the root of confusion, error, and the Spinozistic equivalent of sin. This feature emerges in the discussion of the relationship of the third kind of knowledge to determinism. A logically determined world makes the third kind of knowledge possible, but the first kind of knowledge—the confusion of sense-perception from its taking place in time—makes us prone to error.

The discussants next consider the relationship of mind and body in Spinoza. Van Doren says, "At the same moment that one is making up one's mind to think a certain thing or to do a certain thing, at that very moment the body is determining the result—determining the thought, so far as I can see." Russell, while seeming to agree, sets him straight: "That of course is psychophysical parallelism. He thinks that every event is both a physical and a mental event. It is really the same event essentially" (p. 111). Thus Russell has, in effect, denied that bodily events determine mental events. But it is somewhat misleading to label Spinoza's theory "psychophysical parallelism". That label is inappropriate when the metaphysician holds that only a single substance exists (though, of course, there is a parallelism of attributes). Mind and body, in Spinoza, are merely two aspects of, or ways of conceiving or "looking at", that single substance. Thus what Spinoza holds is a double-aspect theory—as Russell says, every event is both a physical and a mental event, as well as an infinity of other kinds of events, since there are an infinite number of attributes (E1P11). Russell himself held at this time a double-aspect theory, believing that the events common to brain and mind can be viewed either physically or mentally.[21] Instead of faulting him on the label, therefore, we might understand him as not distinguishing the double-aspect theory as one of the theories falling under the general head of psychophysical parallelism, which would cover all those theories in which mind and matter exist either as substance or as Spinozistic attribute, but do not interact.[22] In Spinoza the double-aspect theory extends to *every* event, and we find the discussants remarking in wonder upon Spinoza's proposition (E5P39) that one whose body is apt in many things is to that extent a resident of eternity (pp. 111–12).

At this point Russell objects that too much time is being spent on Spinoza's metaphysic, when it is his ethic that is of "permanent value". As will become plain, it is Spinoza's normative ethic to which he is referring, not his metaethic. Van Doren tries to excuse this approach on the ground that the ethic follows from the metaphysic. Russell's reply is predictable: "I don't think any ethic can ever follow from any metaphysic. And I think his metaphysic is completely wrong from beginning to end" (p. 112). According to Russell, there is a connection between Spinoza's metaphysic and the *imperfection* of his ethic:

> ... where I think his ethic fails is just in the fact that I can't accept his view of a block universe which, if you understood it, would seem to be all good. The universe seems to me partly good and partly bad, and I think you have to have an attitude toward the

bad which doesn't consist of saying, "I don't understand this, but if I did, I should see it to be good." Because there are things that, however well you understand them, will remain bad. Over those I think his ethic fails.... I mean it is just the way Nature works. But Nature works not only for good, as Spinoza thinks, but also for evil. (P. 117)

The others ask Russell to give what he regards as the "bases" of Spinoza's ethic. Russell's reply is not the kind that would satisfy a neutral inquirer; rather, it is the reply of someone who agrees with much of that ethic, and it sets forth the grounds for reaching that agreement. The grounds lie in personal experience:

... one can discover by experience that there is a certain kind of way of living which seems to most of those who have tried it to be a good way and which is the way which Spinoza recommends—a way in which you get rid of indignation and fear and irrational hope and a number of things that produce anxiety and perturbation in life, and acquire a certain kind of calm. The kind of calm which Spinoza recommends is, I think, attainable without adopting his metaphysic. (Pp. 112–13)

Buchanan then immediately, though vaguely, draws a connection between the pursuit of three objects: "calm", the practice of psychoanalysis, and the "intellectual love of God". He sees Spinoza's recommendation, therefore, just as Spinoza saw it, as a "remedy" (E5P20S). Russell does not reject the mention of psychoanalysis, but he does insist that the matter is not "medical" or even "psychiatric": "... it isn't to be assumed that a person is diseased because he doesn't live the life of a perfect saint, nor is it to be presumed that it is a medical man who will get him out of it. He may get out of it, as I say, through listening to music or through a hundred different things—whatever it is that appeals to that particular man" (p. 113). It was Russell who drew a connection between Spinoza's idea of calm and the intellectual love of God. Buchanan, knowing Russell's love for mathematics, tries repeatedly to identify the method of attaining the state of calm with the study of mathematics. These attempts bring Russell to identify that state with one in which you have the intellectual love of God. The "remedy", Russell holds, is "[n]ot necessarily mathematics—that depends upon who you are. You might get it just as well from history, or you might get it from music, or you might get it from poetry. There are a hundred ways of getting the kind of thing which Spinoza calls the intellectual love of God" (p. 113).[23] Asked if he would regard the "unity and ecstasy about a certain kind of mathematical technique and success" as the intellectual love of God, Russell assents. In doing so he terms it an "emotion", which "you can experience without taking on Spinoza's metaphysics" (p. 115). Then Buchanan asks Russell whether he agrees that mathematical intuition is what Spinoza is talking about. Russell reiterates his view that the third kind of knowledge is not merely mathematical in a passage disclosing that in his view logical determinism is irrelevant to the third kind of knowledge:

> ... I think it applies in all kinds of knowledge. I'm speaking now psychologically, not metaphysically; but in all kinds of knowledge, when you get a certain familiarity, there comes a moment when the imagination seizes hold upon the total of some body of knowledge that you possess, and suddenly you realize it; you suddenly see it in a kind of vision; and that, I think, is Spinoza's third kind of knowledge. It is not confined by any means to mathematics. (P. 115)

We are faced, therefore, with the conclusion that the concept of the intellectual love of God is being explained here as the concept of an emotional state—a state of the emotion of calm; moreover, that such a state occurs while one is in a state of understanding—but not just any state of understanding, but one in which a whole is grasped. You may recognize having had moments of such a state; but it is a very different matter for such a state to persist indefinitely. Its connection with the avoidance of "anxiety and perturbation in life" is left obscure.

Russell wants to leave God "entirely" out of it at this stage: "My point about Spinoza is that a great many of the things he says have psychological truth when restated in other language than his, but do not have metaphysical truth so long as you stick to his language" (p. 115). When the discussants go on to explore possible defects in Spinoza's ethic, we find Russell rejecting the monistic view that understanding the universe results in seeing that all is good. But Spinoza's analysis of the emotions themselves draws Russell's praise: "I like his definitions of the emotions—they are interesting" (p. 117), and he agrees with Spinoza's evaluation of pity as an emotion not to be encouraged. The transcript of the programme ends with the discussants disagreeing over whether or not understanding a toothache lessens its pain. Despite trying very hard, Russell has never found that it did any good. The pain persists. Hence he believes that evil in the form of pain is an ineradicable feature of the universe. We shall find that in *A History of Western Philosophy* Russell still adheres to the argument from eternity in explaining that ineradicableness.

29 *A History of Western Philosophy*: Preliminary Aspects

We come now to *A History of Western Philosophy*. In the present section we shall examine a sheet of notes for the chapter on Spinoza; the manuscript of the chapter; its introductory pages; and various passages concerning Spinoza elsewhere in the volume. In 30 we shall examine the bulk of the chapter itself, which is devoted primarily to Spinoza's metaphysic and ethic.

A History of Western Philosophy and its Connection with Political and Social Circumstances from the Earliest Times to the Present Day is a controversial work, with the reputation of being an undisciplined record of merely personal tastes and opinons.[24] Yet the charge that the *History* is undisciplined is by no means a just one. In the preface to the first edition only (1945), Russell states that his "purpose is to exhibit philosophy as an integral part of social and political life" (p. ix). This purpose has an interesting result for our study. Russell continues: "One consequence of this point of view is that the importance which it gives to a philosopher is often not that which he deserves on account of his philosophic merit. For my part, for example, I consider Spinoza a greater philosopher than Locke, but he was far less influential; I have therefore treated him much more briefly than Locke" (*ibid.*). There are, in the first edition, 12 pages devoted to Spinoza, and 44 to Locke, including 7 on his influence. Given Russell's stated purpose, and the relative influences of Spinoza and Locke, the proportions seem just; and given Russell's admiration for Spinoza and his ethic, discipline in awarding these proportions is quite in evidence.

It is not known precisely when Russell wrote the chapter on Spinoza,[25] but preserved with the manuscript of the *History* is a single sheet of notes Russell took on reading some of Spinoza's writings. The sheet, headed "*Life of Spinoza*", begins with these notes: "p. 55 Rabbis and Christian magistrates / 63–4 Tidily dressed / 71 Spinoza's Talk".[26] The page numbers are those of *The Oldest Biography of Spinoza*, edited by A. Wolf.[27] These notes are followed by the heading "Spinoza, Bohn, I" and considerably more notes. The fact that

Russell was reading a life of Spinoza and making notes on the Elwes translation of his works—for it is that translation which was published in the Bohn Library[28]—is indicative of his making preparations to write on Spinoza. The discussion programme might not have justified reading to that extent. And the only substantial piece of writing on Spinoza in the early 1940s is the *History* chapter. Furthermore, two references in popular articles can help to date the notes (and the chapter) a little more precisely.[29] It seems likely, therefore, that Russell wrote his Spinoza chapter in 1942 or 1943.

According to Wolf, the biography in question was probably written by one Lucas—at any rate by someone who knew and loved Spinoza—within a year or two of his death (Wolf, p. 19). As a student Russell had probably read the later life by Colerus in Pollock's book; it is interesting that he should have gone to another primary source when several fuller but more recent lives were available.[30] Lucas's life is very short—only 35 pages in Wolf's edition. The note about the rabbis and Christian magistrates concerns how the latter collaborated with the former in driving Spinoza out of Amsterdam after his excommunication. The passage about Spinoza being tidily dressed is amusing to look up, since that quality is said to be rare in a philosopher. Of "Spinoza's Talk", Lucas records that "his conversations had such an air of geniality and his comparisons were so just that he made everybody fall in unconsciously with his views. He was persuasive although he did not affect polished or elegant diction. He made himself so intelligible, and his discourse was so full of good sense, that none listened to him without deriving satisfaction" (Wolf, p. 71). Against my assumption that the notes were preparatory to writing the chapter is the fact that Russell's scant two paragraphs on Spinoza's life in the *History* do not appear to owe anything to his reading of Lucas. Even Spinoza's dates were taken from Elwes's introduction (vol. I, pp. x, xx), if that inference may be made from the fact of a common error.[31] However, later in the chapter there is an appreciative account of Spinoza's persuasive ability in argumentative discourse (*History*, p. 574; p. 557), which may owe something to reading Lucas.

The remainder of the notes concern the *Tractatus Theologico-Politicus, Tractatus Politicus, Treatise on the Improvement of the Understanding*, and Elwes' selection of the correspondence. Russell's comments on the first of the treatises are, in both the notes and the chapter, very few. Some of the notes concern ethics, but they are not worked into the chapter (the political part of the first treatise being more generously treated). There is a curious absence of any use of more positive statements on the role of the state. Russell notes that in the *Tractatus Politicus*, "Commonwealth does wrong when it promotes its own ruin i.e. acts against reason" (Bohn, p. 310), yet he makes nothing of this in his chapter. The doctrine is important because Spinoza is drawing certain pro-rational inferences about how a state should act from its agreed goal, namely independence; and this goal of the state is much like the goal of the individual, that is, independence of the passions through action in accordance with reason. Russell also does not use a passage on slavery and peace which he notes as "eloquent" (Bohn, p. 317).

The notes on *Improvement of the Understanding* are not used either. Since this is the only time Russell refers to this important but unfinished work of Spinoza's, I shall quote them. Russell notes on page 34 of the Bohn edition that "Knowledge of effect is only more perfect knowledge of cause", and on page 36 that "In uncreated things, definition must make existence evident." The first is evidence for Russell's statement that Spinoza holds that "the interconnections of the parts of the universe are *logical*" (p. 572; p. 555). The second is preparatory to Spinoza's proof of the unity of substance, which Russell omits to discuss in the *History*. Russell's notes on Spinoza's correspondence likewise go unused. None of them concerns ethics, except perhaps the note pointing out a passage in which Spinoza remarks on Leibniz. Spinoza wrote in part: "As far as I could conjecture from his [Leibniz's] letters, he seemed to me a man of liberal mind, and versed in every science. But yet I think it imprudent so soon to entrust my writings to him"[32] (Ep. 68b, 18 Nov. 1675). However, there is no evidence that Russell is noting this passage in particular.

In addition to the chapter itself, *A History of Western Philosophy* is rich in references to Spinoza. There is an enlightening discussion of the idealist ethic of Hegel in contrast to that of Spinoza, with which I shall deal in 31. Generally the allusions to Spinoza are of a personal nature, though some are philosophical. The characters of Spinoza and Plotinus are compared and praised. Leibniz, on the other hand, "was wholly destitute of those higher philosophic virtues that are so notable in Spinoza" (p. 581; p. 563). There has been a criticism that "love of the eternal is characteristic of a leisure class, which lives on the labour of others. I doubt if this is true. Epictetus and Spinoza were not gentlemen of leisure" (p. 786; p. 751).[33] As a member of the "mathematical party" of philosophers (p. 828; p. 783), Spinoza is part of a very important strain in western philosophy: other members of the party are Plato, Saint Augustine, Thomas Aquinas, Descartes and Kant. In them, "... there is an intimate blending of religion and reasoning, of moral aspiration with logical admiration of what is timeless, which comes from Pythagoras, and distinguishes the intellectualized theology of Europe from the more straightforward mysticism of Asia" (p. 37; p. 56). The mystical element in Spinoza is not forgotten. "There are in Spinoza two unreconciled views on ethics, one that of Hobbes, the other that the good consists in mystic union with God" (p. 644; p. 620). Finally, there is a report of Nietzsche's condemnation of Spinoza, which was in part: "How much of personal timidity and vulnerability does this masquerade of a sickly recluse betray!" Russell unhesitatingly takes Spinoza's side: "Exactly the same may be said of him [Nietzsche] with the less reluctance since he has not hesitated to say it of Spinoza" (p. 767; p. 734).[34] In rounding off the chapter on Nietzsche, Russell constructs an imaginary dialogue between Nietzsche and Buddha on what their ultimate ethical disagreements might be. He might just as well have made it a dialogue between Nietzsche and Spinoza. That he did not do so was probably because Buddha is a better-known representative of the views Russell wished to defend.

30 *A History of Western Philosophy*: Chapter on Spinoza

The main part of the *History*'s chapter on Spinoza begins with an overview of the *Ethics*. It then settles into a summary of his metaphysic and ethic. Finally there is an evaluation of the ethic in the light of Russell's rejection of the metaphysic. In the evaluation Russell tests the remedy of philosophic calm in various problem cases in which that attitude might be adopted. I shall follow Russell's order in dealing with these topics.

The overview is remarkable for its omission of Spinoza's theory of knowledge. Even later, in the discussion of the intellectual love of God, the third kind of knowledge is not introduced, although the subject of knowledge is not entirely neglected. A discussion of the first kind of knowledge, sense-perception, you would think was a necessity in approaching the concept of the intellectual love of God, for the reliance upon the first kind of knowledge is, according to Spinoza (E5P28), one of the barriers to the attainment of that state. In his summary of the *Ethics*, Russell traces two historical connections: "The metaphysic is a modification of Descartes, the psychology is reminiscent of Hobbes, but" (Russell adds) "the ethic is original, and is what is of most value in the book" (p. 570; p. 553). In the framework of a "materialistic and deterministic physics", Spinoza attempted "to find room for reverence and a life devoted to the Good." Russell judges the attempt to be "magnificent".

In Spinoza's metaphysic, Russell continues, there is only one self-subsistent being, "God or Nature". The attributes of thought and extension as modified in terms of "individual souls and separate pieces of matter are, for Spinoza, adjectival; they are not *things*, but merely aspects of the divine Being." Since all determination is negation (E1P8S1; E4Pref.), there can be only one undetermined being, and this being cannot be finite. If he were limited in any respect, he would be the subject of a limitation, and therefore not infinite. "Hence Spinoza is led to a complete and undiluted pantheism" (p. 571; p. 554). The determinism operating in this system is logical, not causal. (It shows a misunderstanding to imagine things as able to happen differently from the way in which they do. It is easy, then, to see how understanding could lead to acquiescence in the *status quo*.) There is an indication that Russell has read at least some of Spinoza's correspondence when he points out that everything ordained by God is good. The question "Was it good that Nero should kill his mother?", which is repeated by Russell in his chapter, is answered in Spinoza's letter to William Blyenbergh of 13 March 1665 (Ep. 36).[35] The vexatious problem of negation is raised by Spinoza's answer, which I shall quote because in the discussion programme Russell said that this was the weak point in Spinoza's ethic:

> Spinoza answers that what was positive in these acts was good, and only what was negative was bad; but negation exists only from the point of view of finite creatures. In God, who alone is completely real, there is no negation, and therefore the evil in what to us seem sins does not exist when they are viewed as parts of the whole. This doctrine, though, in one form or another, it has been held by most mystics, cannot, obviously, be reconciled with the orthodox doctrine of sin and damnation.... Spinoza was too honest to conceal his opinions.... (Pp. 571–2; p. 554)

You may wonder whether the qualifier "most" before "mystics" is meant to allow for the inclusion in that class of people like Russell. For even during the period of his most mystical writings—i.e. during 1910–12—he remains opposed to the notion that if the whole is good, then the bad elements in it disappear. He seems to hold rather that both good and bad disappear. (For his mysticism, see **42**.)

Russell next discusses Spinoza's geometrical method. There is no talk now of coming to "love" it, as he talked of it in 1911 (**24**). But although the method presents grave difficulties to the student, Russell holds that it must not be dismissed as inessential to Spinoza's purpose. A few years later Russell writes that "Spinoza took geometry for his model, and hoped to deduce the nature of the universe from self-evident axioms...."[36] In the *History*, he elaborates:

> It was of the essence of his system, ethically as well as metaphysically, to maintain that everything *could* be demonstrated, and it was therefore essential to produce demonstrations. *We* cannot accept his method, but that is because we cannot accept his metaphysic. We cannot believe that the interconnections of the parts of the universe are *logical*, because we hold that scientific laws are to be discovered by observation, not by reasoning alone. (P. 572; p. 555)

A few pages on, he provides an example of Spinoza's geometrical proofs. What is proved, in the example "that 'love of God must hold the chief place in the mind'" (E5P16), is not so much a "moral exhortation", but something which must happen upon the acquisition of understanding (see **21** for an earlier use of this example).

Part III of the *Ethics* is also treated briefly by Russell, but what he says of it is important for understanding his grasp of Spinoza's system. The psychology of the Part is "egoistic". That is, man's fundamental motive is self-preservation, and the psychology of self-preservation is behind such propositions as "He who conceives that the object of his hate is destroyed will feel pleasure" (E3P20), and that which says we will seek to prevent others from enjoying uniquely possessable goods (E3P32). But "self-preservation alters in character when we realize that what is real and positive in us is what unites us to the whole, and not what preserves the appearance of separateness" (p. 573; p. 555). Self-preservation can, therefore, lead to self-enlargement and away from psychological egoism, in Russell's understanding. This connection is of vital importance, for it allows for the possibility of building a normative ethic on the facts of man's nature. As he told Lady Ottoline in 1918, "it doesn't do to forget the animal in man" (*Autobiography*, vol. II, p. 89), implying then that self-preservation is possible not only at the expense of others (*ibid.*). In the same paragraph of the *History*

Russell quotes E3P43 again: "Hatred is increased by being reciprocated, and can on the other hand be destroyed by love."

Russell comes finally to Parts IV and V. He continues his account of Spinoza's concept of self-preservation and its ethical bearings. "All wrong action is due to intellectual error" (p. 573; p. 555). This conclusion is explained by the adequacy of understanding in Spinoza for right action. A man possessed of adequate understanding "will even be happy in the face of what to another would be misfortune." Although self-preservation governs all human behaviour, "what a wise man will choose as the goal of his self-seeking is different from that of the ordinary egoist." In fact, men who follow reason will agree with one another. Such agreement is fostered by realization of the unreality of time. Russell quotes E4P62: "In so far as the mind conceives a thing under the dictate of reason, it is affected equally, whether the idea be of a thing present, past, or future." It is thus foolish to be more concerned about the future than the past, since the future, because it is also determined, is just as unalterable as the past. Both hope and fear, therefore, are unwise (p. 574; p. 556). In the wise man's contemplation of the world as a whole, evil is nothing but inadequate knowledge (Russell quotes E4P64). Hence the whole is good; and since everything in the whole is necessary to it, everything is necessary to the goodness of the whole. As we might expect, Russell returns to this argument in his critical section. From an individual's perspective, good is what originates in a man, and evil is what is imposed on him from without. This is perhaps the strongest reason for thinking the world as a whole is good—there is nothing that can happen to it from without. Russell summarizes: "In so far as a man is an unwitting part of a larger whole, he is in bondage; but in so far as, through the understanding, he grasps the sole reality of the whole, he is free" (pp. 574–5; p. 557).

Focusing now on the fifth Part, Russell explains how for Spinoza emotions may cease to be "passions"—the only kind of emotion to which Spinoza objects. The mind acquires power over the (passive) emotions by the help of the knowledge that all things are necessary. Then Russell quotes E5P15 as the proposition which "introduces us to the 'intellectual love of God', in which wisdom consists." It is interesting that Russell should consider this proposition—"He who clearly and distinctly understands himself and his emotions loves God, and so much the more in proportion as he more understands himself and his emotions"—as that introduction. The "intellectual love of God" is not actually mentioned until E5P32C, when Spinoza says, "From the third kind of knowledge necessarily arises the intellectual love of God." The intervening propositions concern (*a*) love of God, (*b*) the immortality of the mind, and (*c*) the third kind of knowledge. It must be through (*c*) that Russell understands the link between E5P15 and E5P32C. First let us see what he says here of the intellectual love of God:

> The intellectual love of God is a union of thought and emotion: it consists, I think one may say, in true thought combined with joy in the apprehension of truth. All joy in true thought is part of the intellectual love of God, for it contains nothing negative, and is therefore truly part of the whole, not only apparently, as are fragmentary things so separated in thought as to appear bad.... there is something in "intellectual *love*" which is not mere intellect; perhaps the joy involved is considered as something superior to pleasure. (P. 575; pp. 557-8)

Russell adds later that "The intellectual love of God, when experienced by an individual, is contained in this eternal part of the mind"—i.e. the part which achieves immortality. And the part which achieves immortality is "an idea which expresses the essence of this or that human body under the form of eternity ..." (p. 577; p. 559).

Russell's explanation of the concept of the intellectual love of God is clearly a sympathetic one, as we should expect from his earlier remarks. In this chapter he gives no examples. Earlier in the *History*, however, he explains the concept in the same fashion as on the discussion programme. In the midst of treating Plato's theory of ideas, Russell says:

> Philosophy, for Plato, is a kind of vision, the "vision of truth." It is not *purely* intellectual; it is not merely wisdom, but *love* of wisdom. Spinoza's "intellectual love of God" is much the same intimate union of thought and feeling. Every one who has done any kind of creative work has experienced, in a greater or less degree, the state of mind in which, after long labour, truth, or beauty, appears, or seems to appear, in a sudden glory—it may be only about some small matter, or it may be about the universe. The experience is, at the moment, very convincing; doubt may come later, but at the time there is utter certainty. I think most of the best creative work, in art, in science, in

literature, and in philosophy, has been the result of such a moment. (P. 123; p. 138)

Russell continues the passage with a description of his method of soaking himself in the detail of a subject-matter, and then one day perceiving it whole, with all the parts interrelated. The description is familiar from "How I Write"[37] and other writings, but in them there is no mention of the "intellectual love of God". The alternate analogy of "first walking all over a mountain in a mist, until every path and ridge and valley is separately familiar, and then, from a distance, seeing the mountain whole and clear in bright sunshine" is similar, and familiar to readers of Russell's works.[38]

Russell briefly discusses Spinoza's remedies for emotional turmoil. The most important remedy is clear understanding of the emotions, and seeing how they arise from changing external forces. It is better, then, to attach ourselves to things which are eternal, than to things which are changeable (p. 557; p. 559). The expository section of the chapter ends with the definition of "blessedness" and the last half of the final scholium of Part V.

In his criticism, Russell first separates Spinoza's ethic from his metaphysic. The metaphysic is concerned not only with the concept of substance, but with the concept of a single substance of which every apparently separate thing is logically a part. Russell calls Spinoza's philosophy the best example of logical monism. That is why, in this metaphysic, even to imagine events as able to be otherwise than they are is to commit a conceptual error. Spinoza's doctrine of necessity, argues Russell, makes the limits of human power narrower than they really are. Now, Russell is concerned with anthropocentrism during all the later period, and that attitude tends to inflate men's sense of their own power. As he writes later in the *History*, "To frame a philosophy capable of coping with men intoxicated with the prospect of almost unlimited power ... is the most pressing task of our time" (p. 729; p. 700). But limits do exist, and "Broadly speaking, Spinoza is concerned to show how it is possible to live nobly even when we recognize the limits of human power." Thus to be obsessed by events beyond our power, the fear of death, is a kind of slavery. There are steps to be taken to avoid death in the short term, and they should be taken "calmly", and our thoughts directed elsewhere. "The same considerations apply to all other purely personal misfortunes" (p. 578; p. 560). This is part of what can be accepted even with the rejection of Spinoza's metaphysic.

In coming to the part of Spinoza's ethic which he cannot accept, Russell enters upon a lengthy digression concerning the attitude which is warranted towards the misfortunes of other people, in particular those we love. The context is the case of misfortunes that *have* occurred, not those that might occur in the future. The examples Russell chooses are typical of the time in which he is writing, two of them being "Suppose you are a Jew, and your family has been massacred" and "Suppose your daughter has been raped and killed by enemy soldiers." The question is "Ought you, in these circumstances, to preserve a philosophic calm?" In other words, is acquiescence justified, when respected alternatives are available?

The Christian alternative is discussed. It "does not inculcate calm, but an ardent love even towards the worst of men" (p. 579; p. 561). But despite the fact that he has sometimes observed Quakers practising this alternative—even when they felt the misfortune in question as deeply as it should be felt—he judges that "it is too difficult for most of us to practise sincerely." Russell, in treating the Christian alternative, also deals with Stoicism. The Stoic alternative is to pretend that such injury does not affect one's own striving towards virtue. Russell is thus looking for an alternative with popular appeal, not one available only to a moral elite.

Another alternative—an unrestrained emotional reaction to the type of event in the examples—is the pursuit of revenge. The discussion of revenge appears to be unique in Russell's corpus. It comes possibly as a surprise that the pursuit of revenge should be a serious alternative to philosophic calm. It must be remembered, however, that Russell is discussing alternative attitudes to cases of grievous and deliberate injury to persons in whose lives you are bound up. Revenge is justified in part from the point of view of the mental health of the person possessed of this very strong impulse, and in part because revenge leads to punishment "and punishment is sometimes necessary". But revenge is a dangerous motive, for its dominating force often leads to excess. Spinoza is right that "a life dominated by a single passion is a narrow life, incompatible with every kind of wisdom. Revenge as such is not the best reaction to injury" (p. 579; p. 561).

It is worth noting that Russell omits the alternative of simple but deep suffering until the emotional injury is healed. In his *Autobiography* he relates a case in which this alternative was evidently the one which he employed. The case was that of Crompton Llewelyn Davies, Russell's best friend, who had lost his closest brother, Theodore. Russell relates that Crompton "suffered almost unendurably. I spent the weeks after Theodore's death with him, but it was difficult to find anything to say.* The sight of his unhappiness was agonizing" (vol. I, p. 58). In the footnote Russell cites two letters in the first volume of his *Autobiography*. In the first letter he tells a correspondent that he is with Crompton "to do what I can for him—there is little enough except to sit in silence with him and suffer as he suffers." In the second he tells the same correspondent that "the case was one which admitted of no philosophy at all—I could not see that there was anything to be said in mitigation of the disaster."[39] It was doubtless cases like this one which filled Russell "with a desire almost as profound as that of the Buddha to find some philosophy which should make human life endurable" (vol. I, p. 146).

The alternative Russell settles for in the *History* is a watereddown version of Spinoza's alternative. Russell claims that Spinoza took the Christian attitude and added to it the doctrine that when a sorrow is fully understood it is seen as an inevitable part of the whole order of nature, and therefore as not positively evil. Russell cannot accept this doctrine because he does not believe in the world's ultimate goodness; and we see, finally, the point of the digression:

> Spinoza thinks that, if you see your misfortunes as they are in reality, as part of the concatenation of causes stretching from the beginning of time to the end, you will see that they are only misfortunes to you, not to the universe, to which they are merely passing discords heightening an ultimate harmony. I cannot accept this: I believe that particular events are what they are, and do not become different by absorption into a whole. Each act of cruelty is eternally a part of the universe; nothing that happens later can make that act good rather than bad, or can confer perfection on the whole of which it is a part. (P. 580; p. 562)

Nor can Russell accept the Christian element in Spinoza's answer. There is danger in turning the other cheek to those who have power over you. He quotes E3P43 on hatred being destroyed by love. Now Russell had, at this time, very recently advocated that Britain, in the face of a Nazi invasion, should refuse to fight, despite the most serious provocations.[40] The Nazi terror was to be defused through the return of love for hate. He recanted this position during the Battle of Britain, in May 1940. He wrote now that the wicked cannot be deprived of power by non-resistance (p. 580; p. 562). He does, however, allow for an interesting special case, "where the person hating is completely in the power of the person who refuses to hate in return. In such cases, surprise at being not punished may have a reforming effect." He does not, unfortunately, inform us how to get those who hate us completely into our power.

What Russell does accept in Spinoza's remedy is his "principle of thinking about the whole, or at any rate about larger matters than your own grief". This is once again the familiar spatial image related to the self, or to a self-concern. The point, presumably, about thinking about the whole is to gain perspective on the relative size of the matter of your grief. In wartime, especially, you are unlikely to be unique in any kind of sorrow. This may seem a pale vestige of the 1911 philosophy of "life in the whole" and of self-enlargement through the widening of interests and sympathies, but the concept is fundamentally the same. In closing the chapter Russell repeats what is a common thought in his corpus almost from the beginning: "There are even times when it is comforting to reflect that human life, with all that it contains of evil and suffering, is an infinitesimal part of the life of the universe. Such reflections may not suffice to constitute a religion, but in a painful world they are a help towards sanity and an antidote to the paralysis of utter despair" (p. 580; p. 562). Russell's final attitude towards philosophic calm is, therefore, ambiguous. He appears to accept it as the best of all possible attitudes in the face of disaster, present or impending. He is necessarily less persuasive on its behalf, however, than is Spinoza—because in Russell's metaphysic there is less persuasive material for him to use. Russell's discussion of alternative attitudes does show that he would not condemn those who adopt those attitudes.[41] As for himself, Russell did not, I am sure, practise or even recommend a life of unruffled calm. His emotions and actions in the face of the nuclear threat are sufficient evidence to the contrary. (See **50**; for an evaluation of philosophic calm, see **59**.) But he did display the kind of calm that results in the husbanding and the directing of energy: his moments of anger and heat seem to have been "active" rather than "passive". That, I conclude, is very nearly what his evident praise of Spinoza amounts to earlier in the chapter: "Unlike some other philosophers, he not only believed his own doctrines, but practised them; I do not know of any occasion, in spite of great provocation, in which he was betrayed into the kind of heat or anger that his ethic condemned" (p. 574; p. 557).

31 Miscellaneous References, 1945–64

I mentioned at the end of 29 that the chapter on Hegel in the *History* throws interesting light on Spinoza's conception of the whole, as well as on the conception of the whole to which Russell was attracted in the 1890s.[42] The first point of importance is that Hegel "differed from Parmenides and Spinoza in conceiving the whole, not as a simple substance, but as a complex system, of the sort that we should call an organism" (p. 731; pp. 701–2). Russell previously discussed organic systems in connection with Aristotle's theory of the relation of the individual to the state (p. 186; p. 197). In Hegel, each apparently separate thing has a degree of reality as such. In Hegel's political application, the whole is the state. The individual's membership in the state is crucial to his realization. Russell summarizes: "... the individual only has objectivity, truth, and morality in so far as he is a member of the State, whose true content and purpose is union as such" (p. 740; p. 710). The individual, according to Russell, disappears in the Spinozistic whole, or state; but in the Hegelian whole, or state, "the individual does not disappear, but acquires fuller reality through his harmonious relation to a larger organism" (p. 742; p. 712). Thus the Bradleian idealism discussed in Chapter II seems to be a more direct descendant of Hegelianism than of Spinozism—which is just what we should have expected.[43] But common to the political philosophies of Spinoza, Hegel, and Bradley is the belief that self-realization is best advanced through membership in a suprapersonal community of human beings.

What Russell says here of Spinoza does not seem to be true. Individuals do not disappear in Spinoza's wholes, since his single substance is only manifested as modified attributes in which individuals are always apparent. The intellectual love of God is itself a contemplation of individual things—"The more we understand individual objects, the more we understand God" (E5P24). However, it is not unlikely that monists should disagree about the degree by which individual things are enhanced through absorption into the whole.

After the *History*, there are no new interpretative writings on Spinoza by Russell, although there are interesting passages in which Spinoza figures. And when Russell invokes a largeness of vision, as he does increasingly as the prospect of man's annihilation through nuclear war becomes greater, he brings in Spinoza's views. I shall deal with a selection of the more significant passages in chronological order to complete the account of Russell's lifelong interest in Spinoza.

In *Authority and the Individual* (1949) Russell devotes a chapter to the social role of individuality. It is not Spinoza's philosophy but his life which is referred to here. Practically every task the individual wishes to perform in order to attain a goal of some importance requires the help of a powerful organization. Hence "... the man who works without the help of an organization, like a Hebrew prophet, a poet, or a solitary philosopher such as Spinoza, can no longer hope for the kind of importance which such men had in former days."[44]

Russell enjoyed using Spinoza as an illustration, because it was often possible to refer to his life at the same time as his ethic. "Fortitude",[45] a chapter in *New Hopes for a Changing World*, combines both sorts of references. Spinoza is again employed in a discussion of individuality. Now Russell is discussing the kind of individuality that can lead to conscious social involvement—not political involvement, just simple community feeling. The relevant section begins: "While Russia underestimates the individual, there are those in the West who unduly magnify the separateness of separate persons" (*New Hopes*, p. 182). However, we must say no more until Chapter VI about Russell's proposal for conceiving the individual as less "separate" than is often done. Spinoza is brought in specifically to illustrate the notion of largeness of vision. The following paragraphs come between two discussions on the "separateness" of the individual ego:

> If bad times lie ahead of us we should remember while they last the slow march of man, chequered in the past by devastations and retrogressions, but always resuming the movement toward progress. Spinoza, who was one of the wisest of men and who lived consistently in accordance with his own wisdom, advised men to view passing events "under the aspect of eternity." Those who can learn to do this will find a painful present much more bearable than it would otherwise be. They can see it as a passing moment—a discord to be resolved, a tunnel to be traversed. The small child who has hurt himself weeps as if the world contained nothing but sorrow, because his mind is confined to the present. A man who has learned wisdom from Spinoza can see even a lifetime of suffering as a passing moment in the life of humanity. And the human race itself, from its obscure beginning to its unknown end, is only a minute episode in the life of the universe.
>
> What may be happening elsewhere we do not know, but it is improbable that the universe contains nothing better than our-

selves. With increase of wisdom our thoughts acquire a wider scope both in space and in time. The child lives in the minute, the boy in the day, the instinctive man in the year. The man imbued with history lives in the epoch. Spinoza would have us live not in the minute, the day, the year or the epoch, but in eternity. Those who learn to do this will find that it takes away the frantic quality of misfortune and prevents the trend toward madness that comes with overwhelming disaster. Spinoza spent the last day of his life telling cheerful anecdotes to his host. He had written: "A free man thinks of death least of all things, and his wisdom is a meditation not of death but of life." [E4P67] And he carried out this precept when it came to his own death. (Pp. 189–90)

That organicist phrase, "a discord to be resolved", is suggestive of the very view Russell has hitherto been concerned to reject—the view that evil disappears in a whole which is good. However, the remark does not actually imply that pain becomes good when viewed in the light of the whole—only that even the worst evils should not be permitted to colour all existence. There is no suggestion of an "ultimate harmony" as Russell asserts there is in Spinoza (**30**). *New Hopes* is also the source of one of the best-known passages on the widening of the ego in Russell's writings. I discuss such passages in Chapter VI (see **50** for the passage in *New Hopes*).

In 1956 Russell included in *Portraits from Memory and Other Essays* a short essay titled "A Philosophy for Our Time". This essay is useful for understanding his ethic. Spinoza is mentioned in connection with an antidote to dogmatism. Dogmatism has both intellectual and emotional sources, according to Russell. The emotional source is fear. Once again he employs Spinoza's ethic to combat fear:

> Where danger is real the impersonal kind of feeling that philosophy should generate is the best cure. Spinoza, who was perhaps the best example of the way of feeling of which I am speaking, remained completely calm at all times, and in the last day of his life preserved the same friendly interest in others as he had shown in days of health. To a man whose hopes and wishes extend widely beyond his personal life there is not the same occasion for fear that there is for a man of more limited desires. (Pp. 183–4)

In 1958 G. E. Moore died, and Russell wrote in an obituary that Moore's intellect had been "as deeply passionate as Spinoza's".[46] This is the same phrase he used in writing of the early Moore in his *Autobiography* (vol. I, p. 64). *My Philosophical Development* and *Wisdom of the West* (both published in 1959) contain nothing new on Spinoza. The last mentions of Spinoza by Russell known to me are in two interviews of 1964. One is quoted in **10**. The other says of Spinoza: "I think he's all wrong, but I admire him very much."[47] This statement is on a par with that at the end of the quotation from Russell's 1957 broadcast on "The Pursuit of Truth" (**11**). Russell says there merely that he finds Spinoza's doctrines intellectually unsatisfactory, a view which, because of Russell's non-cognitivist metaethic, does not prevent him from esteeming Spinoza's normative ethic.

32 Summary

This chapter concludes Part A, the survey of Russell's writings on Spinoza. In spanning more than half a century of those writings, the survey has laid bare some inconsistencies and confusions in Russell's understanding of that philosopher. The survey has also revealed a considerable change in Russell's mode of writing on Spinoza—from the quasi-metaphysical attempt at constructing a religious philosophy during the affair with Lady Ottoline, to the less exalted discussions of Spinoza's value by 1940. Much of the material surveyed is little known to philosophers, even those specializing in Russell's development, partly because of the uncollected, and even unpublished, nature of much of those writings. But it is due also to the fact that in some of them Russell is not writing in the capacity of professional philosopher he created for himself. Rather he is writing as someone who has, to a great extent, abandoned the attempt to give reason as large a role in metaethics as has traditionally been the case. Yet much of the material surveyed in Part A—the reviews of Picton's book and of White and Stirling's translation of the *Ethics*, and the *History of Western Philosophy*—was undoubtedly written in Russell's professional capacity. The radio discussion was undertaken in that capacity. And much of what he has to say on Spinoza in that capacity is carried over to the other writings. This is the case in particular with the notions of eternity and determinism, and with his analysis of man's nature as one rooted in the impulse to self-preservation. On the borderline is the notion of the intellectual love of God. Russell thinks there is something important in the notion, after its metaphysical basis in Spinoza has been removed. The "intellectual love of God" seems to be, in the way Russell understands it, a notion familiar to Russell's readers. It seems to be the emotional state accompanying intellectual discovery. That, however, cannot be the whole truth about the concept. Part B will be devoted first to making the notion more precise and to a critical summary of all that Russell derived from Spinoza which has an ethical bearing. Then we shall be well suited to explore Russell's non-Spinozistic writings on ethics to see what of Spinoza is of enduring influence in them, and finally to evaluate Russell's normative ethic.

PART B

Russell's Spinozistic Ethic

CHAPTER V

Amor Dei Intellectualis

33 Introduction to Part B

In examining Russell's writings on Spinoza in Part A, the focus was on Russell's view of Spinoza's importance for normative ethics. Metaphysics, theory of knowledge, and metaethics were included only to convey the scope of Russell's interest in Spinoza. We shall now examine the primary concept involved in Spinoza's ethical influence on Russell, the "intellectual love of God". Part A makes it clear that Russell thought he had found something of ethical importance to him in Spinoza, and Part B is devoted to analyzing just what that was and the exact influence it had on Russell's ethic. At this point it will be well to assess Russell's reading of Spinoza and to sum up our historical and interpretative data with respect to the "intellectual love of God". I contend that Russell's own normative ethic has an underlying conceptual unity through the notion of self-enlargement through impersonality. For Russell, this notion has its origin in his appreciation of Spinoza's *Ethics*.

To sum up Part A, Russell had a lifelong interest in Spinoza. Moreover, as Russell's earliest surviving writings reflect an absorption in problems relating to the self, we are justified in seeing a relation between Spinoza's attractiveness to Russell and some of Russell's central concerns. The survey of his writings on Spinoza has shown the extent to which he was acquainted with Spinoza's life and writings. After the full grounding provided by Pollock's *Spinoza*, Russell's knowledge of Spinoza's life stood fairly static. Russell took Spinoza the man as a moral model, despite his intellectual disagreements with him. As for Spinoza's writings, Russell's effective acquaintance with them—by which I mean his use of them in his own writings—can be stated with greater certainty. The survey shows Russell acquainted with the *Treatise on the Improvement of the Understanding* and the *Tractatus Theologico-Politicus* only when he came to write the Spinoza chapter in *A History of Western Philosophy*. In this work Russell also refers to the *Tractatus Politicus*. There is no evidence of acquaintance with Spinoza's minor works. But the survey did show Russell very closely acquainted indeed with the *Ethics*. He probably read it first early in 1894, in conjunction with Pollock's book. He definitely read the *Ethics* in March 1899, when he was researching his *Leibniz*. It is not known whether he read the *Ethics* in its original Latin, but it seems probable.[1] At this time Russell read other books on Spinoza, including (in 1901) Joachim's *Study*, which he annotated. By 1910 Russell is clear that the import of the *Ethics* is ethical, not metaphysical. But the absolute idealist tradition in which Russell was taught philosophy and in which Joachim was ensconced had a permanent influence on Russell. The idealist conception of the moral self is a wider one than the self that is usually the subject of self-realization (which I call the "narrow self"). The idealists' striving for harmony with society and even the universe requires a "self" that can expand beyond the boundaries of the individual as traditionally conceived.

Russell's writings on Spinoza are various in nature, ranging from student essays through book reviews to correspondence and making Spinoza a character in a work of fiction. The best-known writing is the chapter in *A History of Western Philosophy*, but it is not, to my mind, the most satisfactory. The reason is that Russell allotted space to the classical philosophers on the basis of their influence, and not their interest to him. Spinoza, we found, is the sort of philosopher whom Russell mentions repeatedly in writings not specifically devoted to topics in Spinoza's philosophy—e.g. metaphysics and especially normative ethics. Russell did not publish a theoretical or systematic treatise on his own normative ethic. There are hints that he believed the very abstruseness of such an enterprise would render it ineffective in harmonizing people's values—he complains several times of the inaccessibility of Spinoza's ethical writings. Russell also did not think normative ethics capable of being successfully argued for in treatise-like fashion.

34 Spinoza's Concept of the Intellectual Love of God: Russell's First Interpretation

Spinoza writes that the man guided by reason strives "to conceive things as they are in themselves, and to remove the hindrances to true knowledge, such as hatred, anger, envy, derision, pride ..." (E4P73S). This statement appears to be no more than a plea for impartial judgment through removal of the ordinary obstacles of personal bias. Russell, of course, would heartily agree with the statement. If this plea were all there was to Spinoza, Russell would not have returned to him again and again. It was something more than this plea that caught Russell's ethical imagination, even though he could not accept Spinoza's demonstration of the doctrine involved. Russell's ethic of impersonal self-enlargement is derived, in the main, from Spinoza's concept of the intellectual love of God. We have seen, especially in Chapters III and IV, that Russell often used this term, even when Spinoza is incidental to the discussion at hand, over a period of at least half a century. We should not, however, assume that he always used the term in the same way. Indeed, I shall distinguish a general and a special use or interpretation by Russell. Nor should we assume that, when he uses the term, he understands it precisely in the way Spinoza understood it, or the ways in which commentators understand it. In 1911 Russell told Lady Ottoline that commentators quarrel over what Spinoza meant by the term, but that he felt that he knew what Spinoza meant by it (for the exact quotation, see 24). To understand these "quarrels" and to evaluate Russell's understanding of the concept are the chief aims of this chapter.

I shall examine first what Spinoza says about the "intellectual love of God" to assess whether Russell's interpretations are even possible ones. In preparation, we should be acquainted with at least three ideas used throughout the *Ethics*: "intuitive knowledge", "love", and "God". Spinoza holds in the *Ethics* that there are three kinds of knowing. There is knowledge through sense-perception and imagination—these are the sources of all "inadequate and confused" ideas (E2P41D). There is rational, or deductive, knowledge, mediated by universal concepts, whose conclusions are necessarily true or necessarily false. And there is intuitive knowledge (*scientia intuitiva*), which penetrates at once to the essence of things and thereby avoids the steps of ratiocination. Intuitive knowledge is therefore the direct, or unmediated, apprehension of adequate and clear ideas.[2] Spinoza defines "love" as "joy accompanied with the idea of an external cause" (E3P13S, E3Df.Aff.6), "joy" or "pleasure" (*laetitia*) itself being defined as "the passion by which the mind passes to a greater perfection" (E3P11S). "God" is a much more difficult concept to understand than "love". As Savan has remarked, "The very center of Spinoza's philosophy is his conception of God and the complete dependence of human well-being upon God."[3] The importance of God in Spinoza's ethic would appear to rule out the possibility of non-believers doing anything positive with the ethic. Fortunately, however, Spinoza's concept of God as a non-personal being that is not fundamentally distinct from the world is something that Russell can appreciate without committing himself to a theology and a metaphysic inconsistent with his own. Russell's characterization of Spinoza's God as "somewhat abstract" (*Autobiography*, vol. II, p. 38), while vague, is not erroneous. Spinoza's definition of "God" is the following: "By God, I understand Being absolutely infinite, that is to say, substance consisting of infinite attributes, each one of which expresses eternal and infinite essence" (E1Df.6). Thus God is substance, and the only substance. We are never directly acquainted with God, though in the sense of *natura naturans* (E1P29D) we are acquainted with what belongs to either of the two knowable attributes of God or substance, namely thought and extension. We can, however, have some understanding of God. On an interpretation using the attribute of extension, "the more we understand individual objects, the more we understand God" (E5P24). But Spinoza's emphasis is on God under the attribute of thought. "Objects" in the previous quotation might have to be understood as thought-objects, and God seems at times even to be equated with the body of eternal truths (E5P30).[4]

The term the "intellectual love of God" occurs only in Part V of the *Ethics*, in propositions 32 to 37. In E5P38 "love of God" occurs and is probably to be understood as the intellectual love of God. These propositions are preceded by several on the relationship of eternity and intuitive knowledge (E5P22–31). Two of these propositions are especially important for the intellectual love of God. According to E5P23S, there is an aspect or part of the mind[5] that "cannot be limited by time nor manifested through duration." This aspect of the mind is that which apprehends the truths of the third kind of knowledge. The second proposition is E5P27: "From this third kind of knowledge arises the highest possible peace of mind." The connection between the third kind of knowledge and the "eternal" part of the mind is essential to understanding the concept of the intellectual love of God. There are nine steps comprising the connection between intuitive knowledge and the eternal part of the mind and leading to the intellectual love of God:

(1) Spinoza takes mind for his example of the power of knowledge of the third kind. He wants to "show, by this example, what that knowledge of individual objects which I have called intuitive or of the third kind (Note 2, Prop. 40, pt. 2) is able to do, and how

much more potent it is than the universal knowledge which I have called knowledge of the second kind" (E5P36S). For "the essence of our mind consists in knowledge alone . . ." (*ibid.*).

(2) The parts of mind that serve to individuate us as distinct personalities—imagination and memory (E5P34S)—are not eternal and hence are accidental to the mind's essence. The impersonality of the mind is thus half-way established, i.e. that what is personal is not essential. It remains to establish that what is impersonal is essential.

(3) Spinoza is now ready to show that the pursuit of intuitive knowledge leads, as he puts it, to "our salvation, or blessedness, or freedom" (E5P36S). Whatever we understand by means of the third kind of knowledge, we delight in and think of God as the cause of our delight (E5P32).

(4) "From the third kind of knowledge necessarily springs the intellectual love of God" (E5P32C)—in so far as He is eternal, Spinoza adds. Here the definition of "love" as "joy accompanied with the idea of an external cause" (E3Df.Aff.6) is essential to the proof.

(5) By a dubious use of E1Ax.3, the intellectual love of God is eternal. Spinoza interprets E1Ax.3 scholastically to mean that an effect, love, must be in some essential respects like its cause, God, although the relevant part of E1Ax.3 says only that "From a definite cause an effect necessarily follows. . . ."

(6) Only intellectual love is eternal (E5P34C), since other kinds of love depend upon passions, and they exist only as long as the body does.

(7) "The intellectual love of the mind toward God is the very love with which He loves Himself . . . in so far as He can be manifested through the essence of the human mind, considered under the form of eternity . . ." (E5P36). Spinoza has now shown the connection between the essence of the mind and God. As long as we pursue the knowledge of "objects" in the third way, we share something fundamental with God. Moreover, this pursuit has the reward of reinforcing itself. E5P36, "In so far as the mind understands all things as necessary, so far has it greater power over the affects, or suffers from them" (a proposition Russell marked in his copy of the *Ethic*), shows how the power of the mind's understanding of the emotions can increase the mind's power over the emotions. Filling the mind with intuitive knowledge of eternal things constitutes the second half of the

establishment of impersonality. Neither half alone would be sufficient for the task.
(8) Intellectual love is indomitable (E5P37), there being nothing that can "negate" it.
(9) The "highest possible peace" (E5P38S) arises from the third kind of knowledge, because "the more objects the mind understands by the second and third kinds of knowledge, the less it suffers from those emotions which are evil" (E5P38).

From these steps to the intellectual love of God it is possible to extract a conception of the self which Spinoza does not explicitly set out. With the exclusion of personality-individuating parts of mind such as imagination and memory, features coordinate with our bodily existence in an ordinary sense are dropped from view. What remains is mental power, which, though varying no doubt in degree from individual to individual, is essentially the same in all minds. The "objects" apprehended by the third kind of knowledge are also not those apparently dependent on the accidental circumstances of our bodies. They are therefore impersonal as well. The intellectual love of God seems to remain a phenomenon for individuals, however, as there is no suggestion, except possibly at E5P40S, that our minds coalesce in a single pool of thought. Man's basic psychology of striving for self-preservation—the *conatus*—remains a background assumption of Part V of the *Ethics*.

How, then, does Russell understand the "intellectual love of God", and what does he make of the concept in his ethic? He seems to have two interpretations. The general one is analyzed in the present section. The special one, the "moments of intellectual discovery" interpretation, is treated in the next. He first mentions the term in an 1894 letter to Alys (quoted in **14**) and in a graduate paper (**16**). In the 1907 review Russell claims that Picton "in the main ... successfully extracts his master's teaching on the conduct of life and on the intellectual love of God" (**21**). I quoted the core of what Picton has to say, but on the basis of this brief remark of Russell's we cannot probe further. In the 1910 review, however, Russell writes sufficiently on the concept for us to grasp his understanding of it. First, the concept is based on the knowledge of what is necessary, as in mathematical knowledge. But Russell applies the term "necessary" to more than analytic truths. I noted earlier that Russell is here going beyond what he allowed himself to say in his formal treatments of the concept of cause. Knowledge is the highest good, because knowledge—particularly of necessity—brings you closer to God. Knowledge develops "intellectual love", which is, as Russell says, "coloured by emotion through and through". He does not explain what Spinoza means by "God", but from the remark that the first Part of the *Ethics* contains only pantheism, we may with reservations infer that he understands the key term to mean intellectual love of the world. At one point in the review Russell says that "though immortality in the ordinary sense is an error, the mind is nevertheless eternal in so far as it consists in the intellectual love of God." Although it is difficult to be sure from the context, this seems to be an endorsement by Russell of Spinoza's peculiar doctrine of immortality. When Spinoza characterizes something as immortal, he means that its existence is eternal, at least in the sense Alan Donagan has identified as "necessary omnitemporal existence"[6]—though Spinoza warns us not to confound eternity with any sort of duration (E5P34S).[7] Russell talks about the "reconciliation of the individual with the whole". This notion is probably connected, for him, with the intellectual love of God. We shall be able to see how this is so in the other writings of this period in Chapter VI.

Lady Ottoline was informed by Russell that he felt he knew what Spinoza meant by the "intellectual love of God", despite the quarrels of commentators. Let us look again at what Russell told Lady Ottoline immediately after this remark:

> He thinks men as individuals are not immortal, but in so far as they love God, their love of God is something deathless, but impersonal. He is filled full with an emotion towards the universe which is at once mystical and intellectual—it must have grown up in him through the feeling of god-like calm that comes when one passes from passionate strife to an impersonal reasoned view of the matter of strife. He thinks strife the fundamental evil, and reason informed by love the cure. His heart and mind are always great—he looks at each individual thing always in the light of the whole. (no. 82, p/24 May 1911)

The emphasis on impersonality is important, and it fits what Spinoza writes. The immortal or eternal part of the mind is the impersonal part, that which is characterized by intuitive knowledge. The mortal parts are imagination and memory, which are of a personal nature, i.e. they belong to the individual *qua* individual. As Matson points out, the removal of the criterion of memory for personal identity results in immediate immortality for the "impersonal and atemporal or 'eternal'" intellect, it being nothing more than the ideas known by intuition and reason.[8] In view of what Russell says in the 1940s, the notion of "calm" in the 1910–12 period seems dependent on the surmounting of strife—it is therefore a more political notion (because of its association with peace among men or groups of men) than is the notion of the 1940s, where it appears to be identified with moments of intellectual discovery. Ultimately the two sources of philosophic calm are reconcilable. Moments of intellectual discovery can emerge after periods of intellectual strife, or when you are able to unite the masses of data held in the mind. Still, Russell does not tell us in 1910–12 all that he must have understood Spinoza to have meant by the term. Evidently it was the subject of discussions between Russell and Lady Ottoline, for at one time he tells her: "His [Spinoza's] 'intellectual love of God' is so much the thing we care for...." We may find that Russell's understanding of the notion is completed in the 1912 novella (see 25 and 46).

Nasispo's discourse in "The Perplexities of John Forstice", for the first time in the documents we have studied, introduces the idea of contemplation. Contemplation is as essential to Spinoza's ethical doctrine as it is to Russell's. Contemplation is passionless thinking, entirely unconnected with the need to act. That is not to say there is no urge to act in those who contemplate, but rather that the urge does not interfere with the exercise of thought. In Spinoza's terms, contemplation is an "active emotion". To Nasispo, contemplation that is not "fettered by desire" is independent of time. Spinoza's understanding of this point leads to his doctrine of the immortality of the mind. Russell's understanding is best characterized as psychological, i.e. as based on the standpoint of feeling, or the attitudinal effect upon the individual.[9] Nasispo continues: "The joy and peace of this contemplation is Spinoza's intellectual love of God, that 'infinite love with which God loves himself' [E5P35], and the soul which is filled with the intellectual love of God is at one with all other souls inspired by the same love." This unity of "souls" may be described as self-enlargement or impersonality. It is clear from what Nasispo says, though he does not say it directly, that the affects "peace of mind" (*acquiescentia mentis*) and "self-acceptance" (*acquiescentia in se ipso*) accompany the intellectual love of God.

The first interpretation by Russell of the "intellectual love of God" is complete by 1916. As we noted in 27, it is rounded off by the statements in *Principles of Social Reconstruction*: "Contact with this eternal world—even if it be only a world of our imagining—brings a strength and a fundamental peace which cannot be wholly destroyed by the struggles and failures of our temporal life. It is this happy contemplation of what is eternal that Spinoza calls the intellectual love of God. To those who have once known it, it is the key of wisdom." On this interpretation, the intellectual love of God involves the following elements: (1) the order of the universe is believed to be a determined, or necessary, one; (2) this order is the object of contemplation; (3) contemplation is a passionless activity; (4) to the extent that a person contemplates, he is impersonal; (5) impersonality in contemplation is identical to enlargement of self; (6) the impersonal, contemplative activity of the mind results in a profound feeling of peace. As the "key of wisdom", the notion may lead to much else. What it leads to, in Russell's case, will be explored in Chapter VI.

35 Russell's Second Interpretation

We did not find any occasion on which Russell used or mentioned the term the "intellectual love of God" in his writings of the 1920s. In the 1930s there was the curious statement in his draft autobiography (27) in which he said that the intellectual love of God was the best thing to live by, but that he did not have even Spinoza's God to which to attach his love. The statement is curious because Russell had always interpreted Spinoza pantheistically, i.e. he had attached much importance to Spinoza's claim that God is in some sense identical with the world. Russell could have meant that it was not possible for him (Russell) to love the actual world, since he did not find the actual world to be good—a theme common to his normative ethical writings ever since "The Free Man's Worship". There was also the correlative statement that, "when Spinoza believed anything, he considered that he was enjoying the intellectual love of God." The statements are correlative because they concern the same attitude, namely that of intellectual love toward the world. I think we can detect a diminution in Russell's feeling of exaltation in such beliefs.

There is a more marked change in Russell's understanding of the "intellectual love of God" in the radio discussion programme and the Spinoza chapter in the *History*. First, there is much less use of metaphysical terminology. In common-sense terms Russell declares that the "way of living" Spinoza recommends is a "good" way—"a way in which you get rid of indignation and fear and irrational hope and a number of things that produce anxiety and perturbation in life, and acquire a certain kind of calm." But *how* do you get rid of anxiety-producers? The answer is through the third kind of knowledge, which Russell seems to identify with the intellectual love of God. Thus the "intellectual love of God" seems to have taken on a more restricted meaning, i.e. intellectual discovery, rather than contemplation in which the barriers of personality seem to fall away—although that contemplation is not necessarily excluded. In his own words, "... in all kinds of knowledge, when you get a certain familiarity, there comes a moment when the imagination seizes hold upon the total of some body of knowledge that you possess, and suddenly you realize it; you suddenly see it in a kind of vision; and that, I think, is Spinoza's third kind of knowledge." (Spinoza, of course, would reject any role on the part of imagination.) Earlier in the discussion Spinoza asserts that history or music or poetry would suffice in the place of mathematics: "There are a hundred ways of getting the kind of thing which Spinoza calls the intellectual love of God." For the purposes of a popular programme, then, Russell may simply be suggesting a few of the "hundred ways", and other ways may not be limited to moments of intellectual discovery. There is some doubt, therefore, that Russell is here identifying intuitive knowledge of some subject-matter with production of the intellectual love of God. The psychological difficulty with the narrow interpretation of the "intellectual love of God" is in understanding how the resulting state of calm is to persist sufficiently to ward off the perturbations of ordinary living. The attention would have to return very frequently to grasping subject-matters as wholes. The intellectual love of God seems able, therefore, to provide calm only in those limited areas of life in which intellectual disturbances prevail. Disturbances with emotional origins could be left unresolved. Spinoza might have regarded the former areas as very large through the overlapping of the intellectual and the emotional, but still they would be significantly limited. The Spinozistic experience of calm will be clarified in Chapter VI. It seems that it involves a mystical element, as the quotation from the letter of 24 May 1911 in **34** suggests.

The explanation of the "intellectual love of God" in the *History* is different in some notable respects. In writing on Plato, Russell says that creative intellectual work results in an "intimate union of thought and feeling" which is the intellectual love of God (see **30**). In the Spinoza chapter, however, this interpretation does not appear. True, the intellectual love of God is understood, in practically the same words, as "the union of thought and emotion", or "true thought combined with joy in the apprehension of truth". Although Russell seldom uses the term "third kind of knowledge", the concept is present when he comes to talk about viewing things "under the dictate of reason", that is, *sub specie aeternitatis*. Such a viewpoint, he holds, produces philosophic calm. But in the *History* chapter Russell goes on to include in the notion of the intellectual love of God the seeing of everything as part of the whole, from which, by the privative doctrine of evil, it follows that no part of the whole is really evil.

Russell's task, in the *History*, is to stick close to Spinoza's intention for the phrase, the "intellectual love of God". In his own normative ethic, Russell strips the concept of what he cannot accept, but retains a residue which is essentially Spinozistic. For example, he believes that nothing that happens later can make an act of cruelty good rather than bad. But Spinoza requires, on Russell's view, that the universe as a whole be regarded as good. (Although "good" might not be the appropriate word in view of E4Pref., the intellectual love of God does imply a positive attitude towards the universe as a whole as it is necessarily unfolding, since through understanding sorrow is dissipated [E5P18].) It is clear that philosophic calm is more easily produced under the view Russell attributes to Spinoza than under Russell's own doctrine, which is well known to be one of materialistic pessimism. Nevertheless Russell believes it can be produced under his view. The difficulty is in seeing how moments of intellectual discovery can suffice. If we are to make sense of this later interpretation of the "intellectual love of God", we may have to see in it an implicit recognition of a continuous though subdued appreciation of the necessary order of the universe. Looking at events in this light and in the light of the whole, or at least in a larger context, does, according to Russell, "enlarge the eternal part of you". It seems to me that Russell means by this phrase the growth of the self in an impersonal way. Either we must make such an implicit recognition, or we shall have to include a mystical element in his analysis of the "intellectual love of God".

Thus Russell's two interpretations differ chiefly by the narrower origins ascribed to the intellectual love of God in the later interpretation. They coalesce only if we attempt to read into the later interpretation some provision for wider origins. In that case the intellectual love of God would be produced not only by moments of intellectual discovery—be they of large or small matters—but also by viewing all matters subject to rational and intuitive knowledge in a way that removes temporal elements. Let us turn now to the commentators on

Spinoza to see whether they support either of Russell's interpretations.

36 Other Interpretations: Pollock, White and Picton

Commentators on the concept of the intellectual love of God in the *Ethics* disagree in their interpretations. Both Pollock and White are tentative in their explanations of propositions E5P24–38. For Pollock (his *Spinoza*, Chap. IX), the secularist interpretation of the doctrine of immortality is first evident in his account of Spinoza's conception of the eternal life. The eternal life is actually possible in this life. "Whether it is called the life eternal, the kingdom of God, wisdom, liberation, or *nirvána*, the state of blessedness has been put forward by the great moral teachers of mankind as something not apart from and after this life, but entering into and transforming it" (p. 294). Pollock excuses Spinoza's language by saying that the philosopher is determined to surpass the theologians with their own vocabulary (p. 301). Spinoza provokes the appellation of "mystic", but he is not really one. Instead he is an Aristotelian for holding that "contemplative knowledge is the highest and most proper function of the mind, in respect of which alone it can be said to partake of eternity" (p. 303). The intellectual love of God "is nothing else than conscious acceptance of universal law, the 'welcoming every event' of the Stoics; and ... the secret of blessedness and glory (for those titles are expressly claimed and justified) is none other than a mind steadfastly bent on the truth" (p. 302). Thus in Pollock's interpretation there is no hint of impersonal self-enlargement.

White claims that the intellectual love of God "is the discovery of law or attribute, and the inclusion of the world under it" (*Ethic*, preface, p. lxxxvi). The mind feels a "repose [*acquiescentia*] in the exercise of its true function and in the contemplation of the order of the universe" (*ibid*.). Possibly Spinoza intended more than this, thinks White, but White does not say what it might be. We know from the fact that Russell quoted White's extract from the *Short Treatise* on p. lxxxiv of the preface that Russell read these pages; but he could not have found in them suggestions for his own interpretation, since White has nothing to say about the transcendence of individuality.

Nor, for that matter, could he have found any such suggestions in Picton. I maintain this despite the fact that I ascribed to Russell's authorship a review in which Picton is praised for his understanding of the "intellectual love of God" (21). For although Picton's popularization is a credible one, there is nothing in it for Russell's own interpretation. What Russell probably means, in his commendation, is that Picton's interpretation of Spinoza is reliable enough for the general reader.

37 Joachim

Russell told Lady Ottoline that both Pollock and Joachim were outstanding interpreters for the technical reader. I suggest that Pollock's chief value for Russell lay in opening up the rest of Spinoza's *Ethics* to him, but that, as a self-realizationist, Joachim's was the interpretation of the "intellectual love of God" closest to Russell's. The chief reason for this lies in Joachim's absolute idealism. This is not to say that, without Joachim's *Study of the Ethics of Spinoza*, Russell would not have developed his own interpretation. But it does appear that the monistic idealists' treatment of the self's relationship to the universe, or the whole, was a major stimulant to Russell's interpretation. Joachim's importance to us is primarily as a representative of the idealism that influenced Russell.

Joachim's final chapter, "The Ideal Life as Conscious Union with God", outlines Spinoza's doctrine as follows:

> ... in the most complete thinking of which we, as intelligences, are capable, our thought is God's thought; and God's thought is God thinking so far as he constitutes the essence of *our* mind, i.e. God's thought is *our* thinking. That oneness of our intelligent being with God merges us in the divine thought, and *eo ipso* most fully characterizes us, or gives us our "self." And in that transfusion of our thinking being by God's being, we are "real" with the divine reality, or God is real in, *and as*, us: i.e. we are "eternal." In the glow of that self-realization—which is *at once* the identity of all selves with God, *and* the most fully characterized distinction of all selves from God and from one another—our mind unites or fuses in itself our whole being. (P. 294)

While Russell is on no interpretation a theist, this passage reveals no commitment to a God transcending our impersonal thinking—which is, for Russell, man's most divine characteristic. The phrase "the most fully characterized distinction of all selves from God and from another" is puzzling because it is not obvious why that which provides our unity in God should also provide our individuality. Joachim solves the difficulty a few pages later. He points out that in so far as our minds are composed of adequate ideas, we are fully realized, and that in so far as we have adequate ideas we are identical with God's thought and with each other. What we might take as *prima facie* individuators of the various selves, namely inadequate ideas, are not really individuators because they do not belong to the highest levels of our cognition and, therefore, to our true, or wider, selves. As Joachim puts it:

> These "confused" ideas are—*quâ* confused—not really "ours." They do not constitute the essential nature of our mind; they constitute our mind-in-its-environment. And they indicate not so much what we are, as what we are not; they reveal our limits, the "torn edges" which make us finite.* [*Cf. e.g. E. iii. 3 S.] . . . death is only one way in which we thus "come to ourselves." The essential condition is that we should think clearly and adequately, and think *only* clearly and adequately. In other words, the essential nature of our mind is intelligence; we are really and completely "ourselves," in proportion as "we" are entirely clear consciousness. (Pp. 300–1)

To be most fully ourselves, therefore, we must lose those aspects of our mind which commonly distinguish us from others. Such commonly accepted criteria of personal identity as experience and memory are not true criteria, for they rely on knowledge involving inadequate ideas, namely sense-perception and imagination. When we have the third kind of knowledge, the content of our knowledge is the same for all of us, though the individual acts of knowing remain numerically different because they take place in different minds. Joachim goes on to discuss the life of the "free man", the man whose life is filled with the love of God. "Our 'self' at this stage", he writes, "is that which characterizes all men as such, our 'humanity.' We have a common interest and ideal, a common love of knowledge; and live a common or social life as the means to satisfy that love" (p. 307).

In the Joachim-Russell interpretation of the "intellectual love of God", we are to understand that what each self has in common, or could have in common, is rationality. In so far as we are rational, and pursuing knowledge, other aspects of personality do not serve to individuate us. The pursuit of truth requires the impersonal exercise of reason. But in that exercise we ourselves become impersonal. Becoming impersonal is one way of enlarging self. Other ways of enlarging self come to mind, however—ways which involve dominating others. For this reason I use the term "impersonal self-enlargement" to cover the interpretation that Russell, and neo-Hegelians like Joachim, have of Spinoza's "intellectual love of God". It is admittedly paradoxical that, under this interpretation, we realize ourselves most when we most develop our impersonal side.

38 Wolfson, Bidney, Hampshire and Harris

So much for the commentators we know Russell to have studied. There are others worth discussing. Harry Austryn Wolfson's detailed account of the origins of Spinoza's ideas in *The Philosophy of Spinoza* traces the origin of the "intellectual love of God" to various philosophical and theological predecessors. Drawing upon his immense learning, Wolfson cites Aristotle, Descartes, Leo Hebraeus, and Thomas Aquinas, though he holds that it is "useless to speculate from whom Spinoza took it".[10] Then he brings in Crescas, Maimonides, and the Old Testament. Wolfson thinks Spinoza meant nothing more by the phrase than a love which is not an "animal" or "sensitive" love (p. 306). There is nothing in Wolfson's interpretation relating the concept to selflessness or the wider self.

A "narcissistic" interpretation of the "intellectual love of God" is available in David Bidney's study of the psychology and ethics of Spinoza.[11] He holds that the intellectual love of God is "really identical" with self-satisfaction (p. 173), or human self-love (p. 349). The former term is the usual translation of *acquiescentia in se ipso*. If this identity holds, then the joy accompanying intuitive knowledge would draw a person into himself, resulting in a kind of narcissism, rather than an expansion of himself in the impersonal sense offered by Joachim and Russell.

Hampshire notices the connection between Spinoza's concepts of the intellectual love of God and eternity, explaining it thus:

> ... in so far as I do attain genuine knowledge, my individuality as a particular thing disappears and my mind becomes so far united with God or Nature conceived under the attribute of thought. We feel and know that we are eternal in so far as we conceive things *sub specie aeternitatis*.... In our intellectual life, at the more

successful moments of completely disinterested, logical thought, we have these glimpses of the possibility of living, not as finite and perishing modes of Nature, but identified or "united" with God or Nature as a whole ... the free man's intellectual love of God is the enjoyment of this identification or union of ourselves with nature through reason and the understanding; and this identification we never completely and permanently achieve, but must always pursue.[12]

Hampshire does not draw normative conclusions from this brief insight into the ultimate nature of individuality in Spinoza. What he does say about the life of the free man, however, is instructive (pp. 161–5) for its acccount of the free man's derivative values.

In contrast to Bidney, Errol E. Harris grasps the self-enlarging aspect of the intellectual love of God. He too connects the concept with Spinoza's doctrine of immortality. On the first point Harris writes: "The criticism that Spinoza's ethic is nothing better than enlightened selfishness is finally confuted by this doctrine of intellectual love, which is utterly selfless and wholly absorbed in the obsessive awareness of the infinite object."[13] This statement is in agreement with Russell's statement (quoted in 28) that, while Spinoza assumes psychological egoism, it is not a selfish egoism. But something is not quite right about the obsessive absorption Harris refers to. To be obsessed by *anything* is to Spinoza a bondage. Instead, the free man pursues "the infinite object" (i.e. God) because his understanding has transmuted what could have been a passion into an active emotion, or affection. In connection with immortality, Harris mentions the criticism that absorption of the rational part of the self in God annihilates human individuality (p. 244). Harris replies:

Immortality ... is not a matter of the "survival" by any personality of his body. Nothing "remains" in the sense of continuing *in time*. What remains when we have accounted for the mortal form of experience is an eternal awareness of God's essence and the complex system of the world. It is an awareness enjoyed in his own person by each and every individual who attains to adequate knowledge, and it transforms and perfects his personality by developing it to its fullest moral capacity. So far from being lost or swallowed up in the boundless ocean of substance, the individual personality becomes whole, internally harmonious and perfectly self-determined.... Temporal transience is not felt as an irremediable handicap or an inescapable confine.[14] (P. 245)

Harris, like White, suggests Russell's later understanding of the "intellectual love of God" as intellectual discovery. Harris, however, limits it to one such discovery. "The third level of knowledge", he says, "... is a grasp, in a single apprehension, of the principle of wholeness that governs the detached character of each and every finite mode of substance ..." (p. 202). In criticism, I hold that both Spinoza and Russell have less ambitious discoveries in mind. Russell would agree that it is wholeness that is concerned, but wholeness limited to the body of data at hand. Spinoza hardly made it a condition of the third kind of knowledge that it consist in an apprehension of the wholeness of *everything*.

39 Wetlesen and Wienpahl

The last interpretation of the "intellectual love of God" with which I shall deal is that of some Spinozists[15] interested in Eastern thought: Jon Wetlesen, Arne Naess, and the late Paul Wienpahl. These scholars, despite divergences in other areas of interpretation, find significant parallels between certain doctrines of Spinoza and Buddhist philosophy and religion. Wetlesen and Naess base their interpretation on an extremely close textual examination of the *Ethics*.[16] Wienpahl based his upon Zen and his work in translating and commenting on Spinoza's corpus.[17] Another European scholar interested in Spinoza's mysticism is H. G. Hubbeling, though he is not as prominent.[18] These philosophers do not claim that Spinoza was influenced by Buddhism, but merely that there are parallels with the latter that are useful in understanding the former. Nor do they claim the Spinoza must have had mystical experiences, in the sense of sudden ecstasies in which truth seems to be revealed. I shall examine what Wetlesen and Wienpahl have to say on the intellectual love of God, and then offer the criticism I think Russell would have made of the alleged affinity with Buddhism.

Wetlesen's view, in *The Sage and the Way*, is that the Spinozistic sage uses a form of meditation—body awareness—as the gateway to wisdom. This form of meditation finds parallels in Buddhism (p. xiii). The intellectual love of God is seen as the means to the "selfless" love of oneself. It is a selfless love because

... selfish love is conditioned by the person's attachment to his images of himself in his temporal aspect. Through ignorance this attachment will be increased, but through wisdom it may be decreased. The more he cognizes himself and other modes from the viewpoint of eternity, the less he will be bound by his cognition of these things from the viewpoint of time. Through his love of God, therefore, his love of modes will become more impartial. The more he understands himself and others adequately, through God as the adequate and immanent cause of all, the less he will find any relevant reason for preferring his own good before the good of others, and consequently will, to an increasing extent, love others as much as himself. (P. 185)

Wetlesen holds that Spinoza offers an "ethics of love" (p. 190). We reach this stage of "sageliness" when we undergo the "instantaneous strategy of liberation", which is awareness of our body *sub specie aeternitatis* (pp. 313–14), or the "undoing of the ego" (p. 317). It is clear from the quotation that Wetlesen's interpretation involves first understanding ourselves in an impartial way and then treating others in the impartial way we learn to treat ourselves. This approach is typically Eastern in its initial inner-directedness.

Wienpahl's Buddhist interpretation of Spinoza derives partly from his training in Zen, which, however, I shall not discuss. As for his unpublished translation,[19] I shall give one example to illustrate his "radical" approach. In his attempt to render a translation as close to the original Latin as possible, Wienpahl uses English words with Latin roots. When no Latin words are available, he offers as literal a translation as he can in words of non-Latin origin. An example is the last line of the *Ethics* of which the original is: "*Sed omnia praeclara tam difficilia, quam rara sunt.*" The key word is *praeclara*. Pollock, Elwes, Boyle (Everyman's Library) and Shirley translate it as "excellent", and Wetlesen and White-Stirling as "noble". Wienpahl translates it according to its roots as "very clear",[20] so that the sentence reads, in his deliberately unpolished style which closely follows the Latin syntax: "But all things very clear are as difficult as rare" (*The Radical Spinoza*, p. 256). Wienpahl justifies this literal translation on the ground that "[p]hilosophically speaking, an aim of the ETHIC is clarity, i.e., knowing intuitively" (p. 258). Wienpahl relates knowing clearly to knowing intuitively, since for Spinoza knowing sensually is *not* knowing clearly, and the only other kind of knowing is rational knowing, which can be raised to the intuitive kind. As in E5P24, the more we know particular ("singular" in Wienpahl's translation) things, the more we understand God. Contrary to many other commentators, Wienpahl holds that particular things are to be understood without their relations to anything else (p. 148).[21] Whatever we know in this way we delight in, and think of God as its cause (E5P32). This complex is the affection Wienpahl calls "God's understanding love" instead of the usual "intellectual love of God".[22] Wienpahl holds that "God's understanding love" is just another term for what Spinoza understands by "immortality" and "knowledge of the union of mind with total nature" (p. 150). Back of this theory is the notion of union. The subject of the *Ethics* is, in Wienpahl's words, "clarity: the kind of knowing or perceiving that comes with a true idea of unity, that is, with union" (p. 154). The notion of union leads to the Buddhist doctrine of "egolessness", in which we are no longer "led to think and act as though we were a separated entity confronted by a world external to us" (p. 90).

There is a similarity between Russell's concept, derived from Spinoza, of impersonal self-enlargement, and the Buddhist concept of egolessness. The moral self is no longer seen as a hard and indivisible unit with rigid boundaries. But the ways of achieving impersonal self-enlargement are very different from the ways of achieving egolessness. Egolessness requires meditation directed at the narrow self (for the Buddhists, like Spinoza, do not deny that the narrow self exists in many of us). Impersonal self-enlargement, on the other hand, is outer-directed from the beginning, as we shall see in Chapter VI. Russell writes little on Buddhism, but he does criticize the major religions for their "self-centred isolation".[23] While he agreed with an interviewer that Buddha himself did not preach egoism,[24] he does object to the general Eastern approach to egolessness in the egocentric, or inner-directed, focus of the various ascetic practices that are employed to attain egolessness. Asceticism, Russell came to hold, merely increases self-absorption (see **48**, end).

40 Summary

In this chapter we have analyzed the pivotal concept in Russell's writings on Spinoza. Russell has a consistent general interpretation of the "intellectual love of God" but also a special interpretation involving intellectual discovery. No commentators could be found who share the special interpretation. The general interpretation is, however, shared by Joachim, whose *Study of the Ethics of Spinoza* may have influenced Russell's understanding. But it is more likely that Russell and Joachim shared a common approach to Spinoza, that of the monistic idealists, and that Joachim's work reflected that approach. Despite the fact that Russell, in 1901 when he read the *Study*, was no longer a neo-Hegelian, he probably found much to agree with in the self-realization treatment of the wider self in the *Study*'s last chapter. Other commentators sometimes share the self-enlargement interpretation of the "intellectual love of God", but they do not develop it. An exception is the group influenced by their study of Buddhism. While they devote much attention to the development of the self in Spinoza, they see it as proceeding by way of some form of meditation. We found that Russell, who was surely ignorant of this recent school of interpretation, would have rejected the meditative approach as too self-centred (in the narrow sense of "self"). It is not in reflecting on, and trying to suppress, the shortcomings of self that Russell's way lies; it lies rather in nurturing the growth of interests outside self and thereby enlarging self.[25]

The analysis of the commentators revealed that Spinoza's concept of the immortality of mind is an important adjunct to that of the intellectual love of God. The latter concept provides for the delight experienced by the knowing consciousness, but that experience, in Russell's understanding, must include the element of unity. Spinoza's doctrine of immortality helps to explain that unity, for involved in it is the notion that in so far as we are knowers of the second and third kinds, we are united by love to God. Russell translates this into the psychological language of self-enlargement. Such self-enlargement is impersonal, or approaches impersonality, because, as Spinoza suggests, it is devoid of the personality-individuating characteristics of memory and imagination. Russell, of course, does not take over this aspect literally, but he does accept the analysis of rationality it implicitly conveys. In the next chapter we shall see how Russell uses the concept of impersonal self-enlargement as the foundation of his normative ethic.

CHAPTER VI

Development of the Ethic of Impersonal Self-Enlargement

41 A Developmental Approach

We turn now to Russell's own ethical writings, with the aim of seeing the degree to which they are indebted generally to Russell's reading of Spinoza and specifically to his interpretations of the notion of the intellectual love of God. Since we cannot consider all of Russell's normative ethical writings, we shall take representative writings from various periods that together span the greater part of Russell's life. The chronological approach will be adopted because, in this previously little-worked field of Russell's thought, development takes place and our aim is to reveal the Spinozistic influence upon a philosopher, as opposed to that upon a philosophy that was expressed in this or that publication but perhaps abandoned afterwards by the philosopher. Russell's ethic changes, and emphasis on one period to the exclusion of others might detract from the ethic's essential unity over half a century. The chief periods to be covered are those represented by "The Free Man's Worship" (1903); the correspondence with Lady Ottoline Morrell (1911–12); *Principles of Social Reconstruction* (1916); *The Conquest of Happiness* (1930); and the writings of the Second World War and the nuclear age. The key to Russell's normative ethical writings is their concern with the narrow self: what to do about the egoistic demands that, on the one hand, so often lead to private misery and, on the other, to interpersonal strife and war. The first solution is self-abnegation; the second, impersonal self-enlargement through a kind of union with the world. Certain biographical details are relevant. Russell developed his normative ethic partly to resolve personal problems of his own. Early in *The Conquest of Happiness* he writes:

> Perhaps the best introduction to the philosophy which I wish to advocate will be a few words of autobiography. I was not born

happy.... Now, on the contrary, I enjoy life; I might almost say that with every year that passes I enjoy it more. This is due partly to having discovered what were the things that I most desired, and having gradually acquired many of these things. Partly it is due to having successfully dismissed certain objects of desire—such as the acquisition of indubitable knowledge about something or other—as essentially unattainable. But very largely it is due to a diminishing preoccupation with myself. (Pp. 18–19)

This statement has the appearance of common sense, and certainly the terms employed are ordinary ones. But behind the common-sense façade is the full ethic of impersonal self-enlargement.

Before examining in detail Russell's writings on normative ethics we shall take up the problem of his "mysticism". It is a prominent element in his ethic, and to deal with his ethic satisfactorily we must understand what role he accorded mystical experience.

42 The Element of Mysticism

Russell's normative ethic contains an important mystical element. In his own study of mysticism, he sharply divides it into two aspects, for which Jack Pitt's terms "cognitive mysticism" and "emotive mysticism" are appropriate. While Russell rejects a cognitive element in mystical experience, he does accept an important emotive element. Pitt quotes from "Mysticism and Logic": "... if we are not to be led into false beliefs, it is necessary to realize exactly *what* the mystic emotion reveals. It reveals a possibility of human nature—a possibility of a nobler, happier, freer life than any that can be otherwise achieved. But it does not reveal anything about the non-human, or about the nature of the universe in general."[1] I shall use "mystical experience" in this unusual sense of having no metaphysical or even credal import.

A synonym in Russell for "the mystic emotion" or "mystical experience" is "religious experience", a phrase he uses in replying to Edgar Sheffield Brightman's essay "Russell's Philosophy of Religion".[2] This paper and Russell's reply are of considerable importance in clarifying Russell's views in theory of value. Brightman, he says, does "full justice" to Russell's "own personal religion" ("Reply to Criticisms", p. 726). Brightman singles out four sources as "the profoundest expression of Russell's positive view of religion": "The

Free Man's Worship", "The Essence of Religion", parts of *Principles of Social Reconstruction*, and the chapter "Effort and Resignation" in *The Conquest of Happiness*. Russell replies that it is Chapter VII[3] of *Principles of Social Reconstruction* whose expression of his personal religion is "least unsatisfactory" to him (p. 726). This comment appears to be partly a correction of Brightman's tendency to elevate "The Essence of Religion" above the other sources. Brightman judges—rightly, I believe—that these four sources reveal "genuinely religious ideas and experiences" and "a side of Russell that is unsuspected by many of his readers" (p. 554). On mysticism itself, Brightman finds that "Russell's deepest religious experience is in harmony with the light by which all mystics live", and that Russell is well aware of this. Brightman, however, wishes that Russell would use such mystical or religious experience as a clue to the existence of God. Russell utterly rejects this approach:

> In arguments to God from religious experience there seems to be an unexpressed premiss to the effect that what seem to us our deepest experiences cannot be deceptive, but must have all the significance they appear to have. For such a premiss there seems to me no good ground, if "significance" means "proving the existence of this or that." ("Reply to Criticisms", p. 726)

To this statement, however, Russell immediately adds what is for his theory of value a qualification of the highest importance: "In the realm of value, I admit the significance of religious experience." As Russell has just been defining "significance", what he seems to mean is that religious (or mystical) experience can prove the existence of this or that value.[4] In view of the fact that only a few pages earlier (720–1) he set out his theory of the subjectivity of ethical valuations, I interpret the qualification further to mean that Russell holds that mystical experience can establish this or that value for the individual whose experience it is. The experience does this by providing the subject with a feeling of certainty about various values which, however, cannot, because of the subjectivity of the experience, be communicated to others in terms of objective evidence. Because of that subjectivity, there is no attempt at an intuitionist metaethic here. Russell's method of ethical persuasion is, as I pointed out in 4, that of rousing cherished desires in other persons ("Reply to Criticisms", p. 724). One technique, then, would be to encourage others to put themselves in situations that might lead to similar mystical or religious experience and hence to the establishment of certain values for those persons.

Mystical experience[5] seems to have had this effect on Russell for the greater part of his life, and is of fundamental importance in understanding his ethic. A very late expression of such experience is in the prologue to his *Autobiography*. This piece, written in 1956, contains the statement: "I have sought it [love], finally, because in the union of love I have seen, in a mystic miniature, the prefiguring vision of the heaven that saints and poets have imagined." There are many such allusions to mystical experience in Russell's corpus, but the most important is the well-known experience of 1901, to which we now turn.

Russell and Alys were staying with Alfred and Evelyn Whitehead in Cambridge in February 1901. Clark (p. 86) remarks on the beauty of the location of the Whiteheads' home. Russell was very responsive to natural beauty. Mrs. Whitehead was ill from an apparent heart ailment (though she lived 60 more years). One evening Russell and Alys went to hear Gilbert Murray read his as yet unpublished translation of the *Hippolytus*. Russell was "profoundly stirred" by the poetry (*Autobiography*, vol. I, p. 146). On returning to their hosts' home, they found Mrs. Whitehead in great pain. Russell then had an experience best termed a "mystical" one for its provision of certain insights. There are two narrations of the event. One is reported in Clark, quoting from letters written ten years later to Lady Ottoline. The other is the well-known one in the *Autobiography* in which, as Griffin points out, Russell terms the experience an "emotional set-back" ("Russell's Crisis of Faith", p. 108). In the former account Russell emphasizes how his insights affected his relationship with the Whiteheads. In the latter account he relates his insights less to what he tried to do for the Whiteheads' situation than to the changes they wrought in his own character. In his mystical experience, Russell identified the fundamental human condition as one of loneliness—Mrs. Whitehead was isolated from everyone by "walls of agony". The narration continues:

> Ever since my marriage [in 1894], my emotional life had been calm and superficial. I had forgotten all the deeper issues, and had been content with flippant cleverness. Suddenly the ground seemed to give way beneath me, and I found myself in quite another region. Within five minutes I went through some such reflections as the following: the loneliness of the human soul is

unendurable; nothing can penetrate it except the highest intensity of the sort of love that religious teachers have preached; whatever does not spring from this motive is harmful, or at best useless; it follows that war is wrong, that a public school education is abominable, that the use of force is to be deprecated, and that in human relations one should penetrate to the core of loneliness in each person and speak to that....

At the end of those five minutes, I had become a completely different person. For a time, a sort of mystic illumination possessed me.... Having for years cared only for exactness and analysis, I found myself filled with semi-mystical feelings about beauty, with an intense interest in children, and with a desire almost as profound as that of the Buddha to find some philosophy which should make human life endurable. (Vol. I, p. 146)

The central role of pain in this experience led Russell to think that, since he could in fact surmount his own intense pain, he could make it "a gateway to wisdom"—an ethic on which he worked for some years. Russell comments on the experience:

The mystic insight which I then imagined myself to possess has largely faded, and the habit of analysis has reasserted itself. But something of what I thought I saw in that moment has remained always with me, causing my attitude during the first war, my interest in children, my indifference to minor misfortunes, and a certain emotional tone in all my human relations. (*Ibid.*)

Another thing that remained with Russell was an influence on his evaluation of mysticism. In "Mysticism and Logic" he writes that the greatest philosophers have "felt the need both of science and of mysticism". The attempt to harmonize the two makes philosophy "a greater thing than either science or religion" (p. 1; 1963 ed., p. 9). The essence of mysticism is "little more than a certain intensity and depth of feeling in regard to what is believed about the universe" (p. 3; 1963 ed., p. 10), though mysticism as commonly reported makes various unsubstantiated claims. Science is necessary to a balanced intellectual life, for in its pursuit man is concerned with the facts, thereby demonstrating his "impartial temper" (p. 7; 1963 ed., p. 13). But science does not have a monopoly on impartiality. Mysticism, again in essence, contributes an impartiality of feeling in its refusal to judge things good or bad, "although it is very easily combined with the feeling of universal love which leads the mystic to say that the whole world is good" (p. 28; 1963 ed., p. 27). Scientific philosophy, in its humility with respect to fact, provides the human mind with "the most intimate relation to the outer world that it is possible to achieve" (p. 32; 1963 ed., p. 30). Scientific philosophy promotes self-enlargement, or, in Russell's words, "like every approach to self-transcendence, it brings with it a rich reward in increase of scope and breadth and comprehension" (*ibid.*).

While the essay's chief purpose is to trace the utility of the scientific method in philosophy, its analysis of mysticism appears to be original. Common mystical thought, Russell alleges, despite apparent differences, has four major aspects: the illusoriness of good and evil, the unreality of time (on which I quoted Russell citing Spinoza in 27), the apparent revelation of the union of all things, and conviction of the existence of a way of knowledge known variously as insight, revelation, or intuition. It is not, however, the *conviction* that interests us here, but the *experience* of putative insight, revelation, or intuition.[6] First, there is the "negative" side: "All who are capable of absorption in an inward passion must have experienced at times the strange feeling of unreality in common objects, the loss of contact with daily things, in which the solidity of the outer world is lost, and the soul seems, in utter loneliness, to bring forth, out of its own depths, the mad dance of fantastic phantoms which have hitherto appeared as independently real and living" (pp. 8–9; 1963 ed., p. 14). This side is "merely the gateway to an ampler world": "The mystic insight begins with the sense of a mystery unveiled, of a hidden wisdom now suddenly become certain beyond the possibility of a doubt" (*ibid.*). Russell then analyzes the four aspects of mysticism, as well as the "inessential accretions" of more local and temporary character. It is important to note what he says about the conception for the mystic of a reality totally different from appearance: "This Reality is regarded with an admiration often amounting to worship; it is felt to be always and everywhere close at hand, thinly veiled by the shows of sense, ready, for the receptive mind, to shine in its glory even through the apparent folly and wickedness of Man. The poet, the artist, and the lover[7] are seekers after that glory: the haunting beauty that they pursue is the faint reflection of its sun" (p. 10; 1963 ed., pp. 14–15). For the denial of the reality of evil, Russell alludes to Spinoza in a special way: "Sometimes—for example in Hegel, and at least verbally in Spinoza—not only evil, but good also, is regarded as illusory, though nevertheless the emotional attitude towards what is held to be

Reality is such as would naturally be associated with the belief that Reality is good" (p. 11; 1963 ed., p. 15). Russell seems to have in mind here the same attitude he finds in the intellectual love of God. The above quotation continues with an analysis of the sense of peace:

> What is, in all cases, ethically characteristic of mysticism is absence of indignation or protest, acceptance with joy, disbelief in the ultimate truth of the division into two hostile camps, the good and the bad. This attitude is the direct outcome of the nature of the mystical experience: with its sense of unity is associated a feeling of infinite peace. Indeed it may be suspected that the feeling of peace produces, as feelings do in dreams, the whole system of associated beliefs which make up the body of mystic doctrine. (*Ibid.*)

It is reasonable to identify this feeling of "infinite peace" with what Russell calls "philosophic calm", for the lack of indignation and the feeling of unity are common to both, and both proceed from moments in which there is a "sense of mystery unveiled". Clearly, then, Russell values moments of mystic illumination highly, especially for their "significance" in the area of subjective ethical valuation. To be fully convinced of this claim, however, we shall have to observe how the element of mystical experience functions in his normative ethic. This claim is the contrary of what, e.g., W. T. Stace supposes about Russell, whose writing on mysticism Stace uses as an example of ignorance on the subject.[8]

43 "The Free Man's Worship"

Since I hold that "The Free Man's Worship" is too early to be predominantly Spinozistic, let us approach the essay from the standpoint of Russell's own self-preoccupation. The essay was written around Christmas 1902. The personal background included witnessing the suffering of Evelyn Whitehead, falling in love with her and out of love with Alys, and finding it impossible, because of his friendship for and collaboration with Whitehead, to express his love for Evelyn in any way. As Russell writes in his journal on 10 February 1903: "Two years ago today Gilbert read his *Hippolytus* at Cambridge. A year ago yesterday I told Alys not to be indiscreet. Today 'the free man's worship' came back from the typewriter—the total result of so much suffering." Russell's "conversion" experience, i.e. the mystical experience I described in 42, was based on the spectacle of great pain and his own subsequent experience of it on the emotional level. These experiences led Russell to formulate an ethic viewing the encountering and surmounting of pain as the key to wisdom in dealing with personal misery. The day following the above journal entry he recorded that he spoke to someone "of the revelation through Pain", and went so far two months later as to write in the journal that "only what gives pleasure is wrong, but what gives pain is either right or at least pardonable" (18 April 1903). The insights provided by pain were not forgotten when Russell came to write "The Perplexities of John Forstice" in 1912. He makes his Russian novelist, Chenskoff, the advocate of his ethic of pain—"the infinite pain which I felt to be the ultimate truth of life" (*Collected Stories*, p. 30), leading to "the marriage of pain [in which] the soul dies to self" (p. 31). In this ethic, the value of pain is as a means, not as an end.

The phrase "the marriage of pain" occurs also in "The Free Man's Worship". A great insight is provided by intense pain, through which we are freed from the demands of self:

> In the spectacle of Death, in the endurance of intolerable pain, and in the irrevocableness of a vanished past, there is a sacredness, an overpowering awe, a feeling of the vastness, the depth, the inexhaustible mystery of existence, in which, as by some strange marriage of pain, the sufferer is bound to the world by bonds of sorrow. In these moments of insight, we lose all eagerness of temporary desire, all struggling and striving for petty ends....
> (*Basic Writings*, p. 71)

The demands of self (or "self-assertion" [p. 69]) are what create anxiety and defeat at the hands of superior forces. The essay is full of terms such as "the fierceness of desire" (p. 69), "goods ... fretfully desired" (*ibid.*), "eager wishes" (*ibid.*), "untamed passion" (*ibid.*), "untamed desire" (p. 70 twice, p. 71 twice), "untrained desire" (p. 70), "temporary desire" (p. 71). Personal desires have to be renounced. The free man must "burn with passion for eternal things" (*ibid.*). However he may succumb outwardly in daily affairs to what appears to be inevitable, his spirit remains uncrushed because, through pain, his self has been purged of personal desire. Where these "abandoned hopes" have died, "[t]here Self must die; there the eagerness, the greed of untamed desire must be slain, for only so can the soul be freed from the empire of Fate" (p. 70). This is still the language of self-abnegation.

The passion for eternal things is the worship of the free man. The phrase "the free man" could hardly have been used by Russell without his thinking of Spinoza's free man. But his use of the term is not necessarily a public, or literary, allusion to Spinoza. True, the suppression of eager personal desires fits Spinoza, as does some of the language. At one point Russell writes that "indignation is still a bondage" (p. 69); Spinoza says that "Indignation is hatred towards those who have injured others" (E3Df.Aff.20) and "Hatred can never be good" (E4P45), because under the influence of hatred a man is in bondage to his passions. (Russell may have picked up such language elsewhere, but the similarity is a probable link between him and Spinoza.) Yet Russell refers to "the Stoic freedom in which wisdom consists", and he nowhere mentions Spinoza in the essay. On the other hand, statements such as the following are reminiscent of Part V of the *Ethics*: "But the vision of beauty is possible only to unfettered contemplation, to thoughts not weighted by the load of eager wishes; and thus Freedom comes only to those who no longer ask of life that it shall yield them any of those personal goods that are subject to the mutations of Time" (p. 69). But to construe this as an expression of the intellectual love of God would be going too far. The essay had no doubt many influences upon it, Spinoza's *Ethics* being just one of them, perhaps mostly in its assumption of determinism in human affairs.[9] You do not need to know the *Ethics* to understand Russell's essay.

The first decade of this century—when Russell was age 28 to 38—is his ascetic period. In a journal entry of 1905 he refers to "the incessant checking of every impulse" that he believed he had to undergo. Probably this was for the sake of his marriage to Alys and the writing of *Principia Mathematica*. Years before he wrote the lost book known as "Prisons", he frequently uses the image of imprisonment to refer to the bondage we experience to personal desires, or self. The earliest published versions of "The Free Man's Worship" contain some sentences which are absent in every version published in 1910 and after. One such sentence concerns "another vision of life [that] might be ours, wider, freer, than the narrow valley in which our private life is prisoned."[10] The prison image, and the problem of self, occur frequently in fragmentary essays written in 1902. Although in "The Free Man's Worship" the notion of self-enlargement cannot be identified, it is present to a significant degree in some of the fragments. Two of the longer fragments—one belonging to the reconstructed sequence, "The Return to the Cave", and beginning "These comforters are Courage, Love, and Peace", the other titled "Austerity"—have similar passages about our being "born into the world single, separate, imprisoned as in a dungeon by strong walls of Self."[11] "Austerity" contains a valuable passage worth quoting *in extenso* as showing Russell's view at the time of the fundamental attitude to life to be adopted:

> All greatness of soul is rooted in renunciation—not only of actual and particular goods, but still more of the greed for personal goods of some kind. Not this or that only must be abandoned, but the whole cry of nature for something to make life happy. To be happy is to be callous to all the evil surrounding us, our own circumstances can never justify contentment. If we enlarge our passions, we must enlarge our miseries too, but by universalizing our thoughts we eliminate the restless indignant demand that *we* specially should be happy. Each human being is born single, separate, enclosed as in a dungeon by strong walls of egotism. But self and its happiness are petty things, unless self has broken down the walls of self and taken the whole world into its inmost sanctuary. Through love the wall of self may be broken down; but if we merely substitute another self as the subject for our greed of happiness, we gain little through love. Such love is not yet purified in the fire of renunciation.... Passion, intense and devouring, is necessary to greatness of soul, but passion purged of all greed and all personal dross. And passion, always, in all moments, must be dominated by a calm and godlike reason, judging, criticizing, restraining and purifying. This is the only peace of mind which in an evil world the good man may rightly feel....[12]

Russell is here awarding reason as great a role as Spinoza does, but to passion he awards a much greater role in encouraging it to be strong. We are not told here how to break down "the walls of self". Nor are we told the distinction between "enlarging" and "universalizing" our passions. By "enlarging" a passion Russell seems to mean making it more intense, so that its satisfaction (or lack of it) becomes more intense. By "universalizing" Russell seems to mean that, in the case of desires, you desire not only on your own behalf but on everyone's, which would eliminate the personal reference included in the "demand that *we* specially should be happy". Renunciation of your chances of personal happiness is the ethic of Russell at the age of 30 and most of the next decade. Clearly, as Russell tells Lady Ottoline in 1911, the ethic of the period of "The Free Man's Worship" "is only for people in great unhappiness" (no. 190, p/6 April 1911). By 1910, as we have seen (**22**), Russell was attacking those who would interpret Spinoza as inculcating resignation, or renunciation. In the context of the 1910 review of the *Ethics*, this is an indication that Russell himself no longer considered an ethic of pain and renunciation—in short, of self-abnegation—to be adequate. The prison image, however, continues to be used in the period up to 1910[13] and indeed to the end of his life.

44 "Prisons" and "The Essence of Religion"

The reasons for the change in Russell's ethic by 1910–12 are obscure. Martin, in his thesis, suggests the personal influence of Lady Ottoline (p. 162). Russell writes of their affair that it was the end to nine years of "tense self-denial" (*Autobiography*, vol. I, p. 205) and the end to the belief that he "was seething with appalling wickedness which could only be kept under by an iron self-control." She made him "much less of a Puritan", "less self-centred, and less self-righteous" (*ibid*.). These are important admissions—especially the one concerning self-centredness—but they do not account for the great influx of Spinozism to be found in Russell's ethical writing at this time. It is possible that, because of his love for Lady Ottoline, he reached for a philosophic expression of it and found the most congenial one in the *Ethics*.[14] In **24** I quoted from letters in which Russell states that much of what he has to say is in Spinoza, but he does not disclose at what point his thoughts and Spinoza's started to converge. We know that as early as 1894 there was already a degree of convergence. The 1910 review of the *Ethics* is evidence that a serious convergence had taken place before the affair with Lady Ottoline began in March 1911. Mention should be made of a possible mystical experience by Russell in the summer of 1911 under Lady Ottoline's influence. In 1912 he writes to her of how in the previous summer "the religious things came up and rather overpowered everything else", and that the "main thing I ought to do in the world [is] to make a harmony of intellect and mysticism—not to put them side by side, but to make one fused whole of them" (no. 493, 10 July 1912). During the previous summer he tells her:

I have two views of you—the one of the every-day you, and the other of a sort of prehistoric timeless embodiment of ancient wisdom. Towards the every-day you I feel an infinite tenderness and an intense joy in all you are. But towards the other all my imagination goes out—I have an infinite reverence and a sense of unbelievable peace.... Then sometimes when the mystical absorption is great, I feel you as the gateway into a transfigured world through which all the glory shines before me. You wouldn't believe how "hard" it is for me not to be mythological about you. It is the combination of freedom and compassion that gives you your power with me. (No. 176, [late Aug.? 1911])

The experiences of the summer of 1911 led Russell to write a book on his philosophy of religion. It is difficult to say precisely what was in "Prisons". Russell wrote out a scheme for Lady Ottoline in a letter that Clark quotes (p. 160). The chapter titles were:[15]

I. The Nature and Value of Religion
II. The World of Universals
III. The Physical World
IV. The Past
V. Contemplation and the Emotions
VI. Contemplation and Action
VII. Union with the Universe (no. 173, n.d.)

We cannot be sure that Russell adhered to this scheme, which may have been a preliminary one. At one point he tells Lady Ottoline that he has written a long chapter on "Freedom and Necessity", added a page on justice, and finished the book (no. 169, n.d.). This chapter might have been Chapter VIII or IX, since a surviving manuscript is titled "Chapter X. The Good". The contents of the book can only be surmised from the outlines, this chapter, and the article. One of the outlines is titled "Prisons I", which may be an outline of the first chapter:

Religion consists in union with the universe. Formerly, union was achieved by assimilating the universe to our own conception of the Good . . . we must find a mode of union which asks nothing of the world, and depends solely upon ourselves....

The moralist divides the world into good and bad, and this division is true and important. But besides this dualistic attitude, there is another, wholly compatible with it, but monistic: an attitude which ignores the difference between the good and the bad, and loves all alike. This is the essence of religion; but because it has not been clearly distinguished from the moralist's attitude, it has been supposed, wrongly, to require the belief that the world is good.... Every such demand [that the world shall conform to our standards] is an endeavour to impose Self upon the world.... The essence of religion is union with the universe achieved by subordination of the demands of Self. This subordination is not complete if it depends upon a belief that the universe satisfies some at least of the demands of Self.... Such a religion is possible; and to those who achieve it it gives nearly all, and in some ways more than all, that the religions of the past have given.[16]

In Russell's own terms this passage draws on mysticism, and the sense remains unchanged if we substitute "mysticism" for "religion" in the passage. In an untitled fragment beginning "Prisons", Russell answers his own question, What is prison?

Self-interest, subjectivity, insistence. Why a prison? because shuts out the love, the knowledge, and the attainment of goods otherwise possible. What the universe allows, what it forbids: It forbids the freedom of omnipotence; it permits the freedom of contemplation. It permits the freedom of oneness with it; three forms of union: love, admiration, knowledge. All three are escapes from prison. All three combined give wisdom, peace, virtue; joy in part, infinite melancholy too.[17]

The "freedom of oneness" with the universe is only possible if self is transcended:

Self in all its forms—in thought, in feeling, in action—is a prison: it shuts out the soul from that complete union with the world, in which true freedom consists. To be wholly free from self is not possible to man; his separate body entails always some separateness of mind. But to become progressively freer, to live more and more the larger life of impersonal contemplation, is possible, and is the road by which we pass into the world of freedom from the prison of strife and private hopes.... The loves that make what is best in the natural life survive, but enlarged, harmonized with universal love, not setting up walls of division between the loved and the unloved.... And above all is the contemplative vision: partly sad, partly filled with a solemn joy, wholly beautiful, wholly great: the vision of all the ages of the earth, the depths of space, and the hierarchy of the eternal truths, met and mirrored in one mind whose being ends almost as soon as its knowledge has come to exist. (Pp. 3–4)

We do not know whether Russell is writing here of "the contemplative vision" as a moment of mystic illumination. The vision in question does not seem to be momentary. But I think he would classify it as mystical. In another summary Russell enlarges upon the contemplative vision in an important way. Through contemplation you become less bound to both friend and foe. You become, instead, "a citizen of the universe and not only of one walled city at war with all the rest".[18] The metaphor of military circumvallation is important because it indicates continuity with "The Free Man's Worship". A dominant image in that essay is that of the enlightened soul withdrawing from the strife of the world into the "citadel" of Tragedy, within whose "walls" the soul continues its free but lonely life. In "The Essence of Religion" the walls of self are to be taken down, and the military metaphor of "The Free Man's Worship" is continued: "The world in which it [the life of instinct] finds a home is a narrow world, surrounded by alien and probably hostile forces; it is prisoned in a beleaguered fortress, knowing that ultimate surrender is inevitable. The life of wisdom [on the other hand] ... finds its home everywhere: no lines of circumvallation bar its progress" (*Basic Writings*, p. 575).

The last quotation comes from "The Essence of Religion", but it is also virtually word for word, with one exception, in a fragment titled "IV Wisdom". The exception is that where I have quoted "wisdom", Russell originally had "reason". The fragment covers the final five paragraphs of "The Essence", where Russell sets forth his fundamental division of human nature into the animal and the divine. To the animal part belongs instinct, to the divine part wisdom, or reason. This twofold division lasted only a few years. In *Principles of Social Reconstruction*, he divides man's nature into three parts. Instinct continues to cover the animal in man, but reason becomes bifurcated into mind and spirit. Although instinct is partial and personal, a satisfactory life is impossible if the instincts are ignored: as Russell told Lady Ottoline, it does not do to "... deny the animal in man. The God in man will not be visible, as a rule, while the animal is thwarted.

... Spinoza, always, is right in all these things, to my mind" (8 Aug. 1918; *Autobiography*, vol. II, pp. 89–90). Both mind and spirit are impersonal, the one in thought and the other in feeling. In *Principles* there is a passage celebrating the impersonality of the religious impulse, which starts from spirit and tries to dominate instinct:

> It is possible to feel the same interest in the joys and sorrows of others as in our own, to love and hate independently of all relation to ourselves, to care about the destiny of man and the development of the universe without a thought that we are personally involved. Reverence and worship, the sense of an obligation to mankind, the feeling of imperativeness and acting under orders which traditional religion has interpreted as Divine inspiration, all belong to the life of the spirit. And deeper than all these lies the sense of a mystery half revealed, of a hidden wisdom and glory, of a transfiguring vision in which common things lose their solid importance and become a thin veil behind which the ultimate truth of the world is dimly seen. It is such feelings that are the source of religion, and if they were to die most of what is best would vanish out of life. (Pp. 207–8)

This passage comes from the chapter Russell says is the least unsatisfactory of his writings on religion. The passage demonstrates two things: (1) that, as Russell is still utilizing the concept of mystical experience (compare the terminology with the quotations from "Mysticism and Logic" in **42**), his thought is continuous on this point; and (2) that, although the conceptual framework is a little different, he still accords to the divine part of man's nature the same virtues as "The Essence of Religion". Although we shall not again find him setting out this framework, he never repudiates it and continues to use at least part of it. I shall assume the framework in dealing with his subsequent normative ethical writings.

"The Essence of Religion" divides man's soul into two natures, the "finite self" and the "infinite self".[19] The infinite self is "God-like", "universal", and "impartial". Peace comes to this self through harmony with the whole, by means of an "experience of sudden wisdom". The source of this experience is "impersonal contemplation", requiring a moment of "absolute self-surrender" which brings "death" to the finite self. The contemplative vision results in two attitudinal changes: "universal love" and its attendant desire for the "universal good", and "universal worship" and its attendant joy. The finite self is characterized as "brute", "self-centred", "particular" in its concerns, responsible for "separateness", based on "all those thoughts and desires that cannot, in their nature, be shared by the inhabitant of a different body" and the drive for self-preservation and "dominion" over others, and the builder of "prison walls" around the infinite self. The finite self is familiar to us, but the unfamiliarity of the infinite self justifies quoting Russell's characterization at length. For the infinite self is the upper limit of the self that is enlarged in an impersonal way. The eloquence of the following passage is due to Russell's wish to create in us a desire for this ideal.

> The infinite part of our life does not see the world from one point of view: it shines impartially, like the diffused light on a cloudy sea. Distant ages and remote regions of space are as real to it as what is present and near. In thought, it rises above the life of the senses, seeking always what is general and open to all men. In desire and will, it aims simply at the good, without regarding the good as mine or yours. In feeling, it gives love to all, not only to those who further the purposes of self. Unlike the finite life, it is impartial: its impartiality leads to truth in thought, justice in action, and universal love in feeling. Unlike the nature which man shares with the brutes, it has a life without barriers, embracing in its survey the whole universe of existence and essence; nothing in it is essentially private, but its thoughts and desires are such as all may share, since none depend upon the exclusiveness of *here* and *now* and *me*. Thus the infinite nature is the principle of union in the world, as the finite nature is the principle of division. Between the infinite nature in one man and the infinite nature in another, there can be no essential conflict: if its embodiments are incomplete, they supplement each other; its division among different men is accidental to its character, and the infinite in all constitutes one universal nature. There is thus a union of all the infinite natures of different men in a sense in which there is no union of all the finite natures. In proportion as the infinite grows strong in us, we live more completely the life of that one universal nature which embraces what is infinite in each of us. (*Basic Writings*, p. 566)

The infinite self in Russell at this time is virtually identical to the Spinozistic self enjoying the intellectual love of God. Spinoza, too (as pointed out in 34) discarded the part of the self that is dependent on, or coordinate with, the particular body it has. Russell's infinite self also has the intellectual love of God, partly because much of the above quotation is an expression of what it *is* to have the intellectual love of God, and partly because Russell says as much in the following passage later in the essay concerning the impersonal contemplative vision: "it is the escape from prison that gives to some moments and some thoughts a quality of infinity, like light breaking through some greater world beyond. Sudden beauty in the midst of strife, uncalculating love, or the night wind in the trees, seem to suggest the possibility of a life free from the conflicts and pettiness of our everyday world, a life where there is peace which no misfortune can disturb" (pp. 566–7). This is akin to Russell's later conception of the intellectual love of God. It is based partly on moments of intellectual and emotional discovery, which is how Russell's mysticism comes in. There is not the same element of mystical experience explicit in Spinoza, though Russell, as we have seen in "Mysticism and Logic", considers him a fellow-mystic. "It is this experience of sudden wisdom which is the source of what is essential in religion", he says in "The Essence" (p. 567). Mysticism is wrong, however, to interpret the experience as "the perception of new objects" (*ibid.*). It is instead "a different way of regarding the same objects, a contemplation more impersonal, more vast, more filled with love, than the fragmentary, disquiet consideration we give to things when we view them as means to help or hinder our own purposes" (*ibid.*).

In "The Essence of Religion" a second mystical moment is required, this time for the creation of the contemplative vision. This moment is constituted by the surrender of self at a time of "some inward or outward necessity to abandon the pursuit of the object which has absorbed all our desire" (*ibid.*). Russell's account here is surely autobiographical—either of the experience that led to "The Free Man's Worship", or of his difficult relationship with Lady Ottoline. To my knowledge, this second mystical moment is not discussed again in Russell's normative ethical writings after "Forstice". Such an experience is inessential to his ethic, and something like it is criticized in "Mysticism and Logic" (see n. 30).

Although the term "enlargement" does not have a central role in the expression of the ethic in "The Essence", the concept does. The term is found only in the section on the acquiescence necessary to prevent unhappiness in the face of the inevitable. Such acquiescence requires a "suppression of self and its demands". "This discipline", Russell holds, "is more severe in the absence of all optimistic dogma, but in proportion as it is more severe its outcome is greater, more unshakable, more capable of so enlarging the bounds of self as to make it welcome with love whatever of good or evil may come before it" (p. 573). "Love" is a vital concept in "The Essence". Love is of two kinds: one is selective, and the other—"divine love"—is impartial. The latter corresponds to the emotional part of the infinite self, as opposed to the cognitive part. Divine love—also termed "impartial heavenly love"—is said to free the soul from its "prison", to "break down the walls of self", to promote union with the world. I do not, however, award love the preeminent place in Russell's ethic that Martin and Sams do in their studies. While love, felt strongly and impartially throughout the world, would soon put an end to strife, the real problems are how to foster love, and what conception of man is required to induce assent to an ethic of love.

"The Essence of Religion" drew a number of responses.[20] Most of them attack Russell's dualism in regarding the actual world as bad and unworthy of our worship, and the ideal as good and worthy of our worship. Pringle-Pattison treated "The Free Man's Worship" and "The Essence of Religion" in one of his 1912–13 Gifford lectures, though he dropped the lecture in question as not of "sufficient permanent importance" when the series was published as a book.[21] He compares the essays and finds them inconsistent. Noticing the expanded impersonal self in "The Essence", Pringle-Pattison wonders if Russell is "aware how far a doctrine like the universal soul will carry him" (p. 52). It should, he thinks, carry him as far as the non-selective worship of an all-embracing reality "conceived as good" (p. 60). But he recognizes that Russell gives priority to reforming the real rather than to acquiescing in it. Pringle-Pattison is correct in holding that Russell is inconsistent in wishing to see his ideals realized and in affecting an "impartial worship and love of whatever exists" (p. 62). G. H. Hardy, the mathematician and long-time member of the Apostles, fastens upon Russell's conviction that "the universe is unutterably bad"[22] while advocating an impartial worship of all existence. Russell therefore, in Hardy's view, worships an ideal good. Hardy will not have this: existence "seems to me indeed an essential factor in most of the highest goods" (p. 651). The "impartial worship" of the world with all its good and bad (as opposed to selective worship of its good) is not sufficient to constitute a religion for Hardy. He thinks he knows the experience Russell writes about under the term "impartial worship" and provides several striking examples (and counter-examples). But he denies finding in the experience any transcendent or "supreme degree of" value. Hardy's difficulty is with failing to unite the concept of such experience with self-enlargement. He does not think of the enlarged or "infinite" self "shin[ing] impartially, like the diffused light on a cloudy sea" (*Basic Writings*, p. 566). In the end Hardy admits that his "whole attitude towards Mr. Russell's religion is warped by unconquerable prejudice" (p. 653): he does not want Russell to make him religious. R. F. Alfred Hoernlé surveyed Russell's non-logical writings from 1903 to 1914 for their religious aspect.[23] He, too, finds unsatisfactory Russell's refusal to look for the embodiment of good in the actual world. He also notices a minor resemblance to Spinoza (p. 169) in Russell's attitude to indignation. Hoernlé sets out to trace the ways in which Russell attempts to achieve the union of the mystic and the man of science in "Mysticism and Logic": "The chapters in our story, in brief, are that Mr. Russell began as a Mystic at odds with the world because of its indifference to his moral demands, and that he has ended, so far, as a Mystic at peace with the world by refusing to press his moral demands against it" (p. 162). Hoernlé is correct that Russell's dualism in "The Essence" is "seriously compromised when wishes are allowed to bridge the gap between actual and ideal" (p. 172). It is inconsistent to advocate both acceptance of the actual world and its improvement through embodiment of the ideal world. Hoernlé goes on to compare Russell's religious philosophy with his new epistemology: "It has dissolved 'omnipotent matter' into a logical construction of sense-data, and the infinite soul of man into the solipsist's shivering wraith" (p. 187), not realizing that Russell regards theory of knowledge and theory of value as logically separate.

In the criticisms of Pringle-Pattison, Hardy and Hoernlé, there is the constant theme that only the actual world, when it is good, is worthy of worship. Pringle-Pattison and Hoernlé both want Russell to recognize the actual world as in some way perfect, as a revelation of God. Hardy wants no religion at all. After "The Essence of Religion" Russell's views change. He no longer tries to worship an ideal world, though, unlike most religious philosophers, he does not transfer his worship to the actual world. Russell was soon engaged in active opposition to the First World War; he is not a mystic at peace with the state of human affairs. Both Pringle-Pattison and Hoernlé note that Russell is a meliorist, and from this time—though not necessarily as a result of their criticisms—Russell holds that contemplation of the ideal world is not "enough to constitute a good life" and "must be married to practice" (*New Hopes*, p. 180), i.e. the actual world.

45 The Problems of Philosophy

Hoernlé attentively read the last chapter of *The Problems of Philosophy*. "There he [Russell] speaks of philosophy in the same fervent language in which he speaks elsewhere of religion" (p. 187). This is for no other reason than that, in the chapter on "The Value of Philosophy", Russell is treating the mental or cognitive side of what he calls religion. Indeed, he tells Lady Ottoline that some of the sentences in that chapter came from "Prisons" (no. 173, n.d.). Hoernlé reports Russell's language about the self, but he does not realize that impersonal self-enlargement is the main theme of the chapter.

The chapter's main theme is recognized by King-Farlow in his "Self-Enlargement and Union: Neglected Passages of Russell and Famous Ones of Proust". In Russell's ending *The Problems* "on an almost Spinozistic note" (p. 106), King-Farlow reaches the judgment that Russell is "a curious sort of limited sympathizer with Spinoza's *Ethics*". While Russell is a less limited sympathizer than he supposes, King-Farlow is on the right track. King-Farlow writes: "[A person's] mind is not just capable of the union described before, but capable of a state in which Selfhood dissolves so that he sees himself harmoniously as a mode of Nature" (pp. 110–11). He concludes that "The Value of Philosophy" is valuable for the light it throws on the topic of wisdom. Presumably in this connection, he mentions the notion of self-realization through self-enlargement, but he does not expand upon it.

The value of philosophy, in addition to an intrinsic interest in its study, Russell holds in *The Problems*, is to be found in "its effects upon the lives of those who study it".[24] One effect lies in the student's having to face uncertainty: "The man who has no tincture of philosophy goes through life imprisoned in the prejudices derived from common sense.... To such a man the world tends to become definite, finite, obvious; common objects rouse no questions, and unfamiliar possibilities are contemptuously rejected" (pp. 156–7). Philosophy, by suggesting "many possibilities which enlarge our thoughts and free them from the tyranny of custom", removes "the somewhat arrogant dogmatism of those who have never travelled in the region of liberating doubt" (p. 157). Philosophy's chief value, however, is "through the greatness of the objects which it contemplates, and the freedom from narrow and personal aims resulting from this contemplation" (*ibid.*). Russell starts discussion on his concept of self-enlargement by citing the "instinctive man's" narrow circle of interests. (The instinctive man is the finite self of "The Essence of Religion".) The instinctive man's life is sooner or later going to lie in ruins before the "great and powerful world" (p. 158). Again there is the image of circumvallation: we must "enlarge our interests to include the whole outer world", or "we remain like a garrison in a beleaguered fortress" (*ibid.*). There must be escape from "this prison and this strife". One way of escape is provided by philosophic contemplation because it views the universe impartially, instead of dividing it into good and bad. This is the job of the infinite self in "The Essence" and of spirit in *Principles of Social Reconstruction*. In Russell's normative ethic, we become accustomed to his calling the same thing by different names.

"All acquisition of knowledge is an enlargement of the Self", and "Knowledge is a form of union of Self and not-Self . . ." (p. 159).[25] These statements express the Spinozistic aspect of Russell's theory of self-enlargement. The connection with Spinoza is in the impartiality of the impulse to knowledge. Both hold that it is through the pursuit of knowledge that we escape the bondage of passive emotions (in Spinoza's case) or instinctive desires (Russells). In Spinoza we achieve a union with God through the intellectual love of God that is part of the intellectual love with which God loves Himself (E5P36). One of the great evils to Russell is "self-assertion". Warnings about it are present in his normative ethical writings from "The Free Man's Worship" onwards. In its presence self cannot grow, because in self-assertion we wish to assimilate the world to ourselves. When man as a species asserts himself, Russell calls it "cosmic impiety", since it flies in the face of a cosmic perspective.[26] It is another way of expressing the domination of the finite or instinctive self. This is the means/end distinction of which much is made in his normative ethic. Things outside the self are not to be subordinated to the self's use of them. In "The Value of Philosophy" he writes:

> Self-assertion, in philosophic speculation as elsewhere, views the world as means to its own ends; thus it makes the world of less account than Self, and the Self sets bounds to the greatness of its goods. In contemplation, on the contrary, we start from the not-Self, and through its greatness the boundaries of Self are enlarged; through the infinity of the universe the mind which contemplates it achieves some share in infinity. (P. 159)
>
> The true philosophic contemplation, on the contrary, finds its satisfaction in every enlargement of the not-Self, in everything that magnifies the objects contemplated, and thereby the subject contemplating. (P. 160)

Personal desires distort the object and create a prison for the intellect. There follows a long Spinozistic passage, the last part of which contains ideas Russell later repudiated. Like Spinoza, he decries the knowledge gained through the senses for its dependence on the accidents of your particular biography and the distortions of your sense-organs. This is not what Russell comes later to believe:

> ... I have no longer the feeling that intellect is superior to sense, and that only Plato's world of ideas gives access to the "real" world. I used to think of sense, and of thought which is built on sense, as a prison from which we can be freed by thought which is emancipated from sense. I now have no such feelings. I think of sense, and of thoughts built on sense, as windows, not as prison bars. (*My Philosophical Development*, p. 213)

He goes on to discuss the limitations he has come to think impartiality is subject to (see **59**). What Russell writes in *My Philosophical Development* seems directly in response to this Spinozistic passage in *The Problems of Philosophy*, inasmuch as there are responses to both the issue of the value of the knowledge derived from the senses and the issue of impartiality. The first half of the Spinozistic passage in *The Problems* is the following: "The free intellect will see as God might see, without a *here* and *now*, without hopes and fears, without the trammels of customary beliefs and traditional prejudices, calmly, dispassionately, in the sole and exclusive desire of knowledge—knowledge as impersonal, as purely contemplative, as it is possible for man to attain" (p. 160). Russell's "free intellect" is indistinguishable from Spinoza's free man enjoying the intellectual love of God. The chapter closes with a restatement of the value of philosophic contemplation in achieving the mind's highest good—union with the universe.

Russell does not ignore the relationship of contemplation to action in "The Essence" and *The Problems*. His language on the subject is very similar in both writings:

> The impartiality which, in contemplation, is the unalloyed desire for truth, is the very same quality of mind which, in action, is justice, and in emotion is that universal love which can be given to all, and not only to those who are judged useful or admirable. Thus contemplation enlarges not only the objects of our thoughts, but also the objects of our actions and our affections: it

makes us citizens of the universe, not only of one walled city at war with all the rest. In this citizenship of the universe consists man's true freedom, and his liberation from the thraldom of narrow hopes and fears. (*The Problems*, p. 161)

The "enlarging", i.e. universalizing, effect upon the sphere of action that contemplation can have is something Russell believes in thereafter. Russell had a low estimate of the pragmatists' concern with the actual world (see note 13), whereas Dewey criticized the analytic realists' high estimate of contemplation as aristocratic and escapist.[27] Russell replied to Dewey: "... those to whom contemplative knowledge appears a valuable ideal find in the practice of it the same kind of thing that some have found in religion: they find something that, besides being very valuable on its own account, seems capable of purifying and elevating practice, making its aims larger and more generous, its disappointments less crushing, and its triumphs less intoxicating."[28] Russell noted in his reply that Dewey's remarks were "amusingly inappropriate" to Russell's then present situation, that of a political prisoner. To some philosophers, the whole controversy would have been amusingly inappropriate. Brightman remarks upon the close resemblance between the two "at the zenith of their religion". It seems that Dewey, too, had "a sense of the infinite" and experienced a religious "feeling of membership in the whole".[29]

46 "The Perplexities of John Forstice"

To complete the exploration of Russell's Spinozistic ethic in the 1910–12 period we must consider the final part of "The Perplexities of John Forstice". Russell says of the first of the "two truths" revealed by the mystic vision and alleged to survive critical examination:

The first of these gives a contemplation of the actual world more vast, more free, more impersonal, than the view of daily life: by rising above the mists of desire, away from the belittling, distorting influence of hopes and fears, we can attain at moments, however imperfectly, to the divine all-embracing intuition of the universe, free from the *here* and *now*, free from the prison house of Self, revealing the whole, eternal and infinite in spite of the brevity and limitation of every part when seen in separate isolation.... (*Collected Stories*, p. 42)

The second truth concerns "[T]he possibility of a life here on earth immeasurably greater than the life of the human society as it now exists" (*ibid.*).

In fact, there is not much that is different in "Forstice" from the other religious writings of the period. There is greater emphasis on the power of love to promote self-enlargement, in contrast to that of philosophic contemplation or the pursuit of knowledge. There is a reliance upon mystical experience stemming from passionate love: "There is in all human intercourse, to those who have the power of love, some disquieting hint, some wistful suggestion, of a mystical world where solitude is overcome, where the walls that divide each separate soul from its comrades are broken down, where the division between Self and Other is of no account" (p. 37).[30] This passage comes from the journal of Forstice's uncle concerning his unrequited love for Sister Catherine Belasys. Modelled upon Mother Julian, a strong influence in Lady Ottoline's life, the nun is given the first name of Russell's mother. While Russell's characterization of Uncle Tristram is in terms (p. 34) reminiscent of his own Uncle Rollo (see *Autobiography*, vol. I, p. 24), Tristram's journal speaks for Russell himself. Clark suggests that Tristram's love for Catherine is a mirror of Russell's unrequited love for Evelyn Whitehead; I suggest it is his incompletely requited love for Lady Ottoline. At any rate, we need not be hesitant in judging that the views of the third part of "Forstice" are views that Russell himself entertained. For example, Forstice holds a kind of pessimistic materialism—"that the soul dies at death, that Matter rules the world, that spiritual forces are powerless against natural laws, mere shining bubbles on the surface of the hurrying stream." He has difficulty reconciling this with the insight of universal love in the face of a crowd of "spiritually stunted human beings" (p. 41). He wonders how Mother Catherine's wisdom and the wisdom Russell believed Lady Ottoline to possess can be "disentangled from the God, the life of prayer, the belief in the power of the Spirit, with which in her it was entwined" (*ibid.*). His reconciliation is that of Russell in "The Essence of Religion":[31] the impartial view of the world that loves the world in spite of its division into good and bad, "a way filled with welcoming acceptance". This is the "mystical acceptance of the world", with which most mystics tend to replace the facts of "cruelty and lust" in the world. Forstice's conclusion is the familiar one of "Mysticism and Logic": "if the vision is to have a real place, to be a source of wisdom, not of illusion, it must accept the everyday world, retaining the mystic's feeling without the mystic's belief as to the nature of the universe" (p. 42).[32] The novella concludes with a statement of the role of contemplation and action in the good life, and Forstice himself returns to the study and teaching of physics.

47 Principles of Social Reconstruction

Having devoted considerable space to Russell's writings of 1911–12, we shall be briefer with the writings that follow. Given Russell's output, and his transformation during World War I into a more popular social and moral philosopher, the task is not easy. We have, however, in the extended treatment of the 1911–12 writings, an extensive foundation on which to proceed. The main chapter of *Principles of Social Reconstruction* is Chapter VII, "Religion and the Churches". In 45 I explained Russell's account of human nature in this book in terms of instinct, mind, and spirit. For his account of human motivation only impulse and desire are required. "Only passion can control passion, and only a contrary impulse or desire can check impulse" (p. 12). This basis to human nature is Spinoza's E4P7, already cited in 16. Whereas desire involves an interval of time before satisfaction (p. 13), impulse demands immediate action. Impulses are of two kinds: possessive and creative. Possessive impulses inspire activities that, by definition, cannot be shared; creative impulses lead to activities that all men may enjoy in common.[33] Scope for following impulse is intimately connected with breaking down the walls of the ego, of the hard, separate individuality typical of persons in modern society (p. 29). The destruction of such walls is impossible, it seems, in the absence of that "organic society" in which our goods are interdependent. Russell's theory of man includes another important Spinozistic component. As quoted in 27, Russell in 1922 claims that Spinoza's theory of human nature is identical to his own. The component in this case is the "principle of growth"—in Spinoza's theory, *conatus*—which Russell describes as "an instinctive urging leading them [men] in a certain direction, as trees seek the light" (p. 24). Because of what follows, this aspect of Russell's theory of man could easily classify him as a self-realizationist of the narrow variety:

> This intimate centre in each human being is what imagination must apprehend if we are to understand him intuitively. It differs from man to man, and determines for each man the type of excellence of which he is capable. The utmost that social institu-

tions can do for a man is to make his own growth free and vigorous: they cannot force him to grow according to the pattern of another man.... in the main, the impulses which are injurious to others tend to result from thwarted growth, and to be least in those who have been unimpeded in their instinctive development. (P. 25)

That he cannot be so classified has been discussed in the previous chapter. Russell's emphasis is on the growth of the wider self, not the narrower.

In other chapters of *Principles of Social Reconstruction* Russell covers the state, war, property, education, marriage, and "What We Can Do" ("Utopia", as he called it in an outline sent to C. K. Ogden on 31 July 1915). His analysis of patriotism in terms of the "joyful merging of the individual life in the life of the nation" is intriguing. He finds patriotism unsatisfactory in the end because of its lack of universality. For "[w]hen once men have learnt to subordinate their own good to the good of a larger whole, there can be no valid reason for stopping short of the human race" (p. 57).[34] Many of the terms employed in 1910–12 are present. For example, "reverence", which is given an impersonal application: "the principle of *reverence* [is] that the life of another has the same importance which we feel in our own life" (p. 227). Reverence also features in the principle of growth in Russell's philosophy of education:

> The man who has reverence will not think it his duty to "mould" the young. He feels in all that lives, but especially in human beings, and most of all in children, something sacred, indefinable, unlimited, something individual and strangely precious, the growing principle of life, an embodied fragment of the dumb striving of the world. (P. 147)

The constancy with which Russell held the principle of reverence is apparent in *The Conquest of Happiness* (1930): "... a respect for the personality of the child—a respect which must be not merely a matter of principle, whether moral or intellectual, but something deeply felt with almost mystical conviction to such a degree that possessiveness and oppression become utterly impossible" (p. 203). The principle informs Russell's philosophy of education in *Principles* and later works such as *On Education* (1926). In *Principles* thought is given an important role, as we would suspect, in its ability to bring "vast regions" to a person's attention and to break down "the prison walls of the commonplace" (p. 164). The chapter on "Marriage and the Population Question" applies the ethic of impersonal self-enlargement to personal love. Unless "the hard walls of the Ego" (p. 188) are broken down, "all real mingling of personalities" (p. 190) is impossible, leaving "[t]he fundamental loneliness into which we are born ... untouched" (p. 191). Russell here uses the same word ("mingling") for the intercourse of personalities as Spinoza does for the intercourse of bodies (see Chapter III, n. 33). In *The Conquest*, in speaking of sexual relations based on love, he claims that "... the whole personality of both becomes merged in a new collective personality" (p. 185) and that a person need not feel himself "a hard separate entity like a billiard-ball" (p. 247). This concept of the wider moral self is essential to Russell's normative ethic and is part of the background to *Marriage and Morals* (1929), discussed in the next section.

The passage on mystic insight from *Principles* quoted in **44** was from the chapter "Religion and the Churches", which chiefly concerns the role of spirit in a harmonious individual. Spirit is the universalizing force of impersonal feeling, extending, e.g., sympathy for yourself to sympathy with others, and in every way "suggesting impersonal uses for force [i.e. instinct] of a kind that thought cannot discredit by criticism" (p. 210). The image of "enclosing walls" that must be broken down is used frequently. Even Russell's former ethic of pain makes an appearance. Thought mocks the exclusive life of instinct, but thought is not the highest wisdom, merely "the gateway of pain through which men pass to a new life, where instinct is purified and yet nourished by the deeper desires and insight of spirit" (p. 221). Finally, Russell contrasts his conception of spirit with that of traditional religion:

> The life of the spirit has suffered in recent times by its association with traditional religion, by its apparent hostility to the life of the mind, and by the fact that it has seemed to centre in renunciation. The life of the spirit demands readiness for renunciation when the occasion arises, but is in its essence as positive and as capable of enriching individual existence as mind and instinct are. It brings with it the joy of vision, of the mystery and profundity of the world, of the contemplation of life, and above all the joy of universal love. It liberates those who have it from the prison-house of insistent personal passion and mundane cares. It

gives freedom and breadth and beauty to men's thoughts and feelings, and to all their relations with others. It brings the solution of doubts, the end of the feeling that all is vanity. It restores harmony between mind and instinct, and leads the separated unit back into his place in the life of mankind. For those who have once entered the world of thought, it is only through spirit that happiness and peace can return. (Pp. 222-3)

In the final chapter Russell credits Spinoza for the "key of wisdom" (p. 245) he has used in *Principles* (quoted in 27). Although the terms are constantly shifting, it appears that the "intellectual love of God" is the concept underlying much of the ethic set out in *Principles*. The book ends by relating the ethic to the tragedy of the war then going on. In the war leaders, ". . . the life of the spirit is dead. If it were living, it would go out to meet the spirit in the young, with a love as poignant as the love of father or mother. It would be unaware of the bounds of self; their tragedy would be its own" (p. 248).

48 *The Conquest of Happiness* and *Marriage and Morals*

Despite its lengthy analysis of individual human nature, the purpose of *Principles of Social Reconstruction* was, as the title indicates, social salvation. Russell's "recipes"—his word—for personal salvation are to be found in *The Conquest of Happiness*. This work is personal in more than one sense. He claims that the recipes are those he himself has discovered to be successful (p. 9). Indeed, several incidents from his own life are used as examples, in slightly disguised fashion. Both his grandmothers are alluded to on page 37. There is an allusion to his own despair at the time of "The Free Man's Worship" and during his affair with Lady Ottoline, in that the despairing man "may camouflage his despair by religious phrases, or by the doctrine that contemplation is the true end of man" (p. 235). We may infer that contemplation is no longer valued quite as highly by Russell, though other evidence, such as the last chapter of *The Scientific Outlook*, shows Russell still valuing it considerably. A third example, in which Russell accounts for his early beliefs psychologically, concerns the plight of the emotional orphan (Russell lost his parents before the age of four):

The child from whom for any reason parental affection is withdrawn is likely to become timid and unadventurous, filled with fears and self-pity, and no longer able to meet the world in a mood of gay exploration. Such a child may set to work at a surprisingly early age to meditate on life and death and human destiny. He becomes an introvert, melancholy at first, but seeking ultimately the unreal consolations of some philosophy or theology.... Within the four walls of his library the timid student feels safe.... Such a man, if he had received more affection, would have feared the real world less, and would not have had to invent an ideal world to take its place in his beliefs. (P. 178)

The "four walls" represent the prison of the narrow ego. *The Conquest* is in fact a detailed practical application of Russell's ethic of impersonal self-enlargement. As I noted in 27, the debt to Spinoza is again made explicit. Russell asserts that the following is in essence little different from what Spinoza said:

A man who has once perceived, however temporarily and however briefly, what makes greatness of soul, can no longer be happy if he allows himself to be petty, self-seeking, troubled by trivial misfortunes, dreading what fate may have in store for him. The man capable of greatness of soul will open wide the windows of his mind, letting the winds blow freely upon it from every portion of the universe. He will see himself and life and the world as truly as our human limitations will permit; realizing the brevity and minuteness of human life, he will realize also that in individual minds is concentrated whatever of value the known universe contains. And he will see that the man whose mind mirrors the world becomes in a sense as great as the world. In emancipation from the fears that beset the slave of circumstance he will experience a profound joy, and through all the vicissitudes of his outward life he will remain in the depths of his being a happy man. (P. 226)

The happy man is one who has enlarged his interests in life beyond the merely personal. His desires include the satisfaction of others' desires. Sometimes he has achieved this state of being through personal love, to which there are two sides. On the one hand, "... love is able to break down the hard shell of the ego, since it is a form of biological cooperation in which the emotions of each are necessary to the fulfilment of the other's instinctive purposes" (p. 40). The other side is mystical and has "significance" for the subjective establishment of values: "I do not pretend that love in its highest form is common, but I do maintain that in its highest form it reveals values which must otherwise remain unknown, and has itself a value which is untouched by scepticism, although sceptics who are incapable of it may falsely attribute their incapacity to scepticism" (p. 41). The beneficial effect of love upon the ego is sufficient, according to Russell, to scuttle what he calls "solitary philosophies in the sense that the good is supposed to be something realizable in each separate person, not only in a larger or smaller society of persons" (p. 40).

In *Marriage and Morals* (1929) Russell elaborates on the impersonal value of love, "the principal means of escape from the loneliness which afflicts most men and women throughout the greater part of their lives" (p. 99). In breaking down "the hard walls of the ego", love, Russell actually asserts, produces "a new being composed of two in one". It is difficult to know how to understand this assertion.[35] However, it does undermine further the view that Russell holds that man is a permanently isolated individual, of which society is a simple compound. Indeed, he denies that personal individuality is an end in itself, which is support for impersonality, and he criticizes the great religions for their emphasis on individuality. The end is instead self-enlargement:

> ... love must feel the ego of the beloved person as important as one's own ego, and must realize the other's feelings and wishes as though they were one's own. That is to say, there must be an instinctive and not merely conscious extension of egoistic feeling so as to embrace the other person as well. (P. 102)

One of Russell's aims in *Marriage and Morals* is so to satisfy the sexual impulse that it no longer dominates the imagination. "The glutton, the voluptuary, and the ascetic are all self-absorbed persons whose horizon is limited by their own desires, either by way of satisfaction or by way of renunciation" (p. 228). (*Cf*. Spinoza on obsession, E4P44S, though he does not relate it directly to lack of impersonality.) Russell traces self-absorption to the thwarting of natural impulses instead of "the equal and balanced development of all the impulses essential to a happy life" (p. 229). The ethic advocated in this period is thus no longer one of renunciation, and in *Marriage and Morals* we find Russell arguing against his former ethic of pain. There is already too much sorrow in life to require more of it, despite the qualification that "a few rare spirits know how to transmute it" (p. 236). Evidently Russell is not totally rejecting his old ethic. Indeed, it seems to survive in his new ethic in the form of a considerable and often overlooked element of self-control.

49 Miscellaneous Ethical Writings, 1916–41

Although it is the public expression of Russell's normative ethic we are concerned to trace, it is sometimes useful to note private expressions of it. They help to show the unity of his ethical thought, and at the same time negate the possibility that he may have presented one face towards the world and another away from it. The love correspondences are particularly rich in the expression of the ethic of impersonal self-enlargement. We already know this in the case of the correspondence with Lady Ottoline Morrell. Another notable correspondence is that with Lady Constance Malleson. Very early in their relationship Russell tells her that

> ... there is a world of peace, and one can live in it and yet be active still over all that is bad in the world. Do you know how sometimes all the barriers of personality fall away, and one is free for all the world to come in—the stars and the night and the wind, and all the passions and hopes of men, and all the slow centuries of growth—and even the cold abysses of space grow friendly—"*E il naufrager m'è dolce in questo mare.*"[36] And from that moment some quality of ultimate peace enters into all one feels.... I cannot bear the littleness and enclosing walls of *purely* personal things—I want to live always open to the world, I want personal love to be like a beacon *fire* lighting up the darkness, not a timid refuge from the cold as it is very often. (29 Sept. 1916; *Autobiography*, vol. II, p. 75)

The image of the beacon fire was one Russell used often in corresponding with Lady Constance. It seldom appears in the public writings, but when it does we may assume its personal association. In *New Hopes for a Changing World* Russell writes impersonally of the duty that "the sages of our time" have to perform for posterity, as Boethius did in *The Consolations of Philosophy* when the Roman Empire was breaking up. They must "crystallize the achievements, the hopes and the ideals which have made our time great—to study them with monumental simplicity, so that they may shine like a beacon-light through the coming darkness" (p. 185–6). (The "coming darkness" is a reference to world nuclear war, which Russell considered likely.) Reasonable doubt as to whether Russell includes himself in the task is dispelled by his use of the personal image. Russell writes to Lady Constance several times on the matter of bringing calm into his life, clearly hoping she would provide it. He tries to achieve calm by consciousness of the great stretches of time and space, and by thinking of the abstract world which is timeless and passionless. He expands upon the sort of calm he seeks and its connection with his love for her in his letter of 28 August 1918 (which for copyright reasons cannot be quoted), telling her that her essence transcends the individual and belongs to the world's essence. We do not know what Lady Constance thought of being transcendentally eternal. No doubt she had never had a lover attracted impersonally to her.

During his prison term in World War I Russell wrote excellent reflective letters to other people, including one to Gladys Rinder,[37] who worked for the No-Conscription Fellowship. This letter has Russell's sole mention of the "intellectual love of God" without Spinoza's name in conjunction with it.

> Is it not odd that people can in the same breath praise "the free man's worship" and find fault with my views on the war? The free man's worship is merely the expression of the pacifist outlook when it was new to me.... How could any one, approving the free man's worship, expect me to join in the trivial self-righteous moral condemnation of the Germans? All moral condemnation is utterly against the whole view of life that was then new to me but is now more and more part of my being.... There is a possibility in human minds of something mysterious as the night-wind, deep as the sea, calm as the stars, and strong as Death, a mystic contemplation, the "intellectual love of God." Those who have known it cannot *believe* in wars any longer, or in any kind of hot struggle. If I could give to others what has come to me in this way, I could make them too feel the futility of fighting. But I do not know how to communicate it: when I speak, they stare, applaud, or smile, but do not understand. (30 July 1918; *Autobiography*, vol. II, p. 89)

Russell is here linking his pacifism, "The Free Man's Worship", and the "intellectual love of God". The connection must lie in the nature of the "mystic contemplation" Russell experienced in 1901 and the *sub specie aeternitatis* outlook of those who enjoy the intellectual love of God. Perhaps the connection is that the mystical outlook makes moral outrage impossible psychologically, and hence the conflict that is the result of condemnation.

There are many writings that could be cited in ensuing years. For example, "'Useless' Knowledge" states that "It is from large perceptions combined with impersonal emotion that wisdom most readily springs" (*In Praise of Idleness* [1935], p. 45). *Power* (1938) embodies an unexpectedly strong normative ethical element. The ethic of impersonal self-enlargement is in full bloom. Russell is concerned with what he calls "the great ethical innovators". They have been men such as Buddha, Christ, Pythagoras and Galileo (p. 271): "they have been men who *desired* more, or, to be more acccurate, men whose desires were more impersonal and of larger scope than those of average men" (p. 247). Russell ascribes to such men an "impersonal ethic" based on a (Humean) universal sympathy, which he calls "the analogue, in the realm of feeling, of impersonal curiosity in the realm of intellect; both alike are essential elements in mental growth" (p. 250). Russell might, we are sure, have instanced Spinoza with Buddha and Christ in the above list of ethical innovators. In discussing the kind of power they sought, Russell comments:

> No one of the four sought the kind of power that enslaves others, but the kind that sets them free—in the case of the first two, by showing how to master the desires that lead to strife, and thence to defeat and slavery and subjection; in the case of the second two, by pointing the way towards control of natural forces. It is not ultimately by violence that men are ruled, but by the wisdom of those who appeal to the common desires of mankind, for happiness, for inward and outward peace, and for the understanding of the world in which, by no choice of our own, we have to live. (P. 272)

The idea of self-enlargement has now been found in a variety of writings over many years, but one kind of writing we have not yet examined is the popular article. The next writing falling into this category is titled "On Keeping a Wide Horizon" (1941). It was to be published by the *Reader's Digest*, but the version published there bears little resemblance to what Russell submitted.[38] Russell sets for himself the problem of combating despair in a world full of murderous strife. The solution to the problem is the contemplation of larger matters, and there are larger matters than even a world war: "Everyone agrees that we should not be self-centred, relating everything that happens to ourselves, making ourselves the centre of the universe. But it is also, to a lesser degree, a defect of imagination to make mankind the centre of the universe, or to attempt to measure eternity with a clock" (p. 7). He then cites examples of what he himself contemplates in order to achieve perspective—e.g. the slow growth of a mountain range—and to change "present pain . . . into the larger emotion of tragedy" (p. 8). Despite the impersonality of the examples, he has found them of use in everyday life. Contemplation of them must be sure, he adds, to issue in action. There is enough "vague benevolence" in the world; but "a great deal of it is ineffective for lack of other and more difficult virtues" (p. 10). These more difficult virtues include respect for fact and evidence. While the ethic presented is by no means Russell's complete one, there are sufficient elements of it to make it recognizable.

50 *New Hopes for a Changing World*, *Human Society in Ethics and Politics* and Later Writings

Russell was nearly 80 when *New Hopes for a Changing World* was published. The purpose of the book is topical, and for this reason it has been ignored since shortly after its publication. But the familiar philosophy of man and the Spinozistic language are again present, and the solutions provided for its topical concerns are not themselves topical. "I think there is a view of man and his destiny and his present troubles which can give certainty and hope together with the completest understanding of the moods, the despairs, and the maddening doubts that beset modern men" (p. 5). What he has to offer man is "a way of life", "a way of thinking and feeling" (p. 10), that he says is "scarcely to be called an ethic" (p. 11). (However, we saw in 1 that in *Power* he defined "ethic" in precisely this way.) The way of life recommended is presented casually—for Russell is not writing a philosophical treatise—and of course without my label of "impersonal self-enlargement". In 31 I quoted from *New Hopes* a passage about Spinoza and living in eternity, which I said came in the middle of a discussion of the self. Here is the context of that passage:

While Russia under-estimates the individual, there are those in the West who unduly magnify the separateness of separate persons. No man's ego should be enclosed in granite walls: its boundaries should be translucent. The first step in wisdom, as well as in morality, is to open the windows of the ego as wide as possible. Most people find little difficulty in including their children within the compass of their desires.... But it is not enough to enlarge our sympathies to embrace our own country. If the world is ever to have peace it will be necessary to learn to embrace the whole human race in the same kind of sympathy which we now feel toward our compatriots. And if we are to retain calm and sanity in difficult times, it is a great help if the furniture of our minds contains past and future ages. (P. 187)

[Then follow the two paragraphs on Spinoza, among four other paragraphs.]

I do not mean that the man who is freed from the tyranny of unwisdom will be destitute of emotion—on the contrary, he will feel friendship, benevolence and compassion in a higher degree than the man who has not emancipated himself from personal anxieties. His ego will not be a wall between him and the rest of mankind. He will feel, like Buddha, that he cannot be completely happy while anybody is miserable. He will feel pain—a wider and more diffused pain than that of the egoist—but he will not find the pain unendurable. He will not be driven by it to invent comfortable fairy tales which assure him that the sufferings of others are illusory.... (P. 190)

... Every one of us can enlarge his mind, release his imagination and spread wide his affection and his benevolence. (Pp. 190–1)

Occasionally I have quoted passages in which Russell seems to be applying his normative ethic to political philosophy. There are two thrusts in this direction. The removal of the wall of separation between individuals has the corollary that humans need one another for their full realization. Second, the broadening, or the universalizing, of the scope of our desires has as its limit the whole of humanity. The concept of the individual involved here is more appropriate to a socialistic position than a liberal one. But as this study will stop short of political philosophy, we shall explore the political implications of Russell's ethic no further. The ethic applies first to the individual, to whom we must now return.

The wise man will eventually face the prospect of his personal death. Russell's recommended attitude to this problem is well known.

The usual quotation from *New Hopes* is the following: "An individual human existence should be like a river—small at first, narrowly contained within its banks, and rushing passionately past boulders and over waterfalls. Gradually the river grows wider, the banks recede, the waters flow more quietly, and in the end, without any visible break, they become merged in the sea, and painlessly lose their individual being" (p. 210).[39] While this conveys the idea of expansion of self, the preceding sentence in Russell's text makes the concept much clearer, and brings it into harmony with Russell's normative ethic: "The best way to overcome it [the fear of death]—so at least it seems to me—is to make your interests gradually wider and more impersonal, until bit by bit the walls of the ego recede, and your life becomes increasingly merged in the universal life" (*ibid.*). The wise man in *New Hopes* is identical to the happy man in *The Conquest*.

Human Society in Ethics and Politics (1954) is chiefly metaethical and political. It does, however, involve the normative ethic I have identified. There is much concern, at the metaethical level, with the scope of desires. Religions have generally aimed at universality, but "it has remained an aspiration of a few philosophers and saints."[40] We do not know whom Russell includes among the saints, but we are sure that Spinoza is among the philosophers. There is an interesting illustration of the intuitionist metaethic Russell does not quite succeed in believing. He is concerned with the notion of objective rightness. If it is an indefinable notion, its truth will have to be vouched for by intuition. Russell says that he may claim that he knows by intuition that "the objectively right act is that which probably does most to promote the general good" (p. 81). This is not logically refutable, and on another occasion Russell declares he is not prepared to reject decisively another intuitively "known" theory (p. 111). But if an opponent in argument wishes to substitute for "the general good" the good of a group of narrower scope, Russell says that he can only resort to "vulgar abuse" and reply:

> "Sir, you are misusing terms. Ethical intuition is a noble faculty, of which you are evidently destitute. It is a faculty which teaches disinterestedness, which requires you to get outside Self and view the world with God-like impartiality. It is in the sphere of action what the scientific outlook is in the sphere of thought. But as for you, you are earth-bound, you are fettered to the accidents of your birth, you are a grovelling wretch incapable of emancipation from bondage to the *here* and *now*." (P. 81)

This is hardly, as we have learned in the present chapter, vulgar abuse from Russell. Besides its reiteration of the role of impartiality, it supports the continued reliance of Russell's ethic on the family of experiences variously called "intuition", "insight" and "mystic illumination".

Impersonality of viewpoint as an ingredient of wisdom is reiterated in the broadcast talk "Knowledge and Wisdom".[41] In the same article there is the statement that "Hatred of evil is itself a kind of bondage to evil" (p. 163). Russell is here agreeing with Spinoza on the nature of hatred as a passion (E4P45). A second broadcast article, reprinted in the same volume, is more explicit. We have already noted (in 31) that "A Philosophy for Our Time"[42] instances Spinoza with respect to "the impersonal kind of feeling that philosophy should generate" (p. 170). Philosophy has the function of developing impersonality in the two spheres of thought and feeling:

> Our desires, like our senses, are primarily self-centred. The egocentric character of our desires interferes with our ethics. In the one case, as in the other, what is to be aimed at is not a complete absence of the animal equipment but the addition to it of something wider, more general, and less bound up with personal circumstances.... Ethics, like science, should be general and should be emancipated, as far as this is humanly possible, from tyranny of the here and now.... (P. 168)
>
> If we could feel in our moments of vision as impersonally as a man of science can think, we should see the folly of our divisions and contests, and we should soon perceive that our own interests are compatible with those of others but are not compatible with the desire to bring others to ruin. (Pp. 169–70)

The man who can think and feel impersonally can conquer what is perhaps the worst emotion in Russell's view, namely fear. For fear is dependent on feeling yourself in personal danger, and fear leads to dogmatic conclusions and fanaticism by inhibiting the exercise of impersonal thought and feeling.

One of the last, and best, expressions of Russell's normative ethic is in a popular article of 1959, "The Expanding Mental Universe".[43] In it he does not claim originality for his ethic:

> Seers and poets have long had visions of the kind of expansion of the ego which I am trying to adumbrate. They have taught that

men are capable of something which is called wisdom, something which does not consist of knowledge alone, or of will alone, or of feeling alone, but is a synthesis and intimate union of all three. (*Basic Writings*, p. 397)

Growth in feeling and in knowledge is God-like. But if we had the complete impartiality of God, we could not survive.[44] This point is similar to the one Pater makes in the story Russell read in 1894 (see **16**). Russell follows the actual Spinoza, and not the one of Pater's imagination, in pointing to the instinct for self-preservation as the limiting factor to impersonality. (It is not that they say that we *should* refrain from self-sacrifice, but that we almost always *will* do so.) The value of impersonality is as against the "petty" obstructions in our immediate environment:

But it is possible, and authentic wise men have proved that it is possible, to live in so large a world that the vexations of daily life come to feel trivial and that the purposes which stir our deeper emotions take on something of the immensity of our cosmic contemplations. Some can achieve this in a greater degree, some only in a lesser, but all who care to do so can achieve this in some degree and, in so far as they succeed in this, they will win a kind of peace which will leave activity unimpeded but not turbulent. (P. 397)

This is the calm combined with action that Russell was seeking in his letter to Lady Constance cited in **49**. And although Spinoza is not named, we feel that he must be among the "authentic wise men" of this passage.

The last writing I wish to consider is "The Duty of a Philosopher in This Age", composed in 1964 when Russell was 92. The essay begins in very dour fashion about the duties, if any, of philosophers. "The only way", Russell says, "in which a philosopher can be considered to have a special duty is through the persuasiveness that he may derive from his knowledge and his preoccupations and from such respect as he may command."[45] An early conclusion is that "There is no reason why people subjected to this discipline [that of academic philosophy] should be specially wise or specially noble" (*ibid*.). The only philosopher Russell singles out for praise is Locke, because he sought the temper of mind that issues in tolerance. One thing a philosopher can do is "teach that everything good is bound up with life and that in a lifeless universe there would be neither good nor bad" (p. 17). Another duty of the philosopher "is to persuade mankind that human life is worth preserving and that an opposite view is only open to fanatics" (p. 18). You may wonder why this is a special duty of philosophers. The answer comes a little later, though on the basis of writings already examined we should expect it to be awarded greater priority:

> How, in our modern world, should a philosopher live? Some of the lessons of philosophy are ancient and timeless. He should endeavour to view the world, as far as he is able, without a bias of space and time, without more emphasis on the here and now than upon other places and other times. When he considers the world in which he has to live, he must approach it as if he were a stranger imported from another planet. Such impartiality is a part of the duty of the philosopher at all times. (P. 20)

Thus Russell's penultimate contribution to philosophy[46] still contains the familiar idea of impersonality in thought ("impartiality" here). I have, however, omitted what Russell says here about suspending philosophical activity and replacing it with agitation against the prospect of nuclear war. John G. Slater, in reviewing the essay, claims that it is uncharacteristic of Russell to recommend that the philosopher suspend his essential attitude of impartial contemplation and "focus on the here and now at least until the future is assured".[47] Slater "doubts that Spinoza, who also lived in very uncertain times but maintained his detachment, would agree" (p. 57). In reply, we cannot say what Spinoza would do in response to the threat of universal annihilation, but we may note that he was not above political action himself. There is the incident of the De Witt brothers, and as well his authorship of writings on political philosophy that he knew must be politically dangerous for him. With Russell, the case is different. We know that he views the existence of good as connected with the existence of human beings. Since contemplative activity is a good, you might expect philosophers to take steps to preserve the possibility of that activity, if not for themselves, then for succeeding generations. But there is a greater consideration. Russell does not hold that contemplation should be carried on to the exclusion of action. He holds, rather, that it should lead to action, and that the action to which it can lead is superior because it is informed by the philosopher's impersonal vision. To those persons trained in philosophy who answer Russell's call, it is not a matter of leaving philosophy altogether, much less of putting aside the emotional and cognitive attitudes gained in the study of philosophy. It is of first importance to use those attitudes by continually invoking the perspective in which the termination of man's existence can be given due weight.[48]

51 Summary

Our task in this chapter has been to show that Russell's normative ethic is one of impersonal self-enlargement. We had seen that he derives something of what he considers great value from Spinoza, but, apart from his writings on Spinoza, we had little evidence by which to judge Spinoza's influence on Russell's own ethic. The influence, we suspected, would be exercised chiefly through the concept of the intellectual love of God. In this chapter we examined Russell's fundamental writings in normative ethics from 1902 to 1964. Throughout them all—after 1910—is a concern to achieve impersonality, in both reason and emotion. Except for the first and last writings studied, a somewhat elastic notion of the self is explicit. The person who is living best is one whose ego is enlarged in both the cognitive and emotional directions. The wider the scope of your vision, the wiser you are likely to be. By forgetting self, a kind of union with the world is achieved. In the final chapter I shall formulate the ethic of impersonal self-enlargement more precisely and subject it to a critical evaluation.

CHAPTER VII

Evaluation of a Normative Ethic

52   Introduction: Normative Ethics

We have been investigating Spinoza's influence on Russell's conception of the moral self and trying to identify the latter's ethic. Why should the concept, "impersonal self-enlargement", involve an ethic? Can impersonal self-enlargement be regarded as a doctrine "not of specific duties, but of a way of life, a manner of thinking and feeling, from which it will become plain, without the need of rules, what must be done on each occasion"[1]? Is the ethic an "organic whole of extra-rational decisions"? We would naturally say that Schweitzer held an ethic of reverence for life. Is it equally appropriate to talk of an ethic of self-enlargement? How should we act in accordance with it? Russell might say that we should act in such a way as to give others' interests equal weight with our own. Yet the obligatory nature of this statement can lead to a mischaracterization of the ethic. We should be careful not to see Russell as speaking in terms of moral duties here. Russell's ethic is a means of fostering generosity and rationality among mankind. The ethic concerns the appropriateness to human conduct of feeling and thinking in a certain way about your own and other persons' interests, the impersonal or impartial way. The egocentric focus of desire is so broadened as, in its limiting case, to include all of humanity. With the egocentric, or personal, focus so enlarged, your desires can be called "impersonal". Your self is so enlarged that you consider others' interests with your own. It is "others", however, without distinction to friend and foe, though that distinction may be a stimulus of self-enlargement in the beginning. In addressing the nuclear peril at a time when near-universal annihilation had become a possibility, Russell enjoins, "Remember your humanity, and forget the rest."[2]

The conception of a normative ethic as a way of life is a broad one. Nevertheless, consider this precedent from Hampshire in his *Two*

Theories of Morality, in which he compares the ethic of Aristotle with that of Spinoza:

> This conception of a way of life has to include some social ideal, more or less detailed, depending on the priority that is given to political activities and to social usefulness. It includes also habits of behaviour and manners, observances, rituals of behaviour, which are not so much direct expressions of explicit moral beliefs as expressions of unstated moral attitudes and which can often be identified with difficulty. The term "way of life" has to be vague if only because it represents not only explicit ideals of conduct, deliberately chosen, but also ideals which have not been made explicit, or formulated, and which may be expressions of not fully conscious preferences, feelings, and ambitions.[3]

It should be noted that an ethic is not to be identified with a style of life; a particular life-style may be morally neutral. Impersonal self-enlargement falls within Hampshire's conception of an ethic, though it is less detailed rather than more. As an ethic, impersonal self-enlargement provides a sufficient guide for living. Russell himself regarded what I have identified as his ethic as "a manner of thinking and feeling", "scarcely to be called an ethic, at any rate in the old acceptation of that word, but something which, nonetheless, will save men from moral perplexity and from remorse and from condemnation of others" (*New Hopes*, p. 17). It is an attitude to life which, if adopted, has consequences for both major and minor matters. It has at least one distinguished ancestor in Spinoza and therefore a place in monistic ethics; and it bears family resemblances to other doctrines.

In our critical summary of the ethic, we shall, for two reasons, depart from Russell's text to discuss the ethic on its own terms. One reason is that Russell never sets out the ethic systematically, leaving to others even its identification as well as its development. The other reason is that ideas, like children, have lives of their own, not entirely predictable or controllable by their parents. Anyone is at liberty to develop the implications of another's idea, and "impersonal self-realization" requires our taking this liberty for its full appreciation. It would be astonishing to have an entirely new ethic at this late stage of man's experience with the conflicts he generates for himself. Medical and environmental ethics, for example, are not new "ways of living" or of treating people or animals or things, but merely now more deeply worked areas of concern because of the development of technology.

Russell's ethic does not, in fact, offer new solutions to standard primary problems. The two solutions to the primary problem of conflict are already well known: be more generous, think of others, put yourself in the position of those who will experience the suffering you may inflict; and improve the balance of power. What the ethic of impersonal self-enlargement offers is principally a way of *encouraging* the growth of generous feeling and dispassionate thinking. In other words, Russell is attacking the secondary problem of getting more of us to act in accordance with such an old-fashioned maxim as "love thy neighbour as thyself", suitably modified by respect for self-preservation. Evaluation itself is also something Russell himself never provides for the ethic. Nevertheless, he does (as we saw in **6**) provide general criteria for the evaluation of an ethic, and in our evaluation we shall employ these as well as other criteria. I do not myself entirely agree with the ethic, as will be seen from discussions of the criteria. The ethic has a systematic weakness to it, which I discuss under criterion (13). It is possible, however, that this weakness can be overcome. My main objections to the ethic are set out in **60**. However, as I cannot think of a more appropriate ethic for overcoming the pervasiveness of conflict, which threatens to end human life and that of many other species on earth, my own attitude to the ethic is one of restrained approval.

53 Critical Summary of Russell's Ethic

In characterizing the ethic of impersonal self-enlargement, we shall begin with Russell's central ethical problem. That problem is conflict—conflict among the desires of the individual, and among the dominant desires of different individuals. Russell finds no way of knowing that one desire or individual has a greater right to domination than any other. Though he may feel a strong sense of obligation to do this or that, the non-cognitivist holds that he cannot know, even fallibly, that a given feeling of obligation is more than a personal preference, no matter how widely it is shared. In this non-cognitivist framework Russell is determined to act on his own desire to prevent conflict and produce harmony. He does not *know* that he should act to minimize conflict; he sees merely that great suffering is the result of conflict and he "longs to alleviate the evil" (*Autobiography*, vol. I, prologue).[4] His problem is practical, not theoretical. Even if he could have produced an infallible treatise demonstrating that you *ought* to consider others' interests equally with your own, he knew that its practical effect would be minimal. At best, a few philosophical readers would be convinced, and possibly a few of their non-philosophical friends would be influenced in their way of living. Instead of providing a complex cognitivist treatise, therefore, Russell seeks a simple doctrine, one capable of practical effects. The price of simplicity in philosophy is usually non-acceptance, but in formulating a way of life simplicity is a requirement for popular acceptance. Since Russell's effort in normative ethics is directed to the formation of a non-cognitivist ethic, he has to forgo the element of inescapability or obligation that is intended to accompany an ethic such as Kant's. Instead, therefore, of concentrating upon the avoidance of conflict through pointing out some obligation or other, he emphasizes the enlargement of the scope of your desires so that, in taking the satisfaction of others' interests into account, less conflict will ensue. He concentrates also upon the growth of rationality, confident that much conflict can be avoided through the recognition of enlightened self-interest (taking "self" in the narrow sense).[5]

In discussing his substitution of "satisfaction of interest" for "pleasure" in his naturalistic approach to defining "good", Russell enlarges on the concept of satisfaction. We often derive satisfaction from fulfilling desires to act in ways that are not in our narrow self-interest. Nor do we act thus in order to feel the pleasure of such satisfaction. What is primary is the desire: " . . . the pleasure is due to the desire, not the desire to the expected pleasure" (*Human Society*, p. 146). The supreme ethical problem—at any rate, for this non-cognitivist—is to instill or foster that group of desires whose satisfaction is greater than that of any other group.[6] In this way conflict will be reduced. The less that desires are narrowly selfish, the greater the chance of their compossibility. Let us examine more closely the notion of unselfish desires. Russell writes:

> It is customary among moralists to urge what is called "unselfishness" and to represent morality as consisting mainly of self-abnegation. This view, it seems to me, springs from a failure to realize the wide scope of possible desires. Few people's desires are wholly concentrated upon themselves. Of this there is abundant evidence in the prevalence of life-insurance. Every man, of necessity, is actuated by his own desires, whatever they may be, but there is no reason why his desires should all be self-centred. Nor is it always the case that desires concerned with other people

will lead to better actions than those that are more egoistic. A painter, for example, may be led by family affection to paint pot-boilers, but it might be better for the world if he painted masterpieces and let his family suffer the discomforts of comparative poverty. It must be admitted, however, that the immense majority of mankind have a bias in favour of their own satisfactions, and that one of the purposes of morality is to diminish the strength of this bias. (*Human Society*, p. 146)

To "widen the scope of desires" means to make them less self-centred. (This is "self" in the narrow sense.) Satisfaction of desires of wider scope is intended to benefit more than one person. The widest possible scope a desire can have at present for other persons is for the whole human race. A desire for the survival of the human species—and for the longevity of its present members—is the most compossible desire there is, since it is compossible with more desires than any other.[7]

The heart of the ethic of impersonal self-enlargement is the universalization of the case you make for yourself. Such a universalization is not, however, like the kind involved in applying the categorical imperative—that it is your duty to act in such a way that you are willing that anyone in your place should act similarly. Russell's ethic does not refer to duties. There is no intended obligation to selflessness, except derivatively or instrumentally. Impersonal self-enlargement has its positive basis in feeling, not reason, except in the calculation of consequences. The impersonal standpoint has long been recognized in ethics, though not in metaethics. Your utterances, in order to qualify as moral, must be impersonal. Kant saw this; in our own day, the universalizability principle is a major part of Hare's prescriptivism.

As discussed in 4, Russell's own metaethical analysis contains a principle of universality, or impersonality. It has been, however, the subject of a formidable criticism. D. H. Monro notices that, as only impersonal desires are to be called "moral", impersonality becomes a defining characteristic: "... the man who genuinely wants to make exceptions in his own favour is ruled out, by definition. And to rule him out in this way is, in effect, to assume the objective validity of a basic principle: that one ought not to make exceptions in one's own favour."[8] Monro's point is, or should be, well taken. It may be right for someone, sometime, to make an exception in his own favour on personal grounds, and a mere stipulative definition should not preclude his being right. Monro's point is not to be identified with the Kantian view that the universalizability principle allows me to make an exception in my favour providing that I am willing that you be permitted to make an exception in your favour. On this understanding, the world's best pickpocket need not proscribe pickpocketing, since he will always show a profit in spite of having his own pocket picked, and he will have acted on a maxim that he can will to become a universal law of nature (the first formulation of the categorical imperative). Monro's point is against universalizability itself. He objects to defining "ethics" so as to exclude the possibility of non-universalizable exceptions. This criticism worries Russell only on the metaethical level, however. In practical ethics, he is looking for ways of reducing conflict, and the road to conflict-prevention he has determined to lie in the impersonal approach to both thinking and feeling.

Let us formulate the central notion involved in impersonal self-enlargement as follows:

> The ego (or self) can be expanded to take others' interests into account with our own, as if they were our own.

When Russell uses the term "ego" in his normative ethic, he is not using it in the same sense that he does as a philosopher of mind. Indeed, as indicated by the alternative ways of expressing the ethic, Russell can replace the term "ego" and rephrase the above formulation by such statements as

> We can approach valuing others as much as ourselves,

or The personal focus in desire can be so widened as to include the (narrow) interests of other people.

Through the impersonal enlargement of self purely personal desires are muted or overcome, and even transformed into desires on behalf of others. The personal enlargement of self is also possible, in the sense that egoistic desires can be strengthened. The employment of reason is crucially important in some attainments of impersonality, for to convince another by argument usually involves considerations designed to appeal to any rational agent. We are all subject to attacks of impulsive desires, and while Russell awards a high place to the frequent following of impulse, he by no means grants complete freedom to it. Take, for example, indignation.[9] The kind of indignation Russell and Spinoza oppose is the personal and obsessive kind. Spinoza defines "indignation" as "hatred towards those who have injured others" (E3Df.Aff.20). A man is unbalanced if he pursues one object to the exclusion of all others, and while we are in bondage to indignation we think of the supposed cause of our indignation to the exclusion of all else. Such bondage prevents rational, i.e. impartial, appraisal of the object, and reduces our quality of life during its hold on us. It also reduces our effectiveness in combating the cause of the particular case of indignation. Even cases of justified personal indignation are best dealt with impersonally; otherwise we are giving vent to hatred, from which good rarely comes (in Spinoza, never—E4P45).

The case of indignation leads to the more general problem of obsession, which Russell calls "fanaticism". Fanaticism is the giving of exclusive attention to any sole supposed cause of a situation when disinterested observers would say there is a strong case for a plurality of causes. In Russell's view, fanaticism is the result of the intrusion of self in examining a state of affairs, causing an unbalanced appraisal of that state instead of one unbiased by the desire for a certain kind of result. Obsessional states have their value, however. They often lead to heightened productivity. In the familiar task of having to write something, it may be difficult to begin, but once a substantial beginning is made, the mind seems to dwell on both the subject-matter and the task of completing the job, providing a kind of obsessional groove in which you are carried along to complete the task. The degree of obsession is subject to some control by the individual involved. But the immediate social effects of even controlled obsession or fanaticism are painful ones, and of uncontrolled obsession potentially disastrous.[10]

The unselfishness, or generosity of spirit, advocated in Russell's ethic is not complete unselfishness. Human nature sees to the impracticality of that. Spinoza identified the limiting factor as *conatus*, the desire to strive, or keep on living, in other words self-preservation. Self-preservation prevents almost all self-sacrifice. Probably if we really regarded ourselves as merely one among a number of others, we would have not only less respect for the individual but also less sympathy for the sufferings of others. Indifference to your own suffering is concomitant with indifference to others', as the lives of some of the self-abnegating saints show. The impartiality at which we should aim in our thinking and feeling must not be the impartiality of indifference. One of Russell's better-known sayings is "The good life is one inspired by love and guided by knowledge" ("What I Believe", p. 372). Without the guidance of knowledge, love's actions may be irrational, in the sense of not being calculated to reach its goals. But without the inspiration of love, the impartiality exercised by rationality in its pursuit of knowledge would be indifferent to its ends.

The notion of impartiality used from time to time in setting out the ethic is a near-synonym of "impersonality". The latter term concerns persons directly, while the former does so only in application. When Russell uses the term in phrases such as "impartial reason" or "impartial love", he means that no unequal consideration is being given to oneself or anyone else. But "impartial" cannot replace "impersonal" in the phrase "impersonal self-enlargement". For what I intend to convey by the phrase is the expansion of your interests in ways that are not related to self-centredness, and hence the element of self, or of a particular personality, is diminished. Russell often calls this ability of man "divine". In doing so he is thinking of the impartiality of the vision attributed to a supreme being not limited to a particular time and place, and thus to a particular person or center of self. This vision is also impersonal in the sense that it may not be concerned with persons at all.

The attitude to life characterized by impersonal self-enlargement is claimed by Russell to be associated with a profound sense of peace, a pervasive inner calm. Explaining the association will involve a degree of assessment of the position now rather than later. The source of calm is ascribed partly to belief in "hard" determinism. "Soft" determinism, or compatibilism, is the doctrine that moral responsibility is compatible with the determination of our actions through motives and desires which are ultimately due to the external factors of heredity and environment. In the view that active emotions should, as far as possible, replace passive or external ones, Spinoza is a soft determinist, for he holds that man's freedom can be achieved that way.[11] Otherwise Spinoza is a hard determinist. Hard determinism sees no room for moral responsibility. The reasonable man will not, therefore, condemn or praise others for their actions. Hard determinism is also compatible with our intervention in the world, since we are part of the world (which is also Spinoza's position), but by and large the determinist views the world as unfolding as it must. Hope and regret[12] become somewhat foolish, though not entirely eradicable. Life becomes less fretful. But the peace of mind Russell derived from his ethic came more from his intellectual love of God than from an acceptance of hard determinism, although (as we saw in Chapter V) the intellectual love of God involves the contemplation of that which has been intellectually ordered—a class of things that includes a determined world. Determinism is not to be confused with fatalism. It is possible to change people's behaviour, which is the aim of all moralists whether or not they are determinists. It is, therefore, legitimate for a determinist to advocate a change in behaviour. Our behaviour is in part a result of our beliefs, and to some extent our beliefs can be changed.

The moral benefit derived from not holding people responsible for their actions is that moral condemnation is not justified. We have noted Russell making this point. It makes for tolerance and removes the ground from some hatred of persons and indignation against them, and from reciprocal hatred and indignation. In illustration, let us take a person who continually offends us, personally or impersonally. A common attitude is one of increasing indignation to the point that his offences obsess us. A deterministic attitude would view such transgressions as to be expected. You say to yourself, "Well, that's the way he acts, and indeed that's the way a lot of people do and probably must act in such circumstances." In addition to not treating every moral situation as a new one, there is a second element, namely concentration upon removing the cause of the objectionable behaviour. It may be that the offender lacks the courage to behave morally. Courage is a quality that can be built up. The reforming determinist can, therefore, deal with some moral failures of individuals by attempting to build up the offender's courage instead of trying in effect to crush him through condemnation. And condemnation, in its tendency to create resentment, is often counter-productive.

The relationship of a deterministic attitude to peace of mind in the ethic of impersonal self-enlargement can now be shown. When you believe that things are happening as they must; when you view others' actions towards you and yours towards them as instances of their general behaviour, which has to be the way it is; and when, having put your self aside to do so, you attend to the laws describing their behaviour and yours, your attitude to your own alleged persecution or ill-treatment becomes a less strident one. When you view the entire cosmos as unfolding as it must because of antecedent conditions, then you can adopt a less fretful, even peaceful, attitude to the universe as past, present and even future. It becomes possible to acquiesce in what *has* happened in the universe. Because you understand how things have happened as they must, the impulse to wish things were otherwise is atrophied. There is no need to acquiesce in what merely *may* happen, however, because you are part of the cause of the future and you may seek to "intervene" in an objectionable train of events. Nevertheless, the determinist realizes that the scope of possible intervention is very limited for any individual. People behave as they do because of their characters, not because of a praise- or blameworthy choice they make in every moral situation. This realization reinforces acquiescence and contributes to peace of mind. Another contributor to calm in this ethic is absence of concern over mundane personal matters. Those who live a life of impersonal self-enlargement are not concerned with personal victories. (E.g., you do not try to get the best of every encounter. When Spinoza was the victim of a bad debt, he observed: "I must economize in order to make up this loss. At that price I buy tranquillity."[13]) You do not approach every meeting with extensive plans designed to save your own face if your proposals are all defeated. You do not evaluate proposals—others' or your own—on the basis of their impact on your position, but on their intrinsic merits—though personal impact in general is a factor to be weighed, as is total inability of yourself to live with a proposal. Evaluation of ideas and people on their intrinsic merits falls under the head of impartial, or impersonal, thinking. It is a revolutionary doctrine,[14] and to attempt its implementation would fill a lifetime with moral and political activity. Now, impersonal thought is strongly associated with Russell as one of his chief values. Its advocacy and celebration are traceable, in his educational writings, at least as far back as 1913, to "The Place of Science in a Liberal Education".[15] The possibility and value of impersonal thought are widely accepted. The possibility and value of impersonal feeling are not. And what has gone unrecognized is Russell's combination of the two into the ethic of impersonal self-enlargement.

Attention to the laws describing human behaviour is only one of the ways in which knowledge *per se* is important to impersonal self-enlargement. Growth in understanding results in growth of the impersonal side of self. Philosophical understanding is particularly important. Russell writes:

> ... philosophical knowledge, or rather philosophical thought, has certain special merits not belonging in an equal degree to other intellectual pursuits. By its generality it enables us to see human passions in their just proportions, and to realize the

absurdity of many quarrels between individuals, classes, and nations. Philosophy comes as near as possible for human beings to that large, impartial contemplation of the universe as a whole which raises us for the moment above our purely personal destiny. There is a certain asceticism of the intellect which is good as a part of life, though it cannot be the whole so long as we have to remain animals engaged in the struggle for existence. The asceticism of the intellect requires that, while we are engaged in the pursuit of knowledge, we shall repress all other desires for the sake of the desire to know. While we are philosophizing, the wish to prove that the world is good, or that the dogmas of this or that sect are true, must count as weaknesses of the flesh—they are temptations to be thrust on one side. But we obtain in return something of the joy which the mystic experiences in harmony with the will of God. This joy philosophy can give, but only to those who are willing to follow it to the end, through all its arduous uncertainties. (*An Outline of Philosophy*, pp. 310–11)

The philosopher's joy is the same as that of Spinoza's experiencing the intellectual love of God.

54 Related Theories

Impersonal self-enlargement does not stand in a conceptual vacuum. It has a place in the history of ethical theory, primarily as a self-realization or liberationist ethic, and there are related theories. It is necessary to distinguish two types of self-realization ethics. In discussing the ethic of Lord Byron and D. H. Lawrence in *A History of Western Philosophy*, Russell considers their assumption that self-realization—or "self-development"—is the fundamental principle of normative ethics, and rejects it on the ground that it is unrestrained egoism: "Man is not a solitary animal, and so long as social life survives, self-realization cannot be the supreme principle of ethics" (p. 684; p. 659).[16] I call the ethic Russell criticizes here self-realization or liberation of the "narrow" or "personal" type, and it accompanies self-enlargement in the narrow sense.[17] There is an element of narrow self-realization in Russell, in the "principle of growth" he outlines in *Principles of Social Reconstruction* (**47**). But that is far from the centre of his ethic. It is much more organicist than has been realized and leads to a mild form of collective self-realization. The element he emphasizes is the growth of the impersonal quality in each of us, which provides the type of self-realization I call "impersonal" and which has also been called "collective".

This conception of the moral self is a recognized one. Wayne Proudfoot distinguishes three conceptions of the self in philosophy of religion:[18] the monistic, individualistic and social conceptions. Proudfoot takes as representatives of each conception the theologians Paul Tillich and Austin Farrer and the philosopher Josiah Royce, respectively. The discussion of Tillich (with several references to Spinoza) places Russell's ethical concept of self squarely in the monistic tradition, which is what we should expect after discovering the Spinozistic origin of the concept in Russell. It is termed the tradition of the "centred self"—a use of terminology designed to distract attention from the question of external boundaries (p. 61)—in order to affirm an individualization in the manner of Spinoza without a plurality of substances. Proudfoot characterizes the monistic tradition further:

> The interpretation of man's knowledge of God as a participation in God's self-knowledge is a basic tenet of idealism. Being and knowing accrue to the finite individual through participation in divine being and knowing. In moments of shock or ecstasy men are afforded a glimpse of the divine ground that transcends the structure of subject and object. Such a glimpse is correlative with the experience of finitude. These moments are rare.... In the revelatory moment some image or person or event becomes transparent to the ground in which men recognize their own rootedness. (P. 52)

Proudfoot's investigation champions Royce's social conception of self, but his study is useful in strengthening the supposition that the origin of some of Russell's religious language lies with the idealist philosophers. While Spinoza discusses "self" very little, he too uses a conception best classified under impersonal self-realization. This is the realization of our potentiality to transcend purely personal interests. Of course, in so far as we have such a potentiality, it is part of our self and therefore not "impersonal". But that is to conflate two senses of "self", to ignore Russell's division of impulses and desires into those which are possessive or "selfish", and those which are creative.

The conception of an "enlargeable" moral self is not to be taken metaphysically. By "moral self" I mean little more than a collection of

54 Related Theories

interests and sympathies associated with one person. Understanding the moral self in this way helps to place Russell's ethic in the history of normative ethical theory. Russell rejects the Kantian moral self in favour of the benevolent self, in that it is the latter whose power he wishes to enlarge. Urging people to take an interest in the satisfaction of others' desires is, of course, not a new ethic to be found in Russell, though he develops it extensively. Compare, for example, the attitude to dying in Mill's *Utilitarianism* with Russell's attitude as quoted in 50. Mill writes: "... those who leave after them objects of personal affection, and especially those who have also cultivated a fellow-feeling with the collective interests of mankind, retain as lively an interest in life on the eve of death as in the vigour of youth and health. Next to selfishness, the principal cause which makes life unsatisfactory, is want of mental cultivation."[19] Mill is concerned to defend utilitarianism against the charge of impracticality. In his day and now there are philosophers who wish to limit the degree of unselfishness advocated in that ethic. There is, admittedly, the possibility of a tension between an ethic with a reasonable chance of adoption and one designed to remedy extensive evils. C. D. Broad and J. L. Mackie have tried to cut Mill's unselfish ethic down to size, by means of Broad's notion of "self-referential altruism".[20] Mackie defines it as "concern for others, but for others who have some special connection with oneself; children, parents, friends, workmates, neighbours in the literal, not the metaphorically extended sense."[21] Expecting people to act unselfishly outside this circle is foolish, for it will rarely happen. Yet on this basis conflicts on or approaching a global scale will remain unresolved. The defence that almost everyone who is a neighbour would be affected if a large, random selection of us acted with self-referential altruism is easily resisted, for we can never suppose that so many people will act in the way a given ethicist desires. Moreover, people without neighbours—such as isolated tribes—are ignored in this approach. The more serious difficulty with self-referential altruism is that it does not consider large enough groups of people. We cannot entrust the solution of wide social, economic and political problems to neighbourliness in the literal sense. Some element of submission of my interests or of the interests of others seems a necessary desideratum in matters of conflict. Russell's approach of thinking and feeling as impersonally as possible helps the individual to undergo such submission.

Viewing ethical disputes, like legal matters, without regard to persons is not unprecedented in the history of ethics. I mentioned the utilitarianism of Mill. Another utilitarian was Sidgwick, whose course on ethics Russell attended in 1893. Sidgwick has a maxim of benevolence, which he states as follows: "each one is morally bound to regard the good of any other individual as much as his own, except in so far as he judges it to be less, when impartially viewed, or less certainly knowable or attainable by him."[22] Sidgwick bases the maxim on two considerations, one of which is of interest to us. That consideration is "the self-evident principle that the good of any one individual is of no more importance, from the point of view (if I may say so) of the Universe, than the good of any other; unless, that is, there are special grounds for believing that more good is likely to be realised in the one case than in the other" (*ibid.*). The "viewpoint of the universe" is simply the viewing of things impersonally, without bias to particular persons. A key difference between Sidgwick and Russell is that the former holds that taking the impersonal viewpoint is a moral obligation, whereas the latter hopes merely for an increase in impartiality in respect to persons, through cultivation of the feeling involved.

It is worth taking a brief look at two contemporary theories involving the concept of impersonality. For, as Frankena notes, it appears that, except in relevant circumstances, you have "no business" using words like "right" and "good" unless you are willing to universalize.[23] An interesting application of the conception of impersonality is to be found in John Rawls' *A Theory of Justice*. To arrive at justice as fairness, or what social obligations we would adopt if we did not know our place in society, Rawls imagines a contractual origin to ethics. We put ourselves in what he calls the "original position" in order to vote on the rules. Even our personal characteristics and period in history are hidden from us behind a "veil of ignorance".[24] The purpose is the following:

> Thus it seems reasonable and generally acceptable that no one should be advantaged or disadvantaged by natural fortune or social circumstances in the choice of principles. It also seems widely agreed that it should be impossible to tailor principles to the circumstances of one's own case. We should insure further that particular inclinations and aspirations, and persons' conceptions of their good do not affect the principles adopted. The aim is to rule out those principles that it would be rational to propose for acceptance, however little the chance of success, only if one knew certain things that are irrelevant from the standpoint of

justice.... At any time we can enter the original position, so to speak, simply by following a certain procedure, namely, by arguing for principles of justice in accordance with these restrictions. (Pp. 18–19)

Later Rawls admits that the viewpoint of the original position is equivalent to that of rational deliberation (p. 138). In my view, the viewpoint of rational deliberation is equivalent to that of impersonal thinking. Rawls admits as much when he says that "we can view the choice in the original position from the standpoint of one person selected at random" (p. 139). It is not simply any person who may be selected, however, but any person stripped of his personal characteristics. One of the merits of Rawls's book is its strong awareness of predecessors in the positions it discusses. In connection with the notion of impartiality in ethics, Rawls discusses Kant and Mill at length. Of the notion of the "impartial sympathetic spectator" Rawls says that to Hume "it offered the only perspective from which moral judgments could be made coherent and brought into line" (p. 190).[25] Rawls holds that classical utilitarianism results "in impersonality, in the conflation of all desires into one system of desire" (p. 188), and contrasts it with the mere impartiality, instead of impersonality, of the persons in the original position. In making this contrast he distinguishes between the "disinterestedness", or impartiality, of those in the original position and the self-sacrificing altruism of the impersonal viewpoint. He claims that the original position assumes that individuals have conflicting desires, though they do not know whose desires conflict with whose. The reason is that there is no means of individuating persons in the original position other than numerically. There are just a number of copies of a single, bare "personality". But this rider collapses the distinction between impartiality and impersonality. For what Russell means by "impersonality" is the removal from consideration of qualities serving to particularize the individual. This is what Rawls's veil of ignorance accomplishes and what he admits in the above quotation from page 139.

This section on the place of impersonal self-enlargement in the history of ethical theory has focused on Russell's conception of the moral self and the role of impartiality in ethical feeling. Much more could be said on its place in formal ethical thought—e.g. with reference to Hare's principle of universalizability. But as the originality of Russell's position lies in the emotional rather than the cognitive sphere, I have concentrated on the former. It might seem relevant to discuss here Roderick Firth's theory of the "ideal observer",[26] but that theory depends upon a cognitivist metaethic. Briefly, the ideal observer is one who, being detached, can see the truth more easily than those involved in a moral problem. Firth takes as defining characteristics of the ideal observer: omniscience with respect to non-ethical facts, omnipercipience,[27] disinterestedness or impartiality, dispassionateness, consistency, and normality in other respects. He recognizes that "*any* ideal observer would react in the same way to a particular act" (p. 219) because of the elimination of all factors leading people to diverge in their ethical reactions. Firth asserts that these factors are eliminated from the "personality" of the ideal observer (p. 220), which is the admission to be expected. The ideal observer is impersonal. Independence of personal qualities gives him, not a better view of any supposed objective truth, but the viewpoint of long perspective. Many of our decisions, it is agreed, would be more rational if they were not made under the influence of temporary passions or egocentric desires. In Gilbert Harman's words, this amounts to a kind of "unbiased motivation",[28] though there must still be motivation.

55 Application of Russell's Evaluative Criteria

Evaluating a normative ethic within a non-cognitivist framework is different from evaluating one within a cognitivist framework. For under the assumption of cognitivism we need answer only the question, Is it true, or right? (though formulating and answering the precise question may be extremely difficult). Under the assumption of non-cognitivism the question of ultimate correctness cannot be answered. Instead of the criterion of truth, therefore, we must search for other criteria by which to judge a normative ethic. I shall, for the sake of argument, assume non-cognitivism here and proceed to assess Russell's position within that framework. It will be seen that many of the criteria are applicable to evaluating a cognitivist normative ethic. This is because cognitivism is sometimes unable to provide an infallibilist answer to the question of knowing the truth of an ethic. Hence the good reasons approach will be adopted in the two cases of fallibilist cognitivism and of non-cognitivism. In **6** we saw that Russell himself provides a set of criteria by which an ethic may be judged. I shall apply those criteria (and another he mentions elsewhere) to his own ethic in this section and in the next. In the following sections I shall apply other criteria and offer criticisms.

55 Application of Russell's Evaluative Criteria

In the passage quoted on Aristotle's ethic, Russell proposes the following criteria: (1) the ethic's self-consistency; (2) its consistency with the remainder of the author's views: (3) the consonancy with our own feelings of the ethic's answers to ethical problems. In judging Santayana's ethic Russell proposes the apparently additional criterion of the ethic's "importance". In view of Russell's subjectivist analysis of value terms, the question of an ethic's importance seems ultimately to fall under (3). However, as the question of importance raises matters I do not wish to discuss under (3), I shall deal with it separately as (4) in a new section (**56**).

(1) We have not so far observed logical contradictions in the statement of Russell's ethic. That, however, does not exhaust the criterion of internal consistency, for the question of the consistency of the effects of following the ethic may be included. Rawls, among others, suggests an argument to show that universal altruism would result in a stand-off. There would be no action taken, because everyone would be thinking of everyone else (*A Theory of Justice*, p. 189). The implication is that no serious problems would be tackled. But in reply we may say that there would *be* no serious problems because there would be no conflicts between persons. In fact, there would be no persons in the sense of distinct personalities, though in a world of scarce necessities, for example, there would still be competition between qualitatively identical but numerically distinct persons. The argument suggested by Rawls is trivial for Russell anyway, for impersonal self-enlargers need not be worried by the prospect of a world of totally unselfish persons. In fact, Russell's ethic includes such a strong respect for the desire for self-preservation[29] that perfect altruism is not recommended as a practical measure, and hence conflict among altruists need not be considered. (While Russell is an admirer of martyrs throughout history, his ethic does not include an obligation to sacrifice your life on behalf of others: self-sacrifice in the ultimate sense is an act of supererogation.) A second objection may be raised concerning the place of the desire for impartiality. In Russell himself this was an active desire, not merely a "neutral" attitude remaining when all "partial" desires had been removed. He warned Lady Ottoline of the overwhelming presence of this desire,[30] and in later life, when he admitted that love of England was "very nearly" his strongest emotion (*Autobiography*, vol. II, p. 17), we may take it that this desire was only overcome by the desire to be impartial. The view of the critic raising the objection must be that the truly impartial observer would be not disinterested but uninterested, and

therefore uncaring in his impartiality. In viewing the prospect of nuclear war and its danger to the survival of our species, the truly impartial observer would remain a spectator of the possible event and not act to provide an "impartially human" remedy to international conflict. This analysis reveals that human desires always infect the Russellian viewpoint *sub specie aeternitatis*. Instead of that viewpoint being passionless, as in the review of "The Duty of a Philosopher in This Age" cited in **50**, the impartial observer has at heart a profound concern for humanity. As Russell himself does not specify it, we shall have to admit a typing restriction on his ethic to exclude the desire for impartiality itself from the range of desires we are to be impartial about.

In writing about Santayana's ethic Russell elaborates on the criterion of internal consistency, extending it beyond the purely logical sphere. He asks: "has the system in question been so deeply felt and thought as to possess a comprehensive subjective harmony?" ("The Philosophy of Santayana", p. 454). Our observation of the permanence and scope of the ethic of impersonal self-enlargement in Russell answers this question in the affirmative. The answer does not imply, however, a total subjective harmony.

The modification of the ethic to exclude the desire for impartiality is not the only modification required to resist logical contradictions. There are related problems. Russell is fond of urging us to take a cosmic viewpoint. But that would ignore human desires altogether. Even if there is a cosmic point of view that takes good and evil into account, it is not to be assumed also that humanity is a force for the greater good of the universe. It may well be that if because of a new species-wide concern, we permit ourselves to survive, the long-term effects of humanity's depredations on the solar system and possibly elsewhere will lead to greater suffering than otherwise to any hierarchy of sentient beings other than that which places humanity at the top. An individual or group of individuals living in harmony benefit themselves, but not necessarily those outside the group. Hence, to avoid trouble from the cosmic point of view, the statement of Russell's ethic must be modified to include the human point of view. Anything much wider runs up against the ethic's allowance for self-preservation, i.e. that narrow self-interests will never be completely eradicated.

(2) The criterion of the consistency of Russell's ethic with the remainder of his views is limited to relevant philosophical positions that he holds. It is probably sufficient to confine ourselves to what

Russell says in other contexts on such topics as the nature of the self and the worth of making ethical recommendations. First I shall discuss the relevance of the criterion. The inconsistency of any statement or set of statements *a* with any other statement or set of statements *b* says nothing about the superiority of *a* or *b* over the other. If *a* were Russell's normative ethic and *b* his philosophy of physics, he would be obliged, as a rational thinker, to drop either *a* or *b*; but we do not know which he would drop or which he ought to drop. Other areas of his thought might be brought into the comparison, and *a* might be found to be pitted against the entire remaining body of his beliefs. Still it would not be obvious whether the original *a* or the enlarged *b* should go. A thinker faced with a fundamental conflict in his views might be unable to jettison either, and he might await a synthesis involving a minor or extensive modification on either side. Certainly, however, we tend to rate more highly a single consistent system embodying all the thinker's views. Spinoza's system is obviously of that description in a way that Russell's is not. Russell's main difficulty, as I hope to show, is linguistic rather than substantive, due to his continued use in ethics of language he forbids himself elsewhere.

The reader may have been surprised by the religious vocabulary Russell uses at the time of Lady Ottoline's greatest influence on him. It has to be understood that Russell does not use religious vocabulary with metaphysical implications. Such vocabulary was and still is used in metaphysical discussions as well as in purely religious associations, and from the latter it has acquired and retained a unique expressiveness for some matters of deepest concern to us. Many people find its continued use essential for such expression in the absence of non-religious vocabulary. In addition, some of the value topics dealt with in this study are properly religious, if "religious" is understood without theological implications or reference to the social record of religious institutions.[31] Some critics of Russell's work—for example, Hoernlé, as I pointed out in 45—have made the mistake of assuming that Russell's metaphysical and epistemological work can be analyzed as one corpus with his ethical writings. Instead, there is, as Russell himself holds, a division between his normative ethical theories and his other philosophical work. The terminology, while sometimes identical, expresses incommensurable ideas. The most blatant case in the quotations I have selected is the use of "self" and "ego" and their near-synonyms "soul" and "intimate centre" of the individual. "Soul" means in Russell merely "the cluster of your deepest concerns", or even sometimes "the entity around which are clustered your deepest concerns". There is no suggestion in Russell's writings of a soul that could be immortal, and no one imputes this view to him.

His use of "self" raises a question as to the consistency of his ethic with his philosophy of mind. His mature—i.e. neutral monist—position on the self in philosophy of mind is that the self is nothing more than a collection of objects (sensations and images) whose relationships are primarily mental rather than physical. In his ethics Russell uses "self" to mean the collection of the individual's feelings and valuations. But it seems that he means more than that, that there is something behind the data of experience, as indicated by his use of the term "intimate centre". In metaphysics and philosophy of mind, the search is for a substantial self beyond all appearances. In ethics, religion and psychology the appearances—i.e. what the personal qualities of any individual *are*—are sufficient. It is, in fact, easier to make sense of Russell's ethical and religious writing if we discard his philosophy of mind when we approach his normative ethics. To the charge of inconsistency he would at least be able to make a defence based on the common feature of egocentricity in the two spheres.[32] Beyond that, in the ethical sphere the use of terms like "the walls of the ego" is best treated as a metaphor. Indeed, a statement such as "You need to break down [or widen] the walls of your ego" can be rephrased, as I have indicated in the examples in 53, into terms independent of reference to entities in either philosophy of mind or psychology. The above statement, for example, is capable of being recast as "You should become more generous". I do not, however, deny the possibility of points of contact between his ethics and his philosophy of mind, but to my knowledge they have not been demonstrated.

The value of making ethical recommendations in a non-cognitivist and deterministic framework has been discussed in 4 and 53. Whatever determinism has to say about past deliberation, present deliberation is not affected. For it remains a fact that we can reason, that we can appraise reasoning—whether our own or others'—and that we can act in accordance with reasoned conclusions. Hence we can affect action through our reasoning. We can also affect action through the alteration of desires, whether by chemical means, by painting attractive pictures of alternate goals, or by bringing persuasive considerations to bear. While Russell often forecasts the adoption of the first method, his own method is the second. If the picture is so attractive as to result in a permanent conversion experience, like Russell's own of 1901, so much the better for the subjective establishment of values.

There is an inconsistency between the ethic and Russell's attitude to emotion. Russell is a proponent in principle of the enjoyment of strong emotions. As in his philosophy of literature (see n. 43 below), he wishes to preserve strong emotions so long as they are directed impersonally. In old age he writes that he would often have sacrificed the rest of his life for a few hours of the joy of personal, romantic love (*Autobiography*, vol. I, prologue; see also *Marriage and Morals*, p. 62). True, he holds that in such love the self expands impersonally, but it is specifically the "ecstasy" of love he values so highly in the passage referred to. There is an inconsistency between such a valuation of strong emotion and the pursuit of philosophic calm, and Russell appears to be ambivalent about these alternatives. If the prevention of conflict depended upon the successful pursuit of philosophic calm, mankind would stand little chance: the experiencing of intense emotional states will not be given up—if it could be—by many in exchange for a peaceful but bland existence.

(3) The criterion of the ethic's consonancy with our own feelings or judgments is difficult to apply. Any answer will be subjective and therefore not binding on others. Still, one's own answer may be of interest. Much unhappiness is the result of excessive involvement of self in social interaction. Thus to the extent that we can abstract ourselves from, or become impersonal towards, such interaction, the less chance there is of bruised feelings and uncontrollable dwelling upon the event following its occurrence. A person must abstract self before the encounter. The attitude recommended in impersonal self-enlargement is therefore one of examining the facts or merits of a situation independently of the effect upon oneself. There is a certain freedom to be enjoyed in paying strict attention to intrinsic merit, no matter what the consequences are for the ego of oneself or others. It takes courage, too, for you have to be prepared to accept the consequences of looking at things impartially. Impersonal self-enlargement is more a way of avoiding conflicts than of resolving them, which is a drawback. For it is most unlikely that one or both parties to a quarrel are suddenly going to experience a diminution of egocentric desire— conflict generally intensifies, rather than diminishes, egocentric emotions. Before a conflict is generated there is a chance of reaching a more compossible state of affairs. That is a state in which my interests and yours are so widened as to overlap significantly. Hence their joint realization is more possible than previously.[33]

The impartiality with which we would be treated has to be that difficult one of neutrality combined with caring for the persons involved. Uncaring neutrality, in human affairs, is easier to achieve, since it involves simply the removal of all feeling for the persons involved in a conflict. That form of impartiality is lacking in courage, and thus is not consonant with our ethical feelings. An example of the right combination is justice tempered with mercy. We will not permit computers to dispense justice, and, for the sake of human self-preservation, we should not allow ourselves to approach the computer's form of impersonality. Impersonality must be combined with feeling. The impersonal treatment is not for children, however.[34] Another problem for the consonancy of the ethic is the dilemma of spontaneity versus self-discipline.[35] The impulsive person will satisfy some of Russell's requirements, but yielding to *every* impulse will result in much egocentric behaviour. Discipline for the possessive impulses is therefore needed, but discipline reduces spontaneity. After the realization of our impersonal selves, however, the problem disappears. The path to realization is strewn with much self-discipline, but along the way we learn gradually which impulses may be followed spontaneously and which not. The learning process is incompatible with spontaneity at the time, but not in the end. Another problem with consonancy is that this ethic, like many, projects an ideal moral person. This conflicts with the injunction we often feel that we should take and respect people as they are, instead of wishing they were different. This valuation has to be overridden by appreciation of the wretched states of affairs that our present characters get us into.

As an ethic, impersonal self-realization possesses the feature of universality that several philosophers have pointed out to be a logical feature of ethics. There is also a strong element of self-sacrifice, or altruism, which is required by conventionally idealistic people. We feel that attention to issues rather than persons is more suitable for adults than for children, and living by such an ethic makes great demands on maturity. The ethic's injunctions to disregard temporary desire and to take a cosmic view have a pacifying effect on a turbulent emotional life. The portrayal of a state in which personalities seem to merge as our interests overlap offers the possibility of satisfying the need to experience union with others. Russell himself craved union with, as he put it, "large bodies of human beings" (*Autobiography*, vol. II, p. 38), but his independent judgment almost always stood in the way.[36] The ethic offers also a hope of escape from loneliness and despair, in which Russell also found himself.[37] In all these respects his ethic is not subject to the criticism he levels against Aristotle's: that it omits "the whole sphere of human experience with which religion is concerned". In both cognitive and emotional matters—in the promotion of rationality and generosity, respectively—impersonal self-enlargement presents a way of living and therefore an ethic by which you may live.

56 Russell's Additional Criteria

(4) "Importance" as a criterion for the evaluation of an ethic seems at first impossibly vague. Let us see what Russell might mean by it. As noted in 21, he introduces the concept in the context of evaluating Santayana's philosophy—one that is "fundamentally ethical". He rightly regards the criterion as "less definite" than that of internal consistency, and the full phrase he uses is "the importance of the [philosophy's] point of view". "A lunatic's judgments," he says, "even if they achieve consistency, remain unimportant; Spinoza's, though not wholly consistent, are important" ("The Philosophy of George Santayana", p. 454). But in what way, we are bound to ask, are Spinoza's relatively inconsistent judgments more important than the consistent ones of the lunatic? There is a clue at the beginning of the essay. Russell divides the functions of philosophy into three: (*a*) "the attempt to understand the world"; (*b*) the ability to "enlarge the imagination by construction of a cosmic epic"; and (*c*) the ability to "suggest a way of life less wayward and accidental than that of the unreflective" (p. 453). Critics will agree that the main function of his own philosophy is (*a*). Russell continues: "A philosopher who attempts either of these tasks [i.e. (*b*) and (*c*)] must be judged by a standard of values, aesthetic or ethical, rather than by intellectual correctness. Lucretius and Spinoza may be taken as illustrative of these two types; each has a metaphysic, but neither loses his importance when his metaphysic is discredited" (p. 453). Later Russell adds that Santayana's *The Life of Reason* and *Realms of Being* are "important books—more important than they appear on a cursory reading" (p. 470). What is important about them is that "a comprehensive view of life and the world has been presented, which is all the more valuable because it is very different from any of those that are prevalent in the present age. It is urbane, historical, free from fanaticism, and the expression of an exceptionally sensitive intellectual perception" (*ibid.*). Thus by the importance of an ethical philosophy Russell seems

to mean its ability to offer a comprehensive way of life. And to be comprehensive an ethic must be thoroughly thought out and applicable to a wide variety of circumstances. The applicability of a lunatic's ethic would, presumably, fail on the non-acceptability of its consequences: too much self-sacrifice, or too much harm to others, or too much emphasis on one of life's goods at the expense of others, and so on.

Is Russell's ethic important? Impersonal self-enlargement is a comprehensive proposal for a way of life, though not, I believe, a complete one. (For the criterion of completeness, see (12) below.) It is applicable to a wide variety of circumstances, and thus is important in the relevant sense.

(5) Another criterion is offered by Russell in a book applying normative ethics to philosophy of education. The criterion is the universalizability of the ethic. He contrasts justice and self-sacrifice on behalf of others as ultimate ends. (Russell's language in this practical work ignores fine distinctions, and in saying that one of the ends cannot be a true one he omits to add that, under his metaethic, no ethic can be true.) Justice is incompatible with self-sacrifice because "Every person has a right to a certain amount of room in the world, and should not be made to feel wicked in standing up for what is due him" (*On Education*, pp. 117–18). Thus justice is compatible with a degree of self-assertion. But the point about universalizability concerns the logical extent to which self-sacrifice could be practised. Russell holds that it "cannot be a true doctrine, because it cannot be universal" (p. 118), whereas justice can. Russell does not explain why self-sacrifice cannot be universalized, but presumably the reason is that in the series, A sacrifices his interests for B, B sacrifices his for C, C ... Z, Z has no one for whom to sacrifice his interests.[38] Actually, Z is precluded from sacrificing his interests for A only if they are ultimate interests such as one's life which, once given, cannot be restored. A universal willingness to sacrifice oneself results in what might be called the paradox of perfect altruism: you cannot do more than to sacrifice your life for the benefit of another person, but in a society of perfect altruists no one would remain to reap the benefit. The ethic of impersonal self-enlargement comes close to failing the criterion of universalizability. But impersonal self-enlargers are not perfect altruists. Their own interests count equally with those of every other relevant person. Russell's ethic meets this criterion because it incorporates the requirement of justice.

57 Non-Russellian Criteria

The five criteria applied in **55–6** are insufficient for a complete evaluation of an ethic, though I do not know what a conclusive set of criteria would be. Hampshire's set (**52**), for example, omits at least the personal religious needs. There is almost no literature on the subject.[39] Several more criteria are available, however, which I shall number in sequence with Russell's and discuss below. In (6) I shall discuss the only metaethical criterion I have found to be relevant. Russell's ethic is to be contrasted most with the Kantian variety, by which an action is intended to be necessarily obligated because of man's essential characteristic as a rational being, and though there is a close resemblance between the impersonality of moral thought set out in the ethics of Russell and Kant, the chief comparison remains at the metaethical level. Some of the criteria seem to require empirical data for full validation of the points discussed. The gathering of such data, however, has to be undertaken under controlled conditions, if scientific validity is to be the goal. Unfortunately, for various reasons, it would often be impracticable to conduct the relevant experiments. At the same time we are faced with the necessity of making ethical decisions, of trying to improve the world in which man lives but which man has made so dangerous for himself. In rejecting the alternative of agnosticism concerning solutions to such a problem, it may seem as if we are basing some of the discussions on our own case, or indeed that we are theoretically limited to doing so. We have, of course, only our own experience to go by, but that experience includes reports of the experience of others. In **59** I present two criteria the acceptance of which, I hold, weakens the ethic's overall value.

(6) There is a metaethical criticism to be made of the approach to unselfishness through feeling. Thomas Nagel is opposed to "any demand that the claims of ethics appeal to our interests: either self-interest or the interest we may happen to take in other things and other persons. The altruism which in my view underlies ethics is not to be confused with generalized affection for the human race. It is not a feeling."[40] He proceeds to attack the conative assumption, i.e. that all motivation has its source in desire (p. 27). In doing so he is a consistent cognitivist. For Russell's confinement of motivation to desire limits the role of reason, and hence objectivity, to the calculation of consequences (*Human Society*, preface). Nagel's work has value in exploring the concept of rationality as found in ethics; reasons cannot be expected to appeal unless individual exceptions are

removed. But he misses equally the value of impersonal desire, by which we desire on behalf of all whose human qualities fit them for the situation we ourselves are in, or could be in. Again, however, in Russell's ethic there is no obligation to feel impersonally, which is Nagel's objection to Russell's sort of altruism. Rationalists in ethics object to making right conduct dependent on the contingent existence of right feeling. Despite Monro's criticism, there is widespread agreement among ethicists that the essence of the ethical point of view is universalizability. Peter Singer cites Sidgwick's phrase, "the point of view of the universe", and writes himself: "The ethical point of view does, as we have seen, require us to go beyond a personal point of view to the standpoint of an impartial spectator."[41] Singer sees more sentient creatures from his perspective than Russell does, but both stand back far enough to include the entire human species.

(7) It is no use offering an ethic that is unsuitable to human nature. Yet the criterion of suitability to human nature is very difficult to apply. For example, how long shall we give human nature to adapt to the ethic? Broad shows convincingly that a society of near-perfect altruists would not survive their indulgence in unlimited self-sacrifice of vital interests;[42] hence it is not adaptation to universal readiness for self-sacrifice that we must contemplate. But the prospect is an unreal one, anyway. Talk about human nature must be kept reasonably close to scientific limits, and we can say that man has an impulse to self-preservation sufficient to forestall the realization of mass self-sacrifice. I implied in 55 (3) that suppression of egocentric desires is not to be expected in the presence of those desires. You must work against them in their absence. Such suppression is not to be interpreted as a form of self-abnegation—which we saw was an ideal of the youthful Russell (13). The expansiveness he came to recommend is the psychological opposite of the ascetic attitude. Achievement of impersonal self-enlargement is a matter of degree, and as an ideal to be worked towards any degree of it counts as success. Human nature, through selfishness, cowardice, and bitterness arising from past personal conflicts, imposes upper limits to the achievement of the ethic.

I have assumed all along that Russell's ethic is directed at a genuine primary problem of human conduct, that of strife between individuals or groups of individuals with conflicting, or incompossible or possessive, desires. Does this problem result from a correct analysis of serious strife? An economic or class analysis only shifts the emphasis from one set of desires to another. Strife remains a human problem, and I conclude that the analysis of strife is relevant. It may be objected that some strife or conflict is beneficial to those who engage in it. Conflict may sharpen skills and develop aspects of character you thought you did not possess, with no one the worse for it. The same arguments are urged in favour of the retention of competitiveness in education. Russell himself opposes conflict and competition for their own sakes. It is not obvious that his ethic needs to exclude them, but let us see. In a conflict between A and B, impersonal self-enlargement results in a view of the issues irrespective of either person. If the satisfaction of B's desire is preferred on the basis of total satisfaction of desire, then A is encouraged, through this ethic, to submit to B. If the satisfaction of A's desire is preferred, than A may rightly engage in a struggle for that satisfaction. Impersonal self-enlargement thus does not require sacrifice of self-interest across the board, and hence allows for some conflict. But since it does not allow for conflict for conflict's sake, the amount permitted will not satisfy those who consider conflict essential to the full development of human powers.

If the ethic is suitable to man, what then are its chances of adoption? Optimism is foolish in the face of great odds, but we do not know the odds. Surely some ethic promoting harmony among mankind will have to be adopted if man is to survive, though this ethic may not be sufficient. Our self-interests now so overlap that world-wide cooperation is in man's self-interest. Yet such cooperation is obviously wanting. Either the mutuality of our self-interests has not been sufficiently pointed out, or self-interest is not sufficient. The supreme goad to harmony among nations for the past three decades has been a self-interest argument, namely that of the balance of terror. Although it seems to have worked in so far as global conflict has been prevented, its record is not enough to rely upon. If the balance of terror fails as a self-interest consideration, there will be no chance to try another method. Moreover, the stresses and threats involved in maintaining a balance of terror are repugnant to civilized persons. In the case that self-interest is not enough, an ethic in which we remember our humanity and forget the features individuating us as persons and nations will help. At any rate, optimism over man's becoming more generous and reasonable costs us nothing. I have not, however, attempted to explore further the political application of impersonal self-enlargement. There are indications that it forms part of Russell's political philosophy, but that is another topic.

58 Further Non-Russellian Criteria

Several criteria cluster about the ethic's worth as a philosophical notion. I shall consider (8a) its philosophical productivity, and (8b) its standing in comparison with rival ethical theories.

(8a) There is work to be done in analyzing the concept of self in the ethic, and in educing the patterns of behaviour suggested by it. The notion of impartiality in both feeling and thinking and its relationship to generosity, rationality, and universalizability can be analyzed further. And Russell's predecessors surely number more than our single identification of Spinoza. The concept of impersonal self-enlargement may lead to greater understanding of Russell's thought in any value-laden area to which he contributed. Some such areas are: political philosophy, moral philosophy, philosophy of education, philosophy of literature,[43] sexual morality (the theory, not the practice), and the study of his life. Understanding the theoretical basis of a work such as *The Conquest of Happiness* may help in applying its remedies for human unhappiness. The directing of a person's thoughts away from himself seems to be a promising beginning, at least in non-psychiatric cases.

(8b) Are there strongly held ethical viewpoints in conflict with this ethic? It conflicts in principle with any cognitivist ethic, for at no point does it claim knowledge as to what we ought to do. As a consequentialist doctrine—holding that mankind will be better off if it adopts the ethic—it has affinities with classical utilitarianism, except for the point that utilitarianism assumes that it is a known or demonstrable good for which an act or rule is useful. There are many points in various widely accepted moral codes with which the ethic conflicts, but that does not constitute comparison on equal levels. Probably the greatest conflict is with deontologism, the view that we have duties to be carried out for their own sakes. Impersonal self-enlargement denies any significant efficacy to the deontological motive. Instead, it tries to increase the power of already existing impulses to love and generosity. Russell puts his hope in fellow-feeling rather than in an increased awareness of duty. Another great conflict is with ethical egoism, the view that we should do whatever will please (or, in general, benefit) us most. I have pointed out that impersonal self-enlargement approaches perfect altruism. The conflict with egoism is different from that with deontologism. Deontologism is an attractive alternative, while ethical egoism derives most of its force from an empirical assumption, namely that of psychological egoism—the view

58 Further Non-Russellian Criteria

that we are so constituted as to pursue always our own self-interest. The conflict between impersonal self-enlargement and egoism occurs only when your self-interest is construed narrowly—there being no necessary conflict between egoism and altruism of character.

(9) Another criterion is that of the clarity of the concepts involved. We have noted difficulties with "impersonality". You may become so impersonal as to disregard others' feelings. Is this what is intended by impersonal self-enlargement? On the whole, it is not. What is intended is enlargement of the impersonal side of self—the enlargement of interests and of feelings on behalf of others. The limit to impersonal enlargement of self is the cosmic or divine viewpoint; this viewpoint need not involve the cessation of fellow-feeling; indeed, far from it. Russell's purpose, in intellectual as well as emotional matters, is to transcend the egoistic viewpoint, not the personal altogether, when the "personal" is understood as involving all of us. There may also be difficulties with the concept of that notoriously elusive entity, the self. For most of his life Russell held that there is no self. If there is no self, then enlargement of what is not is impossible, and there cannot be an ethic of impersonal self-enlargement. In his ethical writings, however, Russell is not using "self" in the sense of a "bare subject which thinks and is aware of objects" (*Our Knowledge of the External World*, p. 74). Rather, he is using "self" to mean roughly "the whole assemblage of things that would necessarily cease to exist if our lives came to an end" (*ibid.*), that is, our memories, our desires, our habitual responses, etc. Boundaries between the set of your "assemblage of things" and mine are recognizable even in the absence of an answer to the problem of the existence of the "bare subject". "Expansion of self" in the former sense means widening the reference points of desires and judgmental perspectives. A person with a widened self does not always think of himself first, and does not refer everything to himself.

(10) A separate difficulty of the ethic concerns the claims of kinship, neighbourliness, and patriotism. There is no essential difference between these claims. You may be concerned about the plight of families left without a father. Families without fathers require help, especially financial help. Should you pay large life insurance premiums so that your own family will benefit in the case of your premature demise, or should you devote the same funds to help all families left without a father? There are many situations in which you feel overwhelmingly obliged to help those whom you happen to know and care for as individual persons more than those whose existence

and plight you are assured of but whom you will never know or care for as individuals. At the time of writing the domestic Canadian automobile industry is suffering from a loss of market to imports. We are urged to buy the domestic product because that way our neighbours may be employed. The industry itself would have the government erect greater trade barriers to protect the domestic market. Should you buy domestic or foreign? Finally there is the question of patriotism in war. Least of all to blame in a war are the ordinary townsfolk. Yet we grieve when our towns or those of our allies are bombed and cheer when it is the enemy's turn. Commiseration should instead be directed equally. Which side should you support, the country of your family, friends and neighbours, or that of their enemy? Impersonal self-enlargement does not provide a comfortable solution in its propensity to recommend pacifism.

It may be said that impersonal self-enlargement cannot compete with the impulse for self-preservation. There would certainly be little competition in the case of the well-being of your own family. For some people there would be little competition for the well-being of neighbours and country. To the logically minded, however, impersonal self-enlargement presents intolerable difficulties. The wish to benefit strangers and foreigners not less than kin, neighbours and countrymen is due to the impersonal perspective that removes accidents of birth and personal acquaintance. Any modification of impersonality here will be a lessening of impersonality and hence a mark against the ethic as a simple, coherent doctrine.

(11) Another consideration, related to the foregoing, is the depersonalization that seems to be implied by the ethic. If we look solely at the issues, and ignore the persons involved in the issues, we shall be more likely to reach objective decisions on the issues. But ignoring persons is to depersonalize. It would seem that sometimes we have a right to expect a decision to be made in our favour just because we are ourselves and not somebody else. This is the basis of the complaint of the relative, neighbour or countryman who has lost out on an objective consideration of the issues. It will not do merely to *say*, as Russell does in one of the "Prisons" fragments,[44] that his ethic extends to everyone the fellow-feeling that is felt instinctively for a few. This extension is fine as a goal for an ethic, but it has to be shown that the ethic can *generate* the extension of such a feeling. On the one hand, we do not desire favouritism to be institutionalized in (say) the admission procedures of medical schools; yet never to defer to personalities seems to involve a loss in terms of human warmth. Impersonal

self-enlargement must enlarge fellow-feeling to the extent it enlarges the capacity for objective intellectual judgment. Russell, the proponent of an impersonal perspective in matters of feeling and intellect, holds also that "in human relations one should penetrate to the core of loneliness in each person and speak to that" (*Autobiography*, vol. I, p. 146). Rather than making him inconsistent on ethics, this belief adds weight to the interpretation of impersonal self-enlargement as an ethic concerned to release man from the grip of self, rather than from regard for others.

(12) An important criterion is the completeness of the ethic as a way of living. To be complete, the ethic would be the source of all positive values—at least those of a private nature and probably, also, those of a public nature. Otherwise a person or a society would have to look elsewhere for remaining values. Aside from the question of isolated values—and I do not suppose that anyone's list of positive values would have them all intrinsically connected—there is the question of what cluster of values follows upon the enlargement of self in an impersonal way. Impersonal self-enlargement is basically an ethic trusting in the potential of man's essentially cooperative and concerned nature. Clearly a large question is begged—the question of original sin. Should we expect men to act badly, or will a little trust free a man to act well towards his fellows? If only the inhibitions binding us within our private selves are eliminated, Russell holds, those selves contain enough of the creative impulses and desires to make most of us privately delightful and socially beneficent people. Russell's programme for human liberation presupposes, therefore, a fundamentally decent core in us. This remains in his ethic a matter of faith. The assumption that man's nature is fundamentally good serves to divide normative ethics into liberationist and non-liberationist varieties. To a significant extent impersonal self-enlargement is designed to be a liberator of positive values within us. But we can well imagine some persons whose impersonal attitude would be equivalent to absolute neutrality. Russell's stock example of a person who does not share his ultimate values at any level is Hitler.[45] Neutralization of the Hitlerian type would still be a good thing. But the ethic of impersonal self-enlargement counts more on the liberation of the good forces in the rest of us. Despite the controversial status of this assumption about human nature and the human condition,[46] various historical antecedents and some contemporary expressions of the quest for getting beyond self-concern through knowledge of things for their own sakes and through generous feeling encourage confidence in Russell's ethic.

(13) From time to time we have noted various modifications which must be made to impersonal self-enlargement to keep it viable. One of them is the modification by Russell himself that the fellow-feeling felt instinctively for a few (family, relatives and neighbours) is to be extended to everyone. "Every man is your brother" is another way of expressing it. I do not wish to make the dubious linguistic point based on the contrast theory of meaning that, if everyone is your brother, then no one is. My concern is with the actions that should follow such a modification. In the humble case of the insurance premium (10), an assumption is that the money I have for such a purpose is limited. Trying to spread it around on the basis that all men are brothers, and that all children are your children, would result in an infinitesimal amount of coverage for each child. The result is similar when brotherly love is cashed out in regard to scarce resources, of which love itself may be one. My point is that Russell's modification seems to be arbitrary; it does not seem generated from the essence of the ethic. When apparently arbitrary modifications are made to an ethic, it tends to become an atomistic collection of principles rather than an organically related whole (of extra-rational decisions), as we saw Russell noting in **6**.

59 Impersonal Self-Enlargement and Philosophic Calm

(14) The last claim I shall consider for impersonal self-enlargement is that it produces an exceptional calmness of spirit, or peace of mind. I say "exceptional" because everyone (excluding a few persons whose difficulty is medical) experiences some calm. The problem is we wish we were calmer, or were calm more often, instead of being subject to disturbing alternations of excitement and depression. It is philosophical thought we are taking here to be the agent. Despite Russell's disclaimer to the contrary in the radio discussion programme (**28**), philosophical thought is more highly regarded by him as an agent than the thought of other disciplines. But it is not philosophical thought as regards any particular topic in philosophy, but the general characteristics of philosophical thought. These characteristics are wide perspective, the attempt to remove the bias of the accidental qualities pertaining to the thinker in question, the conceiving of conceptual connections, and the detecting of logical inconsistencies. Wide perspective is not identical to the removal of personal bias. Wide perspective concerns the conceiving and entertaining of alternative worlds.

The removal of personal bias leads not merely to the removal of an individual's egoistic bias, substituting for it the "bias" of any person in general. It leads also to the removal of the anthropocentric viewpoint, to the discounting of all the fetters binding the observer to a particular point in space and time. In other words, in order to encourage patience and nurture the growth of calmness of spirit, impersonal self-enlargement would have us observe things *sub specie aeternitatis*. Yet calmness of spirit is not the criterion of the wise man. Kant has warned us about that error:

> A person who deliberates calmly, controlling his emotions and passions, seems to have all the essential elements of good character. These qualities were highly praised by ancient philosophers, yet they fall short of being absolutely good. Indeed, without a good will they may be extremely wicked. The calm villain is much more dangerous and hateful to us than the blustering one.[47]

Nevertheless the ability to view things without the bias of here and now and of the narrow self is considered by many to be indispensable to wisdom.

Thomas Nagel is an exception here. The removal of the here and now and narrow self can result in the existentialist judgment that human affairs are absurd, that nothing matters. In his paper on "The Absurd" Nagel points out that stepping back and viewing human affairs *sub specie aeternitatis* guarantees that nothing matters from that vantage point.[48] Nevertheless most of us carry on with our lives. It would appear that the perspective from which nothing matters is self-defeating, for if nothing matters then that perspective cannot matter, and if that perspective does not matter then it cannot render everything else unworthy of mattering. Protecting the eternal point of view through a hierarchy of types is unsatisfactory, for proponents of that viewpoint emphatically assert that *it* matters.

Russell's wish to remove personal bias in his normative ethic does approach the total removal resulting in the existentialist's conclusion that human endeavour is absurd. "To achieve such impartiality", he says, "is impossible for us, but we can travel a certain distance towards it. To show the road to this end is the supreme duty of the philosopher" (*My Philosophical Development*, p. 213). "[I]n thought and feeling," he says elsewhere, "to realise the unimportance of time is the gate of wisdom" (*Our Knowledge*, p. 167). Yet despite the impossibility of attaining a divine perspective on human affairs,

Russell's goal is clearly just that. He regards it as desirable to approach that limit as closely as possible. To do so would be to live completely the life of the rationalist. This goal contrasts with that in which people enjoy their passionate states, or at least some of them. We enjoy forgetting our narrow selves—including the effort to be impartial—in the excitement of being led passionately to do this or that, and the life of the detached rationalist at these times leaves us cold, despite the temporary loss of our capacity for impartial judgment.

60 Conclusion

Our analysis of the ethic of impersonal self-enlargement has revealed certain strengths and weaknesses in it. We found the ethic to be self-consistent (after a modification to take care of typing difficulties). The ethic is consistent with the remainder of Russell's views, except for his valuation of strong emotion. The ethic is important in Russell's sense of providing a consistent way of life that is a realistic alternative. It is universalizable. The ethic appears not to require too much of human nature. There is opportunity, particularly in Russell studies, to explore the ramifications of the concept of impersonal self-enlargement in greater detail. When a key term such as "self" is understood so as not to have implications for philosophy of mind, the ethic contains sufficient conceptual clarity. The weaknesses concern the ethic's lack of "organic" wholeness, its pursuit of philosophic calm in place of strong emotion, and its depersonalization. Because of various modifications, the ethic is more realistic than it would otherwise be, but those very modifications detract from its internal unity, giving it an appearance of arbitrariness. The ethic in its pure form cannot allow for the enjoyment of strong emotions, although Russell himself values this aspect of being human and holds that strong emotions must have an outlet. Finally, in its logical extension, the impersonality feature of the ethic does not permit you to distinguish between the good of those you know and of those you do not know. If it were not for Spinoza and Russell's respect for the motive of self-preservation, the impersonal self-enlarger might have such a weakened sense of his own self as to be suicidal. Yet despite these faults, the ethic seems likely to be useful in promoting generosity—selflessness in feeling—and rationality—impartiality in thought. Both are virtues we sorely need.

Notes

Chapter I Introduction

1 Russell, *Power: a New Social Analysis* (New York: Norton, 1938), p. 243.
2 William K. Frankena, *Ethics* (Englewood Cliffs, N.J.: Prentice Hall, 1963), p. 78; 2nd ed. (1973), p. 95.
3 McCloskey, *Meta-Ethics and Normative Ethics* (The Hague: Nijhoff, 1969), p. 3.
4 McCloskey's answer is in the affirmative, for much the same reason as I cite from Hancock below. If a given definist or naturalist metaethic is true, then we know what it is morally good or right to do. See McCloskey, pp. 5–7.
5 Nowell-Smith, *Ethics* (Harmondsworth, Middlesex: Penguin Books, 1954), p. 24.
6 Santayana, "The Philosophy of Mr. Bertrand Russell", in his *Winds of Doctrine* (London: Dent, 1913), pp. 110–54 (at 115–16).
7 Hancock, *Twentieth Century Ethics* (New York: Columbia University Press, 1974), p. 7.
8 Russell, "On Keeping a Wide Horizon", ed. K. Blackwell, *Russell: the Journal of the Bertrand Russell Archives*, nos. 33–34 (spring–summer 1979), pp. 5–11 (at 8).
9 Russell, "Reply to Criticisms", in P. A. Schilpp, ed., *The Philosophy of Bertrand Russell*, The Library of Living Philosophers, vol. V, 4th ed. (La Salle, Ill.: Open Court, 1971), pp. 681–741 (at 726).
10 Quoted thus by Malleson in "Fifty Years: 1916–1966", in Ralph Schoenman, ed., *Bertrand Russell: Philosopher of the Century* (London: Allen and Unwin, 1967), pp. 17–31 (at 21). The sentence before the ellipsis is from Russell's letter of 5 July 1918; it is more accurately quoted in Russell's *Autobiography, 1914–1944* (London: Allen and Unwin, 1968), p. 87. The original is in the Bertrand Russell Archives (abbreviated "RA"), McMaster University (file 711.200313). The sentences following the ellipsis are from his letter of 24 Aug. 1918 (RA 711.200339).
11 Jager, *The Development of Bertrand Russell's Philosophy* (London: Allen and Unwin, 1972), pp. 428ff. John Lewis also connects what he calls Russell's "anarchic individualism" in politics with his metaphysics (*Bertrand Russell* [New York: International Publishers, 1968], p. 82). See also Leslie Armour, "Russell, McTaggart, and 'I'", *Idealistic Studies*, 9 (Jan. 1979), pp. 66–76, who claims that "the Leibnizian image of man and cosmos" is "the connection between Russell's epistemological writings and his social and political writings" (p. 76 n. 15). This is the image of the individual mirroring the world, which is often found in Russell.
12 Russell, "Reply to Criticisms", p. 719. For an alternative, wider conception of philosophy by Russell, see 6. For a discussion of Russell's restricted conception, see John G. Slater, "The Political Philosophy of Bertrand Russell", in J. E. Thomas and K. Blackwell, eds., *Russell in Review* (Toronto: Samuel Stevens, Hakkert, 1976), pp. 135–54. Slater does not consider whether, independently of Russell's views, normative ethical and political thought can be the subject of philosophical analysis. This study of the conceptual connections in Russell's ethic is evidence that it can.
13 Letter to Sir Stanley Unwin, 1 Oct. 1953 (RA). See also the list of proposed contents, dated 27 Sept. [1953], file 210.006820.
14 Aiken, *Bertrand Russell's Philosophy of Morals* (New York: Humanities Press, 1963). Aiken's otherwise reliable study overlooks the tentativeness with which Russell puts forward the naturalistic metaethic of *Human Society* and his later

dissatisfaction with it. After reading Aiken's book Russell wrote her: "I was a little puzzled by your view that I had made a fundamental change in *Human Society in Ethics and Politics*. I was not conscious of making any such important change. I gather that you do not think much of the idea of compossibility among objects of desire, but I do not quite know why" (26 Aug. 1963; in *Dear Bertrand Russell*, ed. B. Feinberg and R. Kasrils [Boston: Houghton Mifflin, 1969], p. 99). For other such expressions, see n. 18 and the letter to *The Observer* (6 Oct. 1957) quoted by Paul Edwards, "Russell, Bertrand Arthur William: Ethics and the Critique of Religion", *The Encyclopedia of Philosophy*, ed. Edwards (New York: Macmillan and the Free Press, 1967), vol. 7, pp. 251–6 (at 253). Russell's later naturalism has been linked to his early, unpublished metaethic. See Harry Ruja, "Russell on the Meaning of 'Good'", *Russell*, n.s. 4 (summer 1984): 137–56, and **16**.

15 Russell, *A History of Western Philosophy* (New York: Simon and Schuster, 1945), p. xxi; 2nd ed. (London: Allen and Unwin, 1961), p. 20.
16 *Ibid.*, p. 729; p. 700. This is the form I shall use in citing the two editions of the *History* which are in print.
17 Russell sketches a cognitivist metaethic on the datum of individual desires—just as, in *Human Knowledge*, he bases science on the datum of individual percepts. Russell's suggestion is further explored in John L. McKenney, "Concerning Russell's Analysis of Value Judgements", *Journal of Philosophy*, 55 (1958), pp. 382–9, and in Kai Nielsen, "Bertrand Russell's New Ethic", *Methodos*, 10 (1958), pp. 151–81. Nielsen calls Russell's ethics "emotive utilitarianism", because it is "a subtle combination of a mixed emotive theory and universalistic utilitarianism" (p. 156). In commenting on this and another article by Nielsen, Russell told him that he has never felt sure of the soundness of his "ethical opinions", i.e. his metaethic (letter of 13 June 1959).
18 Russell, "Notes on *Philosophy*, January, 1960", *Philosophy*, 35 (1960), pp. 146–7. Russell's notes on metaethics concern D. H. Monro's "Russell's Moral Theories", which is reprinted in D. F. Pears, ed., *Bertrand Russell: a Collection of Critical Essays* (Garden City, N.Y.: Anchor Books, Doubleday and Co., 1972), pp. 325–55. For further discussion of Monro's article, see **53**.
19 This implication is drawn, for example, in George P. Grant, "Pursuit of an Illusion: a Commentary on Bertrand Russell", *Dalhousie Review*, 32 (1952), pp. 97–109, and William S. Sahakian, *Ethics: an Introduction to Theories and Problems* (New York: Barnes and Noble Books, 1974), pp. 207–11 (esp. 210). In defence of Russell, see Edwards, "Russell: Ethics and the Critique of Religion", pp. 253–4, and *The Logic of Moral Discourse* (New York: The Free Press, 1955), pp. 213–15.
20 Russell, *Religion and Science* (New York: Oxford University Press, 1961; 1st ed., 1935), pp. 235–7. Here Russell believes that ethical expressions are more accurately rendered by the optative mood.
21 *The Philosophy of Bertrand Russell*, p. 720. Russell does not think he is "guilty of any logical inconsistency in holding to the above interpretation of ethics and at the same time expressing strong ethical preferences" (p. 724). He does not offer grounds for this view. However, see Ruja, p. 153.
22 It is similar to R. M. Hare's "universalizability" principle. In Russell's case the "universal" element is intentional, while in Hare's it is descriptive. For Russell, the expression of moral desire is universal in scope. To say "x is good" is to wish that everybody desired it (*Religion and Science*, pp. 235–6). In Hare's case the "universalizable" element is logical, i.e. it is necessarily part of the descriptive function of all ethical statements (*Freedom and Reason* [Oxford: Clarendon Press, 1952], pp. 10–15).
23 The examples are mine, not Russell's.
24 Stanley Hauerwas, "Sex and Politics: Bertrand Russell and 'Human Sexuality'", *Christian Century*, 95 (19 April 1978), pp. 417–22.
25 In Russell's *Unpopular Essays* (London: Allen and Unwin, 1950).

26 Barber, "Solipsistic Politics: Russell's Empiricist Liberalism", in George W. Roberts, ed., *Bertrand Russell Memorial Volume* (London: Allen and Unwin, 1979), pp. 455–78 (at 474). For a list of works concerning Russell's political philosophy, see my "A Secondary Political Bibliography of Bertrand Russell", *Russell*, nos. 33–34 (spring–summer 1979), pp. 39–44.
27 The best attempt so far to view Russell as a normative thinker is Justus Buchler, "Russell and the Principles of Ethics", in Schilpp, *The Philosophy of Bertrand Russell*, pp. 513–35.
28 For example, Grant writes concerning some broadcast talks which became part of Russell's *New Hopes for a Changing World* (1951):

> If I did not know their author and was trying to describe him, I would say he must be a man with the worldly wit and cultivated style of the aristocrat, combined with a preacher's hatred of man's sin and desire to improve men; but that these excellent qualities were marred by continual contradictions and a failure to reduce any question to principles. Indeed, I would say that the author was a good man and a clever man, but not a philosopher. This is the dilemma in which Russell is inevitably entangled by the contradiction between the moral scepticism which he holds in principle and the moral fervour which he adopts in practice. Because of his moral fervour he wants to speak out and convince men to be good; because of his moral scepticism he cannot speak in principles and therefore cannot speak clearly. ("Pursuit of an Illusion", p. 98)

29 See McShea's "Spinoza in the History of Ethical Theory", *Philosophical Forum*, 8 (1976), pp. 59–67. For a survey of various and sometimes incompatible ethical theories to be found in Spinoza, see Jay Newman, "Some Tensions in Spinoza's Ethical Theory", *Indian Philosophical Quarterly*, n.s. 7 (April 1980), pp. 357–74. I do not treat Spinoza's metaethic in this study—as C. D. Broad does not treat Spinoza's normative ethic in his study of Spinoza's metaethic. Broad ignores the doctrine of the "intellectual love of God" because it is "the expression of certain religious and mystical experiences" (*Five Types of Ethical Theory* [London: Routledge and Kegan Paul, 1930], p. 15). Because these experiences in Russell's case (and perhaps in Spinoza's) affect his normative ethic profoundly, I am obliged to discuss them. For influential discussions of Spinoza's metaethic, see E. M. Curley, "Spinoza's Moral Philosophy" in Marjorie Grene, ed., *Spinoza: a Collection of Critical Essays* (Garden City, N.Y.: Anchor Books, Doubleday, 1973), pp. 354–76, and William K. Frankena, "Spinoza's 'New Morality': Notes on Book IV", in Eugene Freeman and Maurice Mandelbaum, eds., *Spinoza: Essays in Interpretation* (La Salle, Ill.: Open Court, 1975), pp. 85–100.
30 Russell, *A History of Western Philosophy*, p. 787; pp. 752–3.
31 Russell, "The Philosophy of George Santayana", in Schilpp, ed., *The Philosophy of George Santayana*, The Library of Living Philosophers, vol. II (Evanston and Chicago: Northwestern University, 1940), p. 454.
32 Robert F. Davidson, in *Philosophies Men Live By*, 2nd ed. (New York: Holt, Rinehart and Winston, 1974), quotes part of this passage against Aristotle "though one is rather surprised to find [it]" (p. 213). In Aristotle's defence against Russell, see W. F. R. Hardie, *Aristotle's Ethical Theory*, 2nd ed. (Oxford: Clarendon Press, 1980), pp. 119–20.
33 *The Autobiography of Bertrand Russell, 1872–1914* (London: Allen and Unwin, 1967), p. 146.
34 Santayana's opinion is to be found in *Winds of Doctrine*, pp. 113–14.
35 Russell to Lady Ottoline Morrell, no. 165a, 6 Aug. [1911], Morrell papers, Harry Ranson Humanities Research Center, University of Texas at Austin (microfilm in RA). Russell's letters to Lady Ottoline will be cited in the text in the following form: no. (if any) and date (prefixed by "p/" if the date is that of the postmark on the envelope).

36 "The Twilight of the Absolute", *The Nation*, London, 12 (22 Feb. 1913), p. 864. Carl Spadoni drew my attention to this passage. Russell's authorship is known because on 26 Feb. 1913 he told Lady Ottoline that if there was a review of Bosanquet in the *Nation* that week, then it was by him. On 3 Feb. he had said he had written a review of Bosanquet.
37 Bradley, *Ethical Studies*, 2nd ed. (Oxford: Clarendon Press, 1927), pp. 160–206.
38 Russell, *The Problems of Philosophy* (New York: Oxford University Press, 1959; 1st ed., 1912), p. 161. This passage is quoted by John King-Farlow in "Self-Enlargement and Union: Neglected Passages of Russell and Some Famous Ones of Proust", *Theoria to Theory*, 11 (1977), pp. 105–15, from which I have obtained the term "self-enlargement".
39 Feuer writes: "But a mathematical façade may conceal an inner being which is riven with deep conflict. A logical surface may enclose seething, warring impulses of a thinker who is striving for self-mastery. The mathematical method was for Spinoza, as it is for Bertrand Russell, an expression of an emotional longing toward realities beyond formulae. The geometrical method was an over-compensation for an inner nonlogical world of emotional turmoil" (*Spinoza and the Rise of Liberalism* [Boston: Beacon Press, 1958], p. 199).
40 Hampshire, "Autobiography of Bertrand Russell—II", in his *Modern Writers and Other Essays* (New York: Knopf, 1970), p. 123. In reviewing the first volume, Hampshire noted: "... it is now easier to see why he [Russell] sometimes wished that he had been a contemporary of Spinoza, and had been able, with a good conscience, to constuct a metaphysical system" (*ibid.*, pp. 116–17). His review of the third volume contains the unexplained remark that Spinoza was one of Russell's "predecessors and peers in public philosophy" ("Russell, Radicalism, and Reason", in Virginia Held, Kai Nielsen, and Charles Parsons, eds., *Philosophy and Political Action* [New York: Oxford University Press, 1972], p. 262). Hampshire, as a Spinozaphile, may be prone to imagine connections between Spinoza and other philosophers; but then, as a Spinozalogue, he is well placed to see connections.
41 Rescher notes Russell's "prolonged flirtation with the philosophy of Spinoza, a marked feature of *Mysticism and Logic* and vividly at work in the splendid essay on 'A Free Man's Worship'" ("Russell and Modal Logic", in Roberts, pp. 139–49 [at 140]). I exclude those who, like Curley, merely refer to Russell in exegeting Spinoza (*Spinoza's Metaphysics: an Essay in Interpretation* [Cambridge, Mass.: Harvard University Press, 1969], pp. 4, 163); and those who, like Wallace Matson, simply note Russell's profound respect for Spinoza in *A History of Western Philosophy* ("Russell's Ethics", in Roberts, *Russell Memorial Volume*, pp. 422–7). Matson begins his short essay on Russell's metaethic by quoting the first three sentences of the chapter on Spinoza in *A History of Western Philosophy*. His other mention of Spinoza is the following: "Like Aristotle's, Spinoza's and John Stuart Mill's, Russell's idea of the happiness that ought to be the aim of conduct is not titillation but the untrammelled development and exercise of innate powers: vitality" (p. 423). "Titillation" is a translation of Spinoza's word *titillatio*.) Without referring to the *History*, Louis Greenspan notes that "Russell praised Spinoza for his Stoic ethic" (*The Incompatible Prophecies: an Essay on Science and Liberty in the Political Writings of Bertrand Russell* [Oakville, Ont.: Mosaic Press/Valley Editions, 1978], p. 48).
42 The earliest recognition of any kind is in a letter of 1910 to Russell from William Hale White, a distinguished translator of Spinoza. I quote and discuss the letter in 22. The recognition is confined to Russell's sympathetic understanding of Spinoza. The first published suggestion of a connection is in a comment on Russell's paper "The Essence of Religion", all that survives from the completed book on religious philosophy which Russell wrote in 1911. A commentator, A. S. Pringle-Pattison, remarks that "The Essence of Religion" "is written in a calmer spirit [than "The Free Man's Worship"]—shall I say with less bravado?—and seeks to develop the

idea of acquiescence, on lines very often reminiscent of Spinoza, into a species of religious worship" ("'The Free Man's Worship': a Consideration of Mr. Bertrand Russell's Views on Religion", *Hibbert Journal*, 12 [1913–14], pp. 47–63 [at 51]). This article is cited by R. F. Alfred Hoernlé in "The Religious Aspect of Bertrand Russell's Philosophy", *Harvard Theological Review*, 9 (1916), pp. 157–89 (at 169), who goes on to say: "Instead of being called on to transfigure the world in the crucible of the imagination, we are reminded, in the spirit of Spinoza, that to understand the unalterable necessity of things is to be cured of indignation and protest." (For more discussion of Pringle-Pattison and Hoernlé, see **44** and **45**.) A few years later another parallel is drawn between Russell and Spinoza, this time by a thesis writer. He, too, is commenting on "The Essence of Religion": "To describe religion as seeking 'union with the universe by subordination of the demands of self' is reminiscent of Spinoza" (Rees Higgs Bowen, "A Constructive Study of the Religious Philosophies of S. Alexander, L. T. Hobhouse, and Bertrand Russell" [unpublished PH.D. dissertation, Yale University, 1924], *c.* p. 218 [the pages being unnumbered]).

See my "A Secondary Bibliography of Russell's 'The Essence of Religion'", *Russell*, n.s. 1 (1981–82), pp. 143–6.

43 O'Connor, "Bertrand Russell", in O'Connor, ed., *A Critical History of Western Philosophy* (New York: The Free Press, 1964), pp. 473–91 (at 491).

44 The thesis writers are Gladys G. Leithauser, Duncan Martin, and Richard Sams. Leithauser's work, "Principles and Perplexities: Studies of Dualism in Selected Essays and Fiction of Bertrand Russell" (unpublished PH.D. dissertation, Wayne State University, 1977), contains the discovery that a figure in a fictional work by Russell is a mouthpiece for Spinoza. The novella "The Perplexities of John Forstice" was written in Russell's most Spinozistic period, 1910–12. She writes: "The admiration that Russell feels for Spinoza, whom he describes elsewhere as 'the noblest and most lovable of the great philosophers' (HWP [*History of Western Philosophy*], p. 569), is implied in the choice of Spinoza's view for quintessential expression in the story" (p. 153). Leithauser is unaware of the theoretical inheritance Russell received from Spinoza—namely, the conception of the expandable impersonal self. Martin's thesis, "The Role of Love in Determining the Religious Attitudes of Bertrand Russell" (unpublished M.A. thesis, McMaster University, 1979), concerns the development of Russell's sense of self. It is psychologically oriented. Spinoza is seen as an important figure for Russell during the period 1911–14. The sense of self that is seen as developing is a more psychiatric one than that with which the Spinoza–Russell notion of self-enlargement is concerned. Martin is chiefly occupied with the integration of Russell's personality in his relationship with Lady Ottoline Morrell, but he links the integration to Russell's study of Spinoza in the years 1910–12. Martin holds that Spinoza's "union of the mind with God or Nature was the essential prerequisite for personal equilibrium, moral goodness, and political unity" (p. 169). Through "understanding of the self as a coherent being" (pp. 170–1), Spinoza's doctrine of self-preservation took shape in Russell. Martin's major claim that "In Ottoline, he was blessed with a living representative of Spinoza's alluring philosophical system" (p. 155) is suggestive but unconvincing. Sams' thesis, "Bertrand Russell's Spiritual Development and the Victorian Crisis of Faith, 1888–1914" (unpublished M.A. thesis, McMaster University, 1980), concerns Russell's struggle to live with himself and credits Spinoza's notion of the intellectual love of God for any success Russell had. But Sams is overly sanguine about the inevitability of man's realization of his wider self (p. 18), and his Spinozistic thesis is unsupported by any references to Spinoza's writings. Sams' analysis of Russell's conversion experience of 1901 is valuable for the connections it traces in the writings of William James on religious experience, with which Russell was familiar (Chap. VII).

45 Sessions, "Panpsychism versus Modern Materialism: Some Implications for an

Ecological Ethics" (unpublished mimeographed typescript, 1974), n. 45. See also his "Spinoza and Jeffers on Man and Nature", *Inquiry*, 20 (1977), pp. 481–528. I have corrected the quotation (see Chap. IV, n. 15). Only one of the reviews of *The Conquest of Happiness* mentioned Spinoza, and then briefly. "At many points, his matter and manner suggest Spinoza, whom he occasionally quotes" was the comment by Henry Neumann in his review ("How to be Happy with Russell", *Survey*, 65 [1930], p. 284). See also F. C. S. Schiller's review in *Mind*, 40 (1931), pp. 238–41.

Chapter II   The Early Period (1888–1901)

1 *The Life and Times of Bertrand Russell* (London: British Broadcasting Corporation, 1964), shot list, pp. 12–13 (RA). *Cf.* the quotation referenced at Chap. III, n. 22.
2 My quotations from Spinoza's *Ethics* are usually from the White and Stirling translation. When a passage seems obscure, I check an unpublished translation (with copious notes) by Paul Wienpahl. (His translation of the axioms, definitions and propositions has been published in his *The Radical Spinoza* [New York: New York University Press, 1979].) As a relatively literal translation, it is useful when Spinoza's Latin needs to be examined. The concise form of reference to passages in Spinoza is derived from Arne Naess and Jon Wetlesen. "E2P49S" means "*Ethics*, [Part] 2, proposition 49, scholium". A complete list of such abbreviations for Spinoza's works is in Wetlesen's *The Sage and the Way: Spinoza's Ethics of Freedom* (Assen, The Netherlands: Van Gorcum, 1979), p. xv. I have frequently consulted Elwes' translation and, less frequently, the Latin editions edited by van Vloten and Land (in Russell's library at McMaster) and by Gerhardt and the new translation by Shirley.
3 *The Life and Times of Bertrand Russell*, draft transcript of unedited interview, p. [45].
4 Russell, "Books That Influenced Me in Youth, VI: the Pursuit of Truth", in his *Fact and Fiction* (London: Allen and Unwin, 1961), pp. 43–4. The essay was first published in 1957.
5 Russell, "What Shall I Read?" (notebook listing books read, 1891–1902, by date, author and title). In *The Collected Papers of Bertrand Russell*, vol. 1: *Cambridge Essays, 1888–99*, ed. K. Blackwell, A. Brink, N. Griffin, R. A. Rempel and J. G. Slater (London and Boston: Allen and Unwin, 1983), p. 353.
6 Russell to Alys Pearsall Smith, 28 Jan. 1894 (microfilm, RA; original in possession of Barbara Halpern, Oxford). For a survey of "Philosophy in Russell's Letters to Alys", see the article by Spadoni, *Russell*, nos. 29–32 (1978), pp. 5–31.
7 Russell, "Why I Took to Philosophy", in his *Portraits from Memory and Other Essays* (London: Allen and Unwin, 1956), p. 19.
8 Russell, "Greek Exercises", 14 April, 30 July 1888, respectively; *Autobiography*, vol. I, pp. 49–50, 55; *Cambridge Essays*, pp. 8, 18. The selections published by Russell are unreliable.
9 Russell, "A Locked Diary", 31 Aug. 1890 (microfilm, RA; original in possession of B. Halpern, Oxford); *Cambridge Essays*, p. 56. There is a reference to this diary in *Autobiography*, vol. I, p. 82. For an analysis of Russell's loss of faith, see Kirk Willis, "The Adolescent Russell and the Victorian Crisis of Faith", *Russell*, n.s. 4 (summer 1984), pp. 123–35.
10 Russell, "A Turning Point", *Saturday Book*, 8 (1948), pp. 142–6 (at 143–4).
11 Russell, "Books That Influenced Me in Youth, VI: the Pursuit of Truth", p. 45.
12 Pollock, *Spinoza: His Life and Philosophy* (London: Kegan Paul, 1880; reprint ed., Dubuque, Iowa: Reprint Library, n.d.), p. 403. My point is not that Russell may have read Shelley's translation of Spinoza, but merely to describe an association of persons and ideas in order to convey a certain *milieu*. For Russell and Shelley

generally, see Leithauser, "The Romantic Russell and the Legacy of Shelley", *Russell*, n.s. 4 (summer 1984), pp. 31–48.
13 April 1889. We have his recollection that at this time he "loved natural beauty with a wild passion" (Russell, *My Philosophical Development* [London: Allen and Unwin, 1959], p. 35). For Wordsworth's possible influence on Russell, see Martin, Chap. II.
14 "On Scientific Method in Philosophy", in Russell's *Mysticism and Logic and Other Essays* (London: Longmans, Green, 1918), p. 107; new ed. (London: Allen and Unwin, 1963), p. 82. The essay was written in 1914.
15 "Examination for Major and Minor Scholarships, Exhibitions, and Sizarships", Trinity College, 15 Dec. 1890 (original in possession of B. Halpern, Oxford).
16 The doctrine has ecological implications, and Spinozistic ecologists have not failed to notice them. See, e.g., George Sessions, "Spinoza and Ecophilosophy", *Ecophilosophy: an Informal Newsletter*, no. 1 (April 1976), pp. 1–5, and "Panpsychism versus Modern Materialism"; and Arne Naess, "Spinoza and Ecology", in *Speculum Spinozanum 1677–1977*, ed. Siegfried Hessing (London: Routledge and Kegan Paul, 1977), pp. 418–25. For a critique, see E. M. Curley, "Man and Nature in Spinoza", in Jon Wetlesen, ed., *Spinoza's Philosophy of Man: Proceedings of the Scandinavian Spinoza Symposium 1977* (Oslo: Universitetsforlaget, 1978), pp. 19–26.
17 Russell, "A Locked Diary", 14 July 1890; *Cambridge Essays*, p. 55. Russell's interest in Thomas à Kempis evidently became well known to his family. At the end of 1894, when he married Alys, they received as wedding gifts two copies of *The Imitation of Christ*. One was from his Aunt Agatha, who always tried to control his moral development. See Sheila Turcon, "A Quaker Wedding: the Marriage of Bertrand Russell and Alys Pearsall Smith", *Russell*, n.s. 3 (winter 1983–4), pp. 103–28 (at 125). Neither copy is still in Russell's library.
18 Gordon S. Haight, *George Eliot, a Biography* (Oxford: Clarendon Press, 1968), pp. 172, 199–200. Had it been published when written, Eliot's translation would have been the first into English of the *Ethics*. Her translation is now available, edited by Thomas Deegan, in Salzburg Studies in English Literature, no. 102 (Universität Salzburg, 1981).
19 Leo Sherley-Price, trans., *The Imitation of Christ* (Harmondsworth, Middlesex: Penguin Books, 1952), Introduction, pp. 22–3.
20 Sherley-Price, p. 25.
21 Thomas à Kempis, *The Imitation of Christ*, in F. C. Happold, *Mysticism: a Study and an Anthology*, rev. ed. (Harmondsworth, Middlesex: Penguin Books, 1970), pp. 300–5.
22 See Herbert Spiegelberg, "Good Fortune Obligates: Albert Schweitzer's Second Ethical Principle", *Ethics*, 85 (1975), pp. 227–34.
23 George Eliot, *The Mill on the Floss* (New York: University Edition, Sully and Kleinteich, n.d.), Part I, pp. 430–1.
24 Russell to Lady Ottoline Morrell, 8 Aug. 1918, *Autobiography*, vol. I, p. 90.
25 Russell, graduate lecture notebook, "Stout's History of Philosophy", October 1893–Lent term 1894, I. Spinoza and Hobbes, p. 130 (RA). I have expanded Russell's abbreviations. Pollock's statement is in his *Spinoza*, p. 218.
26 Graduate lecture notebook, "Ward's History of Philosophy", Lent term 1894, p. 28.
27 Stout, *Mind*, n.s. 4 (1895), p. 259.
28 Johann Eduard Erdmann's *Grundriss der Geschichte der Philosophie* appeared in its third edition in 1878 (2 vols. [Berlin: Verlag von Wilhelm Hertz, 1878]). An English translation of this edition of vol. II, *Philosophie der Neuzeit*, was available, but Russell used the original, annotating the first 200 pages of his copy. My quotations are from the translation (*A History of Philosophy*, ed. and trans. Williston S. Hough, 3 vols. [London: Swan Sonnenschein, 1890–93]). Erdmann's is a

comprehensive, scholarly account of the history of philosophy to the mid-nineteenth century. John Dewey, in reviewing the English translation, said that it "was a genuine history of philosophy, tracing, in a genetic way, the development of thought in its treatment of philosophic problems. Its purpose is to develop a philosophic intelligence rather than to furnish information" (Dewey, *The Early Works*, ed. Jo Ann Boydston, 5 vols. [Carbondale, Ill.: Southern Illinois University Press, 1969], vol. III: *1889–1892*, p. 186). Erdmann was also editor of Leibniz's *Opera Philosophica* (1840); this edition had been superseded by the time of Russell's study of that rationalist a few years later, but he did make use of the *Geschichte* in *The Philosophy of Leibniz* (1900).

29 E.g., Erdmann, trans., p. 71; original, pp. 60–1.

30 Translation, p. 82. The original passage marked by Russell was:

> ... so stellt sich dagegen seine Ethik die Aufgabe: zu zeigen, wie die Wenigen, welche des Staates nicht bedürfen, und denen eben darum die bürgerliche Freiheit nicht genügt, sich zu der höchsten, der Geistesfreiheit erheben, die eine Privattugend ist (Tract. polit. I, 6). (Pp. 69–70)

31 Translation, pp. 82–3. The original passage marked by Russell was:

> Eben darum steht man dem Verstandenen als einem Selbstgebilligten oder gewollten, d. h. frei, gegenüber; mit wachsendem Verständniss wächst also die (Geistes-) Freiheit, denn um so mehr ist Solches da, dessen ich Herr bin. Umgekehrt, je mehr ich verstehe, um so mehr muss ich mir, als nicht von mir selbst gebilligt, gefallen lassen, also um so beschränkter bin ich. Dieser Gegensatz zwischen Beschränktheit (*servitus*), welche *Spinoza* im vierten, und der Geistesstärke und Geistesfreiheit (*libertas*), die er im fünften Buche seines Hauptwerks behandelt, ist der Cardinalpunkt seiner Ethik, die eben deswegen der Sache nach nichts Andres ist als, wie er eine frühere Schrift genannt hatte, ein *Tractatus de intellectus emendatione*. (P. 70)

32 Translation, p. 86. The original passage marked by Russell was:

> Hält man dies fest, dass Begreifen Billigen oder Selbstwollen ist, so ist es ganz erklärlich, dass *Spinoza* bei allem seinem Fatalismus doch behaupten kann, dass, ja den Weg zeigen wie, der Mensch zu immer grösserer Freiheit kommen, und sich von jedem Leiden befreien kann. (P. 73)

33 Pollock's chief field was jurisprudence, and he was the author of many distinguished legal books and editor of several legal journals. He had studied classics and mathematics at Trinity College. In addition he was a mountaineer, fencer, picture fancier, and connoisseur of music. As members of the Cambridge society "The Apostles", Russell and Pollock became acquainted, though the process was apparently gradual. In 1902 Russell notes, "I was introduced to Sir F. Pollock for the fourth time: he (foolish old man) tried to explain the circular points of Infinity to Gertrude Bell ..." (Journal, 13 Nov. 1902 [original in Morrell papers, Texas]). Pollock, in writing to Oliver Wendell Holmes, Jr., in 1912 on *The Problems of Philosophy*, remarked: "we fudged even the binomial theorem in our youth, so Russell once told me." After the First World War, which was publicly opposed by Russell, Pollock's tone changed: "Bertrand Russell is a mighty clever philosopher, too clever I think. His theodicy so far as I can make out consists in being angry with the gods for not existing, because if they did he would like to break their windows" (*The Pollock-Holmes Letters: Correspondence of Sir Frederick Pollock and Mr. Justice Holmes, 1874–1932*, ed. Mark DeWolfe Howe [Cambridge, U.K.: Cambridge University Press, 1942], vol. II, letters of 24 Sept. 1912 and 2 July 1928, respectively). But despite their acquaintance and mutual interest in Spinoza,

Russell and Pollock seem not to have corresponded with one another (Sir George Pollock [grandson] to me, 9 Feb. 1979).

34 The first edition of Pollock's *Spinoza* appeared in 1880, a time, like now, of considerable academic interest in Spinoza, for it was soon after the bicentenary of his birth and there was much sympathy with monistic metaphysics. A second edition appeared in 1899 (a copy, unmarked except for Russell's signature and date, is in his library), with a corrected re-issue appearing in 1912 and a reprint in 1936.
35 Russell to Helen Thomas (later Flexner), 11 Nov. 1902 (original in Flexner papers, American Philosophical Society).
36 "Spinoza's Moral Code", *The Nation*, London, 1 (13 April 1907), p. 276; an unsigned review of J. Allanson Picton's *Spinoza*. For evidence of Russell's authorship, see **21**.
37 Russell, "Spinoza", *The Nation*, 8 (12 Nov. 1910), p. 278; review of White and Stirling's translation (4th ed.) of Spinoza's *Ethic*. For a discussion of Joachim's book, see **18**.
38 Later, when Lady Ottoline had read Pollock's book, Russell commented: "Pollock doesn't fully understand him. He is misled partly by friendship with W. K. Clifford, partly by a wish to modernize him and compare him with Spencer. Clifford was a very great man, who died young.... Pollock loved him, and his Spinoza is coloured by that—it was written after his death. Pollock has splendid things buried away—I have heard him at the Society's dinner perfectly wonderful" (no. 375, p/10 March 1912).

Despite this qualification, Russell esteemed Pollock's book. So did H. H. Joachim, whose *Study of the Ethics of Spinoza* is technically superior. He wrote in contributing to the British Academy's obituary of Pollock:

> ... the greatest merit of Sir F. Pollock's book on Spinoza is that it succeeds, to an astonishing degree, in satisfying the demands of this larger public as well as those of the specialist and expert....
>
> It is true, no doubt, that, in his account of Spinoza's philosophy Pollock passes too lightly over some of the technical difficulties, or is too easily content to offer criticisms and solutions, which would hardly be endorsed or accepted by those who have made the study of philosophy and its history their main concern. His whole treatment, e.g., of Spinoza's conception of the Attribute of thought, is obviously unsatisfactory.... It is, beyond all question, the best general introduction to the study not only of Spinoza's life but of his philosophy as well.

Quoted in Henry D. Hazeltine, "Sir Frederick Pollock, Bart.", *Proceedings of the British Academy*, 35 (1949), pp. 233-56 (at 253).
39 Revised and published as *An Essay on the Foundations of Geometry* (1897).
40 For example, in *The Problem of China* (London: Allen and Unwin, 1922), p. 241; *Principles of Social Reconstruction* (London: Allen and Unwin, 1916), p. 30.
41 The passage is from Goethe's autobiography, *Aus meinem Leben, Dichtung und Wahrheit*, Book xiv. It is not known whether Russell read this work; it is not listed in "What Shall I Read?". The passage and Goethe's relationship to Spinoza are discussed in K. R. Eissler, *Goethe: a Psychoanalytic Study, 1775-1786* (Detroit: Wayne State University Press, 1963), vol. II, pp. 930-51 (esp. 933-4).
42 Russell, "Spinoza", p. 280.
43 Russell ignores here the additional factor that in 1894 he became convinced of the validity of the ontological argument for the Absolute's existence ("My Mental Development", in Schilpp, ed., *The Philosophy of Bertrand Russell*, p. 10). See Spadoni, "'Great God in Boots!—The Ontological Argument Is Sound!'", *Russell*, nos. 23-4 (autumn-winter 1976), pp. 37-41. It was psychologically not difficult to attribute religious qualities to the Absolute.
44 Russell, "Reply to Criticisms", p. 726.

45 Russell, "On Keeping a Wide Horizon", p. 8.
46 Russell, *Which Way to Peace?* (London: Michael Joseph, 1936), p. 220.
47 Hume summed up his account as "Reason is, and ought only to be the slave of the passions, and can never pretend to any other office than to serve and obey them" (*A Treatise of Human Nature*, ed. L. A. Selby-Bigge [Oxford: Clarendon Press, 1888; reprinted 1968], II.iii.3 [p. 415]).
48 See "The Elements of Ethics", sec. iv, in Russell's *Philosophical Essays*, 2nd ed. (London: Allen and Unwin, 1966; 1st ed., 1910), p. 38.
49 Russell, "Hopes and Fears as Regards America", in *Bertrand Russell's America*, vol. I: *1896–1945*, ed. Barry Feinberg and Ronald Kasrils (London: Allen and Unwin, 1973), p. 223. The essay was first published in 1922.
50 The notion of remedies is taken up by Wienpahl, "Spinoza and Mental Health", *Inquiry*, 15 (1972), pp. 64–94.
51 *Cf*. Russell's advice in old age: "You should have an attitude of welcoming to everybody"—which in effect is only a little less general than the advice of the Stoics. (I no longer have the source of the statement, which was in a newspaper interview, but I am positive that my recollection of it is accurate.)
52 Russell, "Paper on History of Philosophy", Feb. 1894, *Cambridge Essays*, p. 141.
53 "Having been reading pantheism, I announced to my friends that I was God. They placed candles on each side of me and proceeded to acts of mock worship" (*Autobiography*, vol. I, p. 68). *Cf*. Spadoni, "Philosophy in Russell's Letters to Alys", pp. 25–6.
54 Russell, "Paper on Descartes II", May 1894, *Cambridge Essays*, p. 181.
55 Russell, "Paper on Hobbes", n.d., *Cambridge Essays*. Nicholas Griffin drew my attention to the cancelled passage quoted later in the paragraph.
56 First published in *Imaginary Portraits* (1887); reprinted in W. Pater, *The Works*, vol. IV: *Imaginary Portraits and Gaston de Latour* (London: Macmillan, 1900), pp. 81–115. Russell recorded in "What Shall I Read?" that he read one of the other portraits in September 1894; he may have read "Sebastian van Storck" then as well.
57 I. C. Small, "The Sources for Pater's Spinoza in 'Sebastian van Storck'", *Notes and Queries*, n.s. 25 (Aug. 1978), pp. 318–20. Pater's chief source of information about Spinoza was Pollock's *Spinoza*, according to Small's convincing evidence.
58 There is a valuable account, with full documentation, of Russell's early philosophical influences in Spadoni, "Russell's Rebellion against Neo-Hegelianism" (unpublished PH.D dissertation, University of Waterloo, 1977).
59 The letter (RA, file 710.110946) is dated merely "Friday" but contains a request to play tennis on Tuesday the 27th and refers to a book published in April 1892. Spadoni and Griffin (who is engaged in a study of Russell's idealist apprenticeship) have used this information to date the letter 27 September 1892. The capitalization of titles in my quotation follows the original.
60 Russell, *My Philosophical Development*, pp. 37–8.
61 Spadoni, "Russell's Rebellion", p. 105.
62 Russell, "Cleopatra or Maggie Tulliver", read to the Apostles, Nov. 1894, *Cambridge Essays*, p. 98.
63 Bradley, *Ethical Studies*, p. 196.
64 *My Philosophical Development*, p. 35.
65 "Russell's Rebellion", pp. 59–60.
66 For an account of the Apostles, see Paul Levy, *G. E. Moore and the Cambridge Apostles* (London: Weidenfeld and Nicolson, 1979). See also Griffin's review, "The Acts of the Apostles", *Russell*, n.s. 1 (summer 1981), pp. 71–82.
67 Quoted in "Russell's Rebellion", p. 70.
68 *Cambridge Essays*. There is no evidence the paper was published, but it seems written for publication.
69 Providing that happiness is taken as equivalent to satisfaction of desire.

Notes to pages 47–50

70 Russell, "Ethical Axioms", Feb. 1894, *Cambridge Essays*, p. 228. Stewart Candlish is interesting on the interrelationships of aspects of Bradley's philosophy here:

> ... Bradley's later hostility to the whole notion of external relations takes in the *Studies* the form of a curious mixture of an intellectual dislike of individualism, grounded in the belief that people are internally related to one another (p. 171), and a moral dislike of those who stand apart from society and who, presumably, both refuse to accept society and to recognize and accept their own necessary involvement in it. A further feature of this point is that the obscure injunction of Essay II *to realise oneself as an infinite whole*, and the even obscurer explanation of this (p. 78), begin to take on some sense when viewed in the light of the doctrine of internal relations. ("Bradley on My Station and Its Duties", *Australasian Journal of Philosophy*, 56 [Aug. 1978], pp. 155–70; my italics)

71 Spadoni, "Russell's Rebellion", p. 190.
72 Published in Russell, *Why I Am Not a Christian*, ed. Paul Edwards (New York: Simon and Schuster, 1957), and *Cambridge Essays*. The paper was included in the former collection presumably because, as a definite departure from the idealist metaphysics of Bradley and McTaggart, the paper opposes the claim there is religious value in philosophy. It is wrongly dated 1899 in Edwards' collection.
73 Idealists would disagree about what constitutes experience. M. J. Cresswell quotes Bradley: "Reality is experience and is nothing but experience" (*Appearance and Reality*, 2nd ed., 1897), and goes on to claim that this is the correct interpretation ("Reality as Experience in F. H. Bradley", *Australasian Journal of Philosophy*, 55 [Dec. 1977], pp. 169–88).
74 "Self-Appreciation", *The Golden Urn*, no. 1 (March 1897), p. 31 (published pseudonymously); *Cambridge Essays*, p. 73. The other man is Ferdinand Lassalle (1825–1864), the German socialist. He occupies a chapter in Russell's *German Social Democracy* (1896).
75 2nd ed. (London: Allen and Unwin, 1937; 1st ed., 1900). For the genesis of Russell's *Leibniz*, see Walter H. O'Briant, "Russell on Leibniz", *Studia Leibnitiana*, 11 (1979), pp. 159–222.
76 Russell's index contains only half of the 36 references to Spinoza made in the course of the book.
77 "What Shall I Read?". Russell also mentions in a letter to Alys of 9 March 1899 that he is reading Spinoza: "Moore came to dinner, and we talked at length about everything. I am reading Spinoza's Ethics, which I have nearly finished. It contains the most delightful pedantic cynicism on the Passions, with which I greatly amused Moore. It is the sort of thing Logan [Pearsall Smith] would love. I will read thee bits when thee comes home."
78 Both works are still in Russell's library, but neither is annotated.
79 Pollock's translation on p. 224 is quoted in *Leibniz*, p. 195 n. 1. White and Stirling's translation of E2P49 is quoted in *Leibniz*, p. 200 n. 2.
80 Alexander Louis, Count Foucher de Careil, *Réfutation inédite de Spinoza par Leibnitz, précédée d'un mémoire par A. Foucher de Careil* (Paris, 1854), and Ludwig Stein, *Leibniz und Spinoza. Ein Beitrag zur Entwicklungsgeschichte der leibnizischen Philosophie* (Berlin, 1890). We learn from "What Shall I Read?" that Russell read Stein's book in March 1899.
81 Georges Friedmann disputes this account of Leibniz's role *vis-à-vis* the Church (*Leibniz et Spinoza* [Paris: Gallimard, 1962], p. 336).
82 After his book was published, the researches of Couturat fundamentally altered this view. The second view is that "every true proposition is analytic" (*Leibniz*, 2nd ed., preface, p. v), though not always necessary, thus dissolving Russell's 1900 category of non-necessary existential (or contingent) propositions. The elaboration of this view occupies the preface to the second edition, and it persuaded Russell that

Leibniz was a better logician than he had thought. He came to this view in 1903 in reviewing Couturat's *La Logique de Leibniz* (1901) and as well as his *Opuscules et fragments inédits de Leibniz* (1903) (in *Mind*, 1903 and 1904). It is also asserted, in a more popular style, in *A History of Western Philosophy*. G. H. R. Parkinson's *Logic and Reality in Leibniz's Metaphysics* (Oxford: Clarendon Press, 1965), which is an evaluation of Russell's reductionist thesis, fails to see the revolution in his views caused by Couturat's work (p. 2). The best exposition of Russell's two interpretations is Curley, "The Root of Contingency", in Harry G. Frankfurt, ed., *Leibniz: a Collection of Critical Essays* (Garden City, N.Y.: Anchor Books, Doubleday, 1972), pp. 69–97. Curley rejects Russell's later view as an interpretation of Leibniz, holding that his "early interpretation in the *Critical Exposition*, though based on less evidence than his later discussions, is still the soundest guide to Leibniz's thought on the principle of sufficient reason and the problem of contingency" (p. 97).

83 Russell's claim has been disputed by Martha Kneale, who quotes this passage in "Leibniz and Spinoza on Activity", in Frankfurt, ed., *Leibniz*, pp. 215–37 (at 215–16). Although she carefully distinguishes the various senses in which Leibniz uses the terms "activity" and "passivity", and suggests that the similarities between Spinoza and Leibniz are overstated by Russell and "could be accounted for by common origin rather than by influence" (p. 236), she succeeds, to my mind, in showing just how closely related, and indeed how sometimes very nearly identical, were their uses of these terms. She makes the error of ascribing to Spinoza "the notion of interaction between substances" (p. 225). For "substances", of course, we must read not even "attributes" but "modes". Leibniz's monads are akin (in one important way) to Spinoza's attributes, in that they never interact, though between them there is a harmony. Since Spinoza's system is a determined system, it is, in effect, as pre-established as Leibniz's. Activity and passivity enter into things in respect of the monads' apparent relation of acting upon other monads, or suffering the action of other monads. Although Kneale finds passages to the contrary, Russell has a selection warranting the conclusion that Leibniz holds, like Spinoza, that in so far as we are active, we are in a state of understanding, rather than of confusion; and in so far as we are active, we are progressing towards perfection (p. 195).

84 Joachim, *A Study of the Ethics of Spinoza (Ethica Ordine Geometrico Demonstrata)* (Oxford: Clarendon Press, 1901; reprinted New York: Russell and Russell, 1964). It was published in September 1901 and read by Russell two months later ("What Shall I Read?"). Harold Henry Joachim (1868–1938) was known to Russell before he embarked on the study of philosophy. (Joachim's sister was married to Russell's uncle, Rollo Russell.) Joachim was an Aristotelian specialist as well as a Spinozist, and his book *The Nature of Truth* drew two reviews from Russell (in *Mind* and the *Independent Review*, 1906). In that book there is a lengthy section on Spinoza's coherence theory of truth, on which, however, Russell did not comment in his reviews. Nor is Russell known to have commented on (or even seen) Joachim's posthumously published *Spinoza's "Tractatus de Intellectus Emendatione": a Commentary* (1940). The two philosophers corresponded over *The Nature of Truth* (Russell is acknowledged as having replied in detail to the draft criticism of his views in the second chapter). Unfortunately, no correspondence on either side survives from the time of Joachim's *Study*: none was saved by Russell; and I am assured by Joachim's son-in-law, L. J. Beck, that none of Russell's letters to Joachim is extant (letter of 1 Feb. 1978).

85 We can examine his copy for marginal annotations. In 1911 he remarked upon the fact that Lady Ottoline had noticed Joachim's *Spinoza* on his shelves (no. 195, *c*. 26 Sept. 1911), but it was not in Russell's library by 1967 when I listed the contents for eventual sale. The copy owned by Russell has come to light in the University of York Library (information from Roland Hall). There are marginalia in Russell's hand on pp. 6, 43, 52, 54, 106 and 186, but none of them concerns the topics of God, self-realization, or the "intellectual love of God". See Chap. III, n. 17.

Chapter III The Middle Period (1907–12)

1 Russell to Gilbert Murray, 28 Dec. 1902 (photocopy, RA; original in Murray papers, Bodleian Library, Oxford); *Autobiography*, vol. I, p. 163.
2 2nd ed. (London: Allen and Unwin, 1937; 1st ed., 1903). The only two mentions of Spinoza in the *Principles* are in connection with the analysis of all propositions into those which ascribe a predicate to the Absolute.
3 Russell, "Religion and Metaphysics", *Independent Review*, 9 (1906), pp. 109–16 (at 116).
4 "Spinoza's Moral Code", *The Nation*, 1 (13 April 1907), p. 276.
5 *Speaking Personally Bertrand Russell*, interviewed by John Chandos (Riverside RLP 7014/7015, 1961), side 3. For Einstein on Spinoza, see his introduction to R. Kayser, *Spinoza: Portrait of a Spiritual Hero*, trans. A. Allen and M. Newmark (New York: Philosophical Library, 1946), and his foreword to *Spinoza Dictionary*, ed. D. D. Runes (New York: Philosophical Library, 1951).
6 London: Allen and Unwin, 1930, p. 226.
7 Russell, "Spinoza", *The Nation*, 8 (12 Nov. 1910), p. 278.
8 Hume, *Treatise*, III i.1 (p. 469).
9 Russell, *Mysticism and Logic*, pp. 26–7; 1963 ed., p. 26.
10 *The Philosophy of George Santayana*, p. 453.
11 For a discussion of "importance" as an evaluative criterion, see 56(4).
12 Russell, "Hopes and Fears as Regards America", *Bertrand Russell's America*, vol. I, p. 223.
13 *Spinoza: a Handbook to the Ethics* (London: Archibald Constable, 1907), p. 67.
14 Picton is described in the *Dictionary of National Biography, 1901–1911*, as "an uncompromising radical of an advanced type".
15 "The Mazzinis, the Garibaldis, the Cobdens, and the Brights of history have not been whining, melancholy pessimists, but men rejoicing in the inspired conviction that they were raising not themselves only but their nation, or even mankind, from a lesser to a larger perfection" (Picton, p. 146). Russell was, in fact, a life-long free-trader and internationalist, less I believe for economic reasons than for ethical ones. Just as the walls of the narrow ego prevent harmony between individuals, so the rigid boundaries between nations discourage peace; and nothing seems so absurd to the free-trader as that peace should be discouraged because of economic favouritism, the preference for the well-being of those persons who live on our side of a boundary over the well-being of those on the other side. For Russell's free-trade activism, see R. A. Rempel, "From Imperialism to Free Trade: Couturat, Halévy and the Development of Russell's First Crusade", *Journal of the History of Ideas*, 40 (July–Sept. 1979), pp. 423–43, and Peter Clarke, "Bertrand Russell and the Dimensions of Edwardian Liberalism", *Russell*, n.s. 4 (summer 1984), pp. 207–21.
16 W. Hale White [to the Editor of the *Nation*], 14 Nov. 1910, RA. The addressee's name was added by Russell.
17 His remarks on *affectus* drew a letter to the editor of the *Nation* from someone who had found a previous use of "affect" in the required sense in Bacon—as if that made the term a common one. See "Spinoza", *The Nation*, 8 (19 Nov. 1910), p. 335; the letter is signed "X". Wienpahl, who uses "Affection" to translate *affectus* and "affection" to translate *affectio* because the former is an affection of the body which increases or diminishes our power of acting, claims in his unpublished translation of the *Ethics*: "The entire character of the ETHIC is altered by the use of this word ['emotion'] for 'affectus'", because the use of the word "emotion" breaks a profound linguistic connection. On White's use of "affect", Wienpahl says it is close, "but it is a technical term in psychology, it does not suggest 'affection' to us, and it does not have the range of meanings which 'affection' does (these include 'mode of being')" (p. 524). Wienpahl's innovation, therefore, appears to be justified

by the standard Russell offers, though complete justification can be made only if Wienpahl's interpretation is correct.

In 1901, when Russell read Joachim's *Study*, he suggested "mood" in the margin next to Joachim's proposal of "emotion" (p. 186).
18 *Mysticism and Logic*, p. 109; 1963 ed., p. 83.
19 *Ibid.*, p. 56; 1963 ed., p. 46.
20 *Ibid.*, p. 73; 1963 ed., p. 58.
21 "Hopes and Fears as Regards America", *Bertrand Russell's America*, vol. I, p. 224.
22 *Mysticism and Logic*, p. 69; 1963 ed., p. 55.
23 For the topics of asceticism and Goethe's praises, see **13** and **15**, respectively. The discussion of Goethe is in response to White's preface, pp. lxxxiv–v.
24 *A Short Treatise upon God*, Part II, Chap. 22. The sentence Russell quotes is quoted in full in White's preface, p. lxxxv. Spinoza's *Short Treatise upon God, Man, and Man's Well-Being* was published in an English translation in January 1910 (ed. A. Wolf [London: Black]). The translation includes a long biography of Spinoza based on the latest research. There is no evidence Russell was acquainted with this volume, whose translation of the quoted passage is markedly different from White's.
25 There is also no evidence that he read Wolf's *Correspondence of Spinoza*, published by Russell's regular British publisher in 1928, despite his fondness for reading letters and Stanley Unwin's presents of philosophical books published by his firm. He later read Elwes' selection of the correspondence (**29**).
26 "How to Read and Understand History", in Russell, *Understanding History and Other Essays* (New York: Philosophical Library, 1957), p. 22. The essay was first published in 1943.
27 The two page markers are (1) a printed review slip (dated "19/9/10") for the book found upon arrival at McMaster between pages 248 and 249, i.e. marking heads 28–32 of E4Ap.; and (2) part of a cheque information stub with the typed date "DEC 27 '41" between pages 102 and 103, the site of the scholium to E2P49, and which had already been marked with a cross against the passage quoted above and a line against the statement "Hence we clearly see how greatly those stray from the true estimation of virtue who expect to be distinguished by God with the highest rewards for virtue and the noblest actions as if for the completest servitude, just as if virtue itself and the service of God were not happiness itself and the highest liberty."
28 Knowledge of Russell's interest in this proposition has been useful in ascribing to him a section in an anti-conscription pamphlet of World War I. There were already grounds for supposing his involvement in the writing of Mrs. Henry Hobouse's "*I Appeal unto Caesar*", but it is useful to know which sections can be ascribed to him with some certainty. In World War II, in the midst of supporting a war whose advent he opposed, Russell discusses the same proposition at some length in *A History of Western Philosophy* (see **30**). The passage is quoted in Jo Newberry, "Russell as Ghost-Writer", *Russell*, no. 15 (autumn 1974), p. 22. Newberry (now Vellacott) picks up the Spinoza reference in *Bertrand Russell and the Pacifists in the First World War* (Hassocks, Sussex: Harvester Press, 1980), pp. 212 and 294 n. 660.
29 As Ronald W. Clark says, "it ranks high among well-documented love-affairs since Russell wrote some 2,000 letters to Ottoline, frequently three a day during the heat of his excitement. She replied with nearly 1,600. Read as a whole, and with the repetitions ignored, the correspondence has the quality of a work of art" (*The Life of Bertrand Russell* [London: Cape/Weidenfeld and Nicolson, 1975], p. 132). See *Autobiography*, vols. I and II; Clark, Chaps. 6–8; *Ottoline: the Early Memoirs of Lady Ottoline Morrell*, ed. Robert Gathorne-Hardy (London: Faber and Faber, 1963); *Ottoline at Garsington*, ed. R. Gathorne-Hardy (London: Faber and Faber, 1974), esp. appendix; Sandra Jobson Darroch, *Ottoline: the Life of Lady Ottoline Morrell* (London: Chatto and Windus, 1976), *passim*. For an interpretation of the Russell–Morrell relationship in terms of the development of Russell's "integrity of self", see

Martin, pp. 129–96. See also Andrew Brink, "Russell to Lady Ottoline Morrell", *Russell*, nos. 21–22 (spring–summer 1976), pp. 3–15.
30 By James Strachey in *The Spectator*, 22 July 1911, and by G. H. Hardy in *The Times Literary Supplement*, 7 Sept. 1911.
31 Clark, pp. 152–3, quotes the proof, though he does not display it in the geometrical manner Russell did.
32 See my "The Early Wittgenstein and the Middle Russell", in *Perspectives on the Philosophy of Wittgenstein*, ed. Irving Block (Oxford: Blackwell, 1981), pp. 9, 14ff; and Clark, pp. 161, 176–7, 195, 202ff.
33 "Physical union" is the term employed in the Russell–Ottoline correspondence. It is also the term employed by Elwes for Spinoza's *miscendi corpora* (E4Ap.20). Other translators use "intercourse", "sexual intercourse", or "connection", with the exception of Wetlesen, Boyle and Wienpahl, who use "uniting bodies". *Cf.* Wienpahl's notes on translating *commiscendis corporibus* (E3Df.Aff.48) (unpublished trans., p. 591).
34 See their correspondence, June–July 1912. The democratic appeal of the wisdom demanded in the novella may have come from Lady Ottoline; she also wrote a lengthy section of the nun's speech (Clark, p. 179). Her views on Spinoza are, therefore, worth recording here. She wrote in her diary on 9 March 1912:

> I am reading Spinoza. He gives one a great deal. The abstract intellectual life which is eternal [sic], but I feel I personally learn and take in so much by my senses. . . . I have read Bertie's paper on Religion, too, and like it very much, except that it does not include and draw into itself the ordinary life of men which after all cannot be left outside religion. Why do they all elaborate philosophies and religions outside the real life we live. . . . Pure intellectual conceptions influence such men as Bertie and Moore and McTaggart, but they are almost worthless to the peasant or the clerk, and it is hard that such men should not be "eternal" in Spinoza's sense. Spinoza says that one must still all passions, know them and connect them as one knows one's body and put them away from one, divert the mind from them; only by developing the intellectual life can one attain God. Yes, that is happiness for those who have time and capacity for it, but it would be useless for the ordinary man. (*Ottoline: the Early Memoirs*, pp. 221–2)

Evidently Russell has taught Lady Ottoline that, according to Spinoza, men can become eternal to the extent that their thoughts are of eternal propositions. See Chap. V.
35 See Russell to Lady Ottoline, no. 1,055, p/22 July 1914.
36 Late in life he attached this rider to any posthumous publication: "While I am satisfied with the first part of the work, the second part represented my opinions during only a very short period. My views in the second part were very sentimental, much too mild and much too favourable to religion. In all this I was unduly influenced by Lady Ottoline Morrell" (*The Collected Stories of Bertrand Russell*, ed. Barry Feinberg [London: Allen and Unwin, 1972], preface, p. 10; the rider is in a letter to his literary executor, Anton Felton, dated 6 April 1968). "Forstice" is divided into three parts. Russell's remarks about "the second part" must have been meant to apply to the third part, as it is the religious part. Commentators who agree are Feinberg, *Collected Stories*, p. 12 n. 2, and Leithauser, "Principles and Perplexities", p. 127. Clark admits that it is "possible" Russell wrote "second" when he meant "third" (p. 682 [note to p. 182]).
37 Forstice's name may also be an allusion to Faustus. See Leithauser, "Principles and Perplexities", p. 122. For the importance of Faust to Russell, see Leithauser, "'A Non-Supernatural Faust': Bertrand Russell and the Themes of Faust", *Russell*, nos. 29–32 (1978), pp. 33–41.
38 "Principles and Perplexities", p. 149.

39 Jager, "Russell and Religion", in *Russell in Review*, ed. Thomas and Blackwell, pp. 91–113 (at 99).
40 *Ibid*.
41 For Russell's fondness for Leopardi, see *Ottoline: the Early Memoirs*, p. 226. In *Power*, pp. 32–3, and *The Impact of Science on Society* (London: Allen and Unwin, 1952), p. 98, Russell quotes *in extenso* two poems by Leopardi. I quote one in Chap. V, n. 36. In *A History of Western Philosophy* Russell calls Lucretius a "great poet" (p. 248; p. 256).
42 One is reminded here of the prologue to Russell's *Autobiography*: "These passions, like great winds, have blown me hither and thither, in a wayward course, over a deep ocean of anguish, reaching to the very verge of despair" (vol. I, p. 13).
43 Quoted by Sams, p. 128.

Chapter IV The Late Period (1914–64)

1 Russell, "The Value of Free Thought", in *Understanding History*, p. 66.
2 Russell to Lady Ottoline Morrell, nos. 961ff., 9 Jan. 1914; Clark, pp. 225–6.
3 Aiken (*Bertrand Russell's Philosophy of Morals*, p. 61) documents the change as taking place in 1915, but "On Scientific Method in Philosophy" is clear evidence that the change had taken place by 1914.
4 Vellacott, *Russell and the Pacifists*, p. 15.
5 *Ibid*., p. 41.
6 For example, Stanley Arthur Gurtoff, "The Impact of D. H. Lawrence on His Contemporaries" (unpublished PH.D. dissertation, University of Minnesota, 1965), pp. 144–232 (at 195–7). Despite this disagreement with Gurtoff, I find his account of the Lawrence–Russell relationship excellent, as I do Paul Delany's *D. H. Lawrence's Nightmare: the Writer and His Circle in the Years of the Great War* (New York: Basic Books, 1978), Chaps. III–V. See also George T. Zytaruk, "Lectures on Immortality and Ethics: the Failed D. H. Lawrence–Bertrand Russell Collaboration", *Russell*, n.s. 3 (1983–84), pp. 7–15; and Michael L. Ross, "Lawrence's Letters", *Russell*, n.s. 3 (1983–84), pp. 54–65.
7 For example, Jager, in *The Development of Bertrand Russell's Philosophy*, p. 507, and in "Russell and Religion, p. 92, omits them.
8 *Principles of Social Reconstruction*, pp. 245–6. For further analysis, see **47**.
9 The first draft of Russell's *Autobiography*, called "My First Fifty Years", was dictated in 1931.
10 Russell, *Roads to Freedom* (London: Allen and Unwin, 1918), p. 129. *Cf*. Russell to Lady Ottoline at the beginning of the war: "I live very much with the thought of Spinoza these days. He very nearly lost his life by making an anti-war speech at a time when the Dutch were mad against Louis XIV" (no. 1113, [22 Sept. 1914]). There is a similar personal political reference to Spinoza in an essay written twenty years later: "... public events impinge upon private lives more forcibly than in former days. Spinoza, in spite of his heretical opinions, could continue to sell spectacles and meditate, even when his country was invaded by foreign enemies; if he had lived now, he would in all likelihood have been conscripted or put in prison" ("On Being Modern-Minded", in *Unpopular Essays*, pp. 91–2).
11 This was the Brotherhood Church incident. See *Autobiography*, vol. II, pp. 31–2; Clark, pp. 325–6; Vellacott, *Russell and the Pacifists*, pp. 170–1. Both Clark and Vellacott quote Russell writing at the time to Lady Ottoline: "The young soldiers were pathetic, thinking we were their enemies. They all believed we were in the pay of the Kaiser" (no. 1468, 28 July 1917).
12 Russell, *An Outline of Philosophy* (London: Allen and Unwin, 1927), p. 249. In *The Analysis of Mind* (London: Allen and Unwin, 1921) Russell quotes William

James quoting Spinoza on belief (E2P49S). Russell points out that James's quotation is inaccurate but does not correct James in quoting him. (The inaccuracy is an unregistered omission in the quotation.)

13 Russell, *Logic and Knowledge*, ed. Robert C. Marsh (London: Allen and Unwin 1956), p. 227. Why Russell said "quite likely" rather than "quite possible" is a mystery. Although the lectures were taken down by a stenographer, we know Russell checked the transcript (I. Grattan-Guinness, *Dear Russell—Dear Jourdain: a Commentary on Russell's Logic, Based on His Correspondence with Philip Jourdain* [London: Duckworth, 1977], pp. 144–5). Also, Russell's letter to Unwin of 23 March 1919 mentions that Russell kept a duplicate copy.

14 Russell, "As a European Radical Sees It", *The Freeman*, 4 (8 March 1922), pp. 608–10 (at 610); John G. Slater drew my attention to this passage. Russell feared that Lady Ottoline would regard his outlook as cynical. Writing to her in 1918, he employed the *Ethics* to buttress an analysis of jealous behaviour towards Siegfried Sassoon by Katherine Mansfield and J. Middleton Murry:

> Murry is mean. I don't like it. Jealousy is at the bottom of it. (Not only *simple* jealousy, but a much more complex kind: see further on). Oh why are people so petty? ... Katherine hates you because Murry has liked you; hating you, she hates S.S. because you don't. Therefore Murry also has to hate S.S. They two are almost a repetition of the Lawrences, a little toned down: You will hate my saying all these things, but they are correct. You will find them proved in the 3rd Book of Spinoza's Ethics! Prop. 42, I think, from memory.   (Letter of 25 July [1918])

Russell's reference to the *Ethics* is a little off. He needs E3P35, with assistance from E3P31C.

15 Russell, *The Conquest of Happiness*, p. 226. The first American edition omits "but" in the phrase "all but students of philosophy" ([New York: Boni and Liveright, 1930], p. 227). Presumably the British edition, which Russell proofread (letter of 18 July 1930 to Unwin), has the wording he intended. For further analysis of this work, see **48**.

16 Russell, "On Youthful Cynicism", in *In Praise of Idleness* (London: Allen and Unwin, 1935), p. 183.

17 Spinoza, *Ethics and De Intellectus emendatione* (London: Dent, 1910), p. xix. The publisher has since replaced Santayana's introduction with one by T. S. Gregory.

18 In reviewing Santayana in 1922, Russell had already connected him with Spinoza: "Mr Santayana is a true philosopher, in that he views everything *sub specie aeternitatis*. ... So says Spinoza [at E4P62]; and accordingly these soliloquies are not unduly disturbed by the fact that the things which their author values are past or passing" ("The Aroma of Evanescence", review of Santayana's *Soliloquies in England, and Later Soliloquies, The Dial*, 73 [Nov. 1922], pp. 559–62 [at 559]).

19 Huntington Cairns, Allen Tate, Mark Van Doren, *Invitation to Learning* (New York: Random House, 1941), p. 418.

20 As reported in the programme's second volume, *New Invitation to Learning*, ed. Van Doren (New York: Random House, 1942), pp. 105–18.

21 In a paper written about 1950, Russell says that "... if we had more knowledge, the physical and psychological statements would be seen to be merely different ways of saying the same thing" ("Mind and Matter", in *Portraits from Memory*, pp. 148–9). In *An Outline of Philosophy* there is a discussion of psychophysical parallelism in relation to Spinoza. Russell understands the term to mean that "to every state of the brain a state of mind *corresponds* and vice versa, without either acting on the other" (p. 249).

22 Douglas Odegard disagrees that Russell's and Spinoza's views on the relationship of mind and matter are so similar. He holds that Spinoza "leaves no room for the concept of an 'intrinsically neutral stuff' by reference to which our mental and

corporeal concepts might be constructed" ("The Body Identical with the Human Mind: a Problem in Spinoza's Philosophy", in Eugene Freeman and Maurice Mandelbaum, eds., *Spinoza: Essays in Interpretation* [La Salle, Ill.: Open Court, 1975], pp. 61–83 [at 66]). But Spinoza's substance *is* just that stuff, viewed either mentally or physically for the purpose of such constructions. Russell's neutral stuff is no longer neutral, either, when it is organized mentally or physically. In neither metaphysic do we have direct access to what is neutral, but only—in Spinoza's case—to modifications of attributes of it, or—in Russell's case—to a "reorganization" of it that transforms its neutral character into that which is either mental or physical.

23 *Cf.* E5P24: "The more we understand particular things, the more do we understand God" (Elwes trans.).

24 The reviews were as controversial as could be expected. But, reviewing in the London *Observer*, A. D. Ritchie was mildly complimentary of the Spinoza chapter. While charging that Russell treats a philosopher according to his liking for him, Ritchie admitted: "Spinoza, whose thought is entirely alien to Lord Russell's, is treated pretty fairly ..." (24 Nov. 1946, p. 4). Isaiah Berlin was very perceptive. He noted that Russell "so far as his own intellectual processes are concerned has a greater kinship with the formal architecture of such systems as that of Descartes and Leibniz than with the disconnected introspective description of Locke and Berkeley." As for the other great seventeenth-century rationalist, "He admires Spinoza, and expresses deep respect for his ethical views which, oddly enough, he considers to be lacking in passion. Spinoza belongs to the martyrs and the minorities—'A good man', says Russell with much feeling, 'hence accused of much immorality'. The exposition of his system, although it is scarcely likely to satisfy Spinozists, is a scrupulous and in places moving attempt to reconstruct the vision of man and the universe provided by rationalism at its best and purest" (*Mind*, 56 [1947], pp. 151–66 [at 161]). Berlin also noted about Russell: "Pure mysticism not adulterated with metaphysical—*i.e.* pseudophilosophical—argument appeals to him as an intense form of genuine personal experience" (pp. 158–9).

25 The manuscript of the *History* was likely completed in late 1943 (Russell's letter of 30 June 1943 to P. A. Schilpp says he will finish it in September). In the prefaces to the American and British editions Russell credits Albert C. Barnes and his foundation in Pennsylvania, where the book was "originally designed and partly delivered as lectures". Russell worked for Dr. Barnes from January 1941 to December 1942, when Barnes fired him. But Wienpahl, in a letter of 5 January 1979 to me, claims that Russell gave a version of his *History* as a lecture course at the University of California at Los Angeles in 1939–40. And a contract with Russell's British publisher for a book on "History of Philosophy (from Bacon or Descartes to James)" was signed on 26 July 1937 (RA). This book became *A History of Western Philosophy*, but we do not know how much of it had been written by the time Russell began working for Barnes.

The manuscript of the chapter on Spinoza is exceptionally free of revisions, even for Russell's manuscripts by this time. I have collated the manuscript with the three editions of the *History* and the last printing in Russell's lifetime of the 1961 edition, and found no variants worth reporting. The number of minor changes made between the first and last versions of the *History* is quite large, but the Spinoza chapter was the subject of almost none of them. Examples of alterations within the ms. are "necessary" for "essential" at p. 572, line 22 (p. 555, l. 8 in the 1961 edition), because "essential" is in the next line; and "when" for "where" at p. 578, l.17 (p. 560, l. 23).

26 File 210.006736, RA.

27 London: Allen and Unwin; New York: Lincoln MacVeagh, The Dial Press, 1927.

28 *The Chief Works of Benedict de Spinoza*, trans. R. H. M. Elwes, 2 vols. (London: G. Bell and Sons, 1883–4; reprinted New York: Dover, 1951, 1955).
29 In "An Outline of Intellectual Rubbish" we are told that Spinoza was against votes for women (*The Basic Writings of Bertrand Russell*, ed. L. E. Denonn and R. E. Egner [London: Allen and Unwin, 1961], p. 84). The relevant passage in the *Tractatus Politicus* is among those Russell noted (*Chief Works*, vol. I, p. 386). In "How to Read and Understand History" (as quoted in 23) Russell asserts that certain lives become nobler the more we learn about them. The first of these articles was published in June 1943 and the second as a pamphlet in the same year. The publisher, E. Haldeman-Julius, received them from Russell in late 1942 or early 1943 (see William F. Ryan, "Bertrand Russell and Haldeman-Julius: Making Readers Rational", *Russell*, nos. 29–32 [1978], pp. 53–64).
30 For example, Lewis Browne, *Bleséd Spinoza* (New York: Macmillan, 1932); A. Wolfson, *Spinoza: a Life of Reason* (New York: Modern Classics, 1932); and the introductions to several of the translations and commentaries.
31 In the *History*'s first editions (1945 and 1946), Spinoza's dates are given as 1634–1677. In the new British edition of 1961, the birthdate is corrected to 1632. But the statement on the first page of the chapter, that Spinoza died at age 43, remains uncorrected.
32 *The Chief Works of Benedict de Spinoza*, vol. II, p. 405. The letter is to G. H. Schaller.
33 Dewey made a similar charge against Russell. See my "Russell's Reply to Dewey", *Russell*, no. 12 (winter 1973–4), pp. 29–30, and **48**.
34 Russell has truncated Nietzsche's full statement, which begins with a slashing attack on the style of Spinoza's *Ethics*: "... the hocus-pocus of mathematical form, by means of which Spinoza has as it were clad his philosophy in mail and mask ..." (quoted by Feuer, *Spinoza and the Rise of Liberalism*, p. 199). Nietzsche's statement is from *Beyond Good and Evil*, trans. Helen Zimmern (Edinburgh: Foulis, 1909), p. 10.
35 *The Chief Works of Benedict de Spinoza*, vol. II, pp. 345–50.
36 "Logical Positivism", in *Logic and Knowledge*, p. 368.
37 *Portraits from Memory*, p. 195; "How I Write" (a different article), *The Writer*, n.s. 14 (Sept. 1954), p. 4.
38 See *Autobiography*, vol. I, p. 145.
39 Russell to Lucy Martin Donnelly, 3 Aug. and 3 Sept. 1905; *Autobiography*, vol. I, pp. 178–9.
40 Interview, *New York Times*, 26 Sept. 1938; quoted by Clark, p. 462. In his *Autobiography*, vol. II, Russell writes: "The doctrine which Tolstoy preached with great persuasive force, that the holders of power could be morally regenerated if met by non-resistance, was obviously untrue in Germany after 1933. Clearly Tolstoy was right only when the holders of power were not ruthless beyond a point, and clearly the Nazis went beyond this point" (p. 192).
41 Nor would Spinoza "condemn" them, but he would say they were definitely incorrect to hold these attitudes.
42 See **16–17**.
43 W. H. Walsh makes valuable observations on Hegel and Bradley in his *Hegelian Ethics* (London: Macmillan, 1969), pp. 72–4.
44 London: Allen and Unwin, 1949, p. 58.
45 It was published first as an article: "If We Are to Survive This Dark Time—", *New York Times Magazine*, 3 Sept. 1950, pp. 5, 17–18. It was reprinted in *New Hopes for a Changing World* (London: Allen and Unwin, 1951), Chap. XVIII, and in *Basic Writings*, pp. 682–7.
46 "Prof. G. E. Moore: Influence on Lord Russell", *The Times*, London, 28 Oct. 1958, p. 14.
47 Milton Marmor's Associated Press interview with Russell, 18 Nov. 1964. The full text (corrected by Russell in typescript) is in RA file 410.140676a, p. 8.

Chapter V Amor Dei Intellectualis

1. Russell read philosophical Latin and drafted the mass of translations from Leibniz's Latin for his *Leibniz*, with Moore revising them (O'Briant, p. 185).
2. David Savan makes the point that Spinoza held that it is extremely difficult, if not impossible, to give precise verbal expression to knowledge of the third kind, since it is the perception of a thing without the mediation of words and images. See Savan's "Spinoza and Language", in Paul Kashap, ed., *Studies in Spinoza: Critical and Interpretative Essays* (Berkeley: University of California Press, 1972), pp. 236–48; also in Grene (n. 6 below), pp. 59–72.
3. Savan, "Spinoza on Man's Knowledge of God: Intuition, Reason, Revelation, and Love", in Barry S. Kogan, ed., *Spinoza: a Tercentenary Perspective* ([Cincinnati]: Hebrew Union College—Jewish Institute of Religion [1979]), pp. 80–103 (at 80). Savan describes Spinoza's God as "not a thing, but unlimited expressive activity" (p. 93).
4. Thomas Carson Mark comes very close to asserting this in his explanation of the steps from intuitive knowledge through Spinoza's conception of immortality to the intellectual love of God (*Spinoza's Theory of Truth* [New York: Columbia University Press, 1972], p. 122).
5. Spinoza's term is *pars Mentis* (E5P40C).
6. Donagan, "Spinoza's Proof of Immortality", in Marjorie Grene, ed., *Spinoza: a Collection of Critical Essays* (Garden City, N.Y.: Doubleday, 1973), pp. 240–58 (at 244).
7. For an interpretation contrary to Donagan's, see H. F. Hallet, *Aeternitas: a Spinozistic Study* (Oxford: Clarendon Press, 1930), who denies that sempiternity is involved. The issue of Spinoza's conception of immortality is notoriously difficult, and Hallet is forced to regard some of Spinoza's statements as "verbal slips" (p. 74).
8. Matson, "Death and Destruction in Spinoza's *Ethics*", *Inquiry*, 20 (1977), pp. 403–17 (at 414). Matson applies the personal identity criterion of memory to the phenomenon of death. This application yields a convincing explanation of Spinoza's view that a corpse is not necessary to death, as in his case of the amnesiac poet (E4P39S). Memory is for Spinoza merely the association of ideas relating to modifications of the body (E2P18). Russell does not adopt loss of memory as a means to the metaphorical death of self in which he is interested.
9. Russell writes in "Mysticism and Logic" of his own attitude to time:

    > The arguments for the contention that time is unreal and that the world of sense is illusory must, I think, be regarded as fallacious. Nevertheless there is some sense—easier to feel than to state—in which time is an unimportant and superficial characteristic of reality. Past and future must be acknowledged to be as real as the present, and a certain emancipation from slavery to time is essential to philosophic thought. The importance of time is rather practical than theoretical, rather in relation to our desires than in relation to truth. A truer image of the world, I think, is obtained by picturing things as entering into the stream of time from an eternal world outside, than from a view which regards time as the devouring tyrant of all that is. Both in thought and in feeling, even though time be real, to realize the unimportance of time is the gate of wisdom. (*Mysticism and Logic*, pp. 21–2; 1963 ed., pp. 22–3)

    The same passage (except for the first sentence) also appears in *Our Knowledge of the External World* (Chicago and London: Open Court, 1914), pp. 166–7.
10. Wolfson, *The Philosophy of Spinoza* (Cleveland: Meridian Books, 1958; 1st ed., 1934), vol. II, p. 306.
11. Bidney, *The Psychology and Ethics of Spinoza: a Study in the History and Logic of Ideas* (New York: Russell and Russell, 1962; 1st ed., 1940).
12. Hampshire, *Spinoza* (Harmondsworth, Middlesex: Penguin Books, 1951), p. 175.

13 Harris, *Salvation from Despair: A Reappraisal of Spinoza's Philosophy*, International Archives of the History of Ideas, vol. 59 (The Hague: Nijhoff, 1973), p. 204.
14 This criticism and reply are also made in the same words in Harris's "Spinoza's Theory of Human Immortality", in Freeman and Mandelbaum, eds., *Spinoza*, pp. 245–63 (at 260–1).
15 By "Spinozist" I understand a philosopher who specializes in the scholarly interpreting of Spinoza, not someone who endeavours to follow his teaching. For example, H. G. Hubbeling is a Spinozist in the former sense, while denying that he is one in the latter sense. See his "The Logical and Experiential Roots of Spinoza's Mysticism—an Answer to Jon Wetlesen", in Siegfried Hessing, ed., *Speculum Spinozanum*, pp. 323–9 (at 323). Hessing, on the other hand, while definitely a Spinozist in the second sense, does not appear to be one in the first sense. It is apparent from Wetlesen's book *The Sage and the Way: Spinoza's Ethics of Freedom* that he is a Spinozist in both senses.
16 See, for example, Wetlesen and Naess, *Conation and Cognition in Spinoza's Theory of Affects: a Reconstruction* (Oslo: Institute of Philosophy, University of Oslo, 1967; Ann Arbor: University Microfilms International, 1979). Their "Eastern" publications include an exchange in Wetlesen, ed., *Spinoza's Philosophy of Man*. Naess's article is "Through Spinoza to Mahayana Buddhism or through Mahayana Buddhism to Spinoza" (pp. 136–58). Wetlesen's reply is "Freedom as Contemplation or Action? A Reply to Arne Naess" (pp. 204–9).
17 The chief published source for Wienpahl's views is his *The Radical Spinoza*. See also his "On Translating Spinoza", in Hessing, ed., *Speculum Spinozanum*, pp. 495–524; "Spinoza and Mysticism", in Wetlesen, ed., *Spinoza's Philosophy of Man*, pp. 211–24; and "Spinoza and Mental Health".
18 Hubbeling's article in the Hessing volume is a rejoinder to Wetlesen's article in the same volume ("Body Awareness as a Gateway to Eternity: a Note on the Mysticism of Spinoza and Its Affinity to Buddhist Meditation", *Speculum Spinozanum*, pp. 479–94). Wetlesen's article is in turn a reply to Hubbeling's "Logic and Experience in Spinoza's Mysticism", in J. G. van der Bend, ed., *Spinoza on Knowing, Being and Freedom* (Assen, The Netherlands: Van Gorcum, 1974), pp. 126–43.
19 In *The Radical Spinoza* Wienpahl provides the Latin original as well as his translation of all of the propositions, definitions, axioms and postulates of the *Ethics*. A serious student of the *Ethics* should have at least this near-acquaintance with the original. Spinoza uses certain key terms in a variety of contexts, and most translators suit their translation to the context. Not Wienpahl, however. In finding the same rendering of each Latin term throughout his translation, the reader is forced to struggle more with Spinoza's concept itself, rather than the translator's understanding of it.
20 Lewis and Short's *Latin Dictionary* describes this meaning as "poet. and very rare". Going to the Latin roots as well as the English makes Wienpahl's "radical" translation radical indeed.
21 Savan, who calls Spinoza "the philosopher of individuality *par excellence*", appears to agree with Wienpahl on this matter ("Spinoza on Man's Knowledge of God", p. 92). Savan would qualify his agreement, however, by adding that particular things are to be seen "*as* an expression of God's activity" (*ibid.*, p. 97).
22 Instead of *amor dei intellectualis* in the original Latin edition of 1677, Wienpahl adopts the equivalent reading in the Dutch edition of the same year, which in Latin is *dei amor intellectualis*. In addition, he understands *dei* in the adjectival sense in which Spinoza speaks of the Hebrew term for God in the *Tractatus Theologico-Politicus*, Chap. I, namely just something very great (*The Radical Spinoza*, pp. 46–7). In trying to verify Wienpahl's claim, I find this sense of a "superlative degree" is indeed one offered by Spinoza (*Chief Works*, trans. Elwes, vol. I, p. 21), but it is only one of five senses he offers. I doubt that Wienpahl is at liberty to select this special sense over the more usual ones.

23 Dilip Kumar Roy, "Bertrand Russell", in his *Among the Great* (Bombay: Nalanda Publications, 1945), pp. 111–49 (at 127). Russell checked the transcript of this 1927 interview (p. 116).
24 *Ibid.*, p. 135.
25 For example, he tells Roy: "... when one takes children in hand one may do a lot by encouraging in them the proper sort of impulses which comprise the whole of life instead of cramping them into dwarfed and bigoted egocentrics.... Children should be taught to enlarge interests in life as much as possible" (p. 127).

Chapter VI Development of the Ethic of Impersonal Self-Enlargement

1 Pitt, "Russell on Religion", *International Journal for Philosophy of Religion*, 6 (1975), pp. 40–53 (at 49), quoting from *Mysticism and Logic*, p. 28; 1963 ed., p. 27. For a criticism of this non-credal approach by Russell, see Nicholas Griffin, "Bertrand Russell's Crisis of Faith", *Russell*, n.s. 4 (summer 1984), pp. 101–22 (at 115–17).
2 In Schilpp, ed., *The Philosophy of Bertrand Russell*, pp. 539–56.
3 Titled "Religion and the Churches". See **47** for a summary.
4 See **48** for the "significance" of personal love in establishing values.
5 By "mystical experience" I do not mean anything supernatural. For a discussion of whether Spinoza had such an experience, see the articles by Wienpahl, Hubbeling, Wetlesen and Naess cited in Chap. V, nn. 15–18. B. F. McGuinness has used Russell's "Mysticism and Logic" in trying to determine whether Wittgenstein had a mystical experience ("The Mysticism of the *Tractatus*", *Philosophical Review*, 75 [1966], pp. 305–28).
6 For Russell's arguments against intuition, and details of a course of lectures he planned on the nature of insight, see n. 30 below.
7 *Cf.* Russell in *The Scientific Outlook* (London: Allen and Unwin, 1931):

> The mystic, the lover, and the poet are also seekers after knowledge.... Wherever there is ecstasy or joy or delight derived from an object there is the desire to know that object—to know it not in the manipulative fashion that consists of turning it into something else, but to know it in the fashion of the beatific vision, because in itself and for itself it sheds happiness upon the lover. ... Love which has value contains an impulse towards that kind of knowledge out of which the mystic union springs. (Pp. 270–1)

Cf. also *Human Society in Ethics and Politics*, p. 17.
8 Stace, *Mysticism and Philosophy* (Philadelphia: Lippincott, 1960), pp. 13–17.
9 The shared determinism is the similarity that Rescher notes (cited in Chap. I, n. 41).
10 The suppressed sentences are quoted in my "The Future of the Russell Archives", in Thomas and Blackwell, eds., *Russell in Review*, p. 29 n. 11.
11 "These comforters are Courage...", unpublished ms. (Morrell papers, University of Texas at Austin), photocopy in RA, Rec. Acq. 266 (xxvii). For a different view of these fragmentary essays—one that sees "The Return to the Cave", "Austerity", and the others as comprising a work mentioned variously in Russell's journal as "The Pilgrimage to the Mountain of Truth" (10 Dec. 1902) and "The Pilgrimage of Life" (14 Jan. 1903)—see Brink, "Bertrand Russell's *The Pilgrimage of Life* and Mourning", *Journal of Psychohistory*, 10 (winter 1983), pp. 311–31. It is probable that these fragmentary essays surviving in Lady Ottoline's papers were included with those Russell sent her on 26 March 1911. He commented then: "They are a set of disjointed reflections, for the most part, with which I tried to solace myself when I much needed solace" (no. 43b).
12 "Austerity", unpublished ms. (Morrell papers, University of Texas at Austin), photocopy in RA, Rec. Acq. 266 (xix).

13 For example, in the final paragraph of "Pragmatism", published first in 1909:

> To sum up: Pragmatism appeals to the temper of mind which finds on the surface of this planet the whole of its imaginative material; ... which desires religion, as it desires railways and electric light, as a comfort and a help in the affairs of this world, not as providing non-human objects to satisfy the hunger for perfection and for something to be worshipped without reserve. But for those who feel that life on this planet would be a life in a prison if it were not for the windows into a greater world beyond; for those to whom a belief in man's omnipotence seems arrogant, who desire rather the Stoic freedom that comes of mastery over the passions than the Napoleonic domination that sees the kingdoms of this world at its feet—in a word, to men who do not find Man an adequate object of their worship, the pragmatist's world will seem narrow and petty, robbing life of all that gives it value, and making Man himself smaller by depriving the universe which he contemplates of all its splendour.

Quoted from *Philosophical Essays*, 2nd ed. (London: Allen and Unwin, 1966), pp. 110–11, and quoted by Russell in his Matchette Foundation lectures (*The Impact of Science on Society*, pp. 103–4). For John Dewey's criticism of the ideal of contemplation, see 45.

14 There is no evidence that Lady Ottoline was acquainted with Spinoza before her affair with Russell.

15 The manuscript was completed, typed out in at least two copies, and possibly destroyed by Russell—for no version is known to be extant. Russell considered calling the book "The Religion of Contemplation" or "On Contemplative Freedom" (no. 173, n.d.). To Lady Ottoline he nicknamed it "Prisons", doubtless because it concerned the means of escape from mental prisons. There are accounts of the book's progress in letters Russell wrote to Lady Ottoline. These letters are seldom dated, but the writing seems to have been done in the month of August 1911, immediately following the drafting of *The Problems of Philosophy*. In September Russell had "Prisons" typed, sending one copy to Lady Ottoline in Vienna, and "the other" (no. 200, 29 Sept. 1911) to Alfred and Evelyn Whitehead. Alfred appears not to have read it—"anything ethical bores him", reported Russell—but Evelyn criticized it severely for its form and matter (Clark, p. 160). Others may have criticized it, too. Eventually, in revised form, the only part of it to be published was the last chapter, as "The Essence of Religion" in the *Hibbert Journal* of October 1912. (In February 1912 Russell tells Lady Ottoline that he is busy with "Prisons" again, "... cutting out odd pages and sticking them in to the chapter on Religion" [no. 355, p/23 Feb. 1912].) The rest of the manuscript appears not to be extant in any form, except for a few outlines, passages and a draft of the final paragraphs of the published article. I do not know of any allusion to the work by Russell after 1912. After discarding the bulk of "Prisons", he changed genres in order to try for success in another way. The first attempt was a "spiritual autobiography", written in the spring of 1912, and then "The Perplexities of John Forstice", which is probably a little less directly autobiographical; the former work also does not survive.

16 "Prisons I", unpublished ms. (Morrell papers, University of Texas at Austin), photocopy in RA, Rec. Acq. 266 (xvii).

17 "Prisons", unpublished ms. (Morrell papers, University of Texas at Austin), photocopy in RA, Rec. Acq. 266 (xviii), p. 2.

18 "Action and Contemplation", unpublished ms. (Morrell papers, University of Texas at Austin), photocopy in RA, Rec. Acq. 266 (xvi), p. 2.

19 This application of the terms "finite" and "infinite" does not seem to be original with Russell, though I have not been able to trace his source. A. S. Pringle-Pattison does not find them strange in his paper on "The Free Man's Worship" and "The Essence of Religion" (cited in Chap. I, n. 42).

20 When Wittgenstein read "The Essence" he let Russell know that he regarded him as

a traitor to the gospel of exactness, that he had wantonly used words vaguely, and that such things were too intimate for print (no. 600, p/11 Oct. 1912). See my "The Early Wittgenstein and the Middle Russell", p. 10. The essay was reviewed anonymously as "Religion without God", *The Nation*, 12 (27 Oct. 1912), pp. 171–2. See also the list of articles in Chap. I, n. 42.
21 See the preface to A. S. Pringle-Pattison's *The Idea of God in the Light of Recent Philosophy* (Oxford: Clarendon Press, 1917; 2nd ed., 1923). His lecture on Russell was published in the *Hibbert Journal* (cited in Chap. I, n. 42).
22 Hardy, "Mr. Russell as a Religious Teacher", *Cambridge Magazine*, 6 (19 and 26 May 1917), pp. 624–6 and 650–3 (at 650). Reprinted in *Russell*, n.s. 1 (1981–82), pp. 119–35. Hardy notes that his essay was written before the war (p. 624).
23 Hoernlé, "The Religious Aspect of Bertrand Russell's Philosophy", cited in Chap. I, n. 42.
24 *The Problems of Philosophy*, p. 152.
25 See the quotation in n. 7 for a later expression of cognitive union.
26 Sessions deals with notion under the term "anthropocentricity". See his "Anthropocentrism and the Environmental Crisis", *Humboldt Journal of Social Relations*, 2 (fall/winter 1974), pp. 1–12, where he cites Russell as a critic of anthropocentrism.
27 Dewey, *Essays in Experimental Logic* (Chicago: University of Chicago Press, 1916), pp. 71–4.
28 Review of Dewey's *Essays in Experimental Logic*, in *Journal of Philosophy, Psychology and Scientific Methods*, 16 (2 Jan. 1919), 5–26 (at 19). The review was written in prison in the summer of 1918. Russell goes on to say: "Escape from one's own personality is something which has been desired by the mystics of all ages, and in one way or another by all in whom ardent imagination has been a dominant force. It is, of course, a matter of degree: complete escape is impossible, but some degree of escape is possible, and knowledge is one of the gateways into the world of freedom. Instrumentalism does its best to shut this gateway" (p. 10).
29 Brightman, "Russell's Philosophy of Religion", pp. 552–3. *Cf.* also Russell's account of Dewey's confession to having valued the pursuit of knowledge for its own sake, and a restatement of his (Russell's) valuation of contemplation, in "Dewey's New *Logic*", in Schilpp, ed., *The Philosophy of John Dewey* (Evanston and Chicago: Northwestern University, 1939), pp. 137–56 (at 155); reprinted in *Basic Writings*, pp. 191–206 (at 205).
30 Two years later, and using the term "intuition" rather than "mystical experience", Russell rejects this way to knowledge: "Apart from self-knowledge, one of the most notable examples of intuition is the knowledge people believe themselves to possess of those with whom they are in love: the wall between different personalities seems to become transparent, and people think they see into another soul as into their own. Yet deception in such cases is constantly practised with success; and even where there is no intentional deception, experience gradually proves, as a rule, that the supposed insight was illusory, and that the slower, more groping methods of the intellect are in the long run more reliable" (*Our Knowledge of the External World*, p. 24).

Some time before writing *Our Knowledge*, Russell planned to give a series of lectures on insight. He sent Lady Ottoline a list of topics. Insight in philosophy was to be illustrated chiefly by reference to Spinoza.
31 Jager notes the connection between the two writings in his "Russell and Religion", in Thomas and Blackwell, eds., *Russell in Review*, p. 113. Jager's discussion of the incarnation of values is useful.
32 *Cf.* also *Our Knowledge of the External World*: "I have no wish to deny it [the mystic's world], nor even to declare that the insight which reveals it is not a genuine insight" (p. 20).
33 Richard Wollheim points out the similarity of Russell's theory of impulse to Mill's distinction between self-regarding and other-regarding desires ("Bertrand Russell

and the Liberal Tradition", in George Nakhnikian, ed., *Bertrand Russell's Philosophy* [New York: Barnes and Noble, 1974], pp. 209–20 [at 214]).

34 Some philosophers (e.g. Albert Schweitzer and Peter Singer) would ask why the boundary should be drawn with the human race. Russell was never confronted with the charge of speciesism, though the human race enjoys an elite status in his normative writings.

35 Griffin, "Russell's Crisis of Faith", pp. 109–10, is helpful: "For it was only through love, he [Russell] came to think, that the intolerable loneliness of the human soul could be overcome. It is as if he were desperately trying to preserve love as an internal relation because without some such internal relation the isolation of the individual would be ineradicable, and human life unendurable and without recourse." Clearly Russell regretted the emotional consequences of his revolt from neo-Hegelianism to an irreducible atomism.

36 This is the last line of Leopardi's poem "L'Infinito". R. C. Trevelyan translates it, "and sweet it seems to shipwreck in this sea" (*Translations from Leopardi* [Cambridge, U.K.: Cambridge University Press, 1941], p. 3). Russell quotes the poem in full in *The Impact of Science on Society*, p. 98, prefacing it thus: "This point of view is well expressed in a little poem by Leopardi and expresses, more nearly than any other known to me, my own feeling about the universe and human passions":

> THE INFINITE
> Dear to me always was this lonely hill
> And this hedge that excludes so large a part
> Of the ultimate horizon from my view.
> But as I sit and gaze, my thought conceives
> Interminable vastnesses of space
> Beyond it, and unearthly silences,
> And profoundest calm; whereat my heart almost
> Becomes dismayed. And as I hear the wind
> Blustering through these branches, I find myself
> Comparing with this sound that infinite silence;
> And then I call to mind eternity,
> And the ages that are dead, and this that now
> Is living, and the noise of it. And so
> In this immensity my thought sinks drowned:
> And sweet it seems to shipwreck in this sea.

37 The letter to Miss Rinder was meant to be circulated, like many other letters Russell wrote from prison. There is no particular reason to think he had discussed Spinoza's *Ethics* with her.

38 See my note introducing "On Keeping a Wide Horizon", p. 5. The *Reader's Digest* published its version as "A Philosophy for You in These Times", 39 (Oct. 1941), pp. 5–7.

39 Quoted, e.g., by Constance Malleson, "Fifty Years: 1916–1966", p. 24. The entire paragraph on death is most recently quoted, with the author's approbation, in Douglas N. Walton, *On Defining Death: an Analytic Study of the Concept of Death in Philosophy and Medical Ethics* (Montreal: McGill–Queen's University Press, 1980), p. 166.

40 London: Allen and Unwin, 1954, p. 36.

41 Published first in *The Listener*, 52 (9 Sept. 1954), p. 390. Reprinted in *Portraits from Memory*, pp. 160–4.

42 Published first in *London Calling*, no. 737 (17 Dec. 1953), pp. 8, 18. Reprinted in *Portraits from Memory*, pp. 165–70.

43 First published in *Saturday Evening Post*, 232 (18 July 1959), pp. 24, 91–3. Reprinted in Richard Thruelsen and John Kobler, eds., *Adventures of the Mind* (New York: Knopf, 1960), pp. 275–85; and in *Basic Writings*, pp. 390–8.

44 His point is similar to mine about perfect altruism—see 55(1).
45 In Eugene Freeman, ed., *The Abdication of Philosophy: Philosophy and the Public Good; Essays in Honor of Paul Arthur Schilpp* (La Salle, Ill.: Open Court, 1976), pp. 15–22 (at 16).
46 The last contribution was "Addendum to My 'Reply to Criticisms'", in Schilpp, ed., *The Philosophy of Bertrand Russell*, 4th ed., pp. xvii–xx.
47 "The Philosopher's Duty in These Times", *Russell*, nos. 35–6 (autumn–winter 1979–80), pp. 55–7 (at 56).
48 Because viewing life as a whole is involved, Russell held even that "the movement against nuclear war may count as philosophy" (1964 interview with Marmor, p. 6, cited in Chap. IV, n. 47).

Chapter VII Evaluation of a Normative Ethic

1 See Chap. I, n. 1, for the source.
2 Russell, "Man's Peril", *Basic Writings*, pp. 729–32 (at 732).
3 Hampshire, *Two Theories of Morality* ([London]: Published for the British Academy by Oxford University Press, 1977), pp. 15–16.
4 Russell, in using the term "evil", is not necessarily slipping into a cognitivist mode. Evil is what *he* desires will not happen. In the case of the "evil" of ordinary suffering, Russell knows he has widespread agreement in regarding it that way.
5 See n. 33 for the extent to which Russell came to see men's interests as overlapping.
6 In *Autobiography*, vol. III, Russell recognizes that the doctrine of compossibility "affords no ultimate solution". The doctrine rests on the assumption that it is better to satisfy the largest group of compossible desires rather than any smaller group. Russell identifies happiness with the satisfaction of the largest group of desires, but has no way of showing that happiness is better than unhappiness (p. 34). (Indeed, the term "better" for Russell can have no meaning independent of the satisfaction of desire.) And he nowhere discusses the problems of defining "largest" in this context. As for the concept of desire, it has been analyzed only with respect to Russell's philosophy of mind. See Pears, "Russell's Theory of Desire", in his *Questions in the Philosophy of Mind* (London: Duckworth, 1975), pp. 251–71; also in Thomas and Blackwell, eds., *Russell in Review*, pp. 215–35.
7 As a desire limited to a species, it is contingently the most compossible; there is always the possibility that more species could be included in the desire's scope.
8 Monro, "Russell's Moral Theories", p. 355. Nowell-Smith makes this point, too (*Ethics*, p. 309).
9 The philosophical literature on this concept and its important moral consequences is small. See, e.g., William Neblett, "Indignation: a Case Study in the Role of Feelings in Morals", *Metaphilosophy*, 10 (April 1979), pp. 139–52. Neblett concludes that "the ideally morally good person" does not feel indignation.
10 See Russell, "Why Fanaticism Brings Defeat", *The Listener*, 40 (23 Sept. 1948), pp. 452–3.
11 Newman has opposed the compatibilist interpretation of Spinoza in his article of that title (*The Personalist*, 55 [1974], pp. 360–8). But he does not take into account the application of E1Df.7—the definition of "freedom"—to Spinoza's theory of active and passive emotions. Active emotions allow you to be free because they are not externally imposed. There are still difficulties, however, and in his later essay, "Some Tensions in Spinoza's Ethical Theory", Newman distinguishes these two concepts of freedom. He holds that they are ultimately incompatible since "whoever is free in the second sense [that of being led by reason and (I would add) active emotions] is simply fortunate to be so" because any such freedom is ultimately due to antecedent conditions over which he has no control (p. 359).
12 Spinoza defines "regret" as "the desire or longing to possess something, the affect

being strengthened by the memory of the object itself, and at the same time being restrained by the memory of other things which exclude the existence of the desired object" (E3Df.Aff.32). He says that the man who regrets an action is doubly wretched. First, he did something presumably bad; and second, he wishes he had not done it, which is to fly in the face of determinism.

13 Quoted by White, preface to *Ethic*, p. xvii, from Lucas's biography of Spinoza. Wolf translates the second sentence as "It is at such a price that one buys fortitude" (*The Oldest Biography*, p. 64).

14 See Russell, "Introduction: On the Value of Scepticism", *Sceptical Essays* (London: Allen and Unwin, 1928), pp. 11–25.

15 Reprinted in *Mysticism and Logic*. Russell's greatest celebration of thought for its own sake is in *Principles of Social Reconstruction*, in a psalm-like passage beginning: "Men fear thought as they fear nothing else on earth . . ." (p. 165). For Russell's comments on this passage, see my "'Perhaps You Will Think Me Fussy . . .': Three Myths in Editing Russell's *Collected Papers*", in H. J. Jackson, ed., *Editing Polymaths: Erasmus to Russell* (Toronto: Committee for the Conference on Editorial Problems, 1983), pp. 99–142 (at 111 n. 12). *Cf.* also *The Scientific Outlook*, *passim*.

16 Russell employs his image of the walls of the ego in writing of the Lawrentian battle against love's propensity of "breaking through the protecting walls of his or her ego" (*History*, p. 682; p. 657).

17 In his philosophy of education Russell warns that "A human ego, like a gas, will always expand unless restrained by external pressure" (*On Education* [London: Allen and Unwin, 1926], p. 117).

18 Proudfoot, *God and the Self: Three Types of Philosophy of Religion* (Lewisburg: Bucknell University Press, 1976).

19 John Stuart Mill, *Utilitarianism*, Chap. II, in *Collected Works of John Stuart Mill*, vol. X: *Essays on Ethics, Religion and Society*, ed. J. M. Robson (Toronto: University of Toronto Press, 1969), p. 215.

20 See Broad's 1953 Herbert Spencer lecture, "Self and Others", in *Broad's Critical Essays in Moral Philosophy*, ed. David R. Cheney (London: Allen and Unwin, 1971), pp. 262–82 (at 279ff.). A. J. Ayer agrees with Broad and Mackie (*Freedom and Morality and Other Essays* [Oxford: Clarendon Press, 1984], p. 49).

21 Mackie, *Ethics: Inventing Right and Wrong* (Harmondsworth, Middlesex: Penguin Books, 1977), p. 132. Mackie also uses the term "confined generosity" (p. 170). This concern is the basis of economic protection, as opposed to free trade (see Chap. III, n. 14).

22 Sidgwick, *The Methods of Ethics*, 7th ed. (London: Macmillan, 1907), p. 382. See Bernard Williams, "The Point of View of the Universe: Sidgwick and the Ambitions of Ethics", *Cambridge Review*, 7 May 1982, pp. 183–91. Williams argues (p. 191) that assuming the point of view of the universe denies one's personal moral identity.

23 Frankena, *Ethics*, p. 25.

24 Rawls, *A Theory of Justice* (Cambridge, Mass.: Belknap Press of Harvard University Press, 1971), esp. sec. 24.

25 Rawls gives no reference for the occurrence of this idea in Hume. Although it does not meet with general acceptance as an interpretation of Hume's ethics, the notion definitely is expressed in certain passages reprinted under the title "The Impartial Spectator Theory" in Richard B. Brandt, ed., *Value and Obligation: Systematic Readings in Ethics* (New York: Harcourt, Brace and World, 1961), pp. 385–403. The passages are *Treatise*, III.i.2, III.iii.1, and *Enquiry Concerning the Principles of Morals*, sec. 9. The impartial spectator interpretation of Hume is defended notably by F. C. Sharp, "Hume's Ethical Theory and Its Critics", *Mind*, 30 (1921), pp. 40–56, 151–71.

26 See Firth, "Ethical Absolutism and the Ideal Observer", *Philosophy and Phenomenological Research*, 12 (1952), pp. 317–45; reprinted in Wilfrid Sellars and John

Hospers, eds., *Readings in Ethical Theory*, 2nd ed. (New York: Appleton-Century-Crofts, 1970), pp. 200–21.
27 By "omnipercipience" Firth means the ability to imagine sympathetically all the different viewpoints relevant to an ethical problem.
28 Harman, *The Nature of Morality: an Introduction to Ethics* (New York: Oxford University Press, 1977), p. 52.
29 In old age Russell held that there is a desire stronger than that for self-preservation—namely, the desire "for extermination of one's enemies" (*Autobiography*, vol. III, p. 154).
30 No. 46, 29 April 1911. Quoted by Clark, pp. 139–40. Russell tells her that his intellect "looks at everything quite impartially, as if it were someone else." (The perspective suggested by the term "someone else" is still personal; the impersonal perspective would be better conveyed by the term "anyone else".)
31 As we saw in **42**, Brightman treats Russell as a religious man, and Russell has no problem in accepting the label providing it is devoid of theological implications and church connections. At any rate, there are religious attitudes—such as reverence towards others and towards existence—that are not dependent upon theism.
32 For Russell's concern with the logic of egocentric vocabulary, see Jager, *The Development of Bertrand Russell's Philosophy*, Chap. 8, sec. B, "Perspectival Privacy and Egocentricity", and sec. C, "Solipsism and Privacy".
33 In old age Russell came to believe that men's unenlarged interests now overlap so extensively that they can only be satisfied together. E.g., *Unarmed Victory* (London: Allen and Unwin, 1963), p. 149: "We are all human beings with very similar needs and desires. Enmity is folly, since nine-tenths of the interests of rival nations are identical. All can be happier if they forget their quarrels." *Cf.* also *Has Man a Future?* (London: Allen and Unwin, 1961), Chap. XI, where similar views are expressed, although less forcefully. However, Russell also believes that you need to develop an impersonal outlook in order to recognize the mutuality of self-interests.
34 Treating children impersonally would likely be unsatisfactory for their growth as persons. See Elizabeth Newson, "Unreasonable Care: the Establishment of Selfhood", in Godfrey Vesey, ed., *Human Values*, Royal Institute of Philosophy Lectures 1976/7 (Hassocks, Sussex: Harvester Press, 1978), pp. 1–26. See H. O. Mounce's review in *Mind*, 89 (April 1980), p. 307. Mounce summarizes: "It is precisely because parents treat their child as a special case that a child acquires a sense of his own worth and the confidence to act as an individual."
35 Howard Woodhouse has developed the implications of this problem in his doctoral dissertation, "The Concept of the Individual in Russell's Educational Thought" (Ontario Institute for Studies in Education, 1980).
36 It has been held that Russell finally achieved such union in his political work of the 1960s. See Ron Goldstein, "Crusader and Cassandra: the Politics of Bertrand Russell" (unpublished M.A. thesis, McMaster University, 1977).
37 See the statement on loneliness in *Autobiography*, vol. II, p. 38.
38 It is assumed that $A \ldots Z$ belong to the same generation.
39 The following textbooks have useful discussions: John Hospers, *Human Conduct* (New York: Harcourt, Brace and World, 1961), and Davidson, *Philosophies Men Live By*.
40 Nagel, *The Possibility of Altruism* (Oxford: Clarendon Press, 1970), p. 3.
41 Singer, *Practical Ethics* (Cambridge, U.K.: Cambridge University Press, 1979), p. 219. In "What I Believe" Russell holds that "In a perfect world, every sentient being would be to every other the object of fullest love, compounded of delight, benevolence and understanding inextricably blended" (*Basic Writings*, p. 373). But in this imperfect world there are many sentient beings who disgust us—"Not to mention human beings, there are fleas and bugs and lice" (*ibid.*). We would be twisting our nature out of shape to attempt to feel in this exalted way towards such beings. This leaves it unclear why our feelings should change in a perfect world.

For Russell's criticism of Schweitzer's reverence for life ethic, see "Does Ethics Influence Life?", a review of Schweitzer's *Civilization and Ethics*, in *The Nation & the Athenaeum*, 34 (2 Feb. 1924), pp. 635–6; also published in *The Dial*, 76 (April 1924), pp. 353–6.

42 "Self and Others", p. 282.
43 See his correspondence with Lucy Martin Donnelly and Helen Thomas Flexner during 1900–10. To the latter he writes on 31 March 1902: "All great literature requires the rare and all but impossible combination of fiery emotion with an intellect capable of viewing it impersonally."
44 The passage is ". . . [the rational Will] does not reject the impulse to save family, friends or country to which the instinctive Will can attain, it rejects only the exclusiveness of this impulse, and extends to the world as a whole the impulse which the instinctive Will feels only towards a few" ("Chapter X. The Good", July 1911, Morrell papers, Texas; RA, Rec. Acq. 385). *Cf.* Derek Parfit, *Reasons and Persons* (Oxford: Clarendon Press, 1984), sec. 150, "Impersonality", who argues that there are cases in which we ought not to give priority to our own children: "Impersonality is again better, even in personal terms. Similar claims apply to our relations to such persons as our parents, friends, neighbours, pupils, or patients" (p. 444).
45 See, e.g., remarks reported in Stephen Toulmin, *An Examination of the Place of Reason in Ethics* (Cambridge, U.K.: Cambridge University Press, 1950), p. 165 n. 2.
46 George Nakhnikian does not share Russell's optimistic assumption. Nakhnikian takes the social remedies outlined in works such as *Roads to Freedom* as presupposing that Russell holds the thesis that "economic and political reform is a sufficient condition for improving human relationships" ("Some Questions about Bertrand Russell's Liberalism", in Nakhnikian, ed., *Bertrand Russell's Philosophy*, pp. 221–6 [at 222]). In addition to the suffering deriving from "physical nature, defects of character, and abuse of power" (p. 225), Nakhnikian holds that there is the suffering due to "spiritual malaise", or the human condition. He criticizes Russell for ignoring this kind of suffering when he deals with political matters. Russell's reply would be twofold. First, he would deny the utility of always treating specifically political evils at the same time as personal ones. He does, however, in two books treat both kinds together—in *Principles of Social Reconstruction* and *New Hopes for a Changing World*. Second, Russell would deny that the human condition is as unalterable as Nakhnikian supposes. The ethic of impersonal self-enlargement is a fundamental attempt to alter the expectations of individual and collective human life.

Russell's daughter does not share his optimism, either. See Katharine Tait, *My Father Bertrand Russell* (New York: Harcourt, Brace, Jovanovich, 1975), pp. 187–8.
47 Kant, *On the Foundation of Morality: a Modern Version of the "Grundlegung"*, trans. Brendan E. A. Liddell (Bloomington: Indiana University Press, 1970), p. 43 (Prussian Academy ed., p. 394).
48 In Steven Sanders and David R. Cheney, eds., *The Meaning of Life* (Englewood Cliffs, N.J.: Prentice-Hall, 1980), pp. 155–65 (at 156); also in Nagel, *Mortal Questions* (Cambridge, U.K.: Cambridge University Press, 1979), pp. 11–23 (at 11–12).

Bibliography

1 Spinoza's Writings

The Chief Works of Benedict de Spinoza. Trans. R. H. M. Elwes. 2 vols. London: G. Bell and Sons, 1883–4. Reprinted New York: Dover, 1951, 1955.
Opera. Ed. J. von Vloten and J. P. N. Land. 3rd ed. 4 vols. The Hague: Martinus Nijhoff, 1914.
Opera. Ed. Carl Gebhardt. 4 vols. Heidelberg: Carl Winters Universitaetsbuchhandlung, 1925.
Correspondence of Spinoza. Trans. and ed. A. Wolf. London: Allen and Unwin, 1928.
Ethics. Trans. George Eliot. Ed. Thomas Deegan. Salzburg Studies in English Literature, no. 102. Universität Salzburg, 1981.
Ethic. Trans. Paul Wienpahl. Unpublished mimeographed typescript, n.d.
Ethic. Trans. W. Hale White; trans. rev. Amelia Hutchison Stirling. 4th ed. London: Oxford University Press, 1910. (Russell's library copy.)
The Ethics and Selected Letters. Trans. Samuel Shirley. Ed. Seymour Feldman. Indianapolis: Hackett, 1982.
Short Treatise on God, Man, and Man's Well-Being. Ed. A. Wolf. London: Black, 1910.

2 Writings on Spinoza

Bidney, David. *The Psychology and Ethics of Spinoza: a Study in the History and Logic of Ideas*. New York: Russell and Russell, 1962; 1st ed., 1940.
Broad, C. D. *Five Types of Ethical Theory*. London: Routledge and Kegan Paul, 1930.
Curley, E. M. "Man and Nature in Spinoza". In Wetlesen, ed., *Spinoza's Philosophy of Man*.
Curley, E. M. *Spinoza's Metaphysics: an Essay in Interpretation*. Cambridge, Mass.: Harvard University Press, 1969.
Curley, E. M. "Spinoza's Moral Philosophy". In Grene, ed., *Spinoza*.
Donagan, Alan. "Spinoza's Proof of Immortality". In Grene, ed., *Spinoza*.
Einstein, Albert. Foreword to D. D. Runes, ed., *Spinoza Dictionary*. New York: Philosophical Library, 1951.
Einstein, Albert. Introduction to R. Kayser, *Spinoza: Portrait of a Spiritual Hero*. Trans. A. Allen and M. Newmark. New York: Philosophical Library, 1946.
Feuer, Lewis S. *Spinoza and the Rise of Liberalism*. Boston: Beacon Press, 1958.

Frankena, William K. "Spinoza's 'New Morality': Notes on Book IV". In Freeman and Mandelbaum, eds., *Spinoza*.
Freeman, Eugene, and Maurice Mandelbaum, eds. *Spinoza: Essays in Interpretation*. La Salle, Ill.: Open Court, 1975.
Freudenthal, Jakob, ed. *Die Lebensgeschichte Spinoza's in Quellenschriften, Urkunden und nichtamtlichen Nachrichten*. Leipzig: 1899.
Friedmann, Georges. *Leibniz et Spinoza*. 2nd ed. Paris: Gallimard, 1962; 1st ed., 1946.
Grene, Marjorie, ed. *Spinoza: a Collection of Critical Essays*. Garden City, N.Y.: Doubleday, 1973.
Hallett, H. F. *Aeternitas: a Spinozistic Study*. Oxford: Clarendon Press, 1930.
Hampshire, Stuart. *Spinoza*. Harmondsworth, Middlesex: Penguin Books, 1951.
Hampshire, Stuart. *Two Theories of Morality*. [London]: Published for the British Academy by Oxford University Press, 1977.
Harris, Errol E. *Salvation from Despair: a Reappraisal of Spinoza's Philosophy*. International Archives of the History of Ideas, vol. 59. The Hague: Nijhoff, 1973.
Harris, Errol E. "Spinoza's Theory of Human Immortality". In Freeman and Mandelbaum, eds., *Spinoza*.
Hessing, Siegfried, ed. *Speculum Spinozanum 1677–1977*. London: Routledge and Kegan Paul, 1977.
Hubbeling, H. G. "Logic and Experience in Spinoza's Mysticism". In J. G. van der Bend, ed., *Spinoza on Knowing, Being and Freedom*. Assen, The Netherlands: Van Gorcum, 1974.
Hubbeling, H. G. "The Logical and Experiential Roots of Spinoza's Mysticism—An Answer to Jon Wetlesen". In Hessing, ed., *Speculum Spinozanum*.
Joachim, Harold H. *A Study of the Ethics of Spinoza (Ethica Ordine Geometrico Demonstrata)*. Oxford: Clarendon Press, 1901; reprinted New York: Russell and Russell, 1964.
Kneale, Martha. "Leibniz and Spinoza on Activity". In Frankfurt, ed., *Leibniz*.
Mark, Thomas Carson. *Spinoza's Theory of Truth*. New York: Columbia University Press, 1972.
Matson, Wallace, "Death and Destruction in Spinoza's *Ethics*". *Inquiry*, 20 (1977), pp. 403–17.
McShea, Robert J. "Spinoza in the History of Ethical Theory". *Philosophical Forum*, 8 (1976), pp. 59–67.
Naess, Arne. "Spinoza and Ecology". In Hessing, ed., *Speculum Spinozanum*.
Naess, Arne. "Through Spinoza to Mahayana Buddhism or Through Mahayana Buddhism to Spinoza". In Wetlesen, ed., *Spinoza's Philosophy of Man*.
Newman, Jay, "Some Tensions in Spinoza's Ethical Theory". *Indian Philosophical Quarterly*, n.s. 7 (April 1980), pp. 357–74.
Newman, Jay. "The Compatibilist Interpretation of Spinoza". *The Personalist*, 55 (1974), pp. 360–8.
Odegard, Douglas. "Spinoza's Theory of Mind". In Freeman and Mandelbaum, eds., *Spinoza: Essays in Interpretation*.

Pater, Walter, "Sebastian van Storck". In his *The Works*, vol. IV: *Imaginary Portraits and Gaston de Latour*. London: Macmillan, 1900.

Picton, James Allanson. *Spinoza: a Handbook to the Ethics*. London: Archibald Constable, 1907.

Pollock, Sir Frederick. *Spinoza: His Life and Philosophy*. London: Kegan Paul, 1880; reprinted: Dubuque, Iowa: Reprint Library, n.d. 2nd ed., 1899; 2nd ed. corrected, 1912.

Savan, David. "Spinoza and Language". In Paul Kashap, ed., *Studies in Spinoza: Critical and Interpretative Essays*. Berkeley: University of California Press, 1972.

Savan, David. "Spinoza on Man's Knowledge of God: Intuition, Reason, Revelation, and Love". In Barry S. Kogan, ed., *Spinoza: a Tercentenary Perspective*. [Cincinnati]: Hebrew Union College—Jewish Institute of Religion, [1979].

Sessions, George. "Spinoza and Ecophilosophy". *Ecophilosophy: an Informal Newsletter*, no. 1 (April 1976), pp. 1–5.

Sessions, George. "Spinoza and Jeffers on Man and Nature". *Inquiry*, 10 (1977), pp. 481–528.

Small, I. C. "The Sources for Pater's Spinoza in 'Sebastian van Storck'". *Notes and Queries*, n.s. 25 (Aug. 1978), pp. 318–20.

"Spinoza". *The Nation*, 8 (19 Nov. 1910), p. 335. A letter to the editor, signed "X".

Stein, Ludwig. *Leibniz und Spinoza*. Berlin: 1890.

Stout, G. F. Review of G. S. Fullerton, *The Philosophy of Spinoza*. *Mind*, n.s. 4 (1895), p. 259.

Wetlesen, Jon. "Body Awareness as a Gateway to Eternity: A Note on the Mysticism of Spinoza and Its Affinity to Buddhist Meditation". In Hessing, ed., *Speculum Spinozanum*.

Wetlesen, Jon. "Freedom as Contemplation or Action? A Reply to Arne Naess". In Wetlesen, ed., *Spinoza's Philosophy of Man*.

Wetlesen, Jon. *The Sage and the Way: Spinoza's Ethics of Freedom*. Assen, The Netherlands: Van Gorcum, 1979.

Wetlesen, Jon, ed. *Spinoza's Philosophy of Man: Proceedings of the Scandinavian Spinoza Symposium 1977*. Oslo: Universitetsforlaget, 1978.

Wetlesen, Jon, and Arne Naess. *Conation and Cognition in Spinoza's Theory of Affects: a Reconstruction*. Oslo: Institute of Philosophy, University of Oslo, 1967; Ann Arbor: University Microfilms International, 1979.

White, W. Hale. Preface to Spinoza, *Ethic*.

Wienpahl, Paul. "On Translating Spinoza". In Hessing, ed., *Speculum Spinozanum*.

Wienpahl, Paul, *The Radical Spinoza*. New York: New York University Press, 1979.

Wienpahl, Paul. "Spinoza and Mental Health". *Inquiry*, 15 (1972), pp. 64–94.

Wienpahl, Paul. "Spinoza and Mysticism". In Wetlesen, ed., *Spinoza's Philosophy of Man*.

Wienpahl, Paul. "Notes and Commentary [to his translation of Spinoza's *Ethic*]". Unpublished mimeographed typescript, n.d.

Wolf, A., ed. *The Oldest Biography of Spinoza*. London: Allen and Unwin, 1927; New York: Lincoln MacVeagh, The Dial Press, 1927.

Wolfson, Harry Austryn. *The Philosophy of Spinoza*. 2 vols. in 1. Cleveland: Meridian Books, 1958; 1st ed., 1934.

3 Russell's Writings

3a UNPUBLISHED

Correspondence with Lady Constance Malleson, Helen Thomas Flexner, Gilbert Murray, Alys Russell (née Pearsall Smith), Paul Arthur Schilpp, Sir Stanley Unwin (all in the Russell Archives, McMaster University) and Lady Ottoline Morrell (Harry Ranson Humanities Research Center, University of Texas at Austin).

"Action and Contemplation". Unpublished ms., n.d. Morrell papers, Texas.
"Austerity". Unpublished ms., n.d. Morrell papers, Texas.
"Chapter X. The Good". July 1911. Morrell papers, Texas.
"Cleopatra or Maggie Tulliver". Nov. 1894. Russell Archives (as are the following, unless otherwise noted). Now in *Cambridge Essays, 1888–99*.
"Ethical Axioms". Feb. 1894. *Cambridge Essays*.
"The Free-Will Problem from an Idealist Standpoint". June 1895. *Cambridge Essays*.
"Greek Exercises". *Cambridge Essays*.
A History of Western Philosophy. Ms.
Interview with Milton Marmor, Associated Press, 1964.
"A Locked Diary". *Cambridge Essays*.
"Journal, 1902–05", Morrell papers, Texas.
"*Life of Spinoza*". Ms. notes.
"Paper on Descartes II". May 1894. *Cambridge Essays*.
"Paper on History of Philosophy". Feb. 1894. *Cambridge Essays*.
"Paper on Hobbes". N.d. *Cambridge Essays*.
"Prisons". Unpublished ms., n.d. Morrell papers, Texas.
"Prisons I". Unpublished ms., n.d. Morrell papers, Texas.
"Stout's History of Philosophy". In Russell's graduate lecture notebook.
"These comforters are Courage . . . ". Unpublished ms., n.d. Morrell papers, Texas.
"Ward's History of Philosophy". In his graduate lecture notebook.
"What Shall I Read?" Notebook, 1891–1902. *Cambridge Essays*.

3b PUBLISHED

"Addendum to My 'Reply to Criticisms' ". In Schilpp, ed., *The Philosophy of Bertrand Russell*.
The Analysis of Mind. London: Allen and Unwin, 1921.
"The Aroma of Evanescence". *The Dial*, 73 (Nov. 1922), pp. 559–62. Review of George Santayana, *Soliloquies in England, and Later Soliloquies*.
"As a European Radical Sees It". *The Freeman*, 4 (8 March 1922), pp. 608–10.
Authority and the Individual. London: Allen and Unwin, 1949.
The Autobiography of Bertrand Russell, vol. I: *1872–1914*. London: Allen and Unwin, 1967.
The Autobiography of Bertrand Russell, vol. II: *1914–1944*. London: Allen and Unwin, 1968.

The Autobiography of Bertrand Russell, vol. III: *1944–1967*. London: Allen and Unwin, 1969.

The Basic Writings of Bertrand Russell. Ed. Lester E. Denonn and Robert E. Egner. London: Allen and Unwin, 1961.

"Books That Influenced Me in Youth, VI: The Pursuit of Truth". In Russell's *Fact and Fiction*. London: Allen and Unwin, 1961.

The Collected Papers of Bertrand Russell, vol. 1: *Cambridge Essays, 1888–99*. Ed. K. Blackwell, A. Brink, N. Griffin, R. A. Rempel and J. G. Slater. London and Boston: Allen and Unwin, 1983.

The Conquest of Happiness. London: Allen and Unwin, 1930.

"[Contribution to discussion of] Benedict de Spinoza, *Ethics*". In Mark Van Doren, ed., *New Invitation to Learning*. New York: Random House, 1942.

"[Contribution to discussion of] Hegel, *Philosophy of History*". In H. Cairns, A. Tate, and M. Van Doren. *Invitation to Learning*. New York: Random House, 1941.

A Critical Exposition of the Philosophy of Leibniz. 2nd ed. London: Allen and Unwin, 1937; 1st ed., 1900.

Dear Bertrand Russell. Ed. Barry Feinberg and Ronald Kasrils. Boston: Houghton Mifflin, 1969.

"Dewey's New *Logic*". In Schilpp, ed., *The Philosophy of John Dewey*. Evanston and Chicago: Northwestern University, 1939. Reprinted in *Basic Writings*.

"Does Ethics Influence Life?" *The Nation & the Athenaeum*, 34 (2 Feb. 1924), pp. 635–6; *The Dial*, 76 (April 1924), pp. 353–6. Review of Albert Schweitzer, *Civilization and Ethics*.

"The Duty of a Philosopher in This Age". In Eugene Freeman, ed., *The Abdication of Philosophy: Philosophy and the Public Good; Essays in Honor of Paul Arthur Schilpp*. La Salle, Ill.: Open Court, 1976.

"The Elements of Ethics". In his *Philosophical Essays*.

"The Essence of Religion". *Hibbert Journal*, 11 (Oct. 1912), pp. 46–62. Reprinted in *Basic Writings*.

"The Expanding Mental Universe". *Saturday Evening Post*, 232 (18 July 1959), pp. 24, 91–3. Reprinted in Richard Thruelsen and John Kobler, eds., *Adventures of the Mind* (New York: Knopf, 1960), and *Basic Writings*.

"The Free Man's Worship". In his *Mysticism and Logic* and *Basic Writings*.

A History of Western Philosophy. New York: Simon and Schuster, 1945. 2nd ed.: London: Allen and Unwin, 1961.

"Hopes and Fears as Regards America". In *Bertrand Russell's America*. Ed. Barry Feinberg and Ronald Kasrils. Vol. I: 1896–1945. London: Allen and Unwin, 1973.

"How I Write". In his *Portraits from Memory*.

'How I write". *The Writer*, n.s. 14 (Sept. 1954), p. 4.

"How to Read and Understand History". In his *Understanding History and Other Essays*. New York: Philosophical Library, 1957.

Human Knowledge: Its Scope and Limits. London: Allen and Unwin, 1948.

Human Society in Ethics and Politics. London: Allen and Unwin, 1954.

The Impact of Science on Society. London: Allen and Unwin, 1952.

In Praise of Idleness. London: Allen and Unwin, 1935.

"Knowledge and Wisdom". *The Listener*, 52 (9 Sept. 1954), p. 390. Reprinted in *Portraits from Memory*.
Logic and Knowledge: Essays 1901–1950. Ed. R. C. Marsh. London: Allen and Unwin, 1956.
"Logical Atomism". In his *Logic and Knowledge*.
"Logical Positivism". In his *Logic and Knowledge*.
"Man's Peril". In his *Basic Writings*.
"Mind and Matter". In his *Portraits from Memory*.
"My Mental Development". In Schilpp, ed., *The Philosophy of Bertrand Russell*.
My Philosophical Development. London: Allen and Unwin, 1959.
Mysticism and Logic and Other Essays. London: Longmans, Green, 1918; Allen and Unwin, 1963.
New Hopes for a Changing World. London: Allen and Unwin, 1951.
"Notes on *Philosophy*, January, 1960". *Philosophy*, 35 (April 1960), pp. 146–7.
"On Being Modern-Minded". In his *Unpopular Essays*.
On Education, Especially in Early Childhood. London: Allen and Unwin, 1926.
"On Keeping a Wide Horizon". Ed. K. Blackwell. *Russell: the Journal of the Bertrand Russell Archives*, nos. 33–34 (spring-summer 1979), pp. 5–11.
"On Scientific Method in Philosophy". In his *Mysticism and Logic*.
"On Youthful Cynicism". In his *In Praise of Idleness*.
Our Knowledge of the External World as a Field for Scientific Method in Philosophy. London: Open Court, 1914.
"An Outline of Intellectual Rubbish". In his *Basic Writings*.
An Outline of Philosophy. London: Allen and Unwin, 1927.
"The Perplexities of John Forstice". In *The Collected Stories of Bertrand Russell*. Ed. Barry Feinberg. London: Allen and Unwin, 1972.
Philosophical Essays. 2nd ed. London: Allen and Unwin, 1966; 1st ed., 1910.
"Philosophy and Politics". In his *Unpopular Essays*.
"A Philosophy for Our Time". *London Calling*, no. 737 (17 Dec. 1953), p. 8. Reprinted in *Portraits from Memory*.
"The Philosophy of George Santayana". In P. A. Schilpp, ed., *The Philosophy of George Santayana*. The Library of Living Philosophers, Vol. II. Evanston and Chicago: Northwestern University, 1940.
"The Philosophy of Logical Atomism". In his *Logic and Knowledge*.
"The Place of Science in a Liberal Education". In his *Mysticism and Logic*.
Portraits from Memory and Other Essays. London: Allen and Unwin, 1956.
Power: a New Social Analysis. New York: Norton, 1938.
"Pragmatism". In his *Philosophical Essays*.
The Principles of Mathematics. 2nd ed. London: Allen and Unwin, 1937; 1st ed., 1903.
Principles of Social Reconstruction. London: Allen and Unwin, 1916.
The Problem of China. London: Allen and Unwin, 1922.
The Problems of Philosophy. New York: Oxford University Press, 1959; 1st ed., 1912.
"Prof. G. E. Moore: Influence on Lord Russell". *The Times*, Lon., 28 Oct. 1958, p. 14.

"Religion and Metaphysics". *Independent Review*, 9 (1906), pp. 109–16. Review of J. M. E. McTaggart, *Some Dogmas of Religion*.
Religion and Science. New York: Oxford University Press, 1961; 1st ed., 1935.
"Reply to Criticisms". In Schilpp, ed., *The Philosophy of Bertrand Russell*.
Review of John Dewey, *Essays in Experimental Logic*. *Journal of Philosophy, Psychology and Scientific Methods*, 16 (2 Jan. 1919), pp. 5–26.
Review of Louis Couturat, *La Logique de Leibniz*. In Frankfurt, ed., *Leibniz*.
Roads to Freedom. London: Allen and Unwin, 1918.
The Scientific Outlook. London: Allen and Unwin, 1931.
"Seems, Madam? Nay, It Is". In his *Why I Am Not a Christian*, ed. Paul Edwards. New York: Simon and Schuster, 1957. In *Cambridge Essays*.
"Self-Appreciation". *The Golden Urn*, no. 1 (March 1897), pp. 30–1. Published under the pseudonym of "Orlando". In *Cambridge Essays*.
Speaking Personally Bertrand Russell. Interview by John Chandos. Riverside 7014/7015, 1961. Phonograph records.
"Spinoza". *The Nation*, Lon., 8 (12 Nov. 1910), pp. 278, 280. Review of Spinoza, *Ethic*, trans. White and Stirling.
"Spinoza's Moral Code". *The Nation*, Lon., 1 (13 Apr. 1907), p. 276. Unsigned review of J. Allanson Picton, *Spinoza*.
"The Study of Mathematics". In his *Mysticism and Logic*.
"A Turning Point". *Saturday Book*, 8 (1948), pp. 142–6.
"The Twilight of the Absolute". *The Nation*, Lon., 12 (22 Feb. 1913), p. 864. Review of Bernard Bosanquet, *The Value and Destiny of the Individual*.
Unarmed Victory. London: Allen and Unwin, 1963.
Understanding History and Other Essays. New York: Philosophical Library, 1957.
Unpopular Essays. London: Allen and Unwin, 1950.
"'Useless' Knowledge". In his *In Praise of Idleness*.
"The Value of Free Thought". In his *Understanding History and Other Essays*.
"What I Believe". In his *Basic Writings*.
Which Way to Peace? London: Michael Joseph, 1936.
"Why Fanaticism Brings Defeat". *The Listener*, 40 (23 Sept. 1948), pp. 452–3.
"Why I Took to Philosophy". In his *Portraits from Memory*.

4 Writings on Russell

4a UNPUBLISHED

Beck, L. J. Letter to K. Blackwell. 1979.
Joachim, Harold H. Letter to Bertrand Russell, [1892]. RA.
White, William Hale. Letter to Bertrand Russell, 1910. RA.
Wienpahl, Paul. Letter to K. Blackwell, 1979.

4b PUBLISHED

Aiken, Lillian W. *Bertrand Russell's Philosophy of Morals*. New York: Humanities Press, 1963.

Anon. "Religion without God". *The Nation*, Lon., 12 (27 Oct. 1912), pp. 171–2. Review of Russell, "The Essence of Religion".
Armour, Leslie. "Russell, McTaggart, and 'I' ". *Idealistic Studies*, 9 (Jan. 1979), pp. 66–76.
Barber, Benjamin R. "Solipsistic Politics: Russell's Empiricist Liberalism". In Roberts, ed., *Bertrand Russell Memorial Volume*.
Berlin, Isaiah. Critical Notice of Russell, *A History of Western Philosophy*. *Mind*, 56 (1947), pp. 151–66.
Blackwell, Kenneth. "The Early Wittgenstein and the Middle Russell". In I. Block, ed., *Perspectives on the Philosophy of Wittgenstein*. Oxford: Blackwell, 1981.
Blackwell, Kenneth. "The Future of the Russell Archives". In Thomas and Blackwell, eds., *Russell in Review*.
Blackwell, Kenneth. " 'Perhaps You Will Think Me Fussy . . .': Three Myths in Editing Russell's *Collected Papers*". In H. J. Jackson, ed., *Editing Polymaths: Erasmus to Russell*. Toronto: Committee for the Conference on Editorial Problems, 1983.
Blackwell, Kenneth. "Russell's Reply to Dewey". *Russell*, no. 12 (winter 1973–74), pp. 29–30.
Blackwell, Kenneth. "A Secondary Political Bibliography of Bertrand Russell". *Russell*, nos. 33–34 (spring-summer 1979), pp. 39–44.
Blackwell, Kenneth. "A Secondary Bibliography of Russell's 'The Essence of Religion' ". *Russell*, n.s. 1 (1981–82), pp. 143–6.
Brightman, Edgar Sheffield. "Russell's Philosophy of Religion". In Schilpp, ed., *The Philosophy of Bertrand Russell*.
Brink, Andrew. "Russell to Lady Ottoline Morrell". *Russell*, nos. 21–22 (spring-summer 1976), pp. 3–15.
Brink, Andrew. "Bertrand Russell's *The Pilgrimage of Life* and Mourning". *Journal of Psychohistory*, 10 (winter 1983), pp. 311–31.
Buchler, Justus. "Bertrand Russell and the Principles of Ethics". In Schilpp, ed., *The Philosophy of Bertrand Russell*.
Clark, Ronald W. *The Life of Bertrand Russell*. London: Cape/Weidenfeld and Nicolson, 1975.
Clarke, Peter. "Bertrand Russell and the Dimensions of Victorian Liberalism". *Russell*, n.s. 4 (summer 1984), pp. 207–21.
Curley, E. M. "The Root of Contingency". In Frankfurt, ed., *Leibniz*.
Darroch, Sandra Jobson. *Ottoline: the Life of Lady Ottoline Morrell*. London: Chatto and Windus, 1976.
Delany, Paul. *D. H. Lawrence's Nightmare: the Writer and His Circle in the Years of the Great War*. New York: Basic Books, 1978.
Edwards, Paul. *The Logic of Moral Discourse*. New York: The Free Press, 1955.
Edwards, Paul. "Russell, Bertrand Arthur William: Ethics and the Critique of Religion". In Edwards, ed., *The Encyclopedia of Philosophy*. New York: Macmillan and The Free Press, 1967. Vol. 7, pp. 251–6.
Grant, George P. "Pursuit of an Illusion: a Commentary on Bertrand Russell'. *Dalhousie Review*, 32 (1952), pp. 97–109.
Grattan-Guinness, I. *Dear Russell–Dear Jourdain: a Commentary on Russell's Logic, Based on His Correspondence with Philip Jourdain*. London: Duckworth, 1977.

Greenspan, Louis. *The Incompatible Prophecies: an Essay on Science and Liberty in the Political Writings of Bertrand Russell*. Oakville, Ont.: Mosaic Press/Valley Editions, 1978.

Griffin, Nicholas. "Bertrand Russell's Crisis of Faith". *Russell*, n.s. 4 (summer 1984), pp. 101–22.

Hampshire, Stuart. "Autobiography of Bertrand Russell—II". In his *Modern Writers and Other Essays*. New York: Knopf, 1970.

Hampshire, Stuart. "Russell, Radicalism, and Reason". In Virginia Held, Kai Nielsen, and Charles Parson, eds., *Philosophy and Political Action*. New York: Oxford University Press, 1972. Review of *The Autobiography of Bertrand Russell*, vol. III: *1944–1967*.

Hardy, G. H. "Mr. Russell as a Religious Teacher". *Cambridge Magazine*, 6 (19 and 26 May 1917), pp. 624–6 and 650–3. Reprinted in *Russell*, n.s. 1 (1981–82), pp. 119–35.

Hauerwas, Stanley. "Sex and Politics: Bertrand Russell and 'Human Sexuality'". *Christian Century*, 95 (19 April 1978), pp. 417–22.

Hobhouse, Mrs. Henry. "*I Appeal unto Caesar*". London: Allen and Unwin, 1917.

Hoernlé, R. F. Alfred. "The Religious Aspect of Bertrand Russell's Philosophy". *Harvard Theological Review*, 9 (1916), pp. 157–89.

Jager, Ronald. *The Development of Bertrand Russell's Philosophy*. London: Allen and Unwin, 1972.

Jager, Ronald. "Russell and Religion". In Thomas and Blackwell, eds., *Russell in Review*.

King-Farlow, John. "Self-Enlargement and Union: Neglected Passages of Russell and Some Famous Ones of Proust". *Theoria to Theory*, 11 (1977), pp. 105–15.

Leithauser, Gladys. "'A Non-Supernatural Faust': Bertrand Russell and the Themes of Faust". *Russell*, nos. 29–32 (1978), pp. 33–41.

Leithauser, Gladys. "The Romantic Russell and the Legacy of Shelley". *Russell*, n.s. 4 (summer 1984), pp. 31–48.

Lewis, John. *Bertrand Russell: Philosopher and Humanist*. New York: International Publishers, 1968.

The Life and Times of Bertrand Russell. London: British Broadcasting Corporation, 1964. Film; also shot list, Russell Archives.

Malleson, Lady Constance. "Fifty Years: 1916–1966". In Ralph Schoenman, ed., *Bertrand Russell: Philosopher of the Century*. London: Allen and Unwin, 1967.

Matson, Wallace. "Russell's Ethics". In Roberts, ed., *Bertrand Russell Memorial Volume*.

McKenney, John L. "Concerning Russell's Analysis of Value Judgements". *Journal of Philosophy*, 55 (1958), pp. 382–9.

Monro, D. H. "Russell's Moral Theories". In D. F. Pears, ed., *Bertrand Russell: a Collection of Critical Essays*. Garden City, N.Y.: Anchor Books, Doubleday and Co., 1972.

Moran, Margaret, and Carl Spadoni, eds. *Intellect and Social Conscience: Essays on Bertrand Russell's Early Work*. Hamilton, Ont.: McMaster University Library Press, 1984. (Articles in this collection are cited from the parallel issue of *Russell*, n.s. 4 [summer 1984].)

Morrell, Lady Ottoline. *Ottoline at Garsington*. Ed. Robert Gathorne-Hardy. London: Faber and Faber, 1974.

Morrell, Lady Ottoline. *Ottoline: the Early Memoirs of Lady Ottoline Morrell*. Ed. Robert Gathorne-Hardy. London: Faber and Faber, 1963.

Nakhnikian, George. "Some Questions about Russell's Liberalism". In Nakhnikian, ed., *Bertrand Russell's Philosophy*. New York: Barnes and Noble, 1974.

Neumann, Henry, "How to be Happy with Russell" [review of *The Conquest of Happiness*]. *Survey*, 65 (1930), p. 284.

Newberry [Vellacott], Jo. "Russell as Ghost-Writer". *Russell*, no. 15 (autumn 1974), p. 22.

Nielsen, Kai. "Bertrand Russell's New Ethic". *Methodos*, 10 (1958), pp. 151–81.

O'Briant, Walter H. "Russell on Leibniz". *Studia Leibnitiana*, 11 (1979), pp. 159–222.

O'Connor, D. J. "Bertrand Russell". In O'Connor, ed., *A Critical History of Western Philosophy*. New York: The Free Press, 1964.

Pears, David. "Russell's Theory of Desire". In his *Questions in the Philosophy of Mind*. London: Duckworth, 1975. Also in Thomas and Blackwell, eds., *Russell in Review*.

Pitt, Jack. "Russell on Religion". *International Journal for Philosophy of Religion*, 6 (1975), pp. 40–53.

Pringle-Pattison, A. S. "'The Free Man's Worship': a Consideration of Mr. Bertrand Russell's Views on Religion". *Hibbert Journal*, 12 (1913–14), pp. 47–63.

Pringle-Pattison, A. S. *The Idea of God in the Light of Recent Philosophy*. Oxford: Clarendon Press, 1917; 2nd ed., 1923.

Rempel, R. A. "From Imperialism to Free Trade: Couturat, Halévy and the Development of Russell's First Crusade". *Journal of the History of Ideas*, 40 (July-Sept. 1979), pp. 423–43.

Rescher, Nicholas. "Russell and Modal Logic". In Roberts, ed., *Bertrand Russell Memorial Volume*.

Ritchie, A. D. Review of Russell, *A History of Western Philosophy*. *The Observer*, Lon., 24 Nov. 1946, p. 4.

Roberts, George W., ed. *Bertrand Russell Memorial Volume*. London: Allen and Unwin, 1979.

Roy, Dilip Kumar. "Bertrand Russell". In his *Among the Great*. Bombay: Nalanda Publications, 1945.

Ross, Michael L. "Lawrence's Letters". *Russell*, n.s. 3 (1983), pp. 54–65.

Ruja, Harry. "Russell on the Meaning of 'Good'". *Russell*, n.s. 4 (summer 1984), pp. 137–56.

Ryan, William F. "Bertrand Russell and Haldeman-Julius: Making Readers Rational". *Russell*, nos. 29–32 (1978), pp. 53–64.

Schiller, F. C. S. Review of *The Conquest of Happiness*. *Mind*, 40 (1931), pp. 238–41.

Schilpp, Paul Arthur, ed. *The Philosophy of Bertrand Russell*. The Library of Living Philosophers, vol. V. 4th ed. La Salle, Ill.: Open Court, 1971; 1st ed., 1944.

Slater, John G. "The Philosopher's Duty in These Times". *Russell*,

nos. 35–36 (autumn-winter 1979–80), pp. 55–7. Review of Russell, "The Duty of a Philosopher in This Age".
Slater, John G. "The Political Philosophy of Bertrand Russell'. In Thomas and Blackwell, eds., *Russell in Review*.
Spadoni, Carl. "'Great God in Boots!—The Ontological Argument Is Sound!'" *Russell*, nos. 23–4 (autumn-winter 1976), pp. 37–41.
Spadoni, Carl. "Philosophy in Russell's Letters to Alys". *Russell*, nos. 29–32 (1978), pp. 5–31.
Tait, Katharine. *My Father Bertrand Russell*. New York: Harcourt, Brace, Jovanovich, 1975.
Thomas, J. E., and Kenneth Blackwell, eds. *Russell in Review: the Bertrand Russell Centenary Celebrations at McMaster University, October 12–14, 1972.* Toronto: Samuel Stevens, Hakkert, 1976.
Turcon, Sheila. "A Quaker Wedding: the Marriage of Bertrand Russell and Alys Pearsall Smith". *Russell*, n.s. 3 (winter 1983–4), pp. 103–28.
Vellacott, Jo. *Bertrand Russell and the Pacifists in the First World War*. Hassocks, Sussex: Harvester Press, 1980.
Willis, Kirk. "The Adolescent Russell and the Victorian Crisis of Faith". *Russell*, n.s. 4 (summer 1984), pp. 123–35.
Wollheim, Richard. "Bertrand Russell and the Liberal Tradition". In Nakhnikian, ed., *Bertrand Russell's Philosophy*.
Zytaruk, George T. "Lectures on Immortality and Ethics: the Failed D. H. Lawrence—Bertrand Russell Collaboration". *Russell*, n.s. 3 (1983), pp. 7–15.

4c DISSERTATIONS AND THESES

Bowen, Rees Higgs. "A Constructive Study of the Religious Philosophies of S. Alexander, L. T. Hobhouse, and Bertrand Russell". Unpublished PH.D. dissertation, Yale University, 1924.
Goldstein, Ron. "Crusader and Cassandra: the Politics of Bertrand Russell". Unpublished M.A. thesis, McMaster University, 1977.
Gurtoff, Stanley Arthur. "The Impact of D. H. Lawrence on His Contemporaries". Unpublished PH.D. dissertation, University of Minnesota, 1965.
Leithauser, Gladys G. "Principles and Perplexities: Studies of Dualism in Selected Essays and Fiction of Bertrand Russell". Unpublished PH.D. dissertation, Wayne State University, 1977.
Martin, Duncan. "The Role of Love in Determining the Religious Attitudes of Bertrand Russell". Unpublished M.A. thesis, McMaster University, 1979.
Sams, Richard. "Bertrand Russell's Spiritual Development and the Victorian Crisis of Faith, 1888–1914". Unpublished M.A. thesis, McMaster University, 1980.
Spadoni, Carl. "Russell's Rebellion against Neo-Hegelianism". Unpublished PH.D. dissertation, University of Waterloo, 1977.

5 Other Published Writings

Ayer, A. J. *Freedom and Morality and Other Essays*. Oxford: Clarendon Press, 1984.

Bradley, F. H. "My Station and Its Duties". In his *Ethical Studies*. 2nd ed. Oxford: Clarendon Press, 1927; 1st ed., 1876.

Brandt, Richard B., ed. *Value and Obligation: Systematic Readings in Ethics*. New York: Harcourt, Brace and World, 1961.

Broad, C. D. "Self and Others". In *Broad's Critical Essays in Moral Philosophy* Ed. David R. Cheney. London: Allen and Unwin, 1971.

Candlish, Stewart. "Bradley on My Station and Its Duties". *Australasian Journal of Philosophy*, 56 (Aug. 1978), pp. 155–70.

Cresswell, M. J. "Reality as Experience in F. H. Bradley". *Australasian Journal of Philosophy*, 55 (Dec. 1977), pp. 169–88.

Davidson, Robert F. *Philosophies Men Live By*. 2nd ed. New York: Holt, Rinehart, and Winston, 1974; 1st ed., 1952.

Dewey, John. *Essays in Experimental Logic*. Chicago: University of Chicago Press, 1916.

Dewey, John. Review of J. E. Erdmann, *A History of Philosophy*. In his *The Early Works*. Ed. Jo Ann Boydston. 5 vols. Vol. III: 1889–1892. Carbondale, Ill.: Southern Illinois University Press, 1969.

Eissler, K. R. *Goethe: a Psychoanalytic Study, 1775–1786*. 2 vols. Detroit: Wayne State University Press, 1963.

Eliot, George. *The Mill on the Floss*. New York: University Edition, Sully and Kleinteich, n.d.

Erdmann, Johann Eduard. *Grundriss der Geschichte der Philosophie*. 3rd ed. 2 vols. Berlin: Verlag von Wilhelm Hertz, 1878. Vol. II: *Philosophie der Neuzeit*. Trans. as *A History of Philosophy*. Ed. and trans. Williston S. Hough. 3 vols. London: Swan Sonnenschein, 1890–93.

Firth, Roderick. "Ethical Absolutism and the Ideal Observer". In Wilfrid Sellars and John Hospers, eds., *Readings in Ethical Theory*. 2nd ed. New York: Appleton-Century-Crofts, 1970.

Frankfurt, Harry G., ed. *Leibniz: a Collection of Critical Essays*. Garden City, N.Y.: Anchor Books, Doubleday and Co., 1972.

Frankena, William K. *Ethics*. Englewood Cliffs, N.J.: Prentice-Hall, 1973; 1st ed., 1963.

Griffin, Nicholas. "The Acts of the Apostles" [review of Levy], *Russell*, n.s. 1 (summer 1981), pp. 71–82.

Haight, Gordon S. *George Eliot, a Biography*. Oxford: Clarendon Press, 1968.

Happold, F. C. *Mysticism: a Study and an Anthology*. Rev. ed. Harmondsworth, Middlesex: Penguin Books, 1970.

Hancock, Roger N. *Twentieth Century Ethics*. New York: Columbia University Press, 1974.

Hardie, W. F. R. *Aristotle's Ethical Theory*. 2nd ed. Oxford: Clarendon Press, 1980.

Hare, R. M. *Freedom and Reason*. Oxford: Clarendon Press, 1952.

Harman, Gilbert. *The Nature of Morality: an Introduction to Ethics*. New York: Oxford University Press, 1977.

Hazeltine, Henry D. "Sir Frederick Pollock, Bart." *Proceedings of the British Academy*, 35 (1949), pp. 233–56.

Hospers, John, *Human Conduct*. New York: Harcourt, Brace and World, 1961.

Howe, Mark DeWolfe, ed. *The Pollock-Holmes Letters: Correspondence of Sir*

Frederick Pollock and Mr. Justice Holmes, 1874–1932. 2 vols. Cambridge, U.K.: Cambridge University Press, 1942.

Hume, David. *A Treatise of Human Nature.* Ed. L. A. Selby-Bigge. Oxford: Clarendon Press, 1888; reprinted 1968.

Kant, I. *On the Foundation of Morality: a Modern Version of the* Grundlegung. Trans. Brendan E. A. Liddell. Bloomington: Indiana University Press, 1970.

Levy, Paul. *G. E. Moore and the Cambridge Apostles.* London: Weidenfeld and Nicolson, 1979.

Mackie, J. L. *Ethics: Inventing Right and Wrong.* Harmondsworth, Middlesex: Penguin Books, 1977.

McCloskey, H. J. *Meta-Ethics and Normative Ethics.* The Hague: Nijhoff, 1969.

McGuinness, B. F. "The Mysticism of the *Tractatus*". *Philosophical Review*, 75 (1966), pp. 305–28.

Mill, J. S. *Utilitarianism.* In *Collected Works of John Stuart Mill.* Vol. X: *Essays on Ethics, Religion and Society.* Ed. J. M. Robson, Toronto: University of Toronto Press, 1969.

Mounce, H. O. Review of E. Newson, "Unreasonable Care". *Mind*, 89 (April 1980), p. 307.

Nagel, Thomas. "The Absurd". In his *Mortal Questions.* Cambridge, U.K.: Cambridge University Press, 1979.

Nagel, Thomas. *The Possibility of Altruism.* Oxford: Clarendon Press, 1970.

Neblett, William. "Indignation: a Case Study in the Role of Feelings in Morals". *Metaphilosophy*, 10 (April 1979), pp. 139–52.

Newson, Elizabeth. "Unreasonable Care: the Establishment of Selfhood". In Godfrey Vesey, ed., *Human Values.* Royal Institute of Philosophy Lectures 1976/7. Hassocks, Sussex: Harvester Press, 1978.

Nietzsche, Friedrich. *Beyond Good and Evil.* Trans. Helen Zimmern. Edinburgh: Foulis, 1909.

Nowell-Smith, P. H. *Ethics.* Harmondsworth, Middlesex: Penguin Books, 1954.

Parfit, Derek. *Reasons and Persons.* Oxford: Clarendon Press, 1984.

Parkinson, G. H. R. *Logic and Reality in Leibniz's Metaphysics.* Oxford: Clarendon Press, 1965.

Proudfoot, Wayne. *God and the Self: Three Types of Philosophy of Religion.* Lewisburg: Bucknell University Press, 1976.

Rawls, John. *A Theory of Justice.* Cambridge, Mass.: Belknap Press of Harvard University Press, 1971.

Sahakian, William S. *Ethics: an Introduction to Theories and Problems.* New York: Barnes and Noble Books, 1974.

Sanders, Steven, and David R. Cheney, eds. *The Meaning of Life: Questions, Answers and Analysis.* Englewood Cliffs, N.J.: Prentice-Hall, 1980.

Santayana, George. Introduction. In B. Spinoza, *Ethics and De Intellectus emendatione.* Everyman's Library. London: Dent, 1910.

Santayana, George. "The Philosophy of Mr. Bertrand Russell". In his *Winds of Doctrine.* London: Dent, 1913.

Sessions, George. "Anthropocentrism and the Environmental Crisis". *Humboldt Journal of Social Relations*, 2 (fall/winter 1974), pp. 1–12.

Sessions, George. "Panpsychism versus Modern Materialism: Some Implications for an Ecological Ethics". Unpublished mimeographed typescript, 1974.
Sharp, F. C. "Hume's Ethical Theory and Its Critics". *Mind*, 30 (1921), pp. 40–56, 151–71.
Sidgwick, Henry. *The Methods of Ethics*. 7th ed. London: Macmillan, 1907.
Singer, Peter. *Practical Ethics*. Cambridge, U.K.: Cambridge University Press, 1979.
Spiegelberg, Herbert. "Good Fortune Obligates: Albert Schweitzer's Second Ethical Principle". *Ethics*, 85 (1975), pp. 227–34.
Stace, W. T. *Mysticism and Philosophy*. Philadelphia: Lippincott, 1960.
Thomas à Kempis. *The Imitation of Christ*. Trans. Leo Shirley-Price. Harmondsworth, Middlesex: Penguin Books, 1952.
Toulmin, Stephen. *An Examination of the Place of Reason in Ethics*. Cambridge, U.K.: Cambridge University Press, 1950.
Trevelyan, R. C. *Translations from Leopardi*. Cambridge, U.K.: Cambridge University Press, 1941.
Walsh, W. H. *Hegelian Ethics*. London: Macmillan, 1969.
Walton, Douglas N. *Defining Death: an Analytic Study of the Concept of Death in Philosophy and Medical Ethics*. Montreal: McGill–Queen's University Press, 1980.
Williams, Bernard. "The Point of View of the Universe: Sidgwick and the Ambitions of Ethics". *Cambridge Review*, 7 May 1982, pp. 183–91.

Index of Citations
Russell's Works

"Action and Contemplation" 225 n. 18
"Addendum to my 'Reply to Criticisms'" 228 n. 46
Analysis of Mind 218 n. 12
"Aroma of Evanescence" 219 n. 18
"As a European Radical Sees It" 219 n. 14
"Austerity": quoted 138
Authority and the Individual: quoted 102–3
Autobiography, 1872–1914 (Vol. I) 104, 189, 205 n. 33, 206 n. 40, 208 n. 9, 215 n. 1, 216 n. 29, 221 n. 38; quoted 69, 75, 81, 94, 99, 132, 171, 199, 212 n. 53, 218 n. 42
Autobiography, 1914–1944 (Vol. II) 132, 203 n. 10, 206 n. 40, 216 n. 29, 218 n. 11, 221 n. 40, 230 n. 37; quoted 112, 143, 159, 160, 185, 190
Autobiography, 1944–1967 (Vol. III) 228 n. 6; quoted 230 n. 29
Basic Writings 221 nn. 29 & 45, 226 n. 29, 227 n. 43, 228 n. 2; quoted 136, 142, 144, 147, 166, 230 n. 41
"On Being Modern-Minded" 218 n. 10
Bertrand Russell's America 212 n. 49, 215 n. 12, 216 n. 21
"Books That Influenced Me in Youth, VI: The Pursuit of Truth" 208 nn. 4 & 11; quoted 104
Cambridge Essays 208 n. 5, 208 n. 9, 209 n. 17, 212 nn. 52, 55, 62 & 68, 213 nn. 70 & 72; quoted 26, 42, 44
"Chapter X. The Good": quoted 231 n. 44
"Cleopatra or Maggie Tulliver" 38, 212 n. 62; quoted 43–5
Collected Papers 208 n. 5; *see also Cambridge Essays*
Collected Stories: quoted 75, 136, **46**, 217 n. 36
Conquest of Happiness 16, 83, 129, 131, **48** 164, 196, 208 n. 45, 219 n. 15; quoted 55–6, 154, 155
Critical Exposition of the Philosophy of Leibniz 5, 210 n. 28, 110; quoted 48–50
Dear Bertrand Russell: quoted 204 n. 14

"Dewey's New *Logic*" 226 n. 29
"Does Ethics Influence Life?" 231 n. 41
"Duty of a Philosopher in This Age" 186; quoted 166–7
Education, On 154, 229 n. 17; quoted 192
"Elements of Ethics" 212 n. 48
Essay on the Foundations of Geometry 211 n. 39
"Essence of Religion" 74, 131, 150, 152, 206 n. 42, 217 n. 34, 225 n. 15; quoted **44**
"Ethical Axioms" 212 n. 70
"Expanding Mental Universe": quoted 165–6
Fact and Fiction 208 n. 4
"Free Man's Worship" 53, 69, 117, 129, 131, **43**, 142, 145, 149, 156, 160, 206 n. 41, 206 n. 42; quoted 63
"Free-Will Problem from an Idealist Standpoint": quoted 45–6
German Social Democracy 213 n. 74
Graduate lecture notebooks: quoted 29–31
"Greek Exercises" 25; quoted 23–4, 26
Has Man a Future? 230 n. 33
History of Western Philosophy 6, 8, 12, 16, 55, 57, 79, 109, 117, 118–19, 179, 206 n. 41, 207 n. 44, 214 n. 82, 216 n. 28, 218 n. 41, 229 n. 16; quoted 31, 35, **29–30**
"Hopes and Fears as Regards America" 212 n. 49, 215 n. 12, 216 n. 21; quoted 58–9, 82–3
"How I Write" 97
"How I Write" (2nd article) 221 n. 37
"How to Read and Understand History" 216 n. 26, 221 n. 29
Human Knowledge 5, 204 n. 17
Human Society in Ethics and Politics 5, 7, 8, **50**, 193, 204 n. 14, 224 n. 7; quoted 37, 172–3
"If We Are to Survive This Dark Time—" 221 n. 45

Russell's Works

Impact of Science on Society 218 n. 41, 225 n. 13; quoted 227 n. 36
In Praise of Idleness 219 n. 16; quoted 161
"Introduction: On the Value of Scepticism" 229 n. 14
"On Keeping a Wide Horizon" 203 n. 8, 212 n. 45; quoted 161–2
"Knowledge and Wisdom": quoted 165
Letter to *The Observer* 204 n. 14
Life and Times of Bertrand Russell 104; quoted 21–2
"Locked Diary" 208 n. 9; quoted 27, 42
Logic and Knowledge 218 n. 13, 221 n. 36
"Logical Positivism" 221 n. 36
"Man's Peril" 17, 228 n. 2
[Marginalia in Joachim's *Study of the Ethics of Spinoza*] 50
[Marginalia in White-Stirling trans. of Spinoza's *Ethic*] 23
Marriage and Morals 83, 155, **48**, 189
"Metaphysics for the Man of Action" [review of Schiller] 54
"Mind and Matter" 219 n. 21
"My First Fifty Years" 218 n. 9
"My Mental Development" 211 n. 43
My Philosophical Development 5, 104, 212 n. 60, 212 n. 64; quoted 150, 201, 209 n. 13
"Mysticism and Logic" 58, 143, 145, 147, 152; quoted 57, 79, 130, 133–5, 222 n. 9
Mysticism and Logic 64, 206 n. 41, 209 n. 14, 215 n. 9, 216 n. 18, 224 n. 1, 229 n. 15; quoted 79–80, 222 n. 9
New Hopes for a Changing World **50**, 205 n. 28, 231 n. 46; quoted 101, 147, 159–60, 170
"Nature of Truth" 214 n. 84
[Notes on Bohn edn.]: quoted 89–90
"Notes on *Philosophy*, January, 1960" 204 n. 18
"Notion of Cause, On the" 64
Our Knowledge of the External World 222 n. 9; quoted 197, 201, 226 n. 30, 226 n. 32
"Outline of Intellectual Rubbish" 221 n. 29
Outline of Philosophy 218 n. 12, 219 n. 21; quoted 178–9
"Paper on Descartes II" 114; quoted 40
"Paper on History of Philosophy" 212 n. 52
"Paper on Hobbes" 41

"Perplexities of John Forstice" 72, 116, **46**, 136, 145, 207 n. 44, 225 n. 15; quoted 74–7
Philosophical Essays 212 n. 48; quoted 225 n. 13
"Philosophy and Politics" 9, 10
"Philosophy for Our Time": quoted 103, 165
"Philosophy for You in These Times" 227 n. 38
"Philosophy of G. Santayana" 83, 186, 191, 205 n. 31; quoted 58, 84
"Philosophy of Logical Atomism": quoted 82
"Pilgrimage of Life": *see* "Return to the Cave"
"Place of Science in a Liberal Education" 178
Portraits from Memory 208 n. 7, 219 n. 21, 221 n. 37, 227 n. 41; quoted 103
Power 2, 162, 218 n. 41; quoted 161
"Pragmatism": quoted 225 n. 13
Principia Mathematica 53, 61, 69, 71, 137
Principles of Mathematics 53–4, 61
Principles of Social Reconstruction 4, 5, 8, 59, 129, 131, 142, 149, **47**, 179, 211 n. 40, 229 n. 15, 231 n. 46; quoted 80–1, 116–17
"Prof. G. E. Moore": quoted 104
"Prisons" 72, 74, 137, **44**, 148, 198
"Prisons I": quoted 140
"Prisons" (untitled fragment): quoted 141
Problem of China 211 n. 40
Problems of Philosophy 15, 71, **45**, 210 n. 33
"Recent Work on the Philosophy of Leibniz" 214 n. 82
"Reply to Criticisms" 5, 7, 14, 131, 203 n. 9, 211 n. 44; quoted 130
"Religion and Metaphysics": quoted 54
Religion and Science 204 n. 20
"Return to the Cave": quoted 138
Review of Couturat's *Opuscules* 214 n. 82
"[Review of] Dewey's *Essays in Experimental Logic*" 226 n. 28
Roads to Freedom 218 n. 10, 231 n. 46
Sceptical Essays 83, 229 n. 14
"Scientific Method in Philosophy, On" 62–3, 209 n. 14; quoted 79–80
Scientific Outlook 83, 156, 224 n. 7, 229 n. 15
"Seems, Madam? Nay, It Is" 80; quoted 47–8

"Self-Appreciation" 213 n. 74
Speaking Personally 215 n. 5
"Spinoza" 22, 68, 114, 139, 211 n. 37, 211 n. 42; quoted 55, 58
"Spinoza, *Ethics*" 117; quoted 28
"Spinoza's Moral Code" 114, 211 n. 36; quoted 22
"Study of Mathematics" 75; quoted 63, 64
"Twilight of the Absolute": quoted 14–15
"Turning Point" 208 n. 10
Unarmed Victory 230 n. 33
Understanding History and Other Essays 216 n. 26, 218 n. 1

Unpopular Essays 204 n. 25, 218 n. 10
" 'Useless' Knowledge": quoted 161
"Value of Free Thought" 218 n. 1
"What I Believe": quoted 176, 230 n. 41
"What Is Truth?" 214 n.84
"What Shall I Read?" 208 n. 5, 211 n. 41, 212 n. 56, 213 nn. 77 & 80, 214 n. 84
Which Way to Peace? 212 n. 46
"Why Fanaticism Brings Defeat" 228 n. 10
Why I Am Not a Christian 213 n. 72
"Why I Took to Philosophy" 208 n. 7
Wisdom of the West 104
"On Youthful Cynicism": quoted 83
"IV Wisdom": quoted 142

Spinoza's Works

For an explanation of the system of abbreviations, see Chapter II, n. 2.

Ethics
E1 70, 73
E1Ax.3 113
E1Df.6 82, 112
E1Df.7 46, 228 n.11
E1P8S1 93
E1P11 82, 86
E1P11D2 50
E1P17 73
E1P28 67
E1P29 74
E1P29D 112
E1P32 74
E1P33 74
E1Ap. 24, 67, 74
E2 70, 73
E2Df.6 57, 58
E2P2 67
E2P18 222 n.8
E2P40 67
E2P40S2 73, 112
E2P41D 111
E2P49 213 n.79
E2P49S 22, 85, 216 n 27, 219 n.12
E2P95 67
E3 24, 70, 73, 82, 83, 94
E3P3S 122
E3P6 38
E3P6–7 30
E3P11S 111
E3P13S 111
E3P20 94
E3P31C 219 n.14
E3P32 67, 94
E3P35 219 n.14
E3P43 67, 95, 99
E3P45 67
E3P57 67
E3Df.Aff.6 111, 113
E3Df.Aff.20 137, 175
E3Df.Aff.32 229 n.12
E3Df.Aff.44Ex. 28
E3Df.Aff.48 217 n.33
E4 32, 66, 73, 82
E4Pref. 50, 67, 93, 119

E4Df.1 57
E4P7 37, 44, 153
E4P18S 67
E4P32 68
E4P35 67
E4P35C1 67
E4P37 67
E4P39S 222 n.8
E3P42 219 n.14
E4P44S 158
E4P45 137, 165, 175
E4P45S 23, 67
E4P46 68, 80
E4P54 68
E4P57S 68
E4P62 79, 95, 219 n.18
E4P64 95
E4P67 66, 103
E4P72S 67
E4P73S 110
E4Ap.20 217 n.33
E4Ap.28–32 216 n.27
E5 32, 39, 66, 68, 73, 82, 114, 137
E5Pref. 44
E5P3 68
E5P6 68
E5P11 57
E5P15 95–6
E5P16 57, 94
E5P18 119
E5P19 35
E5P20S 87
E5P22–31 112
E5P23S 112
E5P24–38 120
E5P24 101, 112, 126, 220 n.23
E5P27 112
E5P28 92
E5P30 112
E5P32–7 112
E5P32 113, 127
E5P32C 95–6, 113
E5P33S 68
E5P34C 113

E5P34S 113, 115
E5P35 77, 116
E5P36 39, 113, 149
E5P36S 113
E5P37 114
E5P38 112, 114
E5P38S 114
E5P39 86
E5P40C 222 n.5
E5P40S 114
E5P42 39
E5P42S 54, 66, 97, 126

Treatise on the Improvement of the Understanding 32, 42, 90, 91, 214 n.84

Letters
Ep.36 93
Ep.68b 91

Short Treatise on God, Man and Man's Well-Being 61

Part II, Chap. 22 65, 120

Tractatus Politicus 90, 91

Tractatus Theologico-Politicus 42, 90, 109

Index of Names

Aiken, L. W. 5, 218 n.3; letter to 203 n.14
Allen & Unwin, George 220 n.25
Apostles ("the Society") 43, 47, 146, 210 n.33, 211 n.38, 212 n.66
Argyll, Duke of 24
Aristotle 42, 85, 101, 123, 170, 191; his ethics 12, lacking in "importance" 13
Armour L. 203 n.11
Augustine, St. 92

Balfour, A. J. 45–6
Barber, B. R. connects Russell's political theory and metaphysics 10
Barnes, A. C. 220 n.25
Beck, L. J. 214 n.33
Bergson, H. 72
Berkeley 85, 220 n.24
Berlin, I. 220 n.24
Bidney, D. 124; on intellectual love of God 123;
Blackwell, K. 205 n.26, 207 n.42, 217 n.32, 221 n.33, 224 n.10, 226 n.20, 227 n.38, 229 n.15
Blake, W. 69
Blyenbergh, W. 93
Boethius 159
Bolt, R. 21–2
Bosanquet, B. 14–15
Bowen, R. H. 207 n.42
Boyle, A. 126, 217 n.33
Bradley, F. H. 15, 29, 33, 43, 45–6, 47, 51, 52, 57, 101, 213 nn.70 & 72–3
Brightman, E. S. 130–1, 151, 230 n.31
Brink, A. 69, 217 n.29, 224 n.11
Broad, C. D. 181, 194; ignores "intellectual love of God" 205 n.29
Brotherhood Church 218 n.11
Browne, L. 221 n.30
Buchanan, S. 28
Buchler, J. 205 n.27
Buddha 13, 92, 99, 127, 133, 161, 163
Byron, Lord 179

Cairns, H. 219 n.19

Cambridge University 26, 29, 42, 210 n.33
Candlish, S. 213 n.70
Carroll, L. 84
Chekhov, A. 76
Clark, R. W. 74, 140, 152, 216 n.28, 217 nn.34 & 36, 218 nn.2 & 11, 211 n.40, 225 n.15, 230 n.30
Clarke, P. 215 n.15
Clifford, W. K. 34, 211 n.38
Colerus, J. 61, 66, 90
Cooper Willis, I. 80
Conrad, J. 74
Couturat, L. 213 n.82
Crescas, H. 123
Cresswell, M. J. 213 n.73
Curley, E. M. 205 n.29, 206 n.41, 209 n.16, 214 n.82

Darroch, S. J. 216 n.29
Davidson, R. F. 205 n.32, 230 n.39
Davies, C. Ll. 99–100
Davies, T. Ll. 99–100
Delaney, P. 218 n.6
Descartes 6, 29, 31, 33, 40, 42, 84, 92, 123, 220 n.24
Dewey, J. 151, 210 n.28, 221 n.33, 225 n.13
Dickinson, G. L. 74
Donagan, A. 115
Donnelly, L. M. 221 n.39, 231 n.43
Dostoyevsky, F. 76

Edwards, P. 204 nn.14 & 19, 213 n.72
Einstein, A. 55
Eissler, K. R. 211 n.41
Eliot, G. 27, 28, 43
Elwes, R. H. M. 90, 126, 208 n.2, 217 n.33
England 185
Epictetus 91
Erdmann, J. E. 31, 40, 42; annotated by Russell 32–3

Farrer, A. 180
Faust 217 n.37

Feinberg, B. 217 n.36
Felton, A. 217 n.36
Feuer, L. S. 15–16, 221 n.34
Firth, R. 184
Flexner, H. T. 211 n.35, 231 n.43
Foucher de Careil, A. L. 49
Frankena, W. 2, 182, 205 n.29
Frege, G. 75
Freud, S. 26, 83
Freudenthal, J. 66
Friedmann, G. 213 n.81
Fullerton, G. S. 31

Galileo 161
Gerhardt, C. I. 208 n.2
Germany 82
Goethe 35, 64
Goldstein, R. 230 n.36
Grant, G. 7, 205 n.28
Grattan-Guinness, I. 219 n.13
Green, T. H. 35, 46
Greenspan, L. 206 n.41
Gregory, T. S. 219 n.17
Griffin, N. 132, 212 nn.55, 59 & 66, 224 n.1, 227 n.35
Gurtoff, S. A. 218 n.6

Haight, G. S. 209 n.18
Haldeman-Julius, E. 221 n.29
Hall, R. 214 n.85
Hallet, H. F. 222 n.7
Halpern, B. 208 n.6
Hampshire, S. 15–16, 169–70, 193; on intellectual love of God 123–4
Hancock, R. 3, 203 n.4
Happold, F. C. 209 n.21
Hardie, W. F. R. 205 n.32
Hardy, G. H. 146–7, 217 n.30
Hare, R. M. 173, 204 n.22
Harman, G. 184
Harris, E. E. on intellectual love of God 124–5
Hauerwas, S. 204 n.24
Hazeltine, H. D. 211 n.38
Hegel 31, 84–5, 91, 101, 135; dialectic 44
Heraclitus 4
Hessing, S. 223 n.15
Hitler, A. 199
Hobbes 29, 30, 33, 92, 93; compared with Spinoza 41
Hobhouse, M. 216 n.28
Hoernlé, R. F. A. 147–8, 187, 207 n.42
Holmes, O. W., Jr. 210 n.33
Hospers, J. 230, n.39

Hubbeling, H. G. 125, 223 n.15, 224 n.5
Hume 57, 85, 161, 183, 229 n.25; on reason 38

Jager, R. 75, 218 n.7, 226 n.31, 230 n.32; epistemological and political individuals 5, 9–10
James, W. 207 n.44, 218 n.12
Jesus 59, 68, 161
Joachim, H. H. 34, 42, **18**, 61, 110, **37**, 123, 128, 211 n.38, 216 n.17

Kant, I. 8, 29, 31, 67, 85, 92, 172, 173, 181, 183, 193, 201
Kayser, R. 215 n.5
King-Farlow, J. 149, 206 n.38
Kneale, M. 214 n.83

Lassalle, F. 213 n.74
Lawrence, D. H. 80, 179, 219 n.14
Lawrence, F. 219 n.14
Leibniz 42, **18**, 72, 85, 203 n.11, 210 n.28, 220 n.24, 222 n.1; on individuals 40; Spinoza on 91; worth reading only when wholly abstract 14
Leithauser, G. 75, 76, 78, 209 n.12, 217 n.36; on "Nasispo" 207 n.44
Leo Hebraeus 123
Leopardi G. 75, 227 n.36
Levy, P. 212 n.66
Lewis, J. 203 n.11
Locke 85, 89, 166, 220 n.24
Lucas, J. M. 66, 90, 229 n.13
Lucretius 75

Mackie, J. L. 181
Maimonides 123
Malleson, C. 159, 160, 166, 227 n.39; letter to 4
Mansfield, K. 219 n.14
Mark, T. C. 222 n.4
Marmor, M. 221 n.47, 228 n.48
Martin, D. 139, 146, 209 n.13, 217 n.29; on Russell's sense of self 297 n.44
Marx, K. 83
Matson, W. 115–16; on Russell's ideas of happiness 206 n.41
McCloskey, H. J. 2, 203 n.4
McGuinness, B. F. 224 n.5
McKenney, J. L. 204 n.17
McShea, R. J. 11
McTaggart, J. M. E. 42, 44, 54, 213, n.72, 217 n.34

Index of Names

Mill, J. S. 22, 24, 183, 206 n.41, 226 n.33; on dying 181; and God 36
Monro, D. H. 6, 173–4, 194
Moore, G. E. 48, 213 n.77, 217 n.34, 222 n.2; his intuitionism 3, 5; and organicism 12; compared with Spinoza 104
Morrell, O. 66, 74, 78, 111, 116, 121, 129, 132, 139, 142, 145, 152, 156, 159, 185, 187, 206 n.36, 207 n.44, 209 n.24, 214 n.85, 217 n.36, 218 n.2, 219 n.14, letters to 14, 34, 36, 39, 48, 55, 56, 61, 94, 115, 140, 211 n.38, 218 n.10; Russell's Spinozistic correspondence with 24
Mounce, H. O. 230 n.34
Murray, G. 132, 135; letter to 53
Murry, J. M. 219 n.14

Naess, A. 125, 208 n.2, 209 n.16, 224 n.5
Nagel, T. 193–4, 201
Nakhnikian, G. 231 n.46
Nation, The 21–2
Nazis 221 n.40
Neblett, W. 228 n.9
Nero 93
Neumann, H. 208 n.45
Newberry, J., *see* Vellacott, J.
Newman, J. 205 n.29, 228 n.11
Newson, E. 230 n.34
Nielsen, Kai, letter to 204 n.17
Nietzsche 12, 92
No-Conscription Fellowship 160
Nowell-Smith, P. H. 3

O'Briant, W. H. 213 n.75
O'Connor, D. J. 16
Odegard, D. 219 n.22
Ogden, C. K., letter to 154

Parfit, D. 231 n.44
Parkinson, G. H. R. 214 n.82
Parmenides 101
Pater, W. 42, 166
Peano, G. 75
Pears, D. F. 228 n.6
Picton, J. A. 21, 114, 211 n.36; on intellectual love of God 120–1
Pitt, J. 130
Plato 42, 69, 73, 85, 92, 96, 118, 150; Platonism 83–4
Plotinus 91
Pollock, F. 23, 25, 30, 31, 15, 48, 55, 56, 61, 66, 71, 73, 90, 110, 126, 209 n.25, 212 n.57; on intellectual love of God 120
Pollock, G. 211 n.33
Pringle-Pattison, A. S. 146, 147, 206 n.42, 225 n.19
Proudfoot, W. 180
Pythagoras 92, 161

Rawls, J. 182–4, 185
Reid, T. 29
Rempel, R. A. 215 n.15
Rescher, N. 16
Rinder, G. 160
Ritchie, A. D. 220 n.24
Ross, M. L. 218 n.6
Roy, D. K. 224 nn.23 & 25
Royce, J. 180
Ruja, H. 44, 75, 204 nn.14 & 21
Russell, Agatha 209 n.17
Russell, Alys 27, 34, 45, 54, 114, 132, 135, 137, 213 n.77; letters to 23, 34, 44
Russell, B., asceticism 1, 137; "conversion" 13, 132–3; denies unity in his ethics 5; begins study of philosophy 29, 42–3; correspondence with Ottoline Morrell 24, view of her 140; feels himself at home among the great philosophers 71; his ethics, attempts at systematizing 9; how he wrote 97; impersonal intellect of 1; importance of romantic love to 189; metaethical development of 5; and the mob 82; not seen as normative philosopher 11, 13–14; old age 1; passions; personal problems 129–30; politics 3; professional capacity 104; regrets his non-cognitivism 8; religious impulses 23–4; politics related to his metaphysic 10; as sage 10–11; seeks philosophy of life 99; and Spinoza: admits influence of 22–3, first studies him 23, 33–4, knowledge of his life 66, 90, one of the most important people in the world 71, reading of 109–10; sure of ultimate values 6; tentativeness of metaethic 203 n.14; two interpretations of intellectual love of God 114; uses personal incidents in books 156
Russell, R. 152, 214 n.84
Russia 162
Ryan, W. F. 221 n.29

Sahakian, W. S. 204 n.19
Sams, R. 146, 207 n.44, 218 n.43
Santayana, G. 83–4, 185, 186, 191; Russell judges ethic of 12–13; and subjectivism 3
Sassoon, S. 219 n.14
Savan, D. 111, 222 nn.2–3
Schaller, G. H. 221 n.32
Schiller, F. C. S. 208 n.45
Schilpp, P. A. 5, 220 n.25
Schweitzer, A. 28, 169, 227 n.34, 231 n.41
Sessions, G. 16–17, 209 n.16, 226 n.26
Sharp, F. C. 229 n.25
Shelley, P. B. 24–5
Sherley-Price, L. 209 n.19
Shirley, S. 126, 208 n.2
Sidgwick, H. 29, 182, 194
Simeon Stylites, St 28
Singer, P. 194, 227 n.34
Slater, J. G. 168, 186, 203 n.12, 219 n.14
Small, I. C. 42
Smith, Alys Pearsall, *see* Russell, Alys
Smith, L. Pearsall 34, 213 n.77
Spadoni, C. 43, 206 n.36, 208 n.6, 211 n.43, 212 nn. 53, 58–9 & 67, 213 n.71
Spencer, H. 29, 211 n.38
Spiegelberg, H. 209 n.22
Spinoza, asceticism 35; bought tranquillity 178; conversation 90; difficulty of his writing 55; duration of influence on Russell 22; ethical naturalism 11; exaltation 83; faces mob at the Hague 66, 81–2; Hebraism 83–4; incident of De Witt brothers 167; as intellectual model 36; and Leibniz 18; lived by his wisdom 102–3; nearly lost his life 218 n.10; needs commentaries 61; precursor of Bradley 29; reception after his death 79; remained calm always 103; spiritual life 74; translation of 223 n.19; unique among modern philosophers 71
Stace, W. T. 135
Stein, L. 49, 66
Stout, G. F. 31, 42, 43; lectures on Spinoza 29–30
Strachey, J. 217 n.30
Synge, J. M. 73

Tait, K. 231 n.46
Tate, Allen 219 n.19
Tennyson, A. 26

Thomas, H., *see* Flexner, H. T.
Thomas à Kempis 23, 27, 28, 209 n.17; and self-repression 27
Thomas Aquinas 92, 123
Tillich, P. 180
Tolstoy, L. 220 n.40
Toulmin, S. 231 n.45
Trelawny, E. J. 73
Trevelyan, R. C. 227 n.36
Tulliver, Maggie 43; and Thomas à Kempis 27
Turcon, S. 209 n.17

U.C.L.A. 229 n.25
United States 58, 82
Unwin, S. 216 n.25, 219 nn.13 & 15; letter to 203 n.13

Van Doren, M. 28
van Vloten and Land 48, 208 n.2
Vaughan, H. 69
Vellacott, J. 218 nn.4 & 11

Walsh, W. H. 221 n.43
Walton, D. N. 227 n.39
Ward, J. 29; lectures on Spinoza 31–2
Wetlesen, J. 208 n.2, 217 n.33, 223 n.15, 224 n.5; on intellectual love of God 39
White, W. H. 82, 124, 206 n.42, 229 n.13; on intellectual love of God 120
White, W. H., and A. H. Stirling, translation of *Ethic* 35, 48, 56, 60, 23, 126, 208 n.2, 211 n.37
Whitehead, A. 132, 135, 225 n.15
Whitehead, E. 75, 132, 135, 152, 225 n.15
Wiener, P. P. 14
Wienpahl, P. 208 n.2, 212 n.50, 215 n.17, 217 n.33, 220 n.25, 224 n.5; on intellectual love of God 39
Williams, B. 229 n.22
Willis, K. 208 n.9
Wittgenstein, L. 76, 224 n.5, 225 n.20
Wolf, A. 89, 90, 216 n.25, 229 n.13
Wolfson, A. 221 n.30
Wolfson, H. A., on intellectual love of God 123
Wollheim, R. 226 n.33
Woodhouse, H. 230 n.35
Wordsworth, W. 25

Zytaruk, G. T. 218 n.6

Index of Subjects

abnegation of self, *see* self-abnegation
Absolute 31, 44, 51, 211 n.43, 215 n.2
absolute idealism: of Joachim 121; permanent influence on Russell 110; *see also* monistic idealism
abstraction of self 189
absurdity 201
acquiescence 15; in past vs. future 177–8; and religious worship 207 n.42
acquiescentia 120
acquiescentia mentis 28, 38, 116
acquiescentia in se ipso 116, 123
activity and passivity 50; in Spinoza and Leibniz 214 n.83
action 37; and contemplation 167
aesthetic satisfaction 47–8
aesthetic value of philosophy 80
aesthetic values 191
affectus 61, 215 n.17
altruism 17, 190; of character, and egoism 197; and feeling 193; of impersonal viewpoint 183; universal 185; *see also* self-referential altruism
amor 37; *see also* love
amor dei intellectualis 223 n.22
analytic philosophy 13–14, 62; *see also* exactness 226 n.20
anarchism 10
animals, slaughter of 67
anthropocentrism 1, 97, 149, 226 n.26
argumentation 174
asceticism 28, 35, 41, 42, 194; cruelty of 64; of intellect 179; mathematical 76; prudential 28; as renunciation of self 78; "rich voluptuous" 23; Russell's 1; and self-absorption 127
ascetics, self-absorbed 158
atomism 10, 30; and individualism 10
attribute(s) 72, 112, 214 n.83; infinite 82; of thought 211 n.38
authoritarianism, moral 8

balance of terror, and international harmony 195
beacon fire, image of 159
beautific vision 48, 224 n.7

beauty 96, 133, 137; in nature 24–6
belief 9; standards of 1
benevolence: Sidgwick's maxim of 182; vague 162
bias, impersonal 201
blessedness 68, 97, 113, 120
bondage 16, 23, 50, 83, 95, 124, 137, 165, 175
Buddhism 125, 128

calm 25, 78, 81, 163; acquired in way of living 87; and activity 166; after conflict 70; arising from third kind of knowledge 112, 118; and determinism 177; as evaluative criterion 200–2; in face of misfortune 98; as goal of mystics 28; and impersonal self-enlargement 176; and impersonality 159; and intellectual strife 116; means of obtaining 87, 160; as optimum attitude 100; as religious peace 590; and value of strong emotion 189; and union 135, 141
categorical imperative 173; and universalizability 174
causality 64
certainty 96; abandoned 130; and values 131
children 154, 163; and enlargement of interests 224 n.25; and impersonality 190, 230 n.34, 231 n.44; and parental affection 156–7
Christianity 68, 98
circumvallation 142, 149
clarity, as subject of *Ethics* 127
clarity of concepts, as evaluative criterion 197
code of conduct, *see* morality
cognitivism 2
collective self-realization 179–80
commiscendis corporibus 217 n.33
common sense 56
competition 195
compossibility 41, 44, 63, 172, 204 n.14; not an ultimate solution 228 n.6
conatus 29, 37, 114, 153; as limit to

unselfishness 175–6; *see also* self-preservation
condemnation, moral 62, 63
conduct, ideals of 170
conflict 62, 70, 129, 174; advantages of 194–5; between desires and between individuals 171–2; and harmony of ends 63; and intellectual love of God 71; its futility 160; nipping in bud 189; and self-referential altruism 181
conscientious objectors 80, 216 n.28
consistency, as evaluative criterion 186–9, 191
consonancy, as evaluative criterion 189–91
contemplation 41, 77, 156, 179; and action 147, 150–1, 167; and calm 77; as ideal activity 39; and immortality 84; and intellectual love of God 116; mysticism of 142; and perspective 162; in philosophy 148; vision of 142, 145
courage in standing alone 46
creativity 96–7, 118
criteria, evaluative, *see* evaluation
cruelty 6, 99, 119, 152
cynicism 82

death 67, 84, 103, 136, 157, 163–4, 222 n.8; attitude to, in Mill 181; fear of 97; to finite self 143;
deontologism 196
depersonalization: as evaluative criterion 198–9
desire(s): alteration of 188–9; as basis of Russell's metaethic 204 n.17; compossible 41; conflicts among 171–2; egocentricity of 165; in "The Free Man's Worship" 136; and knowledge 43–4; in Leibniz 50; Nagel questions conative assumption 193; and philosophy of mind 228 n.1; 'purification' of 63; satisfaction of 44–5, 153, 172; scope of 161, 164, 172–3, 228 n.6; self-regarding 226 n.33; Spinoza defines 37
determinism 22–3, 24, 30, 40, 67, 137; and action 188; and calm 176–7; and ethics 85; hard and soft 176–7; and idealism 45–6; logical 93, 94; irrelevant to third kind of knowledge 88; and knowledge 38; of mind by body 86; and moral condemnation 63; Pollock on 35; and regret 229 n.12
dialectic 44, 47

dogmatism 148, 165; and fear 103
domination, Napoleonic 225 n.13
double-aspect theory 86
dualism, of good and bad 140
duty 43, 173; of philosopher 167

Eastern thought 39
ecology 209 n.16
ecstasy of love 189
education 133
ego, hard 153; like a gas 229 n.17; "undoing of" 126; walls of, as metaphor 188
egocentricity, in ethics and philosophy of mind 188
egoism, ethical 58; psychological 124, 196–7; and self-realization 179
egoistic demands 129
egolessness, and impersonal self enlargement 127
emotion(s) 37, 61, 215 n.17; active 176; active and passive 228 n.11; definitions of 44, 88; passive 149; power over 113; strong 189, 202; turmoil of 97; *see also* affections
emotive element in mysticism 130
emotivism 2, 5
enjoyment of life, Russell's 130
enlargement (of self) 123, 144; through contemplation 149; of eternal parts of oneself 119; of interests 15; through love 145–6; of mind 163; of passions 138; of vision 102, 103
empiricism and liberalism 9
epistemology 10; self in 10
error, and wrong-doing 95
eternality, *see* immortality, intellectual
ethics(s), adoption of 195; contractual origin to, in Rawls 182–3; distinguished from metaethics and morality 2; ecological 16, 170; evaluative criteria in 8; as guide to living 169–70; and intellectual arguments 5; of knowledge 65; Leibniz's 49; of love 2, 126; medical 170; and metaphysics 80, 97; of pain 63, 77, 133, 136, 158–9; as gateway to wisdom 155; of power 2; proper names in 7; and reason 6–7; of resignation 138–9; of self-realization, *see* self-realization, ethic of; universality in 7; *see also* normative ethics
ethical innovators 161

Index of Subjects

Ethics: Ward on how to read 30–1, Stout on 31, Russell on 31
euthanasia 9
evaluation of ethics 8, 12–13, 18; nature of non-cognitivist criteria 184
events 86
evil 228 n.4
existentialism, *see* absurdity 201
expansion of ego 165
experience, personal 87

fallibilism 6
fanaticism 98, 167, 175, 191
fatalism, and determinism 177
favouritism 198
fear 87; and dogmatism 103; and fanaticism 165; foolish 95
feeling(s), community 102; impartiality in 103, 133, 165; monism in 14; as source of religion 143
fellow-feeling, and impersonality 197
free man 122, 124; Russell's 136–7
free trade 9, 59, 64, 215 n.15, 229 n.21
free will 22–3, 23–4, 31; in Spinoza 32, 50, 62
freedom 10, 16, 30, 46, 50, 226 n.28; in Spinoza 228 n.11
freethought 9, 35
friendship 13, 163

generosity 1, 17, 68, 171
geometrical method 22–3, 31, 55, 62, 64, 72; and emotional longing 206 n.39; and impersonality 70; and logical determinism 94; *see also* mathematics
geometry, non-Euclidean 35
God 23–4, 36; approaching his viewpoint 202; concept of, in Spinoza 111–12; existence of, ontological argument for 211 n.43; Joachim's understanding of 51, 121; as impersonal end of life 81; in Leibniz 50; mystic union with 92; in pantheism 26; and self 73; in Spinoza 40; union with, through intellectual love of God 149; uses principle of sufficient reason 40
good, (the) 2, 44, 67, 77; in block universe 86–7; and evil 93; general 164; as illusory 134; and life 166; in Leibniz 50; monistic view of 88; as mystic union with God 92; naturalistically defined 172; and perfection 57–8; and the whole 95
good life 84

good reasons approach 184
growing old 1, 164

happiness 3, 9, 138, 157, 228 n.6; and externality 85; miserable longing for 27; and self-enlargement 83
harmony 68; discord and ultimate 99
hatred 67, 68, 99, 137, 165; and love 80, 95
here and now 164, 167; *see also sub specie aeternitatis*
hope, foolish 95
history 87
human condition 231 n.46
human life: infinitesimal 100
human nature 8, 11, 82–3; division into instinct and reason 142, into instinct, mind and spirit 142; and self-preservation 94; Spinoza's conception of 37; suitability to, as evaluative criterion 194; theory of 153; and valid ethic 58
human species 194
humility 54, 68; of science 134

idealism 14–15; monistic 21, 47; robustness in 28
idealist ethics 91
ideal observer, his characteristics 184
imagination, and knowledge 88; and intellectual love of God 118
immortality 23–4, 79, 115, 127; and contemplation 77, 84; intellectual 39; and intellectual love of God 96, 124; and unity 128
impartial judgment 111
impartial love 17
impartial spectator 183, 229 n.25
impartial understanding of ourselves 126
impartiality 164; as duty of philosopher 167; of feeling, in mysticism 133–4; and impersonality 176; and impulse to knowledge 149; of infinite self 144; its limitations 150; and neutrality 190; of scientific thought 133; and typing restriction 186
imperativeness 143
impersonal feeling 155
impersonal self-enlargement 9; and avoidance of conflict 189; and difficulties with claims of kinship, etc. 198; encourages generosity 171; and large-heartedness 58; in *problems of Philosophy* 45; and self-preservation 94–5; solution to conflict 71

impersonality 7, 17; and children 190; defined 183; and eternal truths 113–14; in Firth 183–4; from geometrical method 70; and imagination and memory 113; and impartiality 176; and individuality 158; of life's ends 81; limited by self-preservation 166; and morality 173–4; in Rawls 182–3; and religion 143, 145; in thought 121, 178
importance, as evaluative criterion 58, 191–2; impulse(s), creative and possessive 63, 180; freedom to follow 175; possessive 154; in Spinoza 59; theory of 153; yielding to 190
incarnation of values 226 n.31
indignation 22, 38, 59, 70, 87, 137, 147, 177, 228 n.9; and mystical outlook 135, 161; as obsession 175
individual(ity) 71; as aspect of divine being 93; epistemological and political 5, 10, 14; and God or Nature 123–4; in Hegel vs. Spinoza 101; Joachim on 51, 122; need of social organization 102; and mankind 156; in politics, Lewis on 203 n.11; and self-preservation 29–30; in Spinoza 223 n.21; and substance 180; and whole 65, 70, 115, 124–5, 158; and world 203 n.11
infallibilism 8
insight 165, 226 n.30
instinct 142
instrumentalism, *see* pragmatism
intellect 73; and love 78; and mysticism 139
intellectual discovery 116
intellectual love of God 17; analysis of, on Russell's first interpretation 117; best thing to live by 81; as contemplation of individual things 101; and creative work 96; and Descartes 41; as emotional state accompanying intellectual discovery 105; as "God's understanding love" 127; as happy contemplation of the eternal 81; and immortality 39; and impartial reason 71; as infinite self in Russell 144; interpreters on: Pollock 120, White 120, Picton 57, 59–60, 120–1, Joachim 51, 37, Wolfson 123, Bidney 123, Hampshire 123–4, Harris 124, Wetlesen 125–6, Wienpahl 126–7; as joy and peace of contemplation 77; as knowledge 65, 73–4; more influential than determinism on impersonal self-enlargement 177; and mysticism 145, 205 n.29; as mystic contemplation 160; narcissistic interpretation 123; and pursuit of calm, 87; and religion 78; Russell's earliest mention 33; Russell's second interpretation 35; Russell thought he knew its meaning 111; same as philosopher's joy 179; and Spinoza's geometrical method, *see* geometrical method; Spinoza's ultimate good 70; steps from third kind of knowledge to 112–14; and understanding 95; as union of thought and emotion 96; and union with God 149; what Russell and Lady Ottoline cared for 71
interests, enlargement of 15; special 7
internal relations 213 n.70
internationalism 9, 215 n.15
intimate centre 188
intuition 111; divine 151; as way to knowledge 226 n.30
intuitionism 2, 5, 164; subjectivist 6, 131–2
"is" – "ought" confusion 57

jealousy 219 n.14
Jews 98
joy 37
justice, and impartiality 182–3, 190; as ultimate end 192

kinship, claims of, as evaluative criterion 197
knowledge, ethic of 65; first kind of, and error 85; as intellectual love 65; theory of 31, 72, 147; third kind of 38–9, 73, 76–7, 111–15, 125, 126–7, and imagination 88, and intellectual love of God 92, and personal identity 122; and verbal expression 222 n.2; three kinds of, in Spinoza 33, 73, 111

laetita 37, 111
liberalism 10; and empiricism 9
liberationist ethics 199
life insurance 172, 197, 200
life-style 170
logic, Russell not always persuaded by 7
logical form 7
loneliness 132–3, 152, 158, 190, 199, 227 n.35
love 17, 67, 83; defined by Spinoza 111; and intellect 78; and knowledge 224 n.7; of mankind 70; and mingling of

Index of Subjects

personalities 226 n.30; personal 157; romantic 189; produces new being of two in one 158; significance of, in establishing values 158; of truth and neighbour 82; universal 134, 150; and walls of self 138; of wisdom, in Plato and Spinoza 96

lying 67

man, not a solitary animal 179
man's existence 167, 168
mathematics 67; and attaining calm 87; and *Ethics* 31; in "Forstice" 76; intuition in 88; model of, in Spinoza 22–3, 24; philosophers and 91–2; and Pollock 210 n.33; value of 64
matter 72
means/end distinction 149
meditation 125–6
memory 222 n.8
mental health, and strong impulses 98
merit, intrinsic 189
metaethics, non-cognitivism in 4; and normative ethics **1**. Russell's **3**–**4**; Spinoza's 205 n.29
meta-metaethics 2–3
metaphysics, and comfort 47–8; and ethics 80, 86–7; idealist 14–15; Spinoza's 82
militarism 80
mind, its power over passions 68
mind and body, relationship of 85–6
miscendi corpora 217 n.33
misfortune, attitudes to 98–9
modes 72, 214 n.83
monism, attitude to time 79; in feeling vs. doctrine 81; logical 97
monistic ethics **7**
monistic idealism 4, 29, 30, 35, 52
monistic metaphysics 85
moral condemnation, and tolerance 177
moral identity 229 n.22
moral reasoning 2
moral responsibility, and determinism 176
moralist, attitude of 141
morality, distinguished from metaethics and normative ethics 2; Puritan 83
motivation 184; and deontologism 196
music 87
mutuality 10
mystery, sense of 134
mysticism 23; Asian compared with European 92; beliefs vs. feelings 152; cognitive vs. emotive 130; and calm 118; and evil 93–4; and God's existence 131; in idealism 14–15; and intellect 139; in intellectual love of God? 119; its joy 65; in knowledge 73–4; and moments of intellectual discovery 145; and personal experience 220 n.24; and personality of child 154; Roman Catholic 26; Russell's analysis of **42**, 134–5; and science 147; and self 141; and surrender 145; in Spinoza 41, 70; truths revealed by vision of 151

natura naturans 112
naturalism, ethical 2, 5, 11, 42, 58, 172, 203, n.14
nature-worship **12**
necessity 33, 60, 68, 73, 84; and causality 64; and God 62, 114–15; of human actions 70; of power over passive emotions 95
negation, and the whole 93
neo-Hegelianism 21, 227 n.35; ethics of 14–15; Russell imbibes 29; studied by Russell 42–3
neutral monism 220 n.22; and the self 188
non-cognitivism 5–6, **4**, 11, 104; and obligation 171–2
non-resistance, *see* pacifism
normative ethics, conceptual connections in 9–10; distinguished from metaethics and morality 2; and metaethics **1**; nature of 2–3; treatises not effective 110
nuclear peril 1, 100, 101, 160, 167, 169, 171, 186; movement against, as philosophy 228 n.48

objectivity, of thought and feeling 17
objective rightness 164
obligation 8, 11, 193; and Kant 172; and non-cognitivism 171
obsessiveness 158; *see also* fanaticism
odium 37
operative mood, and ethics 204 n.20
optimism, Russell's 231 n.46
organicism 11–12, 153, 179, 200
original position 182–3
original sin 199
ought 2

pacifism 198, 220 n.40; and "Free Man's Worship" 160; and Nazis 99; in World War I 147

pain 158–9, 163; as gateway to wisdom 133; ineradicable evil 89; as inevitable part of nature 99; and the whole 103; *see also* ethic of pain
pantheism 24–5, 26, 31, 40, 65, 71, 93, 115, 117
paradox of perfect altruism 192
passion(s) 33, 41, 42, 43, 68, 91, 138; defined 44; emotions may cease to be 95; Spinoza on 37, 213 n.77
passivity, in Santayana 84
patriotism 154, 163, 197
peace of mind, *see* calm
perfection 68, 214 n.83; and good 57–8; of whole 99
personal identity 115–16, 122
personalities, mingling of 155
personality, components of 113, 114; escape from 226 n.28
persuasion 7, 9
philosophical beliefs: heterogeneity in? 9
philosophical productivity, as evaluative criterion 196
philosophical psychology, Spinoza's 29, 33
philosophical thought, and calm 200–1
philosophical understanding, importance to impersonal self-enlargement 178–9
philosophy, access to wisdom? 3; academic 166; cognitive vs. emotive conceptions 79; conceptions of 203 n.12; and conceptual fundamentals 9; defined 11; functions of 191; her misfortunes 84–5; and impartial contemplation 179; and life 62; and mysticism 133–4; and political action 167; and religion 39, 43; and self-enlargement 85; technical 9; its value 148
philosophy of education 154, 192
philosophy of literature 231 n.43
philosophy of mind 14, 188
philosophy of religion 4
philosophy of science 47
physics, Spinoza's 93
pity 88
pleasure, *see* joy
poetic sentimentalism 25–6
poetry 88, 132
poise 70
political philosophy 5, 10, 22, 28, 163; and impersonal self-enlargement 195; self-realization in 101; Spinoza's 32

politics 3, 82–3; individual in 10; and metaphysics 9
power, men's 97; to set men free 161; of the wicked, and non-resistance 100
pragmatism 225 n.13, 226 n.28; and commercialism 82–3; and contemplation 151
prescriptivism 2; and universalizability 173
pride 68
principle of growth 59, 153, 154, 179
principle of sufficient reason 40, 49–50, 213 n.82
prison (of self) 137; built by finite self 144; of narrow ego 157; nature of 141; the senses as 150
professional moralists 83
psychoanalysis 87
psychological approach, Russell's 88, 116, 128; and self-preservation 94
psychology, Spinoza's 30, 92
psychophysical parallelism 86, 219 n.21
purification 63; of love 138; *see also* pain, ethic of
Puritanism 83

Quakers 98

rationality and impersonality 174, 183; and self-interest 172
reason 6, 138, 142; cure to conflict 70; and hatred 68; life of 84; limit to 37, 193
reasonable men, their mutual usefulness 67
regret 229 n.12
relativism 30
religion, and common people 217 n.34; and dogma 69; essence of 140–1; impulses to 23; and individuality 158; its source in feelings 143; in "Forstice" 74; and Lady Ottoline 104; and life of spirit 155; and metaphysics 47; as monism in feeling 14; and nature-worship 12; in philosophy 29; from philosophy 39; Pollock on 35, 36; to promote life 81; Russell's personal 36–7; Russell's philosophy of 4; Russell's positive writings on 130–1; and self-abnegation 13; taken account of in Russell's ethic 191; vocabulary of, used by Russell 187
religious experience, James on 207 n.44; and value 130
renunciation 138–9, 155

Index of Subjects

repentance 68
repression, theory of 45
resignation, ethic of 64–5
revenge 98
reverence 22, 93, 143; and principle of growth 154
reverence for life 230 n.41
right 2, 3
right conduct, and right feeling 193–4
Roman Catholicism 26; and Leibniz 49

sainthood 64
salvation 30; personal 156; selflessness as means of 28
sanity 163
satisfaction of interest 172
scepticism 10, 11; and love's values 158
science, creativity in 96; and humility 134
scientia intuitiva 38
scientific outlook 25
selfishness 65, 75, 181, 194; Maggie Tulliver's 27
selflessness 125–6; Schweitzer's 28
self, its boundaries 127; and compossibility 70; in ethics and epistemology 10; finite and infinite 143–4; as mere fluid nucleus of feeling 43; meaning of 197; moral 180, 181; and moralists 141; in monistic idealism 15, 110; and other 152; in philosophy of mind and ethics 14, 188; as prison 77, 141; purged of personal desire 136; separate, wrongly claiming independence 14–15; in Spinoza 114; surrender of 143, 145; walls of 138; wider 14, 15
self-abnegation 13, 35, 47, 52, 78, 137, 139, 172, 194; and asceticism 41; Russell's first solution to conflict 129; and suicide 42; and universe 45
self-absorption 127, 158
self-assertion 30; as an evil 149; and individuality 71; and justice 192; and self-denial 42
self-centredness 139, 176
self-consistency, as evaluative criterion 185–6
self-control 159; Russell's 139
self-denial, *see* self-abnegation
self-discipline 190
self-enlargement 28, 69, 157; and immortality 77; King-Farlow on 106 n.38; through personal love 152, 155, 158; and scientific philosophy 134; and universe of desire 44
self-forgetfulness 168
self-interest 186, 230 n.33; and global cooperation 195
self-preservation 37, 62, 68, 70, 114, 207 n.44; and impersonality 166; and naturalism 58; not the strongest desire 230 n.29; and perfect altruism 185; and self-sacrifice 175–6; in Spinoza 29; and the whole 94–5
self-realization 15, 46–7, 121, 163; Bradley's ethic of 43; ethic of 2, 179; and "narrow self" 110; in Russell 153; in Spinoza 50; and state 101
self-referential altruism: in Broad and Mackie 181
self-renunciation, *see* self-abnegation
self-sacrifice 166, 175, 185; not universalizable 192; *see also* self abnegation
sempiternity 222 n.7
sense-perception, *see* knowledge, first kind of
separateness of egos 102
sexual love 1, 69, 155, 158; and internationalism 9; as union 217 n.33
significance, of religious experience 131
socialism 10
solipsism 10, 147
solitariness, of man, denied 179
solitary philosophies 158
solitude, *see* loneliness
soul 25, 26, 187
speciesism 227 n.34
spirit 142–3
spontaneity 190
state, the, and reason 91; as whole 101
stoicism 64, 98, 120, 137, 212 n.51; its freedom 225 n.13
strive, *see* conflict
sub specie aeternitatis 39, 81, 102, 119, 123, 126, 161, 186; and calm 201
subjectivism 3, 6; in value theory 185
subjectivity, in ethics 131
subject-predicate analysis of propositions 215 n.2
substance 51, 91, 97; and attributes 86; God as 112
suffering 171; as attitude to misfortune 98–9; indifference to 175; of Russell in 1902 136; and universe 102
suicide 42
sympathy 7; universal 161

Tao, the 2
technology 170
thought, attribute of 32; celebrated by Russell 229 n.15
thought-objects 112
time 76–7, 81, 137, 201; attitude to, in monism 79; and error 85; its reality 222 n.9; and reason 95
titillatio 206 n.41
tolerance 62, 166, 177; and subjectivism 3
tristitia 37
truth, as analytic 72; as evaluative criterion in cognitivist ethics 184; means to 25–6; metaphysical vs. psychological 88
truths, eternal, and god 112; hierarchy of 142
types, hierarchy of 201
typing restriction 186

union, joy of 77; with others 190; physical 217 n.33; three forms of 141; with universe 140
universal life 164
universal nature 144
universal soul 146
universalizability, as evaluative criterion 192; in Hare 204 n.22
universalization 138, 173
universals 67, 111
universe, block 86; of passion 44; and human passions 227 n.36; viewpoint of 182
unselfishness 172; and self-preservation 175–6
utilitarianism 3, 46, 181, 182; emotive 204 n.17; impersonal or impartial? 183; and impersonal self-enlargement 196; and promise-keeping 2

validity, in normative ethics 58
value(s) 6, 196; and Hitler 199; standard of 191; subjective establishment of 131–2, 158, 188–9; theory of 130, 147
Vietnam War 9

war 160
way of life (living) 2, 3, 87, 117, 162, 191; completeness of, as evaluative criterion 199; Hampshire on 168–9
whole, the, and absorption of individuals 101; and evil 93–4, 99; grasping, and intellectual love of God 88; and individual 115; membership in 151; as organism 101; in Russell vs. Spinoza 125; seeing parts in relation to 119; and self-preservation 94; thinking about 100
will 30
wisdom 3, 69; free man's 67; as intellectual love of God 95; intellectual love of God as key to 81, 156; and impersonality 161; a little in world 4; and pain 77; and self-realization 148; as synthesis of knowledge, will and feeling 166; and union 141
women's suffrage 9, 64
World War I 156, 216 n.28
World War II 4, 216 n.28
worship 63–4, 143; not of what is transitory 62; of ideal good 146–7; of ideal vs. actual world 147; of reality 134

Zen 125